Energy plays a crucial role in economic and social development. The analysis of energy issues and policy options is therefore a vital area of study. This book presents a hierarchical modeling scheme intended to support energy planning and policy analysis in developing countries.

The authors introduce the concept of "Integrated National Energy Planning" (INEP), and examine the spreadsheet models, optimization models, and linear planning models which energy planners use. Environmental considerations are also introduced into the analysis. Techniques are then applied to two important energy subsectors, electricity and fuelwood, before problems of integration and policy implementation are discussed. Throughout the book the authors examine actual practice in developing countries. Illustrative case material is drawn from Egypt, West Africa, Sudan, Pakistan, Colombia, India, Sri Lanka, and Morocco.

This book will be of interest to students and practitioners of energy planning, and to those concerned with the wider development implications of energy policy.

Energy policy analysis and modeling

CAMBRIDGE STUDIES IN ENERGY AND THE ENVIRONMENT

EDITOR

CHRIS HOPE   *Judge Institute of Management, University of Cambridge*
JIM SKEA   *Science Policy Research Unit, University of Sussex*

We live in a time when people are more able than ever to affect the environment, and when the pace of technological change and scientific discovery continues to increase. Vital questions must continually be asked about the allocation of resources under these conditions. This series aims to provide readers interested in public policies on energy and the environment with the latest scholarship in the field. The books will address the scientific, economic and political issues which are central to our understanding of energy use and its environmental impact.

Other titles in the series:

Energy efficiency and human activity: past trends, future prospects
Lee Schipper and Stephen Meyers

Oil trade: politics and prospects
Jack Hartshorn

Energy policy analysis and modeling

MOHAN MUNASINGHE
World Bank, Washington, DC

and

PETER MEIER
IDEA, Inc., Washington, DC

CAMBRIDGE
UNIVERSITY PRESS

Published by the Press Syndicate of the University of Cambridge
The Pitt Building, Trumpington Street, Cambridge CB2 1RP
40 West 20th Street, New York, NY 10011-4211, USA
10 Stamford Road, Oakleigh, Victoria 3166, Australia

First published 1993

Printed in Great Britain at the University Press, Cambridge

A catalogue record for this book is available from the British Library

Library of Congress cataloguing in publication data

Munasinghe, Mohan, 1945–
Energy policy analysis and modeling/Mohan Munasinghe and Peter Meier.
    p.   cm. – (Cambridge energy studies)
Includes bibliographical references.
ISBN 0 521 36326 8
1. Energy policy – Developing countries – Case studies.
2. Energy policy – Developing countries – Mathematical models.
I. Meier, Peter, 1942–   .   II. Title.   III. Series.
HD9502.D442M845 1992
333.79'09172'6 – dc20   91-42849   CIP

ISBN 0 521 36326 8 hardback

To Srimal and Erika

Contents

Preface

One way of defining the scope of a volume such as this is to develop a consistent view of the audience. We have three primary categories of readers in mind, and have attempted to make the organization and presentation of the material, and the level of mathematics in the exposition, consistent with their presumed needs. The first group of readers that we seek to reach are those who arc responsible for energy planning activities in the developing countries themselves. The typical head of a national energy planning institution and his senior staff, often has an academic background in engineering, and work experience in an electric utility or an oil company. It is they who are responsible for the analytical focus of the planning activity, and it is they who interact with foreign counterparts in technical assistance projects. What they frequently lack in discussions with foreign consultants, and in evaluating technical approaches for modeling and analysis, is an objective yardstick based on experience in other countries. Much of the case material, and guidance we provide on the selection and content of models, is directed at this audience. This may not be a very large audience, numerically, but it is nevertheless a very important one.

Secondly, we hope that the book might serve as a text in courses at the graduate, as well as post-graduate, level. The authors have served a faculty in a wide variety of courses sponsored by Universities in several countries, and by both multilateral and bilateral assistance agencies, that, over the last 15 years, have helped train many thousands of officials from some 70 countries. Nevertheless, despite the many monographs that cover individual aspects of energy planning, there still exists no text that provides an integrated and consistent framework for national energy policy analysis and planning for developing countries. To be sure, one would still need to augment the text with additional case material and detailed articles, but we hope that the book might provide such courses with a readable central focus.

Finally, we hope to reach those in the broader development community who continue to improve the effectiveness of energy policy analysis and planning, as a legitimate and effective activity that can contribute substantively to the development process.

Perhaps the most helpful background for a reader to have is an undergraduate training in science, engineering, and/or economics and several years of practical experience in government, in consulting, or in an electric utility or oil company. It is not likely that most readers would find relevant to their day-do-day problems, esoteric mathematical discussions of econometric models or the details of optimization algorithms. Rather, what is relevant is a broad experience in discussion of issues, alternative analytical approaches and problem resolution procedures.

We owe a great debt to the many individuals who have attended our courses in the past, for it is the interaction with them that has primarily enriched our own knowledge of developing country energy planning problems. They will surely forgive us if we cannot list them all by name.

Many others also have contributed to this volume, with generous advice and comments at various stages, especially Richard Eden, Ken King, Shishir Mukherjee, and Adelaide Schwab. Anne Rix edited the text with great patience and skill. Gurpreet Singh and Emaad Burki provided invaluable research assistance. Nevertheless, as always, the responsibility for the accuracy, content, and opinions, is ours alone.

M.M.
P.M.
May, 1992

Abbreviations

AFBC	Atmospheric Fluidized Bed Combusion
BCR	Benefit-Cost Ratio
BESOM	Brookhaven Energy Systems Optimization Model
CEA	Central Electricity Authority (of India)
CEB	Ceylon Electric Board (of Sri Lanka)
CIF	Cost, insurance, freight
CPC	Ceylon Petroleum Corporation
EA	Environmental Assessment
EIA	Environmental Impact Assessment
EDF	Electricité de France
EPRI	Electric Power Research Institute (of the United States)
FGD	Flue Gas Desulfurization
GDP	Gross Domestic Product
GEF	Global Environmental Fund
GNP	Gross National Product
IEA	International Energy Agency
INEP	Integrated National Energy Planning
IRR	Internal Rate of Return
LNG	Liquified Natural Gas
LOLP	Loss of Load Probability
LP	Linear Programming
LPG	Liquid Petroleum Gas
LRMC	Long-Run Marginal Cost
MEM	Ministry of Energy and Mines (of Morocco)
MOC	Marginal Opportunity Cost
NEA	National Energy Administration (of the Sudan)
NPV	Net Present Value
ONGC	Oil and Natural Gas Commission (of India)
RES	Refeence Energy System
SEB	State Electricity Board (of India)

SPD	Planning and Documentation Service (of the Morocco Ministry of Energy and Mines)
SRMC	Short Run Marginal Cost
T&D	Transmission and Distribution
TERI	Tata Energy Research Insitute (of India)
TOU	Time of Use
UNEP	United Nations Environment Programme
UNDP	United Nations Development Programme
USAID	United States Agency for International Development
WHO	World Health Organization
WAPDA	Water and Power Development Agency (of Pakistan)

PART I

Conceptual framework

CHAPTER 1

Introductory ideas

Energy plays a pervasive and critically important role in economic and social development. The identification and analysis of energy issues, and the development of energy policy options, are therefore important areas of study by governments, researchers, and the development community. But until the first oil price shock of 1973, neither developed nor developing countries conducted sector-wide energy planning: such planning as was done was left to the subsectoral institutions with little attempt at coordination or central planning. All that changed, of course, in the aftermath of the first oil crisis, and countries everywhere struggled with the establishment of effective policies and institutions to deal with energy sector problems. This effort intensified in the aftermath of the second oil price shock, and by the early 1980s most developing (and developed) countries had established some formal energy planning activity. Very simply put, the sharp increase in the real oil price resulted in severe macroeconomic consequences to the low-income, oil-developing countries, to which appropriate responses needed to be developed.

As the price of oil began to fall, gradually in the first half of the 1980s, then collapsed in 1986, other issues joined the forefront of energy planning activity. In many developing countries the question of the linkages between fuelwood use and deforestation gained increasing attention, and energy planners took leading roles in the formulation and implementation of policies to arrest rates of deforestation by promoting more efficient use of fuelwood. More generally, energy related environmental concerns that have emerged recently are likely to dominate in the 1990s and beyond. The need to deal with investment planning issues as problems of capital mobilization to expand the infrastructure of energy supply and distribution, especially electricity, also has become more acute.

The impact of the oil import bill
Expressed as percentages of both imports and exports, table 1.1 indicates the stress that increasing oil import bills have placed upon the

Table 1.1 *Oil imports and merchandise trade for oil-importing countries*

	Oil bill as % of exports		Oil bill as % of imports	
	1973	1983	1973	1983
Philippines	8.8	35.4	9.2	21.8
Thailand	11.1	27.3	8.5	110.9
Pakistan	5.7	32.0	5.6	18.5
Morocco	10.0	42.8	4.8	24.0
India[a]	10.6	70.0	9.6	40.5
Bangladesh	8.6	39.4	9.6	13.2

Note: [a] data shown is for 1980 not 1983; since then increased domestic production has significantly reduced the foreign exchange burden.

merchandise trade balance of developing countries. Many energy planning agencies in developing countries were created in the mid to late 1970s in response to the general recognition that the established subsectoral institutions did not have the inclination or ability to deal with the oil import problem, much less could individual institutions that generally dealt with a single fuel (the electric utility, the gas or coal companies, etc.) deal with the fuel substitution policies that would be necessary to lessen dependence on oil.

Thus the energy planner became involved in the analysis of a complicated and interrelated set of possible policy responses, from the launching of initiatives to promote energy conservation to the articulation of coherent, sector-wide pricing policies. Almost everywhere the search began for domestic fossil resources, oil, coal, and gas, to replace imported oil: in a great number of developing countries these programs met with much success (Thailand, Bangladesh, Pakistan, India, Egypt), but in others with failure (Sri Lanka, Morocco, Sudan, Senegal).[1] Because of the strength of established subsector institutions for electricity and oil, the primary role of the sector-wide planner in these areas has tended to be limited to coordination and integration: but in renewable energy, and in the promotion of energy efficiency and other demand management initiatives, the energy planning agency has often been thrust into a lead role in the implementation of such programs.

---

[1] In some cases early indications of major resources met with bitter disappointment because detailed studies showed reserves to be only marginally exploitable (such as the Meskala Gas Field in Morocco), or because political circumstances prevented commercial exploitation (such as the crude oil discovered in the south central Sudan in the late 1970s by Chevron).

In the early 1980s the price of oil remained roughly constant in dollar terms, implying a decrease in the real price to the United States. Yet this period also marked a period of sharp appreciation in the value of the dollar relative to other currencies, which in large measure offset the constant dollar price. But in 1986 the world price of oil collapsed, reaching as low as $10/bbl before stabilizing in the $15–17/bbl range. But, while this afforded some relief to the oil-importing developing countries, to others the net impact on their balance of payments was just the opposite. As we shall see in the case of Pakistan (in an example presented in chapter 10), while the increase in the value of remittances from Pakistani workers in the middle east exceeded the increase in the oil import bill in the 1979–82 period (meaning that the net impact of the oil price increase was an *increase* in foreign exchange availability due to direct oil-related factors), in the late 1980s precisely the opposite occurred as the economies of the Gulf States contracted: now the fall in worker remittances exceeded the decrease in the oil import bill. Even worse has been the impact of the Iraqi invasion of Kuwait: in late 1990 worker remittances to many South Asian countries have fallen at the same time as the oil price increased. Pakistan, India, Sri Lanka, and Bangladesh were particularly hard hit.[2]

In fact in the mid 1980s the question of how to deal with oil price *decreases* caused as much controversy as the question of how to deal with the price increases of the previous decade: in the immediate aftermath of the 1986 oil price collapse, the responses of governments ranged from maintaining the domestic oil price at the 1985 level and keeping the windfall entirely for itself (as occurred in Morocco) to that of the United States where the retail oil price was allowed to fall as a consequence of price deregulation policies introduced by the Reagan administration in the early 1980s. Most governments adopted policies somewhere in between.

One might add that the problems faced by lower-income, oil-exporting developing countries are not really any different. The need to use domestically produced oil at an economically efficient level is just as great, since oil that is so saved can be exported to earn foreign exchange. Thus Egypt, Indonesia, and Nigeria, for example, all need to grapple with domestic oil consumption issues, and the need for energy conservation, and for the development of other indigenous resources (coal in Indonesia, gas in Egypt and Nigeria) is no less important.

---

[2] Egypt, a net oil exporter, benefitted from the increase in oil price, but suffered a double blow to its foreign exchange balance: in addition to sharp declines in worker remittances, even before the outbreak of the Gulf War in January 1991 Egypt suffered a dramatic decline in foreign tourism, with losses just in the period August–December 1990 estimated at over $1billion.

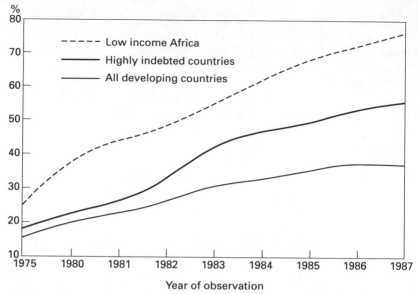

Figure 1.1   Developing country debt as a fraction of GDP

Capital mobilization problems

The second major concern relates to the energy intensiveness of the energy sector, particularly for electricity, and the increasing difficulties of mobilizing the necessary investment resources. The sector has been a major contributor to the external indebtedness of many countries (especially in Latin America), with correspondingly grave macro-economic consequences. Figure 1.1 indicates how developing country debt as a fraction of GDP has risen alarmingly in the 1975–87 period, from an average of 15% in 1987 to about 35% in 1987. In the highly indebted countries of Latin America, the ratio of debt to GDP had increased to an average of 50% by 1987.

Despite some anomalies, the link between energy demand and GDP is well established. Electric power, in particular, has a vital role to play in the development process, with future prospects for economic growth being closely linked to the provision of adequate and reliable power supplies. Figure 1.2 is an indicative example of this relationship between electricity use and income in a sample of fourteen developing countries. A more systematic analysis of World Bank and UN data over the last two or three decades indicates that the ratio of percent age growth rates (or elasticity) of power system capacity to GDP in developing countries is about 1.4.

Assuming no drastic changes in past trends with respect to demand

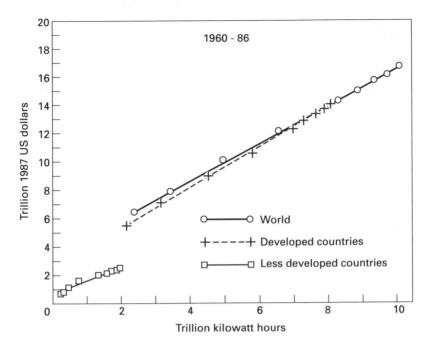

Figure 1.2   Electricity consumption and income

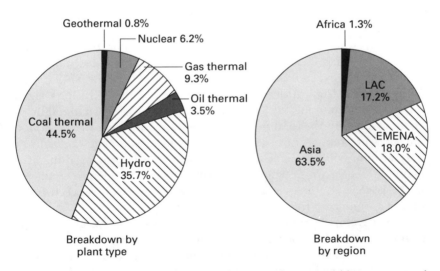

Figure 1.3   Breakdown by plant type and region of capacity additions expected in developing countries in the 1990s
Source: World Bank (1990).

8   *Conceptual framework*

Table 1.2 *Regional breakdown of capital expenditures in the 1990s (in billion $)*

	Asia	EMENA[a]	LAC[b]	Africa	Total
Generation	277	82	83	6	448
Transmission	39	8	32	2	81
Distribution	100	23	27	2	152
General	39	11	13	1	64
Total	455	124	155	11	745
%	61.1	16.6	20.8	1.5	100

Notes:
[a] Europe, Middle East and North Africa (Mediterranean region).
[b] Latin America and the Caribbean.
Source: World Bank (1990).

management and conservation, the World Bank's most recent projections indicate that demand for electricity in developing countries will grow at an average annual rate of 6.6% during the period 1989–99 (World Bank, 1990). This compares with actual growth rates of 10% and 7% in the seventies and eighties, respectively. As indicated in figure 1.3, the Asia region requirements dominate with almost two-thirds of the total, and where coal and hydro are the main primary sources. Both coal and hydro have significant environmental problems associated with their use.

The investment needs corresponding to these indicative projections are also very large. Table 1.2 shows the projected breakdown of power sector capital expenditure in the 1990s. Of a total of $745 billion (constant 1989 US$), Asia (which includes both India and China) again dominates, accounting for $455 billion or over $45 billion annually. In comparison with the total projected annual requirement of $75 billion, the present annual rate of investment in developing countries is only around $50 billion. Even this present rate is proving difficult to maintain. As shown in figure 1.1, developing country debt rose sharply in the 1980s, and investments in the capital-intensive power sector have played a significant role in this observed increase.

If the developing countries follow this projected expansion path, the environmental consequences are also likely to increase in a corresponding fashion. There is already a growing concern about the environmental consequences of energy use in developing countries. At a recent workshop on acid rain in Asia, participants reported on a wide range of environmental effects of the growing use of fossil fuels, especially coal,

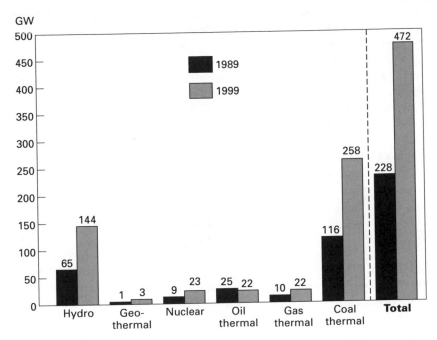

Figure 1.4   Comparison of 1989 and projected 1999 installed generating capacities in developing countries
Source: World Bank (1990).

in the region (Foell and Green, 1991). For example, total 1985 sulphur dioxide emissions in Asia were estimated at around 22 million tons,[3] and these levels, coupled with high local densities, have led to acid deposition in many parts of Asia.

However, the developing countries feel that any attempts to mitigate these environmental effects should not be allowed to jeopardize the critical role played by the energy sector in economic development. Similarly, the allocation of resources to environmental programs in developing countries can only increase the already formidable funding requirements for conventional power system expansion. Thus, energy and environmental policy-makers in the developing countries face difficult trade-offs, a topic to which we return in greater depth in chapter 7.

Optimal investment planning under growing capital and environ-

[3] This level of SO$_2$ emissions for all of Asia might be compared to the 20 million tons of SO$_2$ that is presently emitted in the United States: in chapter 7 we examine the equity implications of this comparison in more detail as part of our discussion of the role of environmental objectives in energy planning.

mental constraints therefore represents the second major area of activity for developing country energy planners. It is of course true that the implementing agencies (the electric utility, the refinery, and so on) generally take the lead in formulating investment plans for their subsector. Yet the consequences of a misallocation of limited investment resources are potentially so severe that coordination and coherence of subsectoral investment plans to some overall view of sector development is generally recognized as requiring a sector-wide planning function as well.

Finally, it might also be noted that recent attempts to increase the role of the private sector in the capital-intensive electricity and oil development subsectors by no means lessens the need for coherent sector-wide planning. Particularly in Asia the attempt to carve out a role for the private sector in power generation has been very difficult and often frustrating for all parties concerned. In the electric sector, for example, establishing the clear regulatory and institutional environment necessary for the successful integration of private sector generating plants into predominantly publicly owned and operated grids requires strong leadership and a coherent vision of the future course of electricity development by the responsible planning entity.

Book outline

This volume is organized into five parts. Part I presents the overall conceptual framework. In chapter 2 the concept of integrated national energy planning (INEP) is introduced, which provides the background to the hierarchical modeling scheme that is the central focus of this book. The role of modeling in the energy planning and policy analysis process is explained in chapter 3.

In part II basic techniques are introduced, starting with a discussion of energy balances in chapter 4. With so much of the analysis now conducted by energy planners being done in a spreadsheet environment, particular attention is paid to the rudiments of good spreadsheet model design and error-checking procedures. A simple model of the Egyptian energy balance is used to illustrate the key points. Energy demand projection is the subject of chapter 5, and optimization models are introduced in chapter 6, using a simple linear programming model of a West African refinery to illustrate the basic concepts. Chapter 7 deals with the crucial problems of how environmental issues may be incorporated into energy planning and decision-making.

In part III we discuss planning issues in two selected energy subsectors. Space limitations preclude a discussion of all of the important subsectors. Among commercial sectors, the singling out of electricity (chapter 8) was dictated by its universal importance in light of its high capital intensity, and by its technical complexity. While all countries need to deal with electrification problems, coal, oil, and natural gas resources, each of which merits its own discussion, do not occur in every country. The analysis of some of the subsectors omitted in this section are covered elsewhere in this book (like the discussion of refinery optimization models in chapter 6), while other areas, such as the use of decision analysis in oil and natural gas exploration and development, are well treated in other works.

The selection of the fuelwood sector (chapter 9) was fairly compeling in view not only of the serious problems of deforestation faced by many developing countries, but also by virtue of the fact that, in the absence of a strong subsectoral institution, energy planners have often been thrust into the lead role in the analysis, definition, and even implementation of fuelwood programs. The Sudan provides the illustrative case material here.

In part IV integration problems are addressed. Chapter 10 begins with a comprehensive discussion of pricing, which is presented as a two stage process: the determination of economically efficient prices in the first and adjustments to reflect other objectives in the second. Chapter 11 deals with energy-economic linkages; models from Pakistan, Colombia, and India are used as illustrative examples. In chapter 12 integrated energy sector models are discussed, including a presentation of some software packages for integrated energy planning.

Finally, part V deals with the implementation of the policy modeling process. A central concern here is the institutional framework (chapter 13), not just in terms of the organization of the energy planning activity, but of the sector itself. In chapter 14 some of the main issues of implementation are discussed, with emphasis on the importance of consistency across all levels of the planning hierarchy, and the concomitant need to align the modeling process with the institutional arrangements on how to deal with uncertainty, and on the special problems imposed by a process increasingly dependent on microcomputers. The book concludes with two more detailed case studies: Sri Lanka in chapter 15, and Morocco in chapter 16.

CHAPTER 2

Integrated national energy planning (INEP)

Because of the many interactions and non-market forces that shape and affect the energy sectors of every economy, decision-makers in an increasing number of countries have realized that energy sector investment planning, pricing, and management should be carried out within an integrated national energy planning (INEP) framework which helps analyze a whole range of energy policy options over a long period of time (Munasinghe, 1980). It must however be emphasized that, while INEP provides primarily a conceptual framework for policy analysis and energy strategy formulation, policy implementation should rely mainly on market incentives and decentralized competitive forces; this point, too, is taken up in greater detail later on.

The development of the concepts and methodology of INEP and its subsequent application can be traced to the energy crisis of the 1970s. Before this period, energy was relatively cheap, and any imbalance between supply and demand was invariably dealt with by augmenting supply. The emphasis was more on the engineering and technological aspects. Furthermore, as noted previously, planning was confined to the various energy subsectors such as electricity, oil, coal, etc., with little coordination among them.

From the mid 1970s onwards, the rapidly increasing cost of all forms of energy, led by the world oil price, stimulated the development of new analytical tools and policies (Munasinghe, 1980). First, the need became apparent for greater coordination between energy supply and demand options, and for the more effective use of demand management and conservation. Second, energy-macroeconomic links began to be explored more systematically. Third, the more disaggregate analysis of both supply and demand within the energy sector offered greater opportunities for interfuel substitution (especially away from oil). Fourth, the analytical and modeling tools for energy subsector planning became more sophisticated. Fifth, in the developing countries, greater reliance was placed on economic principles, including the techniques of shadow pricing. Finally, heightened environmental concerns have led to a better understanding of energy-environmental interactions.

INEP makes use of all these separate threads. Some early attempts at comprehensive energy planning were made, particularly in the second half of the 1970s. However, it was soon recognized that the constraints imposed by limited data, skilled manpower, and time posed formidable problems, especially in third world countries. Many of the early planning models were designed to be all-encompassing and, therefore, proved to be too large and unwieldy to be used successfully in the policy analysis process. On the other hand, more specific models tended to overlook important energy sector or macroeconomic linkages. Finally, most models were not policy-oriented, and were often treated as mere academic exercises. This initial learning process led to a more hierarchical analytical framework that recognizes at least three distinct levels of analysis – energy-macroeconomic, energy sector, and energy subsector – as well as the interactions among them. This approach also gives a better policy focus. More recently, the availability of microcomputers has provided developing country analysts with a relatively cheap, powerful, and flexible tool to develop and apply some of these ideas (Meier, 1985a and Munasinghe, 1986).

Coordinated energy planning and pricing require detailed analyses of the interrelationships between the various economic sectors, and their potential energy requirements, versus the advantages and disadvantages, including their environmental impacts, of the various forms of energy such as electric power, petroleum, natural gas, coal, and traditional fuels (e.g., firewood, crop residues, and dung) to satisfy these requirements. Non-conventional sources, whenever they turn out to be viable alternatives, must also be fitted into this framework.

The INEP concept is equally applicable to both industrialized and developing countries. In the former, the complex and intricate relationships between the various economic sectors, and the prevalence of private market decisions on both the energy demand and supply sides, make analysis and forecasting of policy consequences a difficult task. In the latter, substantial market distortion, shortages of foreign exchange as well as human and financial resources for development, larger numbers of poor households whose basic needs somehow have to be met, greater reliance on traditional fuels, and relative paucity of energy as well as other data, add to the already complicated problems faced by energy planners everywhere.

The broad rationale underlying planning at the national level and policy-making of all kinds in the developing countries is the need to ensure the best use of scarce resources in order to further overall socio-economic development and improve the welfare and quality of life of citizens. Energy planning in particular is therefore an essential part of national economic planning, and should be carried out and implemented in close coordination with the latter. However, the word "planning," whether applied to the national economy or the energy sector in particular, need not imply some rigid framework along the lines of centralized and fully planned economies. Planning, whether by design or deliberate default, takes place in every economy, even where so-called free market forces reign supreme. In energy planning and policy analysis, the principal emphasis is on the detailed and disaggregated analysis of the energy sector, its interactions with the rest of the economy, and the main interactions within the various energy subsectors themselves. Energy policy analysis and planning must be developed to meet the many interrelated and often conflicting overall national objectives as effectively as possible. Specific goals usually include: (a) determining the detailed energy needs of the economy and meeting them to achieve growth and development targets, (b) choosing the mix of energy sources needed to meet future energy requirements at the lowest costs, (c) minimizing unemployment, (d) conserving energy resources and eliminating wasteful consumption, (e) diversifying supply and reducing dependence on foreign sources, (f) meeting national security and defense requirements, (g) supplying the basic energy needs of the poor, (h) saving scarce foreign exchange, (i) identifying specific energy demand/ supply measures to contribute to possible priority development of special regions or sectors of the economy, (j) raising sufficient revenues from energy sales to finance energy sector development, (k) attaining price stability, and (l) preserving the environment.

The scope of INEP

The scope of INEP, policy analysis, and supply-demand management may be clarified by examining the hierarchical framework depicted in figure 2.1 (Munasinghe, 1980, 1988). Although INEP is primarily country focussed, it is useful to begin by recognizing the global consequences of energy use. Individual countries are embedded in an international economic and environmental matrix. Thus both the world economy (through trade and financial linkages) and the natural resource base (through interactions involving resource depletion or global climate change) will impose exogenous constraints and conditions on national-level decision-making.

The next hierarchical level indicated on figure 2.1 treats the energy

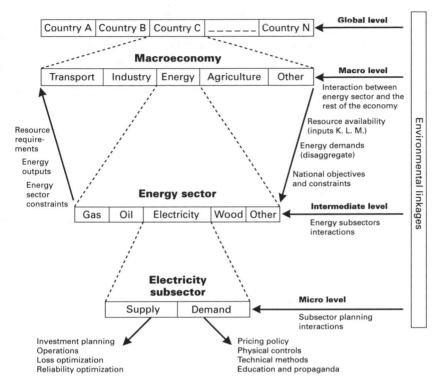

Figure 2.1   Hierarchical conceptual framework for integrated national energy planning (INEP) and environmental analysis

sector as a part of the whole economy. Therefore, energy planning requires analysis of the links between the energy sector and the rest of the economy. Such links include the input requirements of the energy sector, such as capital, labor, raw materials, and environmental resources (such as clean air, water, or space), as well as, in relation to national objectives, energy outputs, such as electricity, petroleum products, woodfuel, and so on, and the impact on the economy of policies concerning availability, prices, taxes, etc.

Energy is so fundamental to the functioning of modern economies that it is often difficult to define neat boundaries of planning responsibility. In the case, say, of transportation fuels, the boundary between energy policy and transportation policy is not distinct: the transportation system must be developed in light of the energy consequences of particular modal choices, while the energy system must be developed in light of the evolution of the transportation system. Thus, specific policies affecting the transport sector, such as subsidies to public transport, construction or non-construction of super-highways or airports, the level of license fees for vehicles or relative excise taxes on diesel versus gasoline vehicles, tax credits for energy conservation, pollution control legislation or specific end-use planning policies may have as profound an impact on energy demands as more broad-based energy pricing, allocation or supply management policies. Similar interfaces occur in the case of non-commercial energy, and fuelwood use in particular, an issue that might be considered a part of integrated rural development planning as much as one of integrated energy planning.

The third level of INEP treats the energy sector as a separate entity that integrates the subsectors such as electricity, petroleum, and so on. It is at this level that one analyzes the interaction among the different energy subsectors with particular emphasis on substitution possibilities and the resolution of any resulting policy conflicts, such as competition between natural gas, bunker oil or coal for electricity production, diesel or gasoline for transport, kerosene and electricity for lighting, or woodfuel and kerosene for cooking.

The last and most disaggregate level pertains to planning within each of the energy subsectors. Thus, for example, the electricity subsector must determine its own demand forecast and long-term investment program; the petroleum subsector, its supply sources, refinery outputs, distribution networks, and likely demands for oil products; the woodfuel subsector, its consumption projections and detailed plans for rotation or reforestation, harvesting of timber, and so on.

In practice, the various levels of INEP merge and overlap considerably. Energy-environmental interactions (represented by the vertical bar on figure 2.1) also tend to cut across all levels, and need to be incorporated into the analysis, as will be described in chapter 7. Finally, spatial disaggregation is rather important in larger and regionally diverse countries.

One example of overlapping arises where a single subsector institution may be responsible for a substantial share of total national export earnings – this is the case, say, for the oil companies of Indonesia and Egypt – thus their production schedules become of express interest to national macroeconomic planning. Experience shows that in these countries sector-wide planning becomes especially difficult because of the independence and power of such national oil companies, whose chairmen often report directly to the head of state, not just nominally, as is frequently the case for electric utilities and oil companies, but in fact as well.

More important however, is the merging between sectoral and

subsectoral planning activities. Indeed, it is a sign of a successful sectoral energy planning process when, for example, the planning cells of utilities and oil companies work closely with the demand forecasting group of a national energy planning agency, and the distinction between what is the demand forecast of the electric utility and what is the demand forecast of the national energy planning agency becomes irrelevant.

INEP in the large developing countries

The compact INEP conceptual framework summarized in figure 2.1 is more relevant to small- and medium-sized countries, and needs to be extended to apply to the very large developing countries such as China, India, and Brazil, where planning at the regional and state levels is an additional consideration that greatly complicates the overall institutional arrangements. Thus, in a small country, a single hydro-electric scheme which may account for a substantial share of total public investment may enter into national macroeconomic planning considerations: in a country such as India, the individual project has essentially no impact at the national macroeconomic level (although major projects may well come to the forefront of national consciousness as a result of major environmental and socio-economic impacts – as typified, say, by the controversy over the Mathura refinery and its potential impact on the Taj Mahal). As we shall see later on, such questions of scale have a substantial impact on the choice of appropriate modeling techniques.

What complicates energy sector planning in these countries is a parallel hierarchial structure for individual subsectors. In India, for example, electricity planning is conducted at the national level by the Central Electricity Authority (CEA), which plans the expansion of the electric system at the regional level. These regions in turn consist of several states, each of which have their own State Electricity Boards (SEBs). At the national level, the Planning Commission interacts with the CEA; at the state level, sector-wide energy planning (of which to date there has been relatively little, but with some notable exceptions such as Gujarat) would interact with the SEBs.

Thus the framework for INEP that is the central focus of this book does have applicability to these large countries, but at the state and regional scale, rather than the national scale, so that here one might simply use integrated regional energy planning to supplement INEP. A determination of how such regional planning efforts should be appropriately integrated to the national level in such places is in any event very case specific, and in each of these countries very different institutional arrangements are required. Meanwhile, INEP has direct relevance for the approximately eighty countries of small to medium size that fall into the general category of lower-income developing countries.

Policy instruments

To achieve the basic national goals elaborated earlier, a broad set of policy instruments is available to governments for optimal energy management, including physical controls, technical methods, direct investments or investment-influencing policies, education and pro-motion, and pricing, taxes, subsidies, and other financial incentives. Since these tools are interrelated, their use should be closely coordinated for maximum effect. But this very diversity of instruments, and their interrelationships, is what makes quantification of these linkages and impact assessment so difficult.

Physical controls are most useful in the short run when there are unforeseen shortages of energy. All methods of limiting consumption by physical means, such as load shedding or rotating power cuts in the electricity subsector, reducing or rationing the supply of gasoline, or banning the use of motor cars during specified periods, are included in this category. However, physical controls can also be used as long-run policy tools: for example a number of countries ban the importation of diesel automobiles in an effort to control the demand mix of petroleum products over the longer term.

Technical methods used to manage the supply of energy include the determination of the most efficient means of producing a given form of energy, choice of the least-cost mix of fuels, research and development of substitute fuels, such as oil from shale, coal, or natural gas, the substitution of alcohol for gasoline, and so on. Technology may also be used to influence energy demand, such as introducing more fuel-efficient auto-mobiles or better wood-stoves, and by research into and promotion of solar heating devices.

Investment policies have a major effect on both energy supply and consumption patterns in the long run. The extension of natural gas distribution networks, the building of new power plants based on more readily available fuels, such as coal, or the development of public urban transport networks are just some of these policies. It should be noted that while many of these may well be undertaken by sectors other than energy – examples are investments in transportation facilities or the systematic installation and/or electrification of deep-well irrigation pumps – close cooperation between the energy administration and planning authorities of these other sectors is obviously called for.

The policy tool of education and promotion can help to improve the energy supply situation by making citizens aware of cost-effective ways to reduce energy consumption, of the energy use implications of specific appliances or vehicles, and of the potential for substitution of energy by capital (such as the proper insulation of buildings). Taxation and subsidies are useful policy instruments that can also profoundly affect energy consumption patterns in the long run. For example, countries which have imposed high taxes on gasoline have generally had significant results in terms of reduced automobile use, more efficient vehicle fleets, and so on. Subsidies have similarly encouraged energy-saving capital investments.

Pricing is politically sensitive, but, as discussed later in chapter 9, it is a most effective means of demand management, especially in the medium and long run. However, pricing has limitations and must be skillfully combined with other non-price policy instruments for best results. For example, in the traditional fuels sector, such as fuelwood, where there is no well-developed market, pricing policy may not be effective. Reduction of fuelwood use may require other non-price measures, such as disseminating a more effective domestic cooking stove. In the case of very high-income consumers, who are willing to pay an extremely high price for their comfort (for example by the purchase and operation of air conditioners), high prices might not reduce demand significantly, but could be used instead as a revenue-generating mechanism.

At the other end of the scale, raising prices to low-income energy consumers may simply cause them to have to spend a greater share of their income on energy purchases without affecting their energy consumption, because these consumers are already at the basic needs level and could not do without a minimum amount of energy (such as kerosene for lighting in rural homes). In such cases, energy price increases would cause hardship by limiting the income available to poor households to purchase essential non-energy items. In summary, controlling the use of energy through coordinated use of the various policy tools is the principal goal of energy supply and demand management. Practical aspects of such policy coordination are discussed later.

CHAPTER 3

The role of modeling in energy
policy analysis

Modeling has been an integral part of national energy planning since the mid 1970s when governments instituted such activities on a major scale after the first oil embargo. Large-scale computer models were a central part of the policy analysis and planning functions of the US Department of Energy (and its predecessor, the Energy Research and Development Administration) and were also used extensively from an early date in the major European Countries and by the EEC. At a very early stage it was recognized that the complexity of the energy problem required sophisticated analytical approaches if the policy options that were to be presented to decision-makers were to be based on sound analysis.

Because so much of energy planning in developing countries has been attempted with formal models originally implemented in the 1970s on mainframes, and more recently on successively more powerful generations of mini- and microcomputers, the lessons of this past experience is central to the development of our own framework. Much of this experience mirrors that of energy policy analysis and planning generally – indeed it can be said that the grand failures of computer modeling match the grand failures of energy planning, a correlation perhaps nowhere better illustrated than in the United States, where a vast expenditure on energy models in the late 1970s contributed very little to the resolution of the fundamental policy debates, such as that concerning the relationship between the so-called shortages (notably that of natural gas) and price controls.[1]

In developing countries the analytical problems are no less complex. The macroeconomic and sectoral outlook in many countries continues to be very bleak, and the exploration of new approaches and initiatives

[1] In general the modeling efforts conducted by the Department of Energy and the Energy Information Administration in this period were used primarily for "impact assessment" of Administration proposals, rather than as a planning tool in the formulation of policy. Data and modeling assumptions were often simply forced in such a way that results would be consistent with the authorities preferences, e.g., for regulatory controls rather than price decontrol.

20

requires a sophisticated understanding of the interactions between the energy sector and its macroeconomic context. For example, the impact of policy packages associated with new lending instruments such as sector restructuring loans and structural adjustment loans requires a level of analysis not easily accomplished by manual calculation. Moreover, the levels of uncertainty faced by developing country policy-makers tend to be greater than those experienced in the industrialized countries. Finally, the transition from essentially rural economies dependent on non-traded traditional fuels to urban systems based on commercial fuels puts additional burdens on analysis.

The experience with energy modeling in developing countries over the past fifteen years or so is very uneven. One can identify three stages in the evolution of such modeling activities. In the first stage, when energy planning institutions in developing countries were still in their infancy and largely dependent on foreign consultants to provide analytical support, an attempt was made to adapt mainframe models originally developed in the United States and Europe. While some of these efforts were successful in the more advanced countries, such as Brazil and South Korea, in most low- and middle-income countries the experience can be characterized as quite unsatisfactory (see box 3.1 on page 22).

The establishment of more mature energy planning institutions in developing countries by the early 1980s coincided with the introduction of microcomputers, which heralded the second phase.[2] Much more of the modeling activity was conducted in-country, by better trained analysts, and with a much greater appreciation of the unique problems faced in developing countries. Nevertheless, many of these efforts remained unsuccessful in dealing with the difficult problems that were faced: as we have noted elsewhere, perhaps the main reason being the lack of model integration with the institutional realities.

As one reviews the role of energy modeling in this second phase, it is unclear to what extent the analytical frameworks and modeling tools were in fact useful, be it from the country perspective (e.g., in terms of the contribution made to the definition of national energy strategies) or from the perspective of development agencies (e.g., in terms of clarifying the impacts and benefits of policy packages associated with structural

---

[2] The experience with mini-computers such as the PRIME, that began to become available in the late 1970s, was also quite disappointing. First, while the cost was substantially below that of a mainframe, in the $100,000 to $200,000 price range, it was still beyond the means of most energy planning agencies. The only case we know of an Energy Planning Agency installing its own mini-computer was in the Dominican Republic, in a project funded by the United States Agency for International Development (USAID). By 1985 this machine was no longer in use, having been completely replaced by IBM PCs.

Box 3.1 *Experience with mainframe models of the 1970s*

In general energy planning models based on mainframes have not proven to be very useful to energy planning agencies in developing countries, for which there are several explanations. Indeed, in some countries such models were developed at great expense, yet never used at all.

A first problem related to the "black box" nature of the models. The client was neither part of the model development process, nor of the code development, with the result that the expatriate (and usually absent) consultant was the only individual who had sufficient knowledge of the code to make changes, or indeed to provide decision-makers with a clear understanding of the assumptions and limitations of the model.

A second problem related to training. Many computer modeling projects consumed vast resources for computer programming, model formulation, and debugging, leaving little time for on-the-job training. Typically, models might be ready only toward the end of multi-year projects.

The third problem concerned the mainframe machines themselves. Energy planning agencies were required to install their energy models on machines owned by others, typically the electric utility or a national computing center. Even aside from the problems of being able to get access to such machines during normal office hours (with administrative uses almost always being given higher priority), there remained the issue of location. Since energy agencies are rarely located in the same building as those who owned such machines, the incentive to use the models remained very low. To be sure, in a few rare cases, remote terminals were available, but obtaining paper copy of outputs usually required a trip to another building.

As always, there are some notable exceptions to the general experience. In South Korea, the DFI model (a large-scale general equilibrium model originally developed for the US Department of Energy) has been successfully implemented and modified by a number of government institutes: indeed, many refinements in the current South Korean version were made without expatriate assistance. However, this is a country where there is now a large, well-established cadre of professionals trained at major universities in economics, operations research, and systems analysis.

Such a cadre of professionals, however, is often absent in the lower-income countries of Africa and the Caribbean. Thus, what is reasonable and feasible in countries such as India, Argentina, Taiwan, Brazil, and Mexico may not be possible elsewhere. Indeed it can be asserted that the successful application of mainframe models has been limited to this group of more advanced countries.

---

adjustment loans). Despite the general lack of information, it seems clear from what is available, and from the experience of the UNDP/ World Bank energy assessments, that the scope, appropriateness, and sophistication of energy models varies quite considerably. Sometimes, even when the models developed are useful, the lack of trained local staff or good documentation can be a significant hurdle.

It can be asserted that we are currently in the third phase of this evolutionary process, in which a clear break has been made with most of the historical antecedents that were rooted in the mainframe models of the US and Europe. Many institutions in the third world, especially in India, Brazil, and China, have redefined the frontier of energy models in directions uniquely suited to developing countries.[3] And energy planning activities in many smaller countries, such as Sri Lanka, the Dominican Republic, Costa Rica, and Morocco, have established analytical approaches that show substantial promise in addressing the complex but country specific problems noted above, and are consistent with extant staff capabilities.

The role of models

Nevertheless, it is nothing short of astonishing that despite almost two decades of energy planning experience one still encounters confusion over the role of modeling in policy analysis. The result is that very often models are adopted by energy planning agencies with relatively little idea of how the outputs are to be used; so often models developed in one place go in search of an application in some other place, and there is a rich body of anecdotal evidence about models developed at great expense never being used, or proving to be so complex, or so cumbersome, or so lacking in documentation, that local staff remained completely untrained when expatriate consultants withdrew at the end of technical assistance projects. This is not just a problem in energy sector-wide models, but with models commissioned at great expense by subsectoral institutions as well. It is of course not surprising that this evidence remains anecdotal: the parties obviously have very little interest in documenting fiascoes, and professional ethics puts limits on the ability to publish articles on the *failures* of energy modeling. The result is that only the articles on the successes (and purported successes) get published in the professional literature. To be sure, there is no doubt that modeling *can* be useful, and *can* assist practical decision-making, but the prerequisites for success are in fact quite limiting and as a result quite rare. We hope that this volume makes some contribution to an understanding not just of the techniques themselves, but of the broader set of circumstances that might enable them to be used with some success.

In our experience there is only one role for modeling in support of policy analysis, and that is to assist the evaluation of the impacts of

---

[3] For example, the TEESE model, developed by the Tata-Energy Research Institute (TERI), is reviewed in chapter 11.

alternative policy options. That means that the process must start with a very clear idea of the feasible set of options to be analyzed, and of what the criteria are for comparing these options. In particular to assume that energy models are capable of defining the "optimal" or even "feasible" set of policy options is simply unrealistic. That does not mean that there is no role for optimization models – indeed, we introduce these in this volume in chapter 6 – but somehow in the mythology of energy modeling there remains the impression that complex energy system optimization models relieve senior staff of the necessity to think about options in a realistic way, in the belief that optimal policies will emerge as an output of the modeling process. One might add that this is by no means an illusion restricted to developing country energy officials; in the industrialized countries there has emerged recently, among some, the perception that large-scale linear programming models will provide easy answers to the global warming problem, that somehow the "optimal" mix of technologies to minimize national, continental, or global CO_2 emissions will emerge as solutions. Most of these models are recycled energy system models developed a decade ago, when they were not able to make practical contributions to solving energy policy problems; simply adding "emission coefficients" to such models and using emissions as the objective function to be minimized, will not enable them to succeed in the new environmental application. It is a classic case of models going in search of new applications.

The most fundamental requirement of all is of course that those involved in the planning process have a clear idea of what questions they are supposed to answer. The reader may well take us to task for stating the obvious, yet the reality is all too often that these questions are *not* known with any precision. Often, this is in fact the practical result of deficiencies and/or ambiguities in the institutional structure that will be examined in chapter 13. A good example here is the case of Morocco, where any objective evaluation would conclude that there have been failures as well as successes in energy modeling (an admission that one of the writers, who was involved in both successes and failures, will readily concede). We will visit Morocco a number of times in this book – but a specific example right at the outset will serve to illustrate the nature of this fundamental problem, and the resultant hazards for the unwary aspiring energy modeler.

The institutional structure in Morocco is such that the Energy Directorate of the Ministry of Energy and Mines has nominal jurisdiction over the state-owned subsectoral implementing agencies (although one further complication here is that the electricity distribution companies, also responsible for water supply, the so-called "Regies," come under the jurisdiction of the Ministry of the Interior). There is a five-year planning cycle in Morocco, that serves to coordinate all public sector investment, and it is one of the nominal responsibilities of the Ministry to "review" and assemble the subsectoral investment plans.

Yet the criteria for this "review" have remained ambiguous, and there is no example of the Directorate ever *rejecting* a proposed project as part of this process. In part, of course, this is a result of the subsectoral institutions having great influence and power, that is not altogether unearned because in Morocco both the electric utilities and the refineries are technically very well managed and have served the country well. But, perhaps more importantly, substantial technical criteria could in any event not be defined in the absence of a well-articulated medium- to long-term energy strategy.

Unfortunately the response to this situation in the early 1980s was to construct an all-encompassing energy model that included a macro-economic model based on an input-output table, that drove an energy system model whose main feature was the ability to accommodate the impact of specific supply-side investment projects. All kinds of unrealistic expectations characterized the implementation of this model in the Ministry (more of which in the case study of chapter 16), the most important of which was the belief that the model would identify the "optimal" energy strategy and provide the means for evaluating proposals upon that basis. This was unrealistic on two counts: first, it was always unlikely that such a model could do better than the detailed subsectoral models used for electric utility capacity expansion planning in defining the optimal expansion plan. But, more importantly, a model can never substitute for the development of a long-term energy strategy: a model can only serve in a secondary role, to assist in the analysis of options under consideration.

Criteria for model selection

For almost two decades now since the first oil price shock, analysts have been developing energy sector models. Many have been reported in the literature, many more remain relatively unknown, having been implemented in the far corners of the world. Indeed, when faced with some particular analytical problem, there is always the question of whether some existing model can be taken "off the shelf," or whether a new model should be purpose built for the application in mind. Perhaps ten years ago, before the widespread use of microcomputers, there were always very strong reasons for adapting an existing model if at all possible, because the programming effort involved in using traditional

Table 3.1 *Summary of evaluation criteria*

General criteria
    Ability to respond to key questions of policy and priorities.
    Degree of integration with and replication of the planning process.
    Approach to treatment of uncertainties and the types of uncertainties that can be handled.
Macroeconomic models
    Integration and consistency with government accounts and forecasts.
    Disaggregation between energy and non-energy sectors.
    Geographic disaggregation.
    Alignment of model with available data.
Energy models
    Incorporation of project level information.
    Formulation of demand structures.
    Technical representation of the electric power sector.
    Does output format follow standard conventions?
    Representation of institutional structure.
    Representation of petroleum sector.
    Treatment of non-commercial fuels.
    Extent of financial detail including tariff structures.
Subsectoral models
    Extent to which model accepts data from models at subsectoral level.

programming modalities (BASIC, FORTRAN, Pascal, etc.) was always substantial. Today, however, with microcomputers, modern spreadsheets, and highly efficient programming environments (such as Microsoft Quickbasic, or Borland Turbopascal, and the "macro" programming languages of LOTUS spreadsheets), the choice is more even. In any event, it is clear, as noted throughout this volume, that the choice of model is dictated by the particular and specific needs of some analysis.

Nevertheless, the experience of the past decade does suggest some generally applicable criteria that can be applied to the choice of an energy sector model. Obviously, given the broad scope of energy planning, this could be a very long list indeed. However, the experience in a large number of small- to medium-sized developing countries indicates that a major part of the analytical needs of energy planning entities are (or should be) focused on a relatively limited set of short- to medium-term issues: integration of subsectoral planning efforts to achieve sector-wide consistency and integration with the overall macroeconomy, pricing and demand management, project evaluation, and medium-term investment planning. A summary of the evaluation criteria is presented in table 3.1

Integration with the planning process

Perhaps the most important attribute of a modeling system from the standpoint of the energy planning agency is the degree to which it replicates the institutional realities. If one accepts the premise that a key function of sector level policy analysis and planning is to integrate, rather than duplicate, the planning efforts at the subsector level into a consistent, sector-wide picture, and into the overall macroeconomic planning framework, then it follows that the modeling framework must also be consistent with this function.

This requirement is reflected both in the overall analytical and modeling approach as well as in matters of data and technical detail. Philosophically, given the premise of a hierarchical planning process itself, there follows also a hierarchical modeling framework in which the individual models can be exercised independently. Ideally, the models at the lowest, subsectoral level are run jointly by both the subsectoral institution and the energy sector level planning institution, or at the very least the energy model must have the ability to accept information at the same level of detail as that offered by the subsectoral entity. For example, in the case of the electric sector, the model should have the ability to accept the capacity expansion plan of the electric utility (a subject examined further below).

Treatment of uncertainties

Energy and macroeconomic policy analysis and planning in the typical oil-importing country is beset with a multitude of uncertainties, and the ability to identify energy and investment strategies that are robust under a variety of future outcomes is perhaps the key element in a successful analytical process in support of energy planning. Several fundamentally different types of uncertainty must be faced: (1) the stochastic character of all natural phenomena (such as rainfall and streamflow, or the distribution of oil reservoir sizes), (2) the uncertainties of the international economic and energy environment, over which the decision-makers in typical developing countries have no (or at best only marginal) control, and (3) the uncertainties in the functioning of the domestic economic system (and hence uncertainty in the responsiveness of the system to policy initiatives). Each of these types of uncertainty pose quite different demands on the analytical framework, and each requires its own unique approach. Chapter 14 discusses these points in detail.

Integration with macroeconomic plans

At the macroeconomic level, perhaps the most important concern is to develop a base-case scenario that is consistent with the official government forecast. In most countries there exists an official plan, typically prepared in an annual or five-year cycle by the Ministry of Planning or Finance. While such forecasts may well be in the nature of a set of goals rather than a forecast, and therefore subject to some controversy, it is nevertheless true that as a matter of practice this forecast usually has official standing, and therefore provides the basis for the participation of the macroeconomic planning authorities in sectoral planning efforts.

It follows that the macroeconomic model used for the short to medium term covered by this forecast should have the ability to replicate the official forecast as the baseline for analysis. Ideally, this baseline should then be capable of perturbation to reflect other assumptions in a consistent fashion, particularly if the official baseline is considered unrealistic and could be replaced with a more responsible alternative. Moreover, the presentation should be in a format that closely follows the official guidelines (for example, using the same sectoral disaggregation, even if this poses some difficulties elsewhere in the analysis, e.g., in the demand projections).

By the same token, given that some of the more important impacts of energy sector decisions are on the external accounts, the format and presentation should follow closely that of the central bank and its reporting requirements to the international financial community. All of this implies a high degree of disaggregation: however, it is easier to produce an aggregated measure from the disaggregated categories, than it is to disaggregate a measure in a manner consistent with official statistics. For example, instead of a single variable for external debt in an energy-macroeconomic model, it is helpful to use the same disaggregation as the central bank (short-, medium-, long-term, government, private, etc.), and then assign the energy sector debt service to the appropriate category.

Disaggregation of energy and non-energy sectors

There are two basic approaches to the reconciliation of energy models and highly aggregated macroeconomic models (in which energy and non-energy sectors are either not distinguished at all, or at a level of disaggregation unsuited to energy work), particularly with respect to the evaluation of the macroeconomic impacts of the energy sector. The simple expedient is to run the two models independently, with a comparison of the energy sector impacts derived from the energy model (say the level of energy-derived government revenues, or foreign debt service) against the overall aggregates projected by the macromodel. Of course, since the aggregate includes the energy sector, this approach is both imprecise and inconsistent, although perhaps adequate for a first-order estimate.

A more detailed, but also more difficult, approach is to attempt some explicit disaggregation of the macromodel. Where formal models are concerned this may require extensive changes to the equation structure. On the other hand, where the basis is a macroeconomic accounting framework rooted in the official government plan, it is usually quite easy to subtract out energy sector investment (and debt service) from the aggregate investment projections. Moreover, since the energy sector often contributes a relatively small amount to GDP, its inclusion in other value-added sectors poses few problems and an explicit disaggregation here is not necessary (electricity is usually included in a sector such as municipal services that also includes water and other utilities, while refinery operations are frequently included in the industrial sector).

Alignment of the model to available data

Many macroeconomic models developed for use in energy-economic studies prove to be poorly designed from the standpoint of possessing a level of complexity that is consonant with the available data. Even those models that make no claim of relevance for the short to medium term, but whose focus is the long-run structural adjustment process, frequently use theoretically convenient equations whose coefficients are difficult if not impossible to derive from actual, in-country data. Such models typically use log-log production functions involving constant substitution elasticities (among energy, labor, capital, and other material inputs) that are quite different from the sort of production functions estimated in sectoral studies.

This problem is perhaps most acute in that subset of countries whose economies are still largely agricultural, and whose export earnings depend heavily on a few export crops. Any reasonable and useful formulation of plantation sectors involving perennial crops would need to include in a sectoral production function – beyond only price and energy (and/or fertilizer) inputs – such additional variables as the area under cultivation, and the age distribution of the planting stock. Since in many cases increases in the area under agricultural or plantation cultivation implies a decrease in the natural forest area, there may also exist an indirect link to the fuelwood supply; in some cases (such as rubber), the replanting cycle itself contributes to the fuelwood supply (in Sri Lanka, for example, a significant portion of the urban fuelwood supply in the Colombo area is rubber wood, i.e., trees felled to make way for new plantings). Typically, production functions in macroeconomic models are of the Cobb-Douglas form, which are the simplest that allow factor substitution. One such form is:

$$X = aL^bE^cK^d$$

where X is incremental output, L is the incremental labor input, E is the incremental energy input, K is the previous year(s) investment, and a, b, c, and d are technical coefficients. Yet production functions encountered in typical sectoral studies are frequently of a quite different form, especially for agricultural sectors, including at a minimum variables for land area, fertilizer inputs (of importance anyway to energy planning because of the energy intensiveness of their manufacture), and irrigation/rainfall inputs.

The argument here is not that macroeconomic models should necessarily be encumbered with vast sectoral detail. However, to the extent that macroeconomic models are built to examine the longer-term issues of structural adjustment (and the impact of that adjustment on the energy sector), then maximum use should be made of the sectoral models built by others interested in the rehabilitation or adjustment of major producing or exporting sectors, especially where there are direct links to important energy supply issues as well.

Project level information
One of the most important questions concerning the suitability of a general modeling framework for both the national decision-makers and international lending agencies is the ability to include project-level information. The smaller the country in question, the more important this issue becomes, since a single electric sector project may in such cases account for a major share of public sector investment and debt service. In brief, the need to evaluate project-level information within the broader context of the energy sector and the macroeconomy is not only important to financing institutions, but it is also fundamental to energy sector investment planning on the part of the borrower. It should be noted that this criterion is not met by the simple availability of a project analysis package.[4]

Equally important are questions such as how alternative investment plans are assembled, and, once assembled, how they are integrated into the overall analysis. For example, are project portfolios assembled on an *ad hoc* basis, by ranking of internal rates of return (in fact a possibly misleading procedure if capital is constrained) or by some sophisticated capital budgeting model that maximizes net present value (NPV) subject to capital constraints? Such questions are especially important for the electric sector, where the determination of the optimal capacity expansion path is a matter of considerable complexity. Indeed, just because of the technical complexity of this task, there may be very good reasons

---

[4] Indeed there are many microcomputer based commercial software packages now available for IRR and cost-benefit type calculations.

not to attempt to include much detail in the energy sector model itself, but to focus on how the energy sector model and the more detailed electric sector optimization models (such as WASP and EGEAS) interact.

Demand structures

The adequacy of the demand structures in many models is in some doubt, particularly with respect to the ability to estimate the impact of policy initiatives. Perhaps the best example concerns the electric sector which, in many developing countries, is supply constrained – the major determinant of demand being the ability of the electric utility to extend the system into both previously unconnected rural regions and rapidly expanding urban centers. Yet the traditional econometric formulation of demand as a function of price and income frequently ignores this issue (quite aside from other assumptions such as constant own-price elasticities, and neglect of cross-price elasticities). To be useful for an energy planning and policy exercise, the demand structure needs to consider, beyond just price and income variables, such factors as the extent of energy and peak load accounted for by auto-generation (which is highly sensitive to the level of reliability provided by the central system), the theft rate (as distinct from purely technical losses, which are subject to altogether different types of policy intervention), and the rates of new connections (in turn also related to the considerable costs of distribution system expansion). Uncertainty must also be taken into account.

To be sure, the level of available data, and the unique circumstances facing a particular country, make such generalizations hazardous. Nevertheless, it is the experience in a very wide set of countries that such questions are almost always present. Indeed, they lie at the heart of the controversy over demand projections that are encountered by, and hence merit the attention of, energy planning and policy-making bodies as part of their coordinating functions.

Technical representation of the electric sector

Because of the importance of the electricity sector from the standpoint of investment and debt service, and the inherent technical complexity of the operation of this subsector, an important issue concerns the degree to which an energy model has sufficient technical credibility to demonstrate the impact of multiple, and simultaneous policy and project initiatives. It is not at all uncommon for several multi- and bilateral agencies, and the country government itself, to be simultaneously contemplating the financing of additional generation capacity, the rehabilitation of the distribution system to reduce system losses, and an industrial sector energy efficiency initiative designed to improve power and load factors. It follows that if an energy model is to be useful even from a very narrow perspective, it has to have the ability to demonstrate the interactive impacts of such diverse but parallel initiatives. This in turn requires a level of technical detail that at a minimum includes the ability to replicate the essential features of system load-duration curves and the optimal dispatch of specific generation units.

Output format and data conventions

Since one of the major reasons for using models is to increase the productivity of the staff engaged in the support work for decision-making bodies, it follows that models should as far as possible adopt the usual reporting conventions in their presentation of key results. For example, energy balances should be generated in the form almost universally accepted by international institutions. This may perhaps be a somewhat obvious point, but several existing models not only require manual transcription of energy balances, but in some cases require additional calculations as well. Consideration must also be given to making outputs readily comprehensible to local decision-makers.

Institutional structure

Beyond the question of how the overall modeling system is aligned to the institutional realities as discussed above, is the degree to which an energy model itself is structured around the institutional framework. Since the revenue, tax and subsidy flows that are of major concern to government decision-makers and to an economically efficient pricing system are related to the transactions between specific energy sector institutions, it follows that for the energy model to be useful for short- to medium-term analysis, it should have as its basic building blocks not subsectors (petroleum, electricity, gas, coal), but institutions (the refinery or oil company, the electric utility, the LPG company, etc.).

Petroleum sector representation

The representation of the petroleum sector in energy models is frequently unsatisfactory. Problems range from inadequate disaggregation (which makes them difficult to use as a basis for pricing studies), to an inadequate treatment of refinery flexibility (future petroleum product output from a domestic refinery is estimated by mechanistic multiplication of the crude run by some set of yield coefficients). Indeed, nowhere is the ability of an energy model to interact with a more detailed subsectoral model more important than the petroleum sector.

Simulation model representations of refineries must therefore have either an appropriate interface to a detailed refinery LP, or find some other scheme to deal with refinery capacity expansion and flexibility issues. Treating the refinery as a black box, with product outputs given as linear functions of the crude inputs, is problematic even for simple hydroskimming refineries because crudes can be spiked over quite wide ranges. For example, the Refinery of the Dominican Republic has long used as input a blend of four different Mexican and Venezuelan crudes, plus a reconstituted crude consisting of a blend of butane, naphtha, kerosene, and gasoil; the result is a product mix that matches the domestic demand without the need for separate product imports. Chapter 6 deals with such refinery modeling issues in some detail.

Non-commercial fuels
There are a number of alternative strategies to deal with non-commercial fuels. Many LP energy models simply ignore them. Others include them in the overall scheme for computing energy balances, but with demand projections for fuelwood and charcoal not well integrated with the commercial fuel demand projections (the issue being the inadequate understanding of substitution effects among the commercial and non-commercial fuels). Reference energy system models (see chapter 5) generally do provide a structure to maintain a consistency in such substitutions, but are ill equipped to relate the pace of change to the price environment. In hierarchical systems that include a detailed fuelwood model, there are special difficulties in forcing consistency among projections for electricity, petroleum products, and non-commercial fuels. The unavailability of data is also a reason for not modeling non-commercial fuels.

Data integration with subsectoral models
The proposition that energy models should be linked to more detailed subsectoral models is of course obvious and logically sound, and the claim that a given model is consistent with other models is almost always made. Indeed, as a matter of computer technique, it is not too difficult to transfer data from one model to another. In practice, however, the question is not one of modeling, but of institutional relationships. What matters is not only the technical capability of an energy model to accept subsectoral detail (as argued above in the case of the electric sector capacity expansion plan), but an institutional mechanism that ensures a sufficient dialogue for the transfer to actually take place. In some countries (such as Morocco and Sri Lanka), such a mechanism is present; in others it is notably absent, which makes any modeling effort much more difficult.

Relationship to staff capabilities

Finally, in terms of in-country application, mention must be made of the issue of staff capabilities and training. Even a modeling framework that possesses all of the above attributes is without value unless the capability exists to use it. The working level staff must be sufficiently well trained to be able to understand and operate the analytical tools successfully. One might note that this is not only a matter of training in modeling and the particular software implementation – indeed, this is probably the least important aspect (if the software is well designed). Rather, the central issue is the technical background and experience of the staff. Often, a well-trained engineer or economist, with some years of experience, can usually be trained successfully to use a modeling system, whereas programmers, modelers, and others without experience in a refinery, electric, or gas utility, whatever their computer expertise, rarely have the technical judgment to successfully understand and operate a model ensemble. However, the participation of a programmer/systems analyst may well be desirable if present as part of a broader team.

PART II

Basic techniques

CHAPTER 4

Energy balances

The basic tool of energy analysis is the energy balance table, which has long been used not just for presentation of historical statistics, but also as a means of presenting alternative views of the future. Table 4.1 illustrates the basic scheme: the columns of the table represent different energy forms — electricity, gasoline, and so on — and the rows of the table represent the different stages of energy production, transformation, and consumption.[1] Thus for each column (fuel), the following identity must be satisfied:

Domestic production + imports − exports + stock changes − conversion inputs + conversion outputs = domestic consumption

Note the sign of certain rows: exports, losses, and inputs to energy conversion always have negative signs. It is of course possible to derive such future balances by purely manual means, bringing energy demand into balance with supplies and energy conversion facilities by iterative adjustment based on judgmental estimates of efficiencies, fuel allocations, the electricity generation mix, and so forth.[2] Indeed, perhaps the most widespread use of LOTUS spreadsheets in LDC energy planning is for the presentation of energy balances, in which the spreadsheet performs only addition and tabular cross-checks, and all of the entries, even for future years, is essentially data, entered by hand. In many such spreadsheets the only rubrics estimated by spreadsheet formula are energy imports, which for small oil-importing developing countries without refineries are readily calculated as the residual.

Units
Although energy balances are often displayed in physical units (Kwh for electricity, tons for coal, etc.), for a number of reasons it is

---

[1] This discussion is adapted from Meier (1986).
[2] Many of the early developing country energy assessments conducted in the 1970s, and the World Bank/UNDP Energy Sector Assessments conducted in the early 1980s, relied on purely manual means of assembling both historical balances and scenario balances for future years.

Table 4.1 *Illustrative energy balance*

	Hydro electricity	Electricity	Gasoline	Fuel oil
Domestic production	90			
Imports			220	280
Stock changes			−20	20
Gross supply	90		200	300
Electricity generation				−100
Inputs	−90			
Generation		60		
T&D losses		−12		
Total consumption		48	200	200
Consumption by sector				
Households		28	200	
Industry		20		200

desirable to use a single unit. For one thing, since different columns have different units, only column totals have any meaning in such a table. Second, and more importantly, one of the most important purposes for energy balance tables is to assess substitution possibilities, which means that a single unit, such as joules, or Btu, should be used throughout. However, to the extent that the key focus in almost all developing countries is the potential for substitution of imported oil, the use of an oil replacement unit has become standard: "tons of oil equivalent," or "barrels of oil equivalent". The basis of conversion of non-oil forms is simply the energy content of each, and hence the oil replacement unit itself requires definition in terms of some specific quantity of energy. Absent some particular reason to the contrary, the ton oil equivalent should be defined as being equal to 10.2 million kilocalories (Kcal), the definition in use by the World Bank. The calorific values of the fuels in each country may vary, and need to be established as one of the first activities in any energy planning effort.

The treatment of electricity
The actual thermal equivalent of electricity is 3,412 Btu per kwh. However, since conversion efficiencies typically lie in the range of 25–35%, the amount of thermal energy that must be consumed to generate 1 kwh of electricity is typically three to four times higher. As indicated on figure 4.1A, the best United States fossil fueled plant has a thermal efficiency of just under 38%; the average efficiency of thermal plants owned by the National Thermal Power Corporation of India is

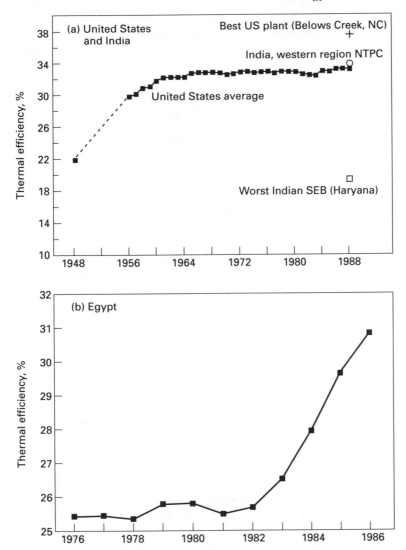

Figure 4.1   Heat rates and thermal efficiency.

about 33%, close to the United States average, but in the State of Haryana (the worst in India) the efficiency is only 19%. Therefore, if one is to provide a useful indication of how much oil is displaced by hydroelectricity, the best approach is to use the existing average, or anticipated future average, efficiency of thermal generation.

Table 4.2 *The treatment of electricity*

	Hydro	Fueloil	Electricity
Supply			
Domestic production	800		
Imports		800	
Total availability	800	800	
Conversion			
Inputs $(-)$	-800	-800	
Outputs $(+)$			400 (34.39)
T&D losses $(-)^a$			-80
Consumption			320 (27.51)

Notes: Units are in 1,000 ton oil equivalent; GWh in parentheses.
^{a} T&D losses assumed at 20% of generation.

The changes in thermal station efficiency over time can be substantial, with important consequences for the energy balance. For example, in Egypt, the average system thermal efficiency in 1976 was 25.38%. A decade later, this had improved to 30.83%, a 20% improvement (see figure 4.1(b))

These points are illustrated further in table 4.2. Electricity consumption is 27.51 GWh, which converts to 320 Ktoe (thousand tons of oil equivalent). Generation is 34.39 GWh, with 20% T&D losses. Fifty percent of the generated electricity is supplied by fueloil, 50% by hydroelectricity. Assume that the efficiency of power generation at fueloil plants is 25% (low compared to the most efficient plants, but not uncommon!); thus the heat input at fueloil plants is 800 Ktoe, which produces a net output of 200 Ktoe of electricity. The other half is produced by hydroelectricity. Using the same 25% conversion efficiency, we see that hydroelectricity displaces 800 Ktoe.

All of this notwithstanding, what is important is that there be a clear understanding of the particular conventions and assumptions used: it does not matter what assumptions are used provided they are explicitly stated. Indeed, it is for this reason (among many others) that energy balances expressed in common energy units should be accompanied by a companion table in physical units.

Table 4.3 illustrates a typical energy balance, taken from the World Bank Energy Assessment of Malawi. In this case hydro is converted to a thermal equivalent using an efficiency of 31.3%, corresponding to a thermal plant heat rate of 10,250 Btu/kwh. Note that fuelwood and

Table 4.3 *1980 energy balance for Malawi*

	Petroleum products	Coal	Hydro	Electricity	Total commercial energy	Fuelwood	Other biomass	Total
Primary supply								
Production			96.1		96.1	3029.0	83.4	3208.5
Imports	148.7	31.2			179.9			179.9
Total	148.7	31.2	96.1		276.0	3029.0	83.4	3388.4
Transformation								
Power Generation	−1.3		−96.1	97.7				
Total supply	147.4	31.2		32.3	210.9	3029.0	83.4	3323.3
T&D losses				−2.8				
Net supply	147.4	31.2		29.5	208.1	3029.0	83.4	3320.5
Final consumption								
Industry	60.4	29.6		21.6	112.6	1526.0	83.4	1722.0
Transport	80.6				80.6			80.6
Commercial	0.1	1.6		3.2	4.9	9.0		13.9
Residential	6.3			4.7	11.0	1493.0		1504.0

Source: World Bank (1982).

biomass account for some 92% of the total primary energy, typical of many low-income developing countries of Africa.[3]

The reference energy system

A useful way of conceptualizing the use of energy in a national economy is as a network, the links of which represent specific uses, transformations, or production of the different energy forms. Such network representations can take a number of different forms, of which one of the most widely used, and perhaps most useful, is the so-called Reference Energy System (RES). This is not just a format for the graphical display of energy balances, but also serves as an analytical framework for demand forecasting (an application presented below, in chapter 5). Originally designed in the early 1970s as a tool for technology assessment in the United States, it has since been used for energy assessments and energy policy and planning studies all over the world, including the

[3] The percentages of the primary energy supply accounted for by fuelwood and other biomass are 87% in Ethiopia, 99% in Rwanda, 79% in Haiti, 45% in the Dominican Republic, 55% in Sri Lanka.

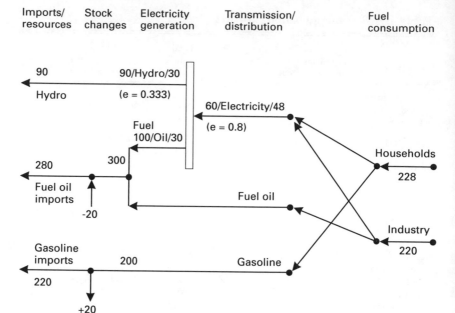

Imports/ resources	Stock changes	Electricity generation	Transmission/ distribution	Fuel consumption

Figure 4.2   Reference energy system presentation of the energy balance

Sudan, Peru, Egypt, Dominican Republic, Sri Lanka, Uruguay, Tunisia, Thailand, India, and Indonesia, among others. Indeed, once one views an energy system as a network of energy flows, the question of what is the *optimal* flow of energy in such a network is amenable to the well established body of mathematical modeling techniques established for network analysis: such extensions are discussed later in chapter 12.

Recall the illustrative energy balance of table 4.1. Suppose that all entries are in tons of oil equivalent, with hydroelectric energy measured in its fossil fuel equivalent, along the lines discussed above. Then the network, RES representation of this balance is portrayed as shown on figure 4.2.

Each link in the network represents some activity – supply, conversion from one energy form to another (such as electric generation), distribution, and use. Some activities involve losses. The notation (e = 0.8) implies an efficiency of 80%; in the above RES, transmission, and distribution of electricity is seen to be 80% efficient. For example, the network link:

$$\frac{60/\text{electricity}/48}{(e = 0.8)}$$

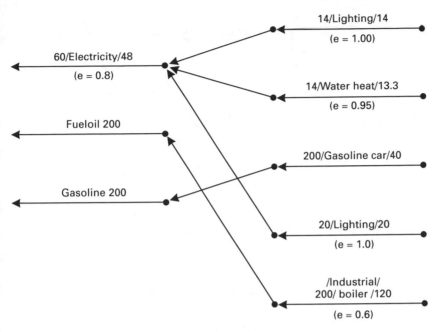

Figure 4.3   RES representation of end-use devices

indicates that net generation of electricity is 60 Toe, the efficiency of transmission and distribution is 80%, and total electricity consumption is 48 Toe. Thus, total losses in transmission and distribution are 12 Toe, equal to 20% of generation.

In such simplified systems, the RES has perhaps little advantage over the tabular balance. However, as soon as the level of information becomes more detailed, particularly by end-use, the advantages of the format become more apparent. Suppose that information is available on the end-use of industrial energy consumption, for example that fueloil is burnt to produce process heat in boilers of 60% efficiency, while electricity is used for lighting (at unit efficiency). The right-hand side of the RES would then appear as shown on figure 4.3

Figure 4.4 illustrates the RES representation of the Malawi energy balance shown on table 4.3.

Modeling energy balances in a spreadsheet: an illustrative model for Egypt

Over the past five years spreadsheets have become the fundamental analytical tool of the energy analyst. Perhaps ten years ago it was still

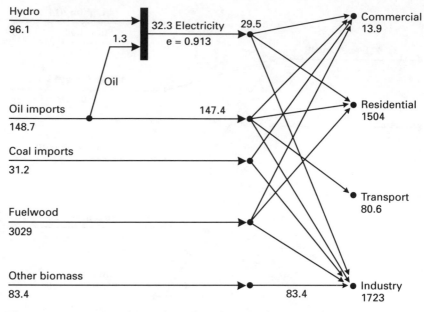

Figure 4.4   1980 RES for Malawi (based on the data in table 4.3)

necessary for the energy planner to have knowledge of FORTRAN or BASIC if he wished to do any quantitative analysis. But today, with microcomputers widely available even in the smallest and most remote developing country, such knowledge of programming languages is no longer necessary. The microcomputer, and the spreadsheet, has revolutionized quantitative analysis at all levels, a revolution that is of course not limited to the energy sector.

Indeed, modern spreadsheets are so powerful that almost all of the energy planning models discussed in this volume can be so implemented. Only where very specialized mathematical algorithms are required – as, say, for linear programming, or for the highly complex procedures to optimize the capacity expansion path for electricity supply – are compiled programs required. Almost everything else needed by the energy analyst can be done in one of the modern spreadsheets such as LOTUS 1-2-3, Quattro Pro, or Microsoft Excell.

Most spreadsheets contain errors. Moreover, the difference between an effective spreadsheet modeling process, and an ineffective one, is the degree to which error checking has been built into the basic design: anyone with extensive experience in spreadsheets will confirm that much more time is spent debugging than creating the basic model itself.

Table 4.4 *The 1985 energy balance for Egypt*

B	C	D — Baseyear Energy Balance: 1985	coal	crude	petr. products	gas	hydro	elec.	total
8		indigenous production		45788.1		3732.9	1935.1		51456.1
9	+C14−@SUM(C10..C13)−C8	imports	747.2	0.0	1794.1	0.0	0.0	0.0	2541.3
10		exports	−12.3	−26753.3					−26765.6
11		marine bunkers			−1480.2				−1480.2
12		stock changes	−4.9		387.4	−40.1			342.4
13									
14	+C21−@SUM(C15..C20)	TOTAL ENERGY REQUIREMENT	730.0	19034.8	701.3	3692.8	1935.1	0.0	26094.0
15									
16		petroleum refineries		−19034.8	17588.2				−1446.6
17		electricity generation			−4057.7	−2101.9	−1935.1	2705.4	−5389.3
18		T&D losses						−393.7	−393.7
19		other losses, own−use, etc.	−80.5		−152.7	−123.3			−356.5
20									
21	+C42+C34+C28	TOTAL FINAL CONSUMPTION	649.5	0.0	14079.1	1467.6	0.0	2311.7	18507.9
22		iron and steel	555.8			168.1			723.9
23		chemical				876.2			876.2
24		non−metallic minerals				308.6			308.6
25		other industry	46.8		5219.5	83.1		1752.2	7101.6
26									
28	@SUM(C22..C27)	total industry	602.6	0.0	5219.5	1436.0	0.0	1752.2	9010.3
29									
30		road			3625.8			7.7	3633.5
31		air			476.1				476.1
32		other			292.0			9.5	301.5
33									
34	@SUM(C29..C33)	total transportation	0.0	0.0	4393.9	0.0	0.0	17.2	4411.1
35									
36		agriculture			497.4			77.4	574.8
37		public/commerce	28.0		158.4			194.4	380.8
38		residential	18.9		2828.8	0.9		270.5	3119.1
39		other				30.7			30.7
40		non−energy use			981.1				981.1
41									
42	@SUM(C35..C41)	total other	46.9	0.0	4465.7	31.6	0.0	542.3	5086.5
43									
44			3328.0	19034.8	57017.7	9563.2	1935.1	9246.8	100125.6
45							row totals>		100125.6
46									
47							errors>		0.00000
48							errors/2>		0.00000
49							delta>		0.00001

Indeed, the main objective of this section is not so much the presentation and discussion of the substance of the Egyptian energy balance, as much as an illustration of how such error-checking principles should be built into *all* spreadsheet models. It is a subject to which few of the numerous books on spreadsheets pay much attention, perhaps in the belief that special purpose "spreadsheet auditing" programs will be used. In fact they rarely are. Much better is to build into the spreadsheet itself some fundamental error-tracking techniques.

Table 4.4 shows a highly aggregated commercial energy balance for Egypt for the year 1985. It corresponds roughly to the format used by the International Energy Agency for its "World Energy Statistics and Balances" publications: the main difference is that here we have separated crude oil from petroleum products.

First an explanation of the first two columns (column B and column C): their sole purpose is to assist the verification of formulae. By copying the formulae in rows G through M into column C, and then using /-range-format-text, LOTUS will display formula rather than the value of the result. Thus, for example, we note that the row "total other" (row 42) is calculated as @SUM(C35..C41). However, this is not very easily interpreted in printed form unless we know which row is which. That is the purpose of column B: in cell B3, for example, we enter the formula @cell("row",B3); this is then copied into all the cells of this column. The result is that we will always know what spreadsheet row we are in when the table is printed out. Experience shows that it is very difficult to verify formula just by looking at the screen: it is much easier to look at printed copy, and hence the use of this device.

Now examine a typical @sum formula – say that used to sum transportation energy demands, namely @sum(C29..C33). Note that we include in the range the rows 33 and 29, which are the lines used to indicate subtotals and/or sections of the table. The reason for doing this is very simple: suppose we had used @sum(C30..C32), and then decided to add another row after "other," which would be the new row 33. Then one would need to go back to the formulas, and change @sum-(C30..C32) to @sum(C30..C33). That is always a potential source of error. However, when one inserts a row (or column) *inside* an existing range, LOTUS adjusts the formula automatically. Even worse, if one were to delete row 32, then any formula that referenced the old row 32 will return ERR. By including the subtotal lines, one can insert and delete rows inside this range without concern over the integrity of the formulae.

The same principle is used for row totals. We include two empty columns, F and M (set to a column width of 1 to make them unobtrusive),

Table 4.5 *Error checking*

B	C	D	E	F	G	H	I	J	K	L	M	N
3		Baseyear Energy Balance: 1985										
5		FORMULA ERROR!										
7					coal	crude	petr. products	gas	hydro	elect.		total
8		indigenous production				45788.1		3732.9	1935.1			51456.1
9	+C14--@SUM(C10..C13)-C8	imports			700.3	0.0	1794.1	0.0	0.0	0.0		2494.4
10		exports			-12.3	-26753.3						-26765.6
11		marine bunkers					-1480.2					-1480.2
12		stock changes			-4.9		387.4	-40.1				342.4
14	+C21--@SUM(C15..C20)	TOTAL ENERGY REQUIREMENT			683.1	19034.8	701.3	3692.8	1935.1	0.0		26094.0
16		petroleum refineries				-19034.8	17588.2					-1446.6
17		electricity generation					-4057.7	-2101.9	-1935.1	2705.4		-5389.3
18		T&D losses								-393.7		-393.7
19		other losses, own--use, etc.			-80.5		-152.7	-123.3				-356.5
21	+C42+C35+C28	TOTAL FINAL CONSUMPTION			602.6	0.0	14079.1	1467.6	0.0	2311.7		18507.9
23		iron and steel			555.8			168.1				723.9
24		chemical						876.2				876.2
25		non--matallic minerals						308.6				308.6
26		other industry			46.8		5219.5	83.1		1752.2		7101.6
28	@SUM(C22..C27)	total industry			602.6	0.0	5219.5	1436.0	0.0	1752.2		9010.3
30		road					3625.8			7.7		3633.5
31		air					476.1					476.1
32		other					292.0			9.5		301.5
34	@SUM(C29..C33)	total transportation			0.0	0.0	4393.9	0.0	0.0	17.2		4411.1
36		agriculture					497.4			77.4		574.8
37		public/commerce			28.0		158.4	0.9		194.4		380.8
38		residential			18.9		2828.8	30.7		270.5		3119.1
39		other										30.7
40		non--energy use					981.1					981.1
42	@SUM(C39..C41)	total other			0.0	0.0	4465.7	31.6	0.0	542.3		5086.5
44					3140.4	19034.8	57017.7	9563.2	1935.1	9246.8		100078.7
45									row totals>			99938.0
47										errors>		140.70
48										delta>		0.00001

(a) Block diagonal

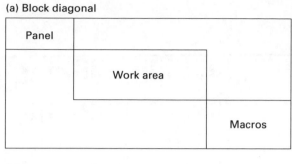

(b) Arrangement by columns

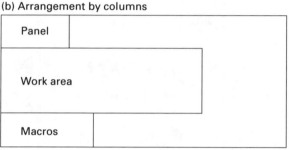

Figure 4.5   Spreadsheet design

and the row totals include these two columns. For example, the formula in cell N8 is @sum(F8..M8), rather than @sum(G8..L8). In this way, if one wishes to insert another column after "electricity," or before "coal," again the totals formulae do not need to be changed manually.

Now examine rows 44 through 48. The most fundamental check is to make sure that the sum of the row totals equals the sum of the column totals ("cross-footing"). This is a requirement even if a column total is not actually needed in the table, as in our example. The column total in cell G44 is simply @sum(G7..G43). We then compare the sum of the row totals with the sum of the column totals, and record any difference in cell N47.

Experience shows, however, that such a cell is often forgotten, particularly since it lies outside the range that is normally printed. A useful device is to include in some cell that is *inside* the usual print range a formula of the type @if((@abs(n47) > delta,"FORMULA ERROR"," "). Delta is some very small number (say 0.00001); a spreadsheet should never test for *exact* zero where formulae may be involved in its calculation, simply because of roundoff error. Note that we format cell N47 to five decimal places!

Most important, however, is that for the cross-foot to be effective as a check, any row sums that are subtotals must be calculated subtotals, not as row sums! For example, cell N14 should be @sum(n7..n13), *not* @sum(f14..m14)!

Let us now examine how these error checks work in an actual example (see table 4.5). We have introduced a deliberate error in the cell G42, entering the formula @sum(G39..G41) in place of @sum-(G35..G41): the result is that the entries 28.0 and 18.9 are not included in the column sum. The result is a cross-foot error, and therefore the cell D6 evaluates to "FORMULA ERROR."

Even in relatively simple spreadsheets some additional design rules will greatly reduce the probability of errors. The first relates to overall structure: whenever possible, a block diagonal organization is recommended, so that rows and columns can be freely added and deleted in individual tables without fear of impacting other tables.[4] Such a structure is illustrated on figure 4.5.

Only in very large models (and by large we mean models with, say, more than 2,000 rows and a twenty-year planning horizon) may there be a need to deviate from this scheme: for reasons not entirely clear from the memory allocation algorithms used in LOTUS, linear structures prove to use less memory than a block diagonal structure. This may be important where other memory resident programs, and LOTUS add-ins, may be required.

A second design rule concerns documentation of macros. The very minimum level of documentation requires that the range-names used in macros be identified in the cells immediately to their left: this also means that the range-names can be created with the /range-name-label-right command.

---

[4] In Version 1 of LOTUS, the memory allocation rules were quite different, and block diagonal structures were to be expressly avoided!

CHAPTER 5

Demand projection

Estimates of future demands are a critical element of energy planning, at both the aggregate sectoral or national level and at the level of some specific fuel, such as electricity. Indeed, one of the most important reasons for making projections of future demand is the lead time required for supply projects. Since a typical baseload electric power plant takes between five and ten years to build, investment decisions must also be made with a five to ten year lead time. Similarly natural gas pipelines, LNG projects, and other capital-intensive energy supply projects invariably are predicated upon some estimate of future demand.

The heavy capital expenditures required to produce and consume energy is another major reason for improving the accuracy of demand forecasting. Errors tend to become expensive – if projections are too low, energy shortages may develop whose costs are usually a large multiple of the volume of energy not supplied, but if forecasts are too high, large amounts of capital with high opportunity costs might be uselessly tied up for long periods of time. Either of these consequences is far more costly to an economy than the resources that would have to be marshalled to undertake detailed and reliable demand studies that could help to avoid such errors.

The larger the time required for new energy supply installations, the greater is the need for forecast accuracy. For example, large thermal power plants may need four to six years to completion, but smaller gas turbines or diesel power plants can usually be commissioned on an emergency basis within one to two years. Consequently, many utility systems use the latter to compensate (at short notice) for initial forecasting errors. Nuclear power plants need eight to twelve years to build, and hydro power plants about five to eight years. Oil and gas fields from initial seismic surveys through exploratory drilling to first production may need five to fifteen years, refineries three to six years, and forest plantations for firewood some five to thirty years. We may conclude that the need for forecast accuracy is directly related to the size, cost, complexity, and irreversibility of projected supply components.

With all of that said, however, it is one of the central fallacies of energy planning (and indeed of planning generally) that demand forecasts should be taken as deterministic. Indeed, one of the main lessons of the energy planning experience over the past two decades is that it is virtually impossible to predict the future with any accuracy: and that applies not just to the world oil price, but to rates of economic growth and household formation, global inflation, the value of the dollar (of particular importance in view of the fact that oil is still priced in dollars), or the evolution of domestic industry and the balance of payments. Experience shows that using single-point forecasts of energy demands as a basis for investment planning is very risky, for the forecasts are almost never correct. Rather, the correct approach is to examine a variety of demand forecasts that reflect different assumptions about factors that cannot be predicted with any accuracy, and then seek the investment plan that is most robust with respect to these uncertainties. This is an extremely important concept that is not just limited to demand forecasts, and will be taken up at greater length in chapter 14. For the present discussion, however, it suffices to say that the real need is not so much for the end result of the forecast to be "accurate," as much as that the forecasting process, or the forecasting model, reflects in the best way possible all of the factors that influence demand. The real question, then, is whether, for example, the relationship between economic growth and energy demand is understood, so that, in turn, the impact of uncertainties over the economic growth rate on energy demand is also understood.

A distinction between demand projections and demand forecasts is sometimes attempted. The former are normative, in the sense that projections often incorporate policy objectives that might or might not be attained, whereas the latter are predictive. In practice, the distinction between what we think *may* happen if such and such occurs (a projection) and what we think *will* happen (a forecast) is not always clear. A better distinction, perhaps, is in terms of the determinants of demand that are within the control of national policy-makers and those over which the decision-maker has no control. Both, of course, are subject to considerable uncertainties. Thus, not only do small oil-importing countries lack control over the world oil price, but this price is itself subject to great uncertainties. On the other hand there are interventions that are clearly within local control, but whose effectiveness in producing the intended result on demand may be uncertain, either because of imperfect understanding of the extraordinary complexity of modern economic systems or because of the inherent randomness of human behavior.

Several approaches are commonly used to derive demand projections: trend analysis; process modeling, and econometric modeling. Each of these is discussed below.

Baseline information

The starting point for demand projections, by whatever method used, is information about current levels of energy consumption. Verification, at least in aggregate terms, is usually possible if reliable data exist either about total supply or total consumption or both. The latter will usually be the case for electricity and natural gas, because supply and consumption, form closed systems with metering at both ends. The only troublesome aspects are autogeneration by non-public enterprises, leakage, transmission and distribution losses, and outright theft. The latter is a serious problem for electric utilities in many countries. For petroleum products and coal, reasonably accurate supply data can usually be obtained from production, refinery, and import and export statistics. However, data will usually be poor or non-existent for both supply and consumption of indigenous energy resources such as wood, charcoal, dung, crop residues, etc.

Verification starts from the necessary equality between supply and consumption per time period. Total production, plus imports, minus exports, minus net additions to storage, minus autoconsumption, processing, and transportation and losses have to be equal to total consumption. In most countries reliable data are available for the supply side, except perhaps for net changes in storage, autoconsumption, and conversion and transportation losses.

On the demand side, reliable consumption data will usually be available only for a few enumerated sectors or activities, although these may account for a substantial percentage of total consumption. Verification problems and estimation errors may arise from illegal diversions of specific energy sources to alternative uses. Another means to check estimated consumption data for their reasonableness is to compare them with published consumption data for similar activities in other countries. Detailed data have become available in recent years in most industrialized nations, and institutions such as the UN, World Bank, OECD, the US Department of Energy, and others regularly publish detailed consumption data for specific activities and production processes. Verification should not be limited to the analysis of past consumption data, since future projections can also be checked, at least for internal consistency with other forecasts.

The need for surveys to augment the available information on consumption levels is almost always a continuing issue. For example, one of the most widespread problems is the disaggregation of gasoil consumption. Total sales are typically available from distribution company statistics, but often little is known about consumption in the individual sectors – agriculture, diesel vehicles for personal transportation, diesel fuel for public transport, and so on.

In essence, surveys consist of a list of more or less sophisticated questions that are put to energy users in order to measure and record their present consumption and future consumption plans. The basic types of questions that might be asked are the following:

How much energy (of each type) do you use per month/year?

What do you use it for?

How much do you pay per unit of energy used (by energy type)?

What do you produce or sell and what is the value added of each major product line?

Can you identify specific energy uses with specific outputs?

What is your net income (for households)?

What are your future expansion plans, and their timing, and what additional energy requirements do they imply?

What additional energy-using appliances or equipment are you planning to acquire in the foreseeable future (identify)?

The major problems afflicting surveys are the following:

They require substantial amounts of time.

They can be costly.

They require skilled interviewers.

Energy users may be unable to provide the information asked because they themselves do not know.

Energy users may be unwilling to provide the information for competitive reasons or because of fear of the consequences of revealing the information, etc.

Energy users may wittingly or unknowingly give inaccurate answers.

Future energy user plans may be vague, or too optimistic/pessimistic.

In brief, the major drawbacks are costs on the one hand, and ignorance, or unwillingness to provide the information, on the other. Because of costs, surveys must generally be limited to major energy consumers such as medium- to large-size industrial plants, mines and smelters, large transportation companies, utility companies, important governmental energy users (e.g., armed forces), etc. Fortunately, these enterprises and activities usually account for a large percentage of total energy consumption in developing countries.

In the industrial sector, energy consumption per unit of output is substantial for only a few activities. Thus, surveys of industrial energy users should first concentrate on those activities that are known to be highly energy intensive per unit of output, and second on those industrial plants and activities that are large relative to the country's industrial sector as a whole. Second, surveys should attempt to evaluate the energy-use implications of new economic development programs, such as irrigation, industrial settlements, mining and hydrocarbon developments, and rural or urban electrification programs, etc. However, care must be taken (and seasoned judgment employed) to assess the realism of these specific projected development programs. Not infrequently, these represent more the dreams of somewhat overoptimistic development planners or politicians than the cold reality of realizable objectives.

The use of surveys will be less practicable for analyzing the consumption of ubiquitous sectors, such as households, farms, and small-scale commercial and industrial enterprises. For these sectors survey costs are generally high, as well as time consuming. They also require the hiring and training of a large number of enumerators – not an easy task in most developing countries. However, energy consumption surveys could be usefully combined with others, such as general population censuses or similar inquiries (such as income studies, etc.). Another limitation is that such surveys usually cannot elicit any useful information from respondents about future energy consumption intentions. Demand projections, therefore, must be developed on the basis of estimated trends using more or less sophisticated methods that take account of the various identifiable energy demand determinants such as disposable income, household formation, etc. In general, the need for surveys of these ubiquitous demand sectors and the required degree of accuracy of the results will depend on the importance of the information thus acquired. If significant and potentially costly decisions must be based on it, requirements for accuracy will be high; but if the information is needed only for statistical record keeping, relatively crude estimates may suffice.

Trend analysis

Trend analysis is a commonly used approach for demand projection. It consists of the extrapolation of past growth trends assuming that there will be little change in the growth pattern determinants of demand, such as incomes, prices, consumer tastes, etc. These trends are usually estimated by a least square fit of past consumption data or by some similar statistical methodology. Depending on the availability of data, they may be estimated either on a national basis for a given energy source (e.g., gasoline) or they may be broken down by region, by consuming sector (e.g., households, commercial enterprises, industry, transportation, etc.), or by both. Frequently, *ad hoc* adjustments are made to account for substantial changes in expected future demands due to specific reasons. For example, this may take the form of projecting on a case-by-case basis the expected demands of new industrial plants or other economic activities. This combination of overall trend projection together with specific adjustments based on survey research is used in many of the smaller developing countries.

The main advantage of this approach is its simplicity. Forecasts can be based on whatever data are available. The major disadvantage is that no attempt is made to explain why certain consumption trends were established in the past. The underlying, and usually unstated, assumption that whatever factors brought about consumption changes in the past will continue unchanged in the future as well is, of course, a rather limiting one in a world in which relative energy prices are changing at rapid rates, and in a direction opposite to that observed until just a few years ago.

Process modeling and the reference energy system: application to the Dominican Republic household sector

The basic idea behind the so-called process modeling approach to demand projection is to examine the specific devices that consume energy. Consider, for example, the case of automobile gasoline consumption. Rather than simply extrapolating the consumption growth trend, in a process model one would examine the number of gasoline powered vehicles (for which we might need, in turn, to examine any changes in the proportion of diesel passenger cars induced by changes in the relative diesel/gasoline price at the retail level, or prohibitions in the import of diesel autos), the changes in the efficiency of gasoline vehicles (that one might quantify in miles per gallon), and the number of vehicle miles driven. Similarly for industrial energy consumption, one would wish to derive fuel demands based on how much process heat is required, then consider the efficiency of boilers, and the fuels used to satisfy the demand. In short, the concept is to shift the estimation process away from fuel consumption itself, to an understanding, and quantification, of the factors that *determine* fuel consumption, and an estimation of the forces that drive energy consumption in the first place. In any event, one of the more important reasons for installing a demand projection capability in an energy planning agency is to be able to analyze the impact of potential policy interventions: a simple trend analysis model of gasoline consumption helps very little in this respect,

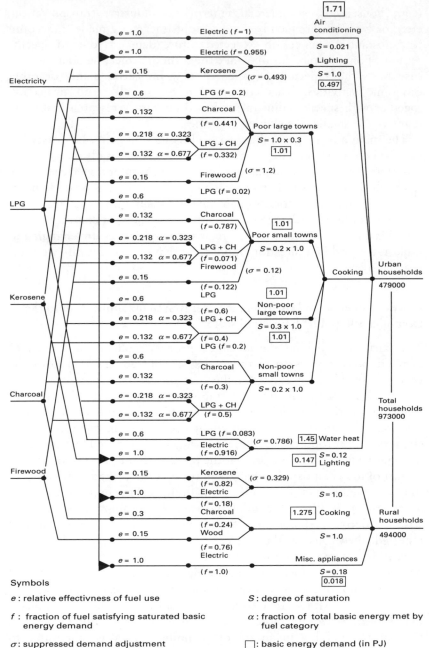

Figure 5.1   A RES network for the household sector of the Dominican Republic

whereas a process model approach in which the impact, say, on the diesel/gasoline fleet mix that might follow from an import prohibition on diesel passenger cars is clearly much more useful.

In the previous chapter we introduced the network flow concept of an energy system, and its implementation as a Reference Energy System (RES). Such a framework proves to be extremely useful for process model demand projections as well. As an illustration of how RES networks have been applied, consider the network of figure 5.1 which represents the household sector of the Dominican Republic.

In conformance with the rules constructing such networks, the driving force for the system is applied to the right-hand side of the network. For the household sector the logical basic driving force is the number of house-holds, which is decomposed into rural and urban. Obviously in larger countries an additional dimension of decomposition would be its regional distribution: in Indonesia, for example, a similar RES constructed for the Directorate for Electricity and Renewable Energy was based on a four-region disaggregation: Java, Sumatra, Kalimanthan, and the rest of the country. Obviously for this sector geographical shifts and the pace of urbanization are fundamental to energy demand projections.

Next are considered the uses of energy; in the rural sector, for example, we consider lighting, cooking, and electric appliance use; in the urban sectors water heating and air conditioning are added to this list. The "saturation level," denoted S on figure 5.1, describes the fraction of house-holds that require the end-use in question. Thus the saturation for cooking and lighting is 1.0 (since all households will require cooking and lighting), but only 0.18 of rural households require miscellaneous appliance use, corresponding to the extent of rural electrification (hence $S = 0.18$).

The next step is to identify for each end-use the so-called "basic energy demand," which identifies how much *useful energy* is required for each household for a particular use. For example, in figure 5.1 the basic energy demand for rural lighting is shown as 0.147, in this case in units of barrels of oil equivalent per year. A problem in specifying such basic energy demands is that they may themselves be a function of the device that is used: in one study of Indonesia, an econometric analysis indicated that households, once they had access to electricity, had much higher levels of lighting than when kerosene lamps were used.

Each end-use may be supplied by one or more different types of devices that use different fuels. Again with reference to figure 5.1, we show that rural cooking could be met either by wood or by charcoal stoves. The *f*-values indicate the fraction of the total number of households (with cookers) that use each device. For example, 76% of rural households use wood for cooking and 82% of households use kerosene for lighting.

Finally, to calculate the fuel consumption, we must divide by the device efficiency (the *e*-values of figure 5.1). Current wood cookers are seen to be 15% efficient, while charcoal cookers have an efficiency of 30%.

Note that the fuel demand for some particular end use, *c*, could be also expressed in equation form as:

$$c = \frac{d \cdot n \cdot S \cdot f}{e} \tag{5.1}$$

where

   c = fuel consumption,
   d = basic energy demand
   n = total number of households,
   S = saturation,
   e = device efficiency,
   f = fraction of households using the device.

Using the current values of these variables, the network of figure 5.1 replicates the *existing* pattern energy and fuel use in the household sector. By using the assumed values for the future year, estimates of the *future* demand can be made. We leave to the reader the task of following through the structure of energy demand in the urban households. Note that, for urban cooking, the survey data permitted a disaggregation by size of town and household income. The urban network is also more complex because many households have more than one device to serve the same end-use. For example, in the category "poor, small towns," 2% of households use only LPG cookers, 78.7% use charcoal, 7.1% possess both charcoal and LPG cookers (with the *a*-value indicating the percentage of time each device is used – for example $a = 32.3\%$ for LPG cookers), and 12.2% use only firewood.[1]

We thus construct a demand estimate for all of the fuels in the household sector based upon a detailed consideration of the end-use devices and their efficiency. Of course, many assumptions must be made in this process, including:

   the number of households in the scenario year (defined by the population growth rate and other demographic variables);

   the degree of urbanization (which some might wish to be subject to policy intervention, but which as a matter of practice may be difficult to influence);

   the saturation level (for example in the case of electricity to rural households, subject to policy decisions on the pace of rural electrification);

   the market shares of different devices (for lighting, again, subject to

---

[1] For further details of these survey results, see Meier (1985b)

Table 5.1 *Representative demand projection variables*

Sector/category	Measure of activity	Utilizing device/activity	Other variables
Industrial			
Iron and Steel	Output (tonnes)	Blast furnace (coke) Process heat	Capacity projections
Petrochemicals	Output (tonnes)	Feedstocks Process heat	Capacity projections
Cement	Output (tonnes)	Burners	Construction projections
Other large	Output (tonnes)	Process heat Electric drive	Industrial value added
Rural small	Output (tonnes)	All	Rural population
Transportation			
Passenger-auto	Passenger-km	Int. comb. engine	Population, disposable income, road km
Ship	Vessel-km	Diesel	
Air	Passenger-km	ICE: Jet	
Truck	Tonne-km	Diesel, ICE	Passenger vs freight travel
Railway	Tonne-passenger-km	Diesel, electric drive	
Pipeline	Thruput, barrels/day	Pump; diesel, electric	Capacity projections
Agriculture			
Soil preparation	Tractor-km	Int. comb. engine	Number of tractors
Irrigation	pump-hours	Diesel pump Electric pump	Agricultural production Number of pumps
Urban households			
Cooking	No of households	Stoves: gas, oil, electric	
Lighting	No of households	Electric lights	Disposable income
Misc. electric	No of households; appliance ownership	Motors, electric devices	Disposable income
Rural households			
Cooking	No of households	Stoves: kerosene & non-commercial	
Lighting	No of households	Electric & gas lamps	Rural electrification
Commercial			
Lighting and appliance	No of establishments and/or floorspace	Vapor compression	Value added in sector
Air conditioning	No of establishments and/or floorspace & saturation	Vapor compression	Value added in sector (including tourism)
Cooking	No of restaurants	Stoves: gas & electric	Value added in sector (including tourism)
Municipal services			
Lighting	Urban population; saturation	Lamps; fluorescent & incandescent	Municipal budgets
Other	Urban population; saturation	Pumps, etc.	Municipal budgets

rural electrification policy; in some other cases, perhaps also amenable to policy interventions, such as the introduction of a new solar cooker or the banning of certain types of hot water heaters);

the device efficiency (note that the search for an improved wood cooker for rural use is the target of most cookstove programs).

In this example of household energy we have used the number of households as the basic driving variable. Other sectors will require different activity measures as the basis for the projection, as suggested in table 5.1.

Econometric multiple correlation forecasting

Econometric forecasting techniques are usually somewhat more sophisticated, and, in theory, hold out the promise of greater forecast accuracy. Past energy demand is first correlated with other variables such as prices and incomes, and then future energy demands are related to the predicted growth of these other variables. However, these methods are frequently nothing more than a special form of trend analysis if the projections of the selected determinants themselves are based on historical trends in turn. The other problem that they encounter is that of data availability. Usually it is difficult, if not impossible, to obtain the required time series that are needed to produce statistically acceptable (i.e., statistically significant) results. Not only are data series often incomplete, they are also subject to changes in definitions over time and, even more frequently, subject to substantial errors. Furthermore, the need for "proving" statistically "significant" results is such that long periods of time have to be covered, periods long enough to have experienced significant changes in the underlying structure of the economy. Hence, confidence in the results must be low, even if they pass the test of statistical significance. However, the advantages of econometric studies are that they can take a number of important, demand-determining variables, such as price, income, number of vehicles, etc., explicitly into account.

The formulation of a typical residential energy demand model would be based on consumer theory in economics. The direct utility function of a consumer, which indicates the intrinsic value derived from the consumption of various goods, may be written:

$$U = U(Q_1, Q_2, ... Q_n; Z) \tag{5.2}$$

where Q_i represents the level of consumption of good i in a given time period (e.g., one year) and Z is a set of parameters representing consumer tastes and other factors. The set of prices $P_1, P_2 \ldots Pn$, for these n consumer goods, and the consumer's income I, define the budget constraint:

$$I \geq \Sigma P_i Q_i \qquad (5.3)$$

Maximization of the consumer's utility U subject to the budget constraint yields the set of Marshallian demand functions for each of the goods consumed by the household:

$$Q = Q_i \, (P_1, P_2, \ldots P_n; \, I; \, Z) \text{ for } i = 1 \text{ to } n. \qquad (5.4)$$

Consider the demand function for a particular fuel (e.g., gas). For this fuel equation (5.4) may be written in the simplified form:

$$Q_g = Q_g(P_g, P_e, P_o, P; I; Z) \qquad (5.5)$$

where the subscript g denotes gas, while subscripts e and o indicate the substitute forms of energy, electricity and oil (e.g., for cooking), and P is an average price index representing all other goods. Next, assuming that demand is homogeneous of degree one in the money variables (i.e., prices and income) we may write:

$$Q_g = Q_g(P_g/P, P_e/P, P_o/P; I/P; Z) \qquad (5.6)$$

Thus, starting from consumer preference theory, we may arrive at a demand function for a given fuel which depends on its own price, the prices of substitutes and income, all in real terms. The effects of other factors Z, such as quality of supply, shifts in tastes, and so on can also be explicitly considered.

The final specification of an equation such as (5.6) could vary widely (Pindyck, 1979). Q_g could be household consumption or per capita consumption; the demand function could be linear or linear in the logarithms of the variables or in the transcendental logarithmic form and could include lagged variables; and Z could include supply-side constraints such as access to supply, and so on.

Analogously, the industrial demand for energy may be derived from production function theory in economics. For example, consider the output of a particular firm or industry over a given time period:

$$X = F(K, L, M, Q_1, \ldots Q_n; S) \qquad (5.7)$$

where K, L, and M represent the inputs of capital, labor and other non-energy materials respectively; Q_i is the input of the i-th form of energy, and S is a set of parameters that represents other factors, such as shifts in technology, industrial policy, and so on. The problem posed in production theory is the minimization of the costs of producing a given quantity of output X, given exogenous prices of inputs. In principle, the solution yields, as in the household case, a set of energy demand functions:

$$Q_i = Q_i(P_K, P_L, P_M; P_M... P_n; X; S) \tag{5.8}$$

As before, we may use one of the non-energy input prices as numeraire, (e.g., P_k) and rewrite Q_i in normalized form:

$$Q_i = Q_i(P_L/P_K, P_M/P_K, P_1/P_K ... ,P_n/P_K; X/P_K, S) \tag{5.9}$$

The demand for energy at time t is therefore a function of its own price, the prices of energy substitutes, the prices of non-energy inputs, and other factors S. Many different choices of variables and specifications of demand function may be used. In this way demand functions for various fuels could be developed for other end-use sectors such as transport, agriculture, and so on. The demand function may be estimated by standard econometric techniques; the estimated equations then form the basis for future demand forecasts. The main difficulties with this approach are:

1 The mechanistic nature of the econometric equations and their extrapolation into the future, which often fails to capture structural shifts in demand growth. Such structural shifts are particularly important in developing countries as a result of the introduction of new technologies (e.g., tractors instead of draft animals, auto manufacturing instead of assembly operations, or rural electricity instead of kerosene lamps).

2 The difficulties of separating out short-run and long-run effects in the analysis of changes in the structure and level of prices (Pindyck, 1979).

3 The lack of an adequate database to make accurate regression estimates. In developing countries this problem is particularly severe because energy price and consumption data by the consuming sector are usually lacking, income data are unreliable or non-existent and do not account for changes in income distribution, and statistical data of output and sales of specific industries are often unobtainable because of their confidentiality if the number of producers is small. Even in industrialized countries with far better data coverage, demand studies should be based on specific processes, rather than broad classifications such as "iron and steel production," or "household use."

4 The inherent limitation of estimating procedures that concentrate on energy prices as demand determinants, but do not account for the prices, availability, life expectancies, and replaceability of the energy-using appliances and equipment that must be utilized with alternative energy sources. This problem is particularly acute under the assumption of homotheticity for all alternative energy sources, since energy

users will base their decisions on total systems cost rather than on energy cost only.

5 The problem that, for almost the whole post-World War II period until the early 1970s, real costs of commercial energy sources were falling, while they have been rising steeply, albeit irregularly, since. Econometric data series, unless they rely on cross-sectional data only (not a practical procedure in developing countries), necessarily utilize the data of these past periods of falling prices. These are unlikely to yield reasonable estimates of future energy demands because of the sharp reversal in relative prices trends.

6 The fact that specific energy resources are often allocated by governmental fiat, or determined by such factors as availability or reliability of supply, rather than observable market price. Another important factor, particularly in developed countries, may be fuel quality, such as the sulphur content of coal.

7 The problem that demand elasticities, even if they were estimated accurately, are likely to change significantly themselves, rather than remain constant, if price changes of energy are large. This is so because for most activities the ability to substitute other resources for energy (including alternative energy resources) is limited.

Because of these problems (see also box 5.1), it is not surprising that the results of various empirical studies of energy demand functions vary by substantial margins even in the industrialized nations. What we might conclude, then, is that many of the more aggregate econometric studies of energy demand are probably of limited value even in industrialized countries and much less useful for developing nations. More specific studies, of clearly defined subsectors, such as urban residential energy demand by city size and income, may be more promising and useful, even if the required disaggregation reduces the more mechanistic measures of statistical significance.

There are, clearly, both differences and similarities between the econometric and process approaches. Both require estimates of *other* variables. For example, in the econometric approach one has explicitly to state future energy prices, while in the process approach (for the transportation sector, for example) one must state the number of vehicle miles traveled. The essential distinction is how technology is considered. In the process approach, the technology of the end-use device must be defined, at least in terms of its efficiency. In the econometric approach, the changes in technology or the improvements in efficiency through conservation are *implicit* in the price response. As prices increase relative to the cost of other inputs, consumers substitute capital and labor for energy, thereby reducing consumption.

Box 5.1 *Misspecification in econometric models*

A most important problem is faulty specification of econometric models: either because important variables are missing, or because the selected functional form is inappropriate, with the result that, despite apparently good statistical fits, the correlation is quite spurious. For example, the following set of models were estimated (by a foreign consultant) to project electricity demand in the Dominican Republic

Industrial demand = 0.0976 (industrial value added)$^{1.4533}$
($R^2 = 0.97$)
Residential demand = 0.0007 (private consumption)$^{1.833}$
($R^2 = 0.96$)
Commercial demand = 7.36 + 0.3124 × residential demand
($R^2 = 0.99$)
Government demand = 0.00169 (GDP)$^{1.5032}$ ($R^2 = 0.97$)

As evidenced by the high values of R^2 such models undoubtedly fit the observed historical data. However their use for projection purposes is highly questionable. Notable is the absence not just of the price variable but of one that measures the number of connections: the result is a gross overestimate of the income elasticity.

Such models completely ignore the conclusions and advice of numerous rigorous studies conducted by donors and others. Sound advice is provided, for example, in a series of studies published in the Interamerican Development Bank Publication Series "Papers on Project Analysis," particularly Westley (1981) and Westley (1984). As he notes in the case of the Dominican Republic, "many studies explain electricity consumption using only a measure of income, a practice that normally inflates the estimate of income elasticity and hence exaggerates the importance of this factor. A proper perspective requires inclusion of other factors, such as the number of users, the price of electricity, the price of substitute fuels, and a measure of outage severity" (Westley, 1984).

On the other hand, in the process approach, prices are implicit. The specification of some new energy efficient technology in place of a less efficient one assumes that the substitution has occurred in response to price incentives. For example, the extent to which air conditioners are installed in households (quantified in our example of the residential sector of the Dominican Republic by the saturation coefficients) depends on both the price of the unit and the cost of running them. Once installed, their use ought to be dependent on the cost of electricity. But we have left unsaid exactly how the many coefficients of the process model are to be determined, leaving it a matter of judgment for the analyst in the construction of the scenarios.

In practice, given the advantages and disadvantages of both

Table 5.2   *Some typical estimates of demand elasticity for electricity*

	Residential		Industrial/commercial	
	Price	Income	Price	Income
Nigeria[a]	−0.310	0.627	−0.679	0.890
Ivory Coast[a]	−0.783	0.279	−0.661	0.494
Togo[a]	−1.022	1.010	−0.701	0.336
Niger[a]	−1.240	1.236	−0.752	0.665
Ghana[a]	−0.195	1.066	−0.459	0.522
Dominican Republic[b]	−0.500	0.450	−0.650	1.250
Costa Rica[b]	−0.500	0.200		
Paraguay[b]	−0.500	0.400		

Sources [a] Glapke and Fazzolare (1985); [b] Westley (1984).

approaches, both are generally used in any given situation. Because it is generally less data intensive, the econometric model is generally built first. It can also be quickly aligned to overall macroeconomic assumptions (e.g., exchange rates, GDP growth) that may set the stage for the energy planning exercise. Using historically estimated elasticities, a first set of energy demands are established under various cases of world oil price and GDP growth rates. Subsequently, on a sector-by-sector basis, process models are built and differences between process and econometric models reconciled. Thus one approach is used as a check upon the other.

Application to Sri Lanka

The demand model recently developed by the Sri Lankan Ministry of Power and Energy is typical of the application of an econometric model embedded in an RES framework for computational convenience.[2] The basic equation at the sectoral level is:

$$Q_j(t) = \epsilon_j(t) \cdot Y(t) \tag{5.10}$$

where

$Q_j(t)$ is the demand for fuel j at time t, in thousand tons of oil equivalent (Ktoe),

$Y(t)$ is the sectoral output at t,

$\epsilon_j(t)$ is the unit demand for fuel j.

The sectoral output in year t is given by the simple growth equation:

$$Y(t) = Y(0)(1 + g_j)^t \tag{5.11}$$

---

[2] For a complete presentation of the Sri Lanka demand model, see Meier and Munasinghe (1984).

where g_j are the assumed sectoral growth rates.

The unit energy demand is assumed to be influenced by two factors: pure price effects and the implementation of a conservation program, $A_j(t)$. Thus if $\lambda_j(t)$ is the price of fuel $_j$ at time t:

$$\epsilon_j(t) = \epsilon_j(0) \cdot \left[\frac{\lambda_j(t)}{\lambda_j(0)}\right]^\beta \cdot A_j(t) \tag{5.12}$$

then (5.10) can be written as:

$$Q_j(t) = \epsilon_j(0) \cdot \left[\frac{\lambda_j(t)}{\lambda_j(0)}\right]^\beta \cdot A_j(t) \cdot Y_0 (1 + g_j)^t$$

$$= Q_j(0)(1 + g)^t \left[\frac{\lambda_j(t)}{\lambda_j(0)}\right]^\beta A_j(t) \tag{5.13}$$

However, such a formulation is poorly suited to those industrial sectors where the growth of output occurs in the form of periodic, large capacity increments (or where major plant closures result in incremental decreases in demand). Thus an additional term, $Q_j^*(t)$, is added to account for such demand increments:

$$Q_j(t) = Q_j(0)(1 + g_j)^t \left[\frac{\lambda_t(t)}{\lambda_j(0)}\right]^\beta A_j(t) + Q_j^*(t) \tag{5.14}$$

One can also write (5.14) in terms of sectoral income elasticities. The energy demand in certain sectors grows much faster than the corresponding increase in income (of which residential electricity demand is the most extreme example). If $\hat{g}$ is the economy-wide GNP growth rate, then it follows that:

$$(1 + g_j)^t = (1 + \hat{g})^{ta_j} \tag{5.15}$$

where a_j is the elasticity of energy demand in the j-th sector with respect to the aggregate real GDP growth rate. Thus in place of (5.14) we can also write:

$$Q_j(t) = Q_j(0)(1 + g)^{ta_j} \left[\frac{\lambda_j(t)}{\lambda_j(0)}\right]^\beta A_j(t) + Q^*(t) \tag{5.16}$$

where a_j is estimated numerically by taking logarithms of both sides of (5.15):

$$t\log(1 + g_j) = ta_j\log(1 + \hat{g}) \tag{5.17}$$

$$a_j = \frac{\log(1 + g_j)}{\log(1 + \hat{g})}$$

Given the current exchange rate policy of the government,[3] the domestic consumer price, in constant terms, can be expressed in terms of the landed cost and a gradually depreciating exchange of the rupee. Thus:

$$\lambda_j(t) = \lambda_j^*(t) \cdot \pi(t) \cdot [1 + m_j(t) + t_j(t)] \qquad (5.18)$$

where

$\lambda_j^*(t)$ is the border price, in \$US,

$\pi(t)$ is the exchange rate,

m_j is the total distribution cost + margin rate,

t_j is the tax rate.

If the exchange rate depreciates at an annual rate of r, then:

$$\lambda_j(t) = \lambda_j^*(t) \cdot \pi(0)(1 + r)^t [1 + m_j(t) + t_j(t)] \qquad (5.19)$$

and the ratio:

$$\frac{\lambda_j(t)}{\lambda_o(t)} = \frac{\lambda_j^*(t)\pi(0)(1 + r)^t [1 + m_j(t) + t_j(t)]}{\lambda_j^*(0)\pi(0)[1 + m_j(0) + t_j(0)]} \qquad (5.20)$$

If the margin rate stays unchanged, then the complete equation is:

$$Q_j(t) = Q_o(1 + \hat{g})^{ta_j} \left[\frac{\lambda_j^*(t) \cdot (1 + r)^t [1 + m_j + t_j(t)]}{\lambda_j^*(0)[1 + m_j + t_j(0)]} \right]^\beta A_j(t) + Q^*(t) \qquad (5.21)$$

The exogenous variables in this model are thus:

the assumed GNP growth rate, $\hat{g}$,

the landed cost, $\lambda_j^*(t)$,

the rate of currency depreciation, r,

whilst the policy variables include:

the conservation goal, $A_j(t)$,

the tax rate $t_j(t)$.

Concluding remarks

A major practical problem for the energy planner is the reconciliation of demand projections among the different sector institutions. With the justification for capital-intensive investment projects often dependent upon some particular level of demand, electric utilities and refineries may resist alternative projections offered by the sector planner. In practice, therefore, if the energy planner is to succeed in his primary function of sector integration, the first step is to attempt to reconcile existing projections, examine any points of inconsistency, and attempt to get agreement by all of the major sector institutions for a common set

[3] Since 1978, when the incoming administration of President Jayawardene introduced extensive economic reforms, the exchange rate was allowed to depreciate in a controlled manner.

of projections based on consistently applied principles. This process of reconciliation and consensus building may in fact have very little to do with formal models.

That said, it is nevertheless very important to avoid errors in demand projections because they often lead to shortages of energy which may have serious repercussions on economic growth and development. The methodologies for demand forecasting include historical trend analysis, process modeling, and econometric multiple correlation methods. In general, the relatively sophisticated econometric and modeling approaches are easier to apply in the developed countries, while data and manpower constraints indicate that the simpler techniques will be more effective in the developing countries. There is no universally superior method of demand forecasting, and the use of several different methods is recommended to cross-check the final result.

CHAPTER 6

Optimization models

As noted earlier in chapter 3, the most fundamental task of energy analysis is to define alternative options – for energy pricing, for energy sector investments, and so on – and quantify their impacts on the objectives established for national energy planning. If, say, two policies are to be evaluated, there must also exist some explicit basis for comparing them, preferably on some ordinal scale of measurement. That is, we are interested not only in a ranking of alternatives, but in general one also wishes to know by exactly how much one alternative is better than another. This may well be an obvious point, yet it is particularly important where multiple objectives must be simultaneously evaluated: policy A may be better to policy option B in terms of, say, some cost-minimization objective, but worse when evaluated on some environmental criterion. But if we know that B is only slightly less good in economic terms, but a great deal better in environmental terms, that is an extremely important piece of additional information for the decision-maker who must ultimately make the trade-off between the two objectives. Examining solutions in the vicinity of the cost-minimizing optimum proves to be very important in such situations, yet it is rarely done.

Indeed, the formal techniques of multi-objective decision analysis have not been used much in energy planning; even in the developed countries, such applications have tended to be somewhat academic, and rarely used by government agencies for the practical problems of supporting energy policy analysis. One important application where they have seen practical use is for power plant siting (Hobbs, 1979, Woodward-Clyde, 1981). Nevertheless, particularly with the growing importance of environmental objectives, and the need to be more explicit about how economic and environmental objectives are to be traded off, the use of such models is bound to increase in the near future. Annex 6.2 presents an introduction to the subject, to which we also return in the discussion of energy-environmental linkages in chapter 7.

All models in fact require objective functions. In the typical spreadsheet simulation model, one or more cells contain the values of the variables of real interest, the results of the calculation: for example, in a fuelwood model, the key variable is the volume of the growing stock, as a proxy for the extent of deforestation that may occur. In the typical energy balance model, there may be several such variables of interest: the quantity of oil imports, the oil import bill, and so on. Thus, in simulation models, different combinations of data and policy assumptions represent the inputs, for which the corresponding set of output variables is computed. If there are, say, six policies to be compared, the model is run six times, and six sets of outputs are examined. Even though this process can to some extent be automated using LOTUS macros or the LOTUS data-table function, the basic principle of the simulation model remains very closely matched to the most important function of energy policy modeling: the evaluation of the impacts of specific options defined in advance by the policy-maker, or defined with the assistance of a technical expert who has experience in formulating programs that are technically feasible and implementable.

Optimization models are different, and seek to get around the most fundamental problem of a simulation model, which is that the *best* combination of inputs may never be looked at. Indeed, there may be thousands of different combinations of projects and policies that might be considered, so that the limited number of policies that are examined would be unlikely to include the "best." An optimization model therefore has two important characteristics: (i) some single function, or objective, whose mathematical minimization (or maximization) provides an unambiguous definition of "best" and (ii) a procedure for finding out which combination of inputs, from the typically almost infinitely large universe of possible input combinations, that produces that "best" solution.

Despite the promise of optimization models as a means of assisting the decision-maker, numerous practical difficulties severely limit their use for energy planning. To be sure, there is no dearth of such models in the literature; yet the reality is that, whatever their academic value, they prove to be difficult to use in practice. First, most optimization models address just a single objective, usually the economic one: yet in practice very few important decisions are made *solely* on such grounds. Second, most optimization models impose very severe limitations on the functional relationships that are permitted in the model, and, as discussed further below, often require linearity. In situations where linearity assumptions are clearly tenuous, modeling results may therefore be subject to doubt. But perhaps most importantly, the presence of an optimization model conveys the impression that that most elusive of beasts, an "optimal energy policy," can in fact be identified. There is no such thing. And it is for this reason that optimization models have to date found their most widespread practical use not for sector-wide planning, where numerous conflicting and political considerations frequently intrude, but for subsectoral planning, where the objectives of cost minimization and "optimality" can be more clearly articulated. Indeed, optimization models have been very successful in this role, making substantial contributions to the management, and investment planning, of the petroleum and electricity subsectors in developing countries.[1] For sector-wide planning, however, much caution needs to be exercised.

Whether for simulation or optimization models, then, how is the economic objective to be captured? Because most planning problems involve streams of costs and benefits that typically span many years, the fundamental issue concerns procedures for taking into account the time value of money. In fact the problem of comparing two policies, or two energy sector investment plans, is no different to the familiar problem of comparing two (or more) individual projects; all of the concepts of traditional benefit – cost analysis are applicable here. In the following discussion we assume that it is some set of policies that are being compared in a simulation model: "project" or "investment plan" could be used equivalently.

The most basic economic criterion for evaluation of a policy is its net present value (NPV), defined as:

$$\text{NPV} = \sum_{t=0}^{T} \frac{(B_t - C_t)}{(1 + r)^t}$$

where B_t and C_t are the benefits and costs in year t, respectively, r is the discount rate, and T is the planning time horizon. Other related criteria such as the internal rate of return (IRR) and benefit to cost ratio (BCR) are described in annex 6.1.

Both benefits and costs are defined as the difference between what would occur with and without the policy being implemented. As described later, for the economic comparisons, B, C, and r are defined in economic terms and appropriately shadow priced using efficiency border prices. In particular, the shadow price of r is the accounting rate

---

[1] That said, however, even here the notion of "optimality," say in an electric sector capacity expansion plan, is coming under increasing question. An investment plan can be said to be "optimal" only for some specific set of exogenous assumptions: if these assumptions turn out to be inaccurate, then very often the investment plan may prove to be distinctly non-optimal. We return to this most important issue in chapter 14.

of interest (ARI). However, for the financial analysis of energy policies B, C, and r may be defined in financial terms. Obviously for a policy to be considered at all it is necessary for its NPV to be greater than zero.

If policies are to be compared or ranked, the one with the highest (and positive) NPV would be the preferred one, i.e., if $NPV_I > NPV_{II}$ (where $NPV_i = $ *net present value for policy i*), then policy I is preferred to policy II. However, a certain caution is required here to account for the scope and scale of the policies being considered: obviously a commitment of investments over a ten year time horizon is likely to have a higher NPV than one for only a five-year horizon.

In the case of most subsectoral models, the benefits in a problem are often viewed as fixed across all alternatives. For example, one might take as given that an electricity capacity expansion plan will need to satisfy a particular demand projection: different investment plans that satisfy the need for that level of electricity will have different costs, but provide the same level of benefits.[2] In this case the comparison is much simplified. Thus:

$$NPV_I - NPV_{II} = \sum_{t=0}^{T} \frac{C_{It} - C_{IIt}}{(1 + r)^t}$$

since the two benefit streams B_{It} and B_{IIt} cancel out. Therefore:

$$\sum_{t=0}^{T} \frac{C_{It}}{(1 + r)^t} > \sum_{t=0}^{T} \frac{C_{IIt}}{(1 + r)^t}$$

implies that $NPV_I < NPV_{II}$.

In other words, the investment plan which has the lower present value of costs is preferred. This is called the least-cost alternative (when benefits are equal). However, even after selecting the least-cost capacity expansion option, it would still be necessary to ensure that any particular project in that plan would provide a positive NPV, greater than for any other project, in order to justify any investment.

The extension to optimization models is obvious: the objective function must be defined as the NPV. In the case of meeting some specified level of benefits, one seeks to minimize the present value of system costs over the planning horizon. In the energy planning context, the specified level of benefits is usually defined by some set of energy demands that must be satisfied at least-cost to meet a particular economic growth target over some particular planning horizon.

---

[2] However even here there are pitfalls: in the case of electricity it is not just the *quantity* of electricity to be supplied that must be held constant, but also its *quality* (meaning the reliability with which it is supplied to the consumer). See chapter 8 for further discussion.

Table 6.1 *Inputs of labor, capital and energy*

Input	Agriculture X_1	Manufactured goods X_2
Labor	10	5
Capital	2	5
Energy	2	4

Sometimes, all the consequences of a project, program, or policy decision cannot be easily quantified in terms of economic costs and benefits, especially environmental externalities of the type discussed in chapter 7. In such cases it is not possible to determine a single-valued objective function, and the techniques of multi-criteria decision analysis may need to be used, as outlined in annex 6.2.

Linear programming

Linear programming is the most widely used optimization technique, not just in the energy sector, but in almost every sector of a modern economy. As its name suggests, what is being optimized is a linear system, in which both the objective function and the constraint set are required to be linear equations. Given the fact that not much of the real world is linear, this may seem to be a somewhat limiting requirement. In fact, however, all manner of techniques have been developed to get around this problem, because more advanced optimization techniques, in which these linearity requirements are relaxed to varying degrees, prove to be very much more complicated, and consume huge amounts of computer time for their solution, even on today's generation of machines.

Linear programming can best be introduced by example.[3] Consider some hypothetical country, which produces only two goods: agricultural products, in the amount X_1, and manufactured goods, in the amount X_2. To produce these two goods three different inputs are required: labor, capital, and energy. Table 6.1 shows the inputs required to produce one unit of X_1 and X_2.

Suppose X_1 and X_2 have the same value, namely one money unit per physical unit of output, and that the economic planning objective is to

---

[3] This follows the discussion of Meier (1985b).

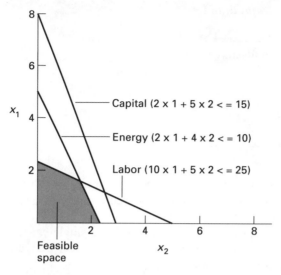

Figure 6.1   Definition of the feasible space.

maximize the value of total output. The objective function, therefore, can be written:

$$\max S = 1.0\, X_1 + 1.0\, X_2$$

This objective is obviously constrained by the fact that the available inputs are limited. Suppose the total supply of labor is 25, of capital is 15, and of energy 10 units. How should these resources be allocated to the two activities in such a way that output is maximized?

The resource constraints can be written in equation form as:

$$10X_1 + 5X_2 \le 25$$
$$2X_1 + 5X_2 \le 15$$
$$2X_1 + 4X_2 \le 10$$

X_1 and X_2 are also real activities, which means that they cannot be smaller than zero. Therefore, $X_1 \ge 0$, $X_2 \ge 0$. This is the so-called "non-negativity" requirement.

Thus we have an optimization problem in which both the objective function and the constraint set are linear equations. Coupled with the non-negativity constraint, such a problem is known as a linear programming problem. When there are only two activities (or "variables"), one can solve this problem graphically. The constraint set can be graphed as shown on figure 6.1: since these are less than or equal constraints, the set

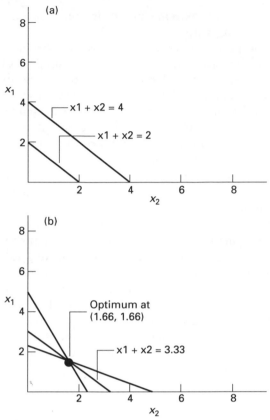

Figure 6.2   Graphical solution

of values of X_1 and X_2 that satisfy each constraint lie to the left of these lines. Combinations of X_1 and X_2 that meet all three constraints simultaneously are represented by the shaded area of figure 6.1: this is the so-called "feasible space." It should be obvious even in the simple two-dimensional problem that there are an essentially infinite number of possible combinations of X_1 and X_2 that lie in the feasible space.

On figure 6.2(a) we now plot various values of the objective function. It should be clear that the optimum value of the objective function is given by superimposing figure 6.2(a) onto figure 6.1, and finding that line which has the slope of the objective function which lies most to the right, but which is still feasible. As indicated on figure 6.2(b), this occurs at one of the corners of the feasible space, at a so-called "extreme point." It can be shown that, if the feasible region is "convex," which will always be the case for a combination of linear constraints, then the optimum will always occur at an extreme point. In our case, the optimum solution is $X_1 = 1.66$, $X_2 = 1.66$, hence $S = 3.333$.

Note that at this extreme point we have used all of the available labor, and all of the available energy; however, we have not used all of the available capital. Thus we say that the labor and energy constraints are "binding," whilst, in this example, capital is not. The implication is that, if either more or less of the binding resources were made available, the optimal solution would change; whereas making more capital available, in this particular example, would shift the capital constraint to the right, which would clearly not affect the optimum solution at all.

Obviously, when there are more than two activities, graphical solution is no longer practical. Indeed, linear programming only became a useful tool with the development by George Dantzig of the so-called "simplex" algorithm: this takes advantage of the fact that the optimum must occur at one of the extreme points. The details of the algorithm need not concern us here: only graduate students in class exams still solve the simplex algorithm by hand. The key is enumerating a sequence of extreme points until the optimum is found: in any event, the computer packages now available embody extremely efficient but also complex procedures that bear very little resemblance to the original simplex algorithm. Indeed, real world problems may have thousands of activities, and thousands of constraints. Those encountered in energy planning typically have a few hundred of each (see chapter 11).

Shadow prices

The value of linear programming as an optimization tool lies not just in the ability to identify that combination of activities that will maximize output. It turns out that it also tells us something about how the inputs should be *priced* in order to ensure that the optimum allocation of resources predicted by the optimization would in fact occur in practice.

Associated with any given LP problem, which we shall call the "primal," there is another LP, called the "dual." If the primal is a maximization problem, then the dual is a minimization problem (and vice versa). If the primal is written, in matrix algebraic form, as:

$$\begin{aligned} \min S \; = \qquad & \underset{(1 \times m)}{c^T} \quad \underset{(m \times 1)}{x} \\ \text{subject to} \quad & \underset{(n \times m)}{A} \quad \underset{(m \times 1)}{x} \quad \underset{(n \times 1)}{\geq b} \\ & x \geq 0 \end{aligned}$$

then the dual of the problem is:

$$\max S = \underset{(1 \times n)}{b^T} \quad \underset{(n \times 1)}{\lambda}$$

$$\text{subject to} \quad \underset{(m \times n)}{A^T} \quad \underset{(n \times 1)}{\lambda} \quad \underset{(m \times 1)}{\leq c}$$

$$\lambda \geq 0$$

Thus there is one variable in the dual for each constraint in the primal; and one constraint in the dual for each variable in the primal.

It turns out that these two problems have the same solution: that is, the value of their respective objective functions is exactly equal at the optimum. More importantly, for every constraint that is binding in the primal, the value of the corresponding dual variable will be non-zero; whereas the value of the corresponding dual variable of non-binding constraints is zero. Indeed, one can show that the value of the dual variables indicate the worth of an additional unit of the resource to the objective function. That is, suppose the value of the dual variable associated with the energy constraint were 0.5. Then, if the supply of energy were increased by one unit, one would expect the value of the objective function to increase by 0.5. Thus, the dual variables can be interpreted as the partial derivative of the objective function with respect to the binding constraint.[4]

Why is this such an important characteristic? It is because it tells us whether or not to expand the supply of energy. For example, suppose the actual cost of expanding the energy supply by one unit in this case is 0.4. That implies that the expenditure of 0.4 to expand the supply by one unit brings a benefit of 0.5 to the system as a whole, with a net gain of 0.1. Indeed, there will be a net gain until the cost of increasing energy production is exactly 0.5. It is for this reason that the values of the dual variable are referred to sometimes as "marginal costs," or more frequently as "shadow prices." Moreover, mathematically they correspond exactly to the so-called "Lagrange multipliers" of classical optimization theory.

Let us return to our numerical example. Ignoring the capital constraint, so that the dual will only have two variables, and can also be solved graphically, the dual can be written:

$$\begin{aligned}
\min S \quad & 25\,\pi_1 + 10\,\pi_2 \\
\text{subject to} \quad & 10\,\pi_1 + 2\,\pi_2 \geq 1 \\
& 5\,\pi_1 + 4\,\pi_2 \geq 1
\end{aligned}$$

---

[4] This is an important point, in so far as the value of the dual variable holds true strictly only in the so-called "epsilon" neighborhood of the optimum. The practical intepretation in our example is very simple: at some point if one added more and more energy to the system, capital might become the binding constraint at the optimum, and energy might become non-binding.

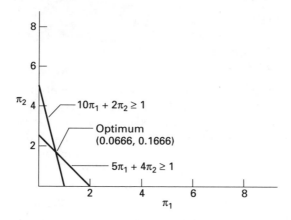

Figure 6.3   Graphical solution of the dual

This can be solved graphically, as shown on figure 6.3. We see that the optimum solution is $\pi_1 = 0.0666$, and $\pi_2 = 0.1666$. This says that an increase of one unit of energy would increase the value of the objective function by 0.1666. The old value of the primal at its optimum was $X_1 = 1.666$, $X_2 = 1.666$, and $S = 3.333$. Therefore we would expect the problem

$$\min S \quad \begin{array}{rcrcl} 1X_1 & + & 1X_2 & & \\ 10X_1 & + & 5X_2 & \leq & 25 \\ 2X_1 & + & 5X_2 & \leq & 15 \\ 2X_1 & + & 4X_2 & \leq & 11 \end{array}$$

to have the solution $S = 3.333 + 0.1666 = 3.5$. We leave to the reader to confirm that the new primal has the solution $X_1 = 1.5$, $X_2 = 2$, and indeed $S = 3.5$, as expected.

Of course in real world problems things are a little more complicated, because the quantity of inputs can themselves be made variables in the LP; and we have been admittedly a little vague here about the difference between "prices" and "costs." This will be explained in more detail in chapter 10, in which we present a more rigorous discussion of energy pricing theory, and in chapter 12, in which we examine the interpretation of the results of energy system optimization models more fully.

Application to refinery optimization

Refinery optimization is one of the classic applications of linear programming, and is widely used by the multi-national oil companies.

Box 6.1 *Glossary*

API: American Petroleum Institute

API Gravity: An arbitrary scale adopted by the American Petroleum Institute for expressing the specific gravity of oils. Its relation to specific gravity is as follows:

$$= \frac{141.5}{Specific\ Gravity\ at\ 60°F} - 131.5$$

FOB Netback: Net Product Worth (NPW) less transportation and insurance for the crude in question from port of loading to refinery site.

Gross Product Worth (GPW): weighted average value of the refined products obtainable from a barrel of crude oil at the refinery gate: it is calculated by multiplying the prevailing spot price for each product by its percentage share in the yield of one barrel of crude oil.

Hydroskimming Refinery: A process with crude distillation and product quality upgrading facilities only as distinct from those with secondary processing units to increase the yield of distillate products.

Liquefied Petroleum Gas (LPG): Light hydrocarbon material, gaseous at atmospheric temperature and pressure, held in the liquid state by pressure to facilitate storage, transport, and handling. Commercial liquefied gas consists essentially of either propane or butane, or mixtures thereof.

Net Product Worth (NPW): GPW less out of pocket operating expenses. Does not include any amortization or depreciation.

Octane Number: The octane number of gasoline is a measure of its anti-knock value. The higher the octane number, the higher the anti-knock quality of the gasoline. The quality is determined in a standard engine by matching for detonation the gasoline under test against a mixture of iso-octane and normal-heptane, both pure hydrocarbons, the percentage by volume of iso-octane in that mixture being noted as the octane number.

Pour Point: The pour point of a petroleum oil is the lowest temperature at which the oil will pour or flow when it is chilled without disturbance under prescribed conditions.

Reforming: A process in which straight-run feedstocks, e.g., benzines or naphthas, are subjected to high temperatures and pressures with the object of changing their chemical structure in such a way as to increase their octane number.

Reid Vapor Pressure: The vapor pressure (q.v.) of petroleum products, e.g., motor spirit, measured at 100°F in the Reid apparatus and reported in pounds per square inch.

Sour Crude: Crude oil containing appreciable amounts of hydrogen sulphide and mercaptans.

Tetra Ethyl Lead (TEL): A colorless stable liquid obtained commercially by the action of lead-sodium alloy on ethyl chloride. When added in small proportions to motor spirit it increases the octane number.

Vapor Pressure: The pressure exerted by the vapor escaping from a liquid. As the temperature of the liquid rises its vapor pressure increases; eventually it exceeds the pressure of the confining atmosphere and the liquid boils. In the petroleum industry vapor pressures are usually reported as "Reid Vapor Pressure."

Visbreaking: Viscosity breaking; lowering or "breaking" the viscosity of residue by cracking at relatively low temperatures.

Table 6.2 *Typical hydroskimming refinery yields*

	Nigerian light	Murban	North Sea	Arab-light	Libya	Venezuela	Kuwait
°API	37.4	39.4	36.3	34.2	37.4	32.5	31.4
% Sulphur	0.11	0.74	0.16	1.7	0.15	1.17	2.5
Yield, % vol.							
LPG	0.95	3.00	1.64	4.51	4.57	2.61	4.22
Gasoline	31.36	27.70	24.28	20.56	21.64	20.58	20.14
Distillate	40.92	40.37	32.20	31.91	28.12	27.85	22.47
Fueloil	22.7	25.10	37.92	39.60	42.16	45.26	49.69
Refinery fuel and losses	4.16	4.03	3.93	3.84	3.83	3.76	3.72
Total	100.00	100.00	100.00	100.00	100.00	100.00	100.00

However, full-scale LP refinery models may be very large, involving hundreds (if not thousands) of constraints and variables, requiring specialized computer codes for solution.[5] The discussion here must again of necessity be limited to a presentation of the basic principles: a number of specialized books on large-scale refinery models should be consulted for further details.[6] We assume the reader has a basic knowledge of crude oil and product characteristics, and of the basic operations in refining.[7] The glossary of box 6.1 on page 79 summarizes some key terms used in this book.

Let us begin with a simple crude choice problem: given the availability of n different crudes that have different yield coefficients, which crudes should be purchased to maximize refining profits? The production of the j-th product, q_j, say gasoline, can be expressed as a function of the crude input as

$$q_j = b.a_j \tag{6.1}$$

where a_j is the "yield" coefficient (with units bbls of gasoline per bbl of crude input), which is a function of the crude concerned: different crudes will have different yield coefficients (see table 6.2).

[5] Such as the IMB-MPSX package for IBM mainframe computers, or the APEX package for CDC machines.

[6] Murtagh (1981) is an excellent work in this respect, as it presents the special computational problems of large-scale LPs in the context of a refinery model example. The major problems of large-scale LPs concern computer storage limitations and the control of round-off error.

[7] Leffler (1979) is recommended as an introduction to petroleum refining for those without prior knowledge: Gary and Handwerk (1975) is a little more technical. D'Acierno and Hermelee (1979) provide an excellent discussion of the oil and gas sector as a whole. All three works belong in every energy library.

In general, if there are n candidate crudes, the quantity of the j-th product produced by the refinery is:

$$q_j = \sum_{i=1}^{n} b_i a_{ij} \qquad (6.2)$$

where b_i is the input of the i-th crude, and a_{ij} the yield of product j from crude i.

The profit to the refinery will be the difference between the sale of products and the cost of crude. Thus if λ_j denotes the ex-refinery price for product j, and c_i is the CIF cost of the i-th crude, the expression to be maximized, the so-called "objective function", evaluates to:

$$\max S = - \sum_{i} b_i c_i + \sum_{j} q_j \cdot \lambda_j \qquad (6.3)$$

$$\begin{bmatrix} \text{cost of} \\ \text{crude} \end{bmatrix} \quad \begin{bmatrix} \text{sales of} \\ \text{product} \end{bmatrix}$$

An additional constraint is necessary to make sure that the sum of crude inputs does not exceed the refinery capacity. Thus we impose the additional: restriction:

$$\sum_{i} b_i \le \bar{b} \qquad (6.4)$$

where $\bar{b}$ is the capacity of the refinery in tons/year. The full algebraic statement of the linear program can now be stated as:

$$\max S = - \sum_{i=1}^{r} b_i c_i + \sum_{j=1}^{k} q_j \lambda_j$$

$$\text{subject to } \sum_{i} b_i \le \bar{b}$$

$$q_i = \sum_{i}^{r} b_i a_{ij} \quad for\ j = 1,...,k \qquad (6.5)$$

$$b_{i,q_j} \ge 0$$
$$for\ i = 1,...,r \text{ and } j = 1,...,k$$

Let us now apply this model to a hypothetical case of a refinery in West Africa that has the choice of using either Nigerian Bonny Light, costing $141.08/ton, or Dubai crude, costing $142.53/ton. The refinery has an annual refining capacity of 1 million tons of crude; the initial assumption is that all refined products must be sold on international markets. The yield coefficients, and product price coefficients, are as in table 6.3.

Table 6.3 *Product yields*

	Yield on Dubai	Yield on Bonny	Product price coefficient
Gasoline	0.200	0.258	183.5
Kerosene	0.094	0.095	169.5
Gasoil	0.239	0.358	144.5
Fueloil	0.383	0.225	74.0

The LP of (6.5) thus becomes:

$$\text{max:} \quad -141.08b_1 \;-142.53b_2 \;+183.50q_1 +169.50q_2 +144.50q_3 +74.0q_4$$

$$
\begin{array}{llllll}
\text{subject to} & 1.0b_1 & +1.0b_2 & & & & \leq 1 \\
& 0.2b_1 & +0.258b_2 & -1.0q_1 & & & = 0 \\
& 0.094b_1 & +0.095b_2 & & -1.0q_2 & & = 0 \\
& 0.239b_1 & +0.358b_2 & & & -1.0q_3 & = 0 \\
& 0.383b_1 & +0.225b_2 & & & & -1.0q_4 = 0 \\
\end{array}
$$

A number of microcomputer packages might be used to solve this LP. One of the most flexible is the LP83 package by Sunset Software: this has the ability to read data for small problems directly from LOTUS 1-2-3 spreadsheets, but also has the ability to use the industry standard MPS data format for large problems. It also has the feature that variables and constraints are identified not by algebraic notation (x_1, x_2, a_{ij}, etc) but by labels, which greatly eases interpretation of output: thus we use "DUBAI" in place of b_1 to identify the first crude.

On table 6.4 we show the layout of a LOTUS 1-2-3 spreadsheet for the above sample problem. Lines 1 through 10 are used to derive the cost coefficients: crude prices are calculated as FOB plus freight, to which is added the operating cost. Since the initial assumption is that products are to be sold on international markets, the product price coefficients (equal to the revenue to the refinery for that product) are taken as CIF Rotterdam minus freight.

Lines 17 through 21 represent the coefficient matrix, which is seen to correspond closely to the algebraic statement of the problem shown above. The LP83 optimizer reads the objective function from line 11 of the spreadsheet, and the coefficient matrix from lines 17 to 21, performs the optimization, then returns the solution into rows 14 through 16, and into the column designated "marginal," to the right of the coefficient matrix (see box 6.2 on page 84).

Table 6.4 *Export refinery – products sold at CIF Rotterdam*

1		Dubai	Bonny	Q (gaso)	Q (kero)	Q (gasoil)	Q (fuel)			
2	FOB, $/bbl	16.00	17.28							
3	FOB, $/ton	118.08	127.53							
4	Discount		0							
5	Freight	9.00	1.00							
6	Clf W. Africa	127.08	128.53							
7	Operating Cost	14.00	14.00							
8	CIF Rotterdam			198.00	184.00	159.00	83.00			
9	Freight			14.50	14.50	14.50	9.00			
10	FOB W. Africa			183.50	169.50	144.50	74.00			
11	Cost coeffs.	− 141.08	− 142.53	183.50	169.50	144.50	74.00			
12	Lower									
13	Upper									
14	Solution									
15	Value	0.00	0.00	0.00	0.00	0.00	0.00	−	0	< S
16	Marginal	25.5695	10.6999							marginal
17	CAPCON	1	1					≤ =	1.00	
18	CGASO	0.2	0.258	− 1				=	0.00	− 183.5
19	CKERO	0.094	0.095		− 1			=	0.00	− 169.5
20	CGASOIL	0.239	0.358			− 1		=	0.00	− 144.5
21	CFUELO	0.383	0.225				− 1	=	0.00	− 74

With the data as shown, the solution is seen to be zero (i.e., all entries in row 14 remain blank), and the value of the objective function is also zero. That means that profits are maximized if no crude is run, since, with the costs as given, refining is unprofitable. LP83 does, however, make entries into row 16. These "marginal" values associated with variables, sometimes termed "reduced costs," give an indication of by how much the corresponding objective function coefficient would have to change for that variable to enter the solution. In the sample problem, Bonny has a reduced cost of $10.699/ton. This means that, if the cost of Bonny Light is less than $131.83 (i.e., $142.53 − $10.699), then refining becomes profitable. Four decimal figures are used only to demonstrate how sensitive LPs are to very small changes in input data.

In table 6.5 we apply a discount of $10.70/ton to the price of Bonny Light (in row 3 of the spreadsheet). As expected, now refining Bonny light becomes profitable, and 1 million tons are treated. The objective

Box 6.2 *Range-name requirements*

For the LP83 software package to be able to locate the cost coefficients and the constraint matrix certain range-names must be used in the spreadsheet. For example, LP83 expects to find the constraint matrix in a range-named 83CONSTRAINT, and expects to find a range-name called 83VA into which it places the optimum solution. The full set of required range-names are as follows:

	83VAR
Optimum solution	83VA
Lower bounds (on variables, if any)	83LOWER
Upper bounds (on variables, if any)	83UPPER
Cost coefficients (objective function coefficients)	83COST
Reduced costs (marginal) for constraints	83VR
Shadow prices associated with constraints	83CR

The layout of these range-names, as used in the examples of this chapter, appear in the spreadsheet as follows:

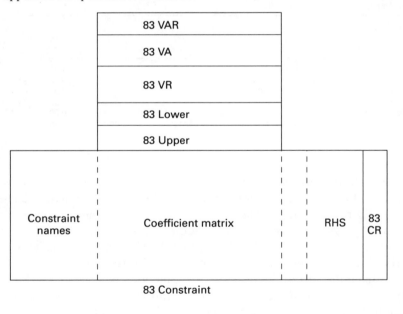

function is positive, showing an annual profit of \$100.[8] Note that the marginal value for Dubai has increased from \$25.5695 to \$25.5696,

[8] Since the right-hand side of the coefficient matrix has units of millions (i.e., the capacity of the refinery is 1 million tons per year), the objective function is seen also to have units of million dollars per year.

Table 6.5 *Export refinery – $10.70/ton discount on Bonny*

1	Dubai	Bonny	Q (gaso)	Q (kero)	Q (gasoil)	Q (fuel)			
2 FOB, $/bbl	16.00	17.28							
3 FOB, $/ton	118.08	127.53							
4 Discount		− 10.70							
5 Freight	9.00	1.00							
6 Clf W. Africa	127.08	117.83							
7 Operating Cost	14.00	14.00							
8 CIF Rotterdam			198.00	184.00	159.00	83.00			
9 Freight			14.50	14.50	14.50	9.00			
10 FOB W. Africa			183.50	169.50	144.50	74.00			
11 Cost coeffs.	− 141.08	− 131.83	183.50	169.50	144.50	74.00			
12 Lower									
13 Upper									
14 Solution		1	0.258	0.095	0.358	0.225			
15 Value	0.00	− 131.83	47.34	16.10	51.73	16.65	− 0.0001		
16 Marginal	25.5695								marginal
17 CAPCON	1	1					≤ =	1.00	0.0001
18 CGASO	0.2	0.258	− 1				=	0.00	− 183.5
19 CKERO	0.094	0.095		− 1			=	0.00	− 169.5
20 CGASOIL	0.239	0.358			− 1		=	0.00	− 144.5
21 CFUELO	0.383	0.225				− 1	=	0.00	− 74

equal to the difference between the first marginal value for Bonny ($10.6999/ton) and the cost actually used ($10.7/ton). The implication is that if the price of Bonny light remains at $131.83, Dubai would have to be offered at a discount of $25.5696 for it to be used in preference to Bonny light.

The conclusion that refining in West Africa to meet product demands in Europe is unprofitable is hardly surprising. But now suppose that some part (or all) of the refinery production can be sold locally, and that the objective is not to maximize refinery profits, but to meet local petroleum product demands at least cost. Since local demands must be met, an additional set of material balances must be added to the problem. If the domestic demand for the j-th petroleum product is denoted d_j, imports of the j-th product i_j, exports e_j and refinery production q_j, then for each product we require that:

$$q_j + i_j = d_j + e_j \qquad (6.6)$$

This ensures that, if refinery production is insufficient to meet the demand for a product, the balance will be imported. It also makes sure that, if one product is produced in excess of local requirements, it will be exported. Indeed, this is a typical condition in developing country refineries, because of the mismatch between the composition of the local product market, and what can normally be produced from a barrel of crude. For example, if just enough crude is run to meet local gasoil demand, then gasoline (or naphtha) must be exported. Conversely, if the crude run is reduced to meet the gasoline demand, then gasoil must be imported.[9] With these additional requirements, the mathematical statement of the LP becomes:

$$\min \sum_i b_i c_i + \sum_j i_j \lambda_j - \sum_j e_j \beta_j$$

$$\text{s.t. } e_j - i_j - q_j = d_j ; \qquad j = 1 \ldots k \qquad (6.7)$$

$$\sum_i b_i \leq \bar{b}$$

$$q_j = \sum_i^r b_i a_{ij} ; \qquad j = 1 \ldots k$$

$$b_i, q_j, i_j, e_j \geq 0$$

The spreadsheet for this revised sample problem is shown on table 6.6. Note that the cost coefficients for imports are FOB Rotterdam plus freight, while for exports they remain at CIF Rotterdam minus freight. We have also returned to the original costs for crude (eliminating the Bonny discount of table 6.5). Local market demands are assumed as follows: gasoline 150,000 tons/year; kerosene 50,000 tons/year, gasoil 300,000 tons/year, and fueloil 400,000 tons/year.

The solution shows that some 837,000 tons of Bonny are refined each year, with refinery production of gasoil exactly equal to the national demand of 300,000 tons/year. Gasoline and kerosene are exported, while fueloil needs to be imported. The solution illustrates an important policy conclusion: even if refining is unprofitable for an export refinery, freight differentials may make local refining part of a least-cost solution to meet national petroleum product demands.

The marginal costs associated with each of the product balance constraints have an important interpretation; they indicate the change to the objective function per unit change in the right-hand side of the

[9] It should be noted that linear programming requires all variables to be greater than or equal to zero. This means that we cannot combine imports and exports into a single variable "net imports," because this may in fact need to be negative (as is the case, typically, for gasoline).

Table 6.6 Refinery to Meet Domestic Market Requirements

	Dubai	Bonny	Q (gaso)	Q (kero)	Q (gasoil)	Q (fuel)	E(gaso)	E(kero)	E(GO)	E(FO)	l(gaso)	l(kero)	l(GO)	l(FO)			marginal
1 FOB. $/bbl	16.00	17.28															
2 FOB. $/ton	118.08	127.53															
3 Discount		0.00									198.00	184.00	159.00	83.00			
4 Freight	9.00	1.00									14.50	14.50	14.50	9.00			
5 CIF W. Africa	127.08	128.53									212.50	198.50	173.50	92.00			
6 Operating Cost	14.00	14.00															
7 CIF Rotterdam							198.00	184.00	159.00	83.00							
8 Freight							14.50	14.50	14.50	9.00							
9 FOB W. Africa							183.50	169.50	144.50	74.00							
10 Cost coeffs.	−141.08	−142.53	0.00	0.00	0.00	0.00	183.50	169.50	144.50	74.00	−212.50	−198.50	−173.50	−92.00			
11 Lower																	
12 Upper																	
13 Solution	0.00	0.83798	0.21620	0.07960	0.3	0.188547	0.06620	0.02960	0.00	0.00	0.00	0.00	0.00	0.21145			
14 Value	14.2360	−119.44	0.00	0.00	0.00	0.00	12.15	5.02	0.00	0.00				−19.45			
15 Marginal									18.5751	18	29	10.4248			=	−121.7	marginal
16 CAPCON	1	1													≤ =	1.00	
17 CGASO	0.2	0.258	−1												= =	0.00	−183.500
18 CKERO	0.094	0.095		−1											= =	0.00	−169.500
19 CGASOIL	0.239	0.358			−1										= =	0.00	−163.075
20 CFUELO	0.383	0.225				−1									= =	0.00	−92.000
21 BGASO			1				−1				1				= =	0.15	−183.500
22 BKERO				1				−1				1			= =	0.05	−169.500
23 BGASOIL					1				−1				1		= =	0.3	−163.075
24 BFUELO						1				−1				1	= =	0.4	−92.000

constraint, and this marginal value is also known as the shadow price (as discussed above). For example, the marginal value shown for gasoline is − 183.5.[10] This means that the objective function will increase by that amount for every unit decrease in the right-hand side of the gasoline constraint: i.e., for every unit decrease in domestic gasoline demand.[11] Suppose, then, that we reduce the gasoline demand by 5%, i.e. from 150,000 tons/year to 142,500 tons/year, equivalent to 0.0075 million tons/year. We would therefore expect the objective function to increase by 183.5 × 0.0075 = 1.376 million dollars.

Table 6.7 shows that this is indeed the case: when domestic gasoline demand is reduced, the objective function (see row 15, far right) improves from − 121.7 to − 120.3, exactly the expected amount.

Some examples of refinery models in developing countries

As noted, very detailed LPs have long been used by the multi-national oil companies. Mobil and Exxon, for example, not only use such models to assist in the day-to-day process optimization of individual refineries, but also use more aggregated models for production planning of sets of refineries in which transportation operations are also included. The use of LPs in the smaller refineries of the developing countries has only become more widespread in the past few years: part of the problem has been that many early efforts resulted in very large models, written by expatriate consultants, that proved to be very poorly matched to the staff capabilities in place. In some of the larger developing countries, however, such LPs have developed to include not just refineries, but also fertilizer production and natural gas utilization, since these are all closely linked; Bhattia (1974) describes such a model for India.

In our two case study countries, such LPs were introduced as part of the overall efforts to improve sector-wide planning: we defer to the case studies of the concluding chapters a discussion of how these were implemented, and how training occurred. However, a few technical comments on the Morocco and Sri Lanka LPs are appropriate at this point.

In the LP for the SCP refinery of Morocco, depicted in simplified form

[10] It can be seen that this is exactly equal to the export price of gasoline: 1 ton less domestic demand means 1 ton more can be exported, which increases revenues by the amount of the export price, per ton. For fueloil, the marginal price is the import price, since one ton less of fueloil demand means one ton less must be imported. In the case of gasoil, however, the marginal cost is $163.07, which lies between the import and export prices (of $144.5 and $173.5/ton, respectively).

[11] In mathematical terms, this is strictly true only of the epsilon neighborhood of the optimum, since it is in fact equal to the partial derivative of the objective function with respect to the value of the right-hand side of the constraint. In the jargon of the classical theory of constrained optimization, it is equal to the value of the corresponding Lagrange multiplier at the constrained optimum.

Table 6.7 Decrease gasoline demand by 10 percent

1	Dubai	Bonny	Q(gaso)	Q(kero)	Q(gasoil)	Q(fuel)	E(gaso)	E(kero)	E(GO)	E(FO)	l(gaso)	l(kero)	l(GO)	l(FO)	≤/=		marginal
2 FOB $/bbl	16.00	17.28									198.00	184.00	159.00	83.00			
3 FOB $/ton	118.08	127.53															
4 Discount	0.00	0.00															
5 Freight	9.00	1.00									14.50	14.50	14.50	9.00			
6 CIF W. Africa	127.08	128.53									212.50	198.50	173.50	92.00			
7 Operating Cost	14.00	14.00															
8 CIF Rotterdam							198.00	184.00	159.00	83.00							
9 Freight							14.50	14.50	14.50	9.00							
10 FOB W. Africa							183.50	169.50	144.50	74.00							
11 Cost coeffs.	−141.08	−142.53	0.00	0.00	0.00	0.00	183.50	169.50	144.50	74.00	−212.50	−198.50	−173.50	−92.00			
12 Lower																	
13 Upper																	
14 Solution		0.83798	0.21620	0.07960	0.3	0.188547	0.06620	0.02960						0.21145			
15 Value	0.00	−119.44	0.00	0.00	0.00	0.00	12.15	5.02	0.00	0.00	0.00	0.00	0.00	−19.45	=	−120.3	
16 Marginal	14.2360		0.00	0.00					18.5751	18	29	29	10.4248				
17 CAPCON	1	1													≤	1.00	
18 CGASO	0.2	0.258	−1												=	0.00	−183.500
19 CKERO	0.094	0.095		−1											=	0.00	−169.500
20 CGASOIL	0.239	0.358			−1										=	0.00	−163.075
21 CFUELO	0.383	0.225				−1									=	0.00	−92.000
22 BGASO			1				−1				1				=	0.1425	−183.500
23 BKERO				1				−1				1			=	0.05	−169.500
24 BGASOIL					1				−1				1		=	0.3	−163.075
25 BFUELO						1				−1				1	=	0.4	−92.000

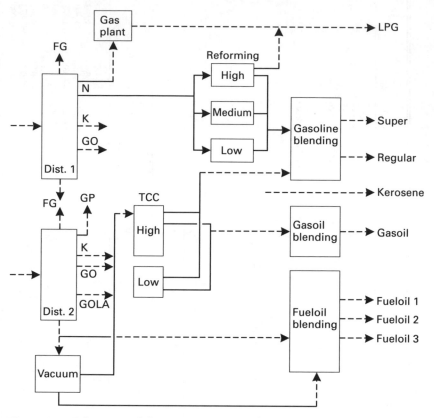

Figure 6.4   Schematic of the Morocco SCP Refinery LP

on figure 6.4, a major issue concerned the severity levels used in the Reformer and the TCC. Indeed, because of the rapid growth of domestic LPG consumption, Morocco has had to import LPG: both refineries had long been operated in such a way as to maximize LPG production in both reforming and cracking operations. Until very recently, LPG was imported in small quantities, in pressurized rather than liquified form, a very expensive proposition. But with the start of imports in liquified form, the issue of optimizing the LPG import/refinery LPG production mix has become of increasing interest.

Because yield patterns are dependent on severity, the model assumes the existence of several hypothetical units, each characterized by its own yield and operating characteristics. The capacity of these two hypothetical units is set equal to the capacity of the actual single unit:

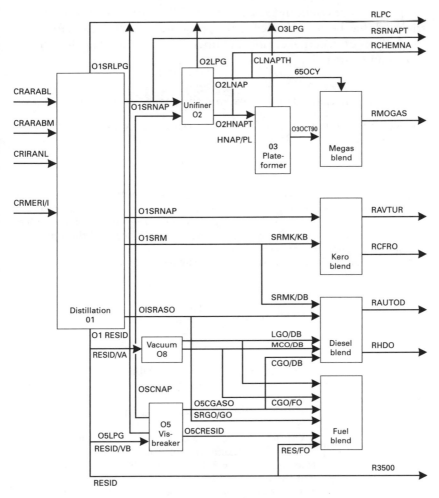

Figure 6.5   Schematic of the Sri Lanka Refinery LP

$$\text{TCC}_{\text{high}} + \text{TCC}_{\text{low}} \leq \text{TCC}_{\text{actual}}$$

The optimum level of severity is then given by the weighted average of the throughputs. Where the severity-yield relationship is strongly non-linear, three hypothetical units may need to be used, as is the case for reforming: if the model is properly formulated, then the optimum solution will show throughput to at most two units (high + medium, or medium + low).

The LP model of the Sapugaskanda refinery of the Ceylon Petroleum

Corporation was built in 1985 to support the National Energy Strategy studies. It has been used since to support crude purchase decisions, and for analyses of debottlenecking and upgrading options. The flowchart is shown on figure 6.5.

Annex 6.1: Internal rate of return and the benefit-cost ratio

Besides NPV, the internal rate of return (IRR) is also used as an evaluation criterion. The value of IRR may be defined by:

$$0 = \sum_{t=0}^{T} \frac{(B_i - C_i)}{(1 + \text{IRR})^t}$$

Thus, the IRR is the discount rate which reduces the NPV to zero. In the case of a specific investment program or project, it would be considered acceptable for financing if IRR > ARI, which in most normal cases implies NPV > 0 (i.e., ignoring cases where multiple roots could arise – which occurs if the annual net benefit stream changes sign several times).

Another frequently used criterion is the benefit-cost ratio (BCR):

$$\text{BCR} = \frac{\displaystyle\sum_{t=0}^{T} \frac{B_t}{(1 + r)^t}}{\displaystyle\sum_{t=0}^{T} \frac{C_t}{(1 + r)^t}}$$

If BCR > 1, then NPV > 0 and the project is acceptable.

Each of these criteria has its strengths and weaknesses, but NPV is probably the most useful, especially in the context of optimizing an objective function. For example, the use of IRR could be misleading for ranking two different programs (I and II), since $\text{IRR}_I > \text{IRR}_{II}$ does not guarantee that $\text{NPV}_I > \text{NPV}_{II}$, and similarly for BCR. On the other hand, a comparison of the IRR versus the discount rate is helpful in making judgments on pricing policy, if the average tariff is used as a proxy for incremental benefits. Also, the IRR and BCR provide some measure of the yield per unit of investment, which may be useful in ranking policies when there is an overall budget constraint. In practice, all the different criteria should be estimated (since they use the same basic data) in order to obtain a balanced decision.

Annex 6.2: Multi-objective decision-making

As explained earlier, traditional economic cost-benefit analysis (CBA) seeks to measure all consequences of a given project in monetary terms and evaluate the result according to some single criterion such as net present value (NPV) or internal rate of return (IRR). When projects and their impacts are to be embedded in a system of broader (national) objectives which cannot be easily quantified in monetary terms, the theory of multi-objective decision-making offers an alternative approach which may facilitate the optimal choice among investment options available.

Once the necessity for change and analysis of a system has been recognized, desirable objectives are specified. Such a set of objectives often exhibits a hierarchical structure. The highest level represents the broad overall objectives (e.g., to improve the quality of life), often vaguely stated and, hence, not very operational. However, it can be broken down into lower-level objectives (e.g., to maximize income) so that the extent to which the latter are met may be practically assessed. For this purpose, one or more comprehensive and measurable attributes have to be assigned to each objective. The relationship between objective (e.g., minimizing costs) and attribute (e.g., $ per year of expenditures) should be as direct as possible. Sometimes only proxies are available (e.g., if the objective is "to enhance recreation opportunities," the attribute "number of recreation days" can be used).

Although some value judgment is required to choose the proper attribute (especially if proxies are involved), in contrast to the single-criterion methodologies, measurement does not have to be in monetary terms. More explicit recognition is given to the fact that a variety of concerns may be associated with planning decisions. In particular, the general multi-objective model can be expressed as:

$$\max Z(x) = f[Z_1(x), Z_2(x), ..., Z_p(x)],$$

such that:

$$g_i(x) \leq 0 \quad \text{for } i = 1,2,...,m$$
$$x_j \geq 0 \quad \text{for } j = 1,2,....,n$$

where $Z(x)$ is an objective function comprised of p objectives (e.g., the lower-level objectives mentioned earlier), x is an n-dimensional vector of decision variables; and $g_i(x)$ is a set of m constraints (containing, for instance, a maximum budget for the alternatives under consideration). In its simplest form the vector x is one-dimensional and specifies the various independent alternatives (e.g., $n = 1$ for alternative 1, etc.). It follows from this characterization that the effects of a given project on each objective have to be estimated separately. Thus a broad range of impacts of the project is revealed explicitly, enhancing the appropriateness of the final decision.

An intuitive understanding of the fundamentals of multi-objective decision-making might be best provided by a two-dimensional graphical exposition. Assume that a project has two non-commensurable and conflicting objectives, Z_1 and Z_2. For a large river basin plan, such objectives could be irrigation and power production. Assume further that six alternative projects or solutions to the problem have been identified as points a to f, all of which are feasible. As depicted in figure 6.6, the distance from the origin along each axis represents the extent to which the relevant objective is met (e.g., hectares irrigated or energy generated). In terms of the decision variable, the alternatives can be represented by $x = 1$ for project a, $x = 2$ for project b, etc.. It can be seen that alternative b is preferred to alternative f in terms of objective Z_1, but that the reverse is true relative to objective Z_2. Therefore it is not possible, at this stage to make a statement concerning the relative superiority of alternatives b and f with respect to both objectives. However, it can be seen that alternative d is preferred to alternative f in terms of both objectives Z_1 and Z_2, and therefore f can be excluded from further consideration (if only one alternative is to be chosen then d dominates f). In general, the set of all non-dominated feasible solution points

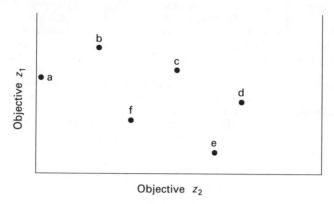

Figure 6.6   Alternative solutions to hypothetical multi-objective problem

forms a Pareto optimal curve (or curve of best options), also called a trans-formation curve or efficient frontier.

For an unconstrained problem, further ordering cannot be conducted without the introduction of value judgments. Specific information has to be elicited from the decision-maker to determine the most-preferred solution. In its most complete form such information may be summarized by a family of iso-preference curves as illustrated in figure 6.7, with the preference level increasing upwards as shown. Each point on a given iso-preference curve indicates a level of achievement of objectives Z_1 and Z_2 which provides the same level of utility or "satisfaction." In other words, the decision-maker will be indifferent between alternatives A and B, but would prefer alternative C to either A or B. The preferred alternative is that which results in the greatest utility – which occurs (for continuous decision variables as shown here), at the point of tangency D of the highest iso-preference curve with the Pareto optimal curve. In this case, the point C is not attainable.

Which practical method in particular is suitable to determine the "best" alternative available, depends on the nature of the decision situation. For instance, interactive involvement of the decision-maker has proved useful in the case of problems characterized by a large number of decision variables and complex causal interrelationships. Some objectives can be dealt with through direct optimization, while others require the satisfaction of a certain standard (e.g., level of particulate emissions from a coal power plant must be below some specified parts per million).

Theory and methods of multi-objective decision-making

Of the existing theoretical developments in multi-objective decision-making, the most common fall roughly into two categories. First, utility theory attempts to directly formalize the decision-maker's preference structure (Chankong and Haimes, 1983). Methodologies that originate from utility theory are most suitable when a set of well-defined alternatives is explicitly given, and the problem structure does not involve interdependence between decision variables.

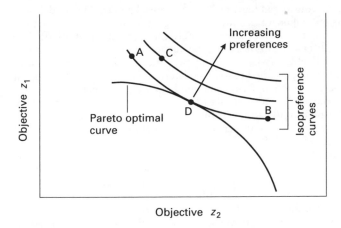

Figure 6.7   Pareto optimal curve and isopreference curves

For instance, planning of a gas fired power plant will include the choice of turbines. A number of producers will be considered as possible suppliers, each of whom may offer various turbines. The alternative solutions are therefore limited, the characteristics of each machine are well-specified, and one type of machine will be chosen. As only this single decision has to be made, the decision vector x is one-dimensional in this example. Each solution will satisfy the decision-maker's multiple objectives to different degrees (e.g., production capacity, cost, maintenance characteristics, service offered by the supplier, etc.). If the analyst succeeds in computing the satisfaction the decision-maker receives from the achievement levels of these individual objectives and their combinations, this will help to determine the preferred turbine. The task can be best accomplished when the nature of the problem results in a set of well-defined and limited alternatives.

Second, when the problem structure is more complex, vector optimization theory is applicable. Numerous planning situations will ask for simultaneous interdependent decisions. For instance the boundaries of the above example can be expanded: the decision-maker may be free to determine project-location, scale, or even institutional structure of the energy sector in addition to just questions of the technical equipment. The system's responses to alternative actions (e.g., a set of simultanous decisions) may be complex and not easily determined. The construction of the preference structure can no longer be based on hypothetical responses of the system. Instead, information about the actual behavior of the system should be presented to the decision-maker whenever this is possible, without overwhelming the individual with technical data. Then preferences can be judged more accurately.

Accomplishments and limitations of multi-objective decision-making

The major accomplishment of multi-objective decision models is that they allow for more accurate representation of decision problems, in the sense that several objectives can be accounted for. However, the question of whose preferences are to be considered has not been addressed so far. The model only aids a single decision-maker (or a homogeneous group). It is assumed that the decision-maker is able to consider appropriately the preferences of all affected people. This difficult task will not always be accomplished in reality. Various interested groups will often assign different priorities to the respective objectives, and normally it may not be possible to determine a single "best" solution via the multi-objective model. Also, the mathematical framework imposes constraints upon the ability to represent effectively the planning problem. Non-linear, stochastic and dynamic formulations can assist in better defining the problem, but impose costs in terms of complexity in formulation and solving the model (Cocklin, 1989).

Nevertheless, in constructing the model the analyst communicates information about the nature of the problem. He specifies what factors are important and how they interact. Liebman (1976) observes that "modeling is thinking made public," and considers this transfer of knowledge to represent perhaps the most important contribution of modeling. With respect to the second point of criticism, diverse preferences, Liebman suggests that there is value to be gained in constructing models from differing perspectives and comparing the results.

Formal applications of multi-attribute decision-making models to practical energy sector planning problems are still quite rare: most applications are to be found in the power sector. Amagai and Leung (1991) examined the trade-offs between economic and environmental objectives in Japan's power sector using a multi-objective LP. Meier and Munasinghe (1992) have applied multi-attribute decision methods to the Sri Lankan power sector, and Crousillat and Hyde (1992) have applied a multi-objective risk/trade-off method to strategic planning in the power sector. However, as noted in the introduction, it is in power plant siting where the application of multi-objective methods has the longest history.

CHAPTER 7

Energy-environmental interactions

Energy is at the very center of many of the current concerns over the global environment and the degradation of local, regional, and national environments. While it is perhaps true that environmental issues have not heretofore occupied a prominent part in developing country energy planning, that situation is changing very quickly. Even aside from purely indigenous concerns over the impact of major energy projects, the International Financial Institutions have begun to pay much more attention to the environmental impacts of major projects than in the past. Moreover, one need only examine the experience of the developed countries in this respect to get some idea of what is to come elsewhere: in the United States, for example, environmental considerations have greatly influenced efforts to change the energy mix from imported oil to domestic coal, domestic oil, and nuclear energy. Epic legislative and legal battles have been fought over conflicts between legislation and programs to promote domestic energy use at the expense of imported oil (such as the Fuel Use Act that sought to increase coal utilization, or the Federal leasing programs for off-shore oil development), and those designed to protect the environment (of which the Clean Air and Water Acts, and the National Environmental Policy Act, are the most important). In the larger developing countries, where the scale of energy resource extraction and air pollution has reached significant levels, environmental concerns are already beginning to influence significantly national and regional energy policies. The environmental impacts of the huge increase in coal output for power generation and industrial boilers in India and China, or the impacts of large-scale hydro development in Brazil and India, are testimony to such trends.

Environmental analysis within INEP

This chapter elaborates on an environmental-economic analytical framework that is very much in the spirit of the INEP approach.

Conceptually, it is of great benefit in terms of long-term sustainability and effectiveness of energy programs and policies to integrate energy and environmental management. By having a better and wider understanding of the nature of environmental interactions and externalities relevant to energy sources and uses, both within and outside the energy sector, decision-makers can integrate such effects into the INEP process.

This kind of environment-oriented INEP recognizes the important and growing role of environmental externalities in determining the abilities of planners to achieve supply targets and requires that a systematic assessment of the order of magnitude, the scale, and the cost implications of a full range of potential environmental effects be made. Although the techniques and data required to do this are still evolving, there are currently tools available that allow a fairly rigorous review to be made of significant factors and, by extension, the costs and benefits of various environmental management options. Increasingly, the most common tool used by planners in the project planning cycle is the environmental impact assessment (EIA). EIA is the explicit tool that has been developed for determining the main environmental concerns that may arise as a result of an energy resource project or program. Governments and international development agencies have, in recent years, elevated EIA to the same level of importance as other analyses involving the more traditional disciplines (e.g., technical, economic, and financial evaluation of projects).

In the energy sector, specific EIAs are being used as a method of determining the impacts of a given policy or project (such as a large hydro dam) on the environment, the energy sector itself, and on related sectors. Increasingly, EIAs are placing greater emphasis also on socio-cultural impacts. At the same time, an EIA can be used as a tool for looking at the impact of indirectly generated externalities on the energy decision in question, i.e., factors resulting from other non-project activities, or management of projects in other sectors.

The wider perspective of EIA involves taking a more regional and multi-sectoral perspective in many instances. For example, from the point of view of environmental management, it is important to know what the effects of catchment deforestation (caused by agriculture or commercial forestry) will have on future reservoir capacity, or on the water inflow regime. This is not an impact of the dam, per se, but a related impact of the dam from additional externalities that may occur in the future. The example given is clearly an integrated planning issue. If the effects of allowing increasing rural populations to colonize the catchment area of a major dam and to practice slash-and-burn agriculture would be large-scale sedimentation and increased periodicity of river inflows, it would obviously be necessary to formulate a policy of catchment protection as an implicit component of dam management. The planning decisions that facilitate such changes might come from the Ministry of Agriculture or the Ministry of Lands, rather than the Ministry of Energy, and apply to a complete region (e.g., a drainage basin) rather than an individual project site. The cost implications of such a strategy for the country as a whole, particularly the opportunity costs of agricultural output foregone, and the social costs to poor landless peasants would need to be accounted for as part of a full project evaluation.

In some cases, the rather narrow outlook of a conventional EIA does not lend itself to such a wide-ranging assessment of issues. A basic problem with most EIAs is that they focus on environmental changes that result from a particular energy sector project, rather than looking for environmental changes that cause problems affecting energy projects. Since the term EIA could have a specific project connotation, one may adopt the more general term of Environmental Assessment (EA) which suggests a more holistic view of the positive (benefits) and negative (costs) impacts of human activities in a range of economic sectors on energy projects and vice versa.

To show that the question of environmental externalities is more than just a local, project-specific problem, this chapter also focusses attention on the transnational and global nature of many energy related environmental issues. Although individual decision-makers in developing countries can often have little direct influence in mitigating the problems causing these issues, they can be still be viewed in the context of the environmental-economic analytical framework developed in previous chapters. Indirectly, through supporting international cooperation and by seeking to address the role played by their own country no matter how small, they can contribute to the worldwide efforts to bring some of these environmental problems under control. We indicate how this can often only be accomplished with the help of external assistance since the costs of environmental management and the short-run benefits foregone by using the environment in a less intensive, environmentally sound manner are too high for resource scarce developing countries to bear alone.

A discussion of the scale and nature of the main energy-environmental interactions of concern to planners is provided next, prior to a more detailed discussion of both the environmental impact assessment procedures and the environmental-economic framework that extends the analytical approaches of previous chapters. Thus the following section sets the environmental context in which the analytical tools must be used.

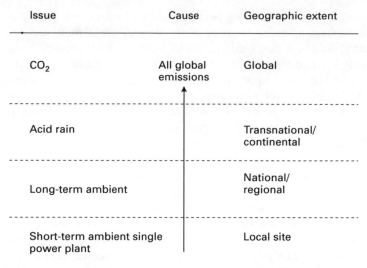

Figure 7.1   The hierarchy of environmental planning

The scale and nature of energy-environmental interactions

Indeed, the hierarchy of energy planning concerns is matched by a hierarchy of environmental concerns, as depicted on figure 7.1; these range from global impacts at the one end to purely project specific impacts at the other. And while it is true that global impacts ultimately result from the sum of individual projects, the institutional frameworks, and the policy initiatives necessary to deal with the problems at the varying scales, are quite distinct. Moreover, just as in energy planning, different levels of the hierarchy require quite different types of modeling for analysis of the policy options.

First, there are the truly global problems, such as the potential worldwide warming due to increasing accumulation of greenhouse gases like carbon dioxide (produced in fossil fuel combustion but not in nuclear power generation), or the pollution of the marine and oceanic environment by oil spills and other wastes. The recent oil spill off the coast of Morocco, which required a major international effort to prevent the slick from reaching the sensitive shoreline, is testimony to the fact that these are very real concerns not just to the developed countries that have borne the brunt of such incidents in the past (such as the Exxon Valdez accident in Alaska), but have the potential for inflicting major *economic* damage to important fishery and tourism industries in developing countries as well.

Second in scale are the transnational issues such as acid rain, or the radioactive fallout in one European country due to fossil fuel or nuclear emissions in a neighboring nation, or the excessive downstream siltation of river water in Bangladesh due to deforestation of watersheds and soil erosion in upstream Nepal. These are generally subcontinental in scale, and typically require bi- or multilateral agreements between governments for their resolution.

Third are the national- and regional-scale issues, typically at the river basin level, such as those involving the Amazon Basin in Brazil or the Mahaweli Basin in Sri Lanka. River basin development is generally for multiple purposes, bringing energy planners and electric utilities concerned with hydroelectric development into contact (and often conflict) with agencies involved with irrigation and regional development.

Finally are the purely local impacts associated with specific projects: acid mine drainage from coal mines, resettlement problems at a hydroelectric dam, the loss of wildlife habitat for a reservoir. Here the pressures for mitigation of the adverse environmental effects are generally driven by local concerns, such as over resettlement and public health impacts at major hydro projects in Africa (Aswan in Egypt, Akosombo in Ghana, Kossou in the Ivory Coast), or the environmentalist opposition to the development of the Bombay High off-shore field in India.

While environmental and natural resource problems of any kind are a matter for serious concern, those that fall purely within national boundaries of a given country are inherently easier to deal with from the standpoint of policy implementation, and are those that will generally be of immediate concern to energy planners, to be addressed in a national energy strategy (see box 7.1 for an example from Pakistan). Even in cases where national energy strategies will have global consequences – particularly in the case of India and China, where present plans for the expansion of their power sectors envisage substantial dependence on coal, the reality is that the most immediate pressures will come from local and national considerations. Just the **local** impacts of increasing coal use for power production in India from 75 million tons/year to 158 million by the year 2000 will force much greater attention to environmental impacts than has heretofore been the case.

The nature of energy-environmental interactions[1]

The environmental and health consequences associated with various cycles of energy production and consumption are, for a large part, very

[1] This review draws heavily on Anderson *Energy and Environment*, World Bank, April 1991, and Bernstein *Review of Environmental Impacts of Energy Use*, Report to USAID by the Energy Center, University of Pennsylvania, 1990.

Box 7.1 *Technology, environment, and domestic energy resources: developing the Lakhra coal field in Pakistan*

The experience of the attempts to develop the Lakhra coal field in Pakistan illustrates how environmental concerns are beginning to influence the development of energy resources in developing countries, and how new technologies may play a role in resolving environmental controversies.

Pakistan has estimated its coal resources at over 9 billion tons, and has for over a decade concentrated its efforts to develop the Lakhra coal field about 200km north of Karachi for large-scale power generation. In the late 1970s a first pre-feasibility study for a 300MW coal-fired electric generating plant was prepared by a Japanese Development Assistance Agency. By 1984, now with the assistance of the United States Agency for International Development (USAID), the American firm of Gilbert-Commonwealth prepared a full feasibility study for 2 × 350MW units as part of an overall long-term plan for the major utility, the Water and Power Development Agency (WAPDA). However, an environmental impact assessment indicated that substantial environmental impacts were likely. With the coal resource consisting mainly of low-grade lignite (30–40% ash, 6,300–8,000 Btu/lb) that also has high sulphur contents in the range of 6–8% by dry weight, the potential for very high SO_2 emissions if the conventional pulverized coal design was not equipped with flue gas desulphurization (FGD) is obvious.

Based on the conclusions of the assessment, electrostatic precipitators were added to the design to reduce particulate emissions, and the project was scaled down to 500MW. Use of FGD, which would increase capital costs by about 20%, was considered to raise to costs to an unacceptable level given Pakistan's problems of capital mobilization. Coal washing was considered, but found not to lower sulphur contents to desirable levels at economic cost. The design was revised further to use tall stacks, 190 metres in height, which would have met World Bank guidelines for maximum ambient twenty-four hour concentrations for SO_2: but since tall stacks are no longer considered acceptable in the developed countries (in the United States, for example, the Environmental Protection Agency and the 1977 Clean Air Act Amendments explicitly preclude tall stacks from being used to meet ambient SO_2 standards for large new utility plants), this too was regarded as an unacceptable option.

The solution has been to look to one of the new "clean coal" technologies: with Chinese financial assistance 3 × 50MW atmospheric fluidized bed combustion (AFBC) of the bubbling bed design have been ordered: this technology has SO_2 emissions comparable to FGD fitted pulverized coal plants, but at a somewhat lower cost, and, perhaps equally important, is much easier to maintain and operate than the FGD alternative

Nevertheless, throughout this debate there were always questions about the ability to develop the coal resource itself. The scaling down from 700MW to the currently planned 150MW has a lot to do with concerns over the ability to develop the necessary mining capacity: at the time of writing in mid 1990, the mine to support even the 150MW plant has yet to be developed.

Source: Wilbanks (1990).

similar among energy sources (see table 7.1). Differences may exist mainly in terms of the magnitude of those effects. Coal and uranium cycles, for example, are considerably more troublesome environmentally than oil and natural gas owing to the quantity and composition of their toxic by-products.

Coal

Major disruptions in the environment and important health impacts are linked to coal from the time it is mined from the ground to the time it is burned. Acid mine drainage and toxic effluents from coal mines have caused serious degradation of streams and rivers (as observed for example in the Appalachian region of the US), while gaseous emissions from coal combustion have seriously threatened air quality.

It has been estimated that coal combustion accounts for 24% and 33% of all NO_x and particulates, respectively, produced by man and yields at least 11% more CO_2 than oil and 67% more than natural gas. NO_x and CO_2 are principal "greenhouse gases"; NO_x when combined with sulphate forms acid rain, or with organic compounds forms photochemical smog. Particulates (e.g., fly ash) can have mutagenic effects; sulphur oxides – the most important air emission from coal combustion in terms of quantity produced – have been linked to increased incidence of respiratory illnesses, cardiovascular diseases and cancers.

Coal-fired power stations make up more than half of the world's thermal generating capacity. They represent the main source of SO_x emissions in many countries; and in developing countries especially the use of high sulphur coals and the resultant emissions of particulates, smoke, and carbon monoxide have created significant health problems in major cities.

Pollution abatement technologies have been developed to combat air pollution caused by the combustion of coal for power generation. Such technological responses to air pollution problems may be grouped broadly into fuel substitution techniques, emission control technologies (e.g., electrostatic precipitators, flue gas desulphurization, or scrubbers) and advanced high-efficiency/low-emission technologies (e.g., fluidized bed combustion, combined gas-steam cycles). Important accomplishments in this area can be summarized from table 7.1 as follows:

Switching from conventional coal-fired power plants to natural gas can reduce particulates and SO_2 emissions by 99.9%.

Use of combined cycle technology in gas-fired power stations (versus conventional coal-fired power plants) can reduce NO_x emissions by 90% per unit of energy produced.

Flue gas desulphurisation can remove 90–7% of sulphurous emissions.

Table 7.1 *Description of environmental and health impacts of energy production and use*

Energy source/ process	Major type of pollution	Health/ecological issues	Pollution control methods
1 Coal Mining and preparation.	Water pollution: acid mine drainage, slurry, toxic heavy metals (e.g., lead, mercury, zinc, cadmium, arsenic, nickel), waste pile runoff.	Contamination of surface/ground-water; siltation of streams and rivers. Zinc and nickel are known carcinogens; pneumoconiosis (i.e., a respiratory disease caused by inhalation of coal mine dusts).	Water effluents control: screens; dissolved air flotation; filtration; pH adjustment/ chemical precipitation; reverse osmosis; etc.
Combustion.	Air pollution: SO_x, NO_x, carbon oxides, fly ash and other particulates, hydrocarbons. Solid wastes: ash, sludge, toxic heavy metals (e.g., arsenic, cadmium, mercury, radionuclides), insoluble inorganic materials.	Acidic deposition; global warming; photochemical smog; adverse impacts on agriculture and forestry (e.g., foliage damage; impaired photosynthesis, possibility of crop losses); impaired visibility.	SO_x control: use of low-sulphur coal; coal beneficiation (sulphur reduction of 46%, ash reduction of 65%, and increase heating value by 20%); flue gas desulphurization – e.g., limestone scrubbing (removal efficiency of 90%), double alkali scrubbing (removal efficiency of 90–97%), magnesia scrubbing (no reliable efficiency data).

Increased lung cancer mortality; pulmonary/respiratory diseases (e.g., asthma, bronchitis, emphysema); cardiovascular diseases; headaches; eye irritation; mutagenic effects.

NO_x control: improvement in burner design (emission reduction of 40–70%); staged combustion (20–30%); selective non-catalytic reduction (40–70%); selective catalytic reduction (80–90%).

Contamination of surface/ground-waters; heavy metals adsorption affects soil processes (e.g., nutrient recycling, soil micro-organisms).

Particulate control: electrostatic precipitators (collection of up to 99.9% of fly ash); wet scrubbers – e.g, venturi scrubbers (nominal efficiency of 99%), moving-bed scrubbers (99%), fabric filters 99.5%).

Cardiovascular diseases; kidney damage; cancers; skin irritation.

Water/thermal pollution: chemical effluents (e.g., sludge, ash leachates – calcium, magnesium sulphate, chloride).

Changes in local aquatic environment (e.g. water temperature, salinity, dissolved oxygen) and impact on marine/freshwater life.

Waste (solid and liquid) disposal management: ponding/sedimentation basins for ash and sludge; landfills for dry wastes; deep-well injection for aqueous wastes; mine disposal; incineration.

2 Oil refining	Air pollution SO_x, CO, hydrocarbons (e.g.Benzo-(a)-pyrene).	Acidic deposition; offensive odors (due to hydrogen sulphide and mercaptans). Benzo-(a)-pyrene is a known carcinogen.	See coal combustion.

Table 7.1 (*cont.*)

Energy source/ process	Major type of pollution	Health/ecological issues	Pollution control methods
	Water pollution raw refinery wastewater contains toxic pollutants (e.g., benzene, toluene, arsenic, cyanide); hydrocarbons, dissolved solids, suspended solids.	Effect on marine or freshwater life if not treated.	Water effluents control: recirculating water for cooling; drainage system designs and use of segregated sewer systems; oil-water separators; dissolved air flotation; aerated lagoon; carbon adsorption; oxidation pond; stripping dissolved gases; electrodialysis; etc.
Tanker operations/ shipping.	Ocean pollution; sea ballasts and tanker washwater containing oil.	Impact on marine/wildlife resources.	Regulation to limit discharges only at a distance of 50 nautical miles from land (1954 International Convention for the prevention of Pollution of the Sea from Oil); "load on top" system; use of segregated ballast tanks.
Combustion.		See coal combustion.	
3 Natural Gas Exploration and production; distribution and storage.	Air pollution: hydrocarbons (e.g., methane), hydrogen sulphide, SO_x.	Pipeline impact of wildlife/aesthetic values; offensive odors. Workers' safety; spills and explosions.	See coal combustion.
Combustion.	Air pollution: primarily NO_x; carbon dioxide, methane.	Contributes to photochemical smog.	

4 Nuclear Uranium mining and processing; fuel conversion and enrichment; routine operation of nuclear power plants.	Radioactive pollution: radioactive wastes (e.g., uranium, thorium, radon gas); gaseous and liquid effluents, radioactive particles, mill tailings.	Risk of groundwater/land contamination of radioactive wastes; catastrophic accidents. Potential threat to workers' health (e.g., cancer, gene mutation).	Radioactive wastes management: heavy shielding and permanent isolation for high/medium-level wastes; shallow land burial in disposal sites for low-level, short-lived wastes.
5 Biomass Gathering of fuelwood; removal of crop residues/ animal dung for fuel.		Overcutting of trees contributes to deforestation, increased incidence of floods, stream sedimentation, decreased water yields from watersheds. Excessive removal of agricultural residues/animal dung affects soil fertility, and exposes soil to increased wind and water erosion.	
Biomass combustion.	Indoor air pollution: carbon monoxide, particulates, NO_x, hydrocarbons (e.g., benzo-(a)-pyrene), dioxins, furans.	Risk of CO poisoning if wood stoves are improperly installed; benzo-(a)-pyrene is a known carcinogen (dioxins and furans cause cancer in animals). Increased background ozone levels in rural areas due to hydrocarbon emissions.	Emission control: improved stove technology; flue gas scrubbers used in thermal power plants/or catalytic converters used in car exhaust systems (too expensive for small-scale, residential use); flue gas treatment (SO_2 and CO reduction of 97%).

Table 7.1 (*cont.*)

Energy source/ process	Major type of pollution	Health/ecological issues	Pollution control methods
6 Renewable energy Exploitation/ power development.	Air pollution; mainly CO_2; ammonia, H_2S. Liquid effluents from cooling towers.	Impacts on land (e.g., opening/ clearing of virgin areas and changes in natural habitats; increased land erosion/land subsidence). Insignificant health risks.	Wastewater disposal methods: direct release to surface water bodies; evaporation; surface spreading to shallow reservoirs; desalination with re-use; reinjection to reservoirs.
Solar energy (e.g., photovoltaic conversion).		Fabrication of photovoltaic cells requires the use of hazardous gases; handling/disposal problems; accidental leakage.	(Solar energy systems do not release air pollutants.)
Solar energy(e.g., thermal conversion).		Requires large areas of land; can affect earth's heat balance if produced on a large scale globally. Reflected light can cause blindness and serious burns; accidental release of heat.	
Wind energy.	Noise pollution.	TV/radio interference; disruption of wildlife. No health risks.	(No air pollutants, water contaminants, thermal pollution or solid wastes.)
Ocean energy (e.g., tidal dams).	Can alter the flow patterns of water and affect aquatic food chain; decreased dilution of solids due to reduced tidal exchanges; thermal releases.		

| Waste energy (e.g., waterwall incinerators, hog-fuel boilers, combined firing systems). | Air pollution: SOx, NOx, carbon oxides, chlorides, hydrocarbons, fly ash (with lead, tin, antimony), bottom ash, particulates. | See coal combustion. |
| Waste-energy (e.g., thermo-chemical or pyrolysis processes). | Air pollution: particulates, HCl, NOx, mercury.

Wastewater from pyrolysis systems can be high in BOD, COD, alcohols, phenols. | See coal combustion. |

Electrostatic precipitators can collect up to 99.9% of fly ash.

Fluidized bed combustion can reduce SO_2 emissions by 85–95%.

Technological improvements in coal combustion have emphasized the development of technologies that would reduce air pollutants to a level nearly as attractive as using natural gas. However, the costs of some of these technologies can restrict their implementation. Flue gas desulphurization, for instance, is a very expensive technology to adopt since its costs would amount typically to 10–15% of generation costs for coal (and also oil).

Nuclear

Generation of radioactive pollutants is the most serious environmental and health issue related to the nuclear energy cycles. From the mining and processing of uranium to the operation of nuclear power plants, significant amounts of radioactive and solid wastes are being produced. For example, it has been estimated that a 1,000MW(e) nuclear plant running at 80% of its capacity can generate 12,000 cubic feet of radioactive wastes per year, and 17,000 cubic feet of ashes and limestones.

As a matter of comparison, nuclear power plants are reportedly more environmentally benign than coal-fired plants in terms of routine air emissions (see table 7.2) and land use. Relatively little land is required for uranium mining and insignificant quantities of air pollutants are produced from nuclear fuel cycles. However, such advantages may still be dwarfed by the risk of catastrophic accidents and the fact that the storage and disposal of radioactive wastes can become extremely

Table 7.2 *Estimates of environmental impacts of energy production and use*

Energy sources	Air emissions	Water/thermal pollution.	Land impacts
1 Coal			
Mining and preparation.	Data from representative underground coal mine in eastern US: $CO = 6.3$ tons/million tons of coal/year $SO_2 = 0.59$ Hydrocarbons $= 0.48$. Data from representative surface coal mine in eastern US: Fugitive dust $= 1,870$ tons/million tons of coal/year $NO_x = 648$ $CO = 135$ $SO_2 = 47$ Hydrocarbons $= 42$ Particulates $= 33$	Solid wastes: e.g., more than 3 billion tons in eastern US in 1979. Land subsidence: e.g., 25% of the 8 million acres of undermined lands in eastern US in 1980 have subsided.	
Combustion.	$CO_2 = 0.21$ lb/1000 Btu. 1,000MW coal-fired plant at 80% capacity: $SO_2 = 45,000$ tons/yr $NO_x = 26,000$ $CO = 750$ Particulates $= 3,500$ $HC = 260$ (See nuclear energy for comparison.)	Solid wastes: ashes and limestone of 200,000 and 300,000 cubic feet/yr, respectively for a 1,000MW coal-fired plant at 80% capacity. (See nuclear energy for comparison.)	

Inorganic trace elements (e.g., arsenic): Mean concentration of 20.3 ppm from combustion of bituminous coal; 22.8 ppm from lignite; 7.67 ppm from anthracite. (See oil combustion for comparison.)

2 Oil Exploration and production.		Water effluents (e.g., drilling muds); a production platform at the height of extraction can generate as much as 400 tons of muds per year.
Off-shore operations and shipping.		Oil pollution in the seas totaled 3.2 million tonnes/year in the 1974–80 period. Industry related sources include:
		Coastal refineries and terminals (6% of total pollution) Tanker accidents = 12%; off-shore exploration and production = 2% tanker operations (e.g., ballasting) = 20%.
Combustion.	Inorganic trace elements (e.g., arsenic): typical levels of 0.26 ppm from combustion of crude oil; 0.36 ppm from residual #6; and 0.085 from distillate.	

Table 7.2 (*cont.*)

Energy sources	Air emissions	Water/thermal pollution	Land impacts
3 Nuclear energy (in the US at present, one ton of enriched uranium produces 180 million kwh of electricity)	Light water reactors (LWR) SO_2 = 1,500 tons/yr NO_x = 900 CO = 25 Particulates = 120 HC = 9. High-temperature gas-cooled reactors (HTGCR) SO_2 = 1,200 tons/yr NO_x = 700 CO = 20 Particulates = 95 HC = 7.	Thermal discharges: e.g., about 70 × 10^6GJ/GW(e)/year at 70% annual capacity. Effluents: radioactivity of 2,000–253,000 curies/yr for a 1,000MW(e) plant at 80% capacity.	Solid wastes: radioactive wastes; solid wastes: radioactive wastes, ashes and limestone of 12,000, 7,000 and 10,000 cubic feet/yr respectively, for a 1,000 MW(e) plant at 80% capacity. Land requirements (e.g., for ore mining, spent fuel storage, exclusion areas): over 400 hectares or about 1,000 acres for a 1,000 MW(e) nuclear plant with a 70% annual capacity.
4 Large-scale wood combustion	NO_x = 0.7 lb/Btu x 10^6 output SO_2 = 0 NC = 0.25 CO = 0.25 Particulates = 8–10 without control) = 0.1 (with control)	Solid wastes: e.g., Bottom ash = 1.39 lb/Btu × 10^6 input. Land requirements: Less than 0.001 acre/Btu × 10^9/yr.	
5 Biomass combustion	Corn: Particulates = 14 lb/ton CO = 108 Hydrocarbons = 16. Oats: Particulates = 21–24 lb/ton CO = 136 Hydrocarbons = 18–33.		

Wheat: Particulates
= 13–22 lb/ton
CO = 108–128
Hydrocarbons =
11–17.

Wet rice:
Particulates = 29
lb/ton
CO = 161
Hydrocarbons =
21.

Sugarcane:
Particulates = 7
lb/ton
CO = 71
Hydrocarbons =
10.

Sorghum:
Particulates = 18
lb/ton
CO = 77
Hydrocarbons = 9.

Forest residues:
Particulates = 17
lb/ton
CO = 140
Hydrocarbons =
24.

Wood in
residential
fireplaces:
Particulate = 20
lb/ton
CO = 120
Hydrocarbons = 5
NO_x = 1.

---

problematic. Although little hard information is available on the health effects of low-level radiation produced during the routine delivery of nuclear energy, there is a general contention that long-term exposure to radiation can cause cancer and gene mutation.

Since the 1950s, nuclear energy has been widely regarded as the main backstop technology to fossil fuels (e.g., coal, oil, and gas) in the event that they become scarce and too expensive to use. But the growth of discoveries of fossil fuel reserves, which has been impressive, indicates that proven reserves are remarkably higher than originally believed. Recent estimates of "ultimately recoverable reserves," for example, are about 650 times the current annual rate of extraction. Owing to the abundance of fossil fuels coupled with the environmental risks linked to nuclear power production, the future role of nuclear energy as a backstop technology is now less certain.

Oil

Air pollution problems resulting from the oil cycles are virtually the same as those associated with the coal cycles, differing only in the amount of pollutants emitted. Oil refining and combustion, for instance, are also important sources of such hazardous emissions like SO_x and NO_x, along with carbon monoxide and hydrocarbons. The composition of water pollutants is obviously quite different between oil and coal – e.g., slurry and acid mine drainage as major effluents from coal mining, brine and drilling mud from oil exploration or heavy metals, and wastewater discharges from refining oil. However, effluents from both sources of energy contain many similar toxic elements that can produce common ecological and health problems – e.g., acidic deposition, contamination of water bodies, carcinogens as by-products.

In oil refineries where water pollution is a major environmental problem, there are three general methods which can be used to reduce pollution levels: (a) in-plant control measures to minimize pollution at the source – e.g., recirculating water for cooling, (b) use of segregated sewer systems for different types of wastewater to avoid complications in treatment procedures, and (c) end-of-pipe treatment – e.g., oil-water separation, removal of dissolved organic material through biological oxidation, aeration and filtration, etc. While water effluents have reportedly been reduced considerably upon adoption of these abatement methods, there are no precise estimates available for the pollution reduction efficiencies associated with them. In addition, these methods have become an integral part of refinery operations in many countries, and it is difficult to assess their impact on costs of production as well as those of pollution.

Meanwhile, off-shore operations and shipping are other aspects of the oil cycles that are notably important with regard to the pollution of oceans. In 1985, the US National Academy of Science reported that oil pollution in the seas averaged about 2.9 million tons of oil per year during the period 1979-80. Of this, around 1.3 million tons were due to the oil industry; tanker operations (e.g., ballasting) and tanker accidents alone were responsible for 0.93 million ton.

In 1954, the International Convention for the Prevention of Pollution of the Sea by Oil was drafted. This convention allowed the discharge of sea ballast and tanker washwater only at a distance of fifty nautical miles from land. More recent efforts to control oil pollution include "load on top system" and use of segregated ballast tanks. "Load on top system" involves treating oily water aboard the ship and recovering oily wastes from emptied tanks during ballasting. To further reduce oil pollution at sea, particularly pollution caused by tanker accidents and spills, the United Nations International Maritime Organization drafted in 1990 an International Convention on Oil Pollution Preparedness, Response and Cooperation. This would entail the creation of national centers for coping with oil pollution, formulation of contingency plans for tanker crews, standardization of spillage combat equipment, and pooling of R&D data on tackling oil spills.

Natural gas
Natural gas production and consumption are fairly benign when compared to the foregoing energy sources, although there are also relatively significant ecological and health issues linked to the natural gas cycles. These may include certain adverse impacts on wildlife and natural habitats in the course of gas exploration or pipeline construction, NO_x emissions during combustion, and occupational hazards.

Conventional hydroelectric power
Hydroelectric dams and reservoirs are used to capture surface energy in order to exploit it in a manageable way over a period of time, and to meet multiple sector uses including drinking, irrigation, electricity generation, transport, flood control, fishing, and so forth (Goodland, 1990). The benefits of dam construction are self-evident. However, they have environmental impacts too. The building of dams may severely affect the environmental equilibrium in the project region and even beyond. Depending on the shape of the landscape, and the height of the dam, large areas of land may become flooded. This will have impacts on human settlements, wildlife habitats, and agricultural lands. From an aesthetic-environmental viewpoint, the loss depends on the uniqueness of the flooded land and on the value placed on it by society (OECD, 1985a). With many dams built in pristine locations, cultural heritage issues are raised since ancient, indigenous populations may be forced to abandon traditional land.

Another basic environmental question to be asked is what irreversible changes might occur in eradicating certain plant or animal species (Maler and Wyzga, 1976). The answer to this question often raises biodiversity related concerns of global scope, thereby superseding the local or national interest. Some of the involved species may contain genetic features which could be of medicinal or agricultural importance for future generations. Comprehensive overviews and case studies of the environmental effects and economic consequences of reservoirs and dams, in World Bank projects, are presented by Dixon *et al.* (1989) and Le Moigne *et al.* (1990). In addition to the above mentioned impacts, these references encompass a broad spectrum of environmental issues dealing with diverse topics such as the preservation of religious and archaeological sites, the inundation of potentially valuable mineral resources, and the risk of induced seismicity and energy-related human diseases. These are all environmental issues raised by the construction of dams which must be considered and reconciled during the INEP process.

Dams, once built, are also the focus of a number of other externality issues. Because of increasing turbidity of runoff water, many reservoirs have lifetimes which are considerably shortened by the accumulation of silt originating from soil erosion in deforested upstream energy catchment areas. The deforestation involved may occur as a direct result of planning decisions made by another government sector, for instance forestry, power, or land management. The conflicts of interest, both in economic and in social terms, must be reconciled as part of an integrated planning process.

Other reservoir-related modifications also may have positive and negative effects. In the case of flood control canals or storm sewers, the engineering project can actually become a synergistic component in environmental resource management or else aggravate the problems of flooding. Maintenance works in flood canals are chronically underfunded and unglamorous. The results of neglect are accumulation of silt and uncontrolled vegetation in the channel beds, thereby increasing the risk of floods. The negative impacts of the latter on the environment are readily understood. Well maintained canals, however, with provision for an artificial floodplain may, on the other hand, contribute by enhancing the environmental value of a floodplain. For example, Williams (1990) argues that the terrace provides space for a walking trail. Planting riparian trees on the banks shades out the channel, which prevents vegetation encroachment, minimizes maintenance, improves energy quality, and creates a continuous corridor for wildlife. Riparian vegetation can also slow bank erosion.

New and renewable sources of energy (NRSE)
Of the wide range of alternative or new and renewable energy sources (see table 7.1), biomass is so far the most important in terms of its widespread uses. Biomass – e.g., fuelwood, crop residues, and animal dung – is an indispensable energy source for many developing countries and serves as an alternative energy source for developed ones. Biomass provides 12–14% of the world's total energy consumption, and accounts for one-third of total energy demand in developing countries. Other renewable energy sources include geothermal, solar, wind, ocean, and waste energy. For most of these energy sources the production technologies are still subject to much research for improvement or development.

As is the case with the other sources of energy discussed earlier, much information concerning the potential impacts on human health and the environment of production and use of renewable energy is oftentimes presented in the form of scientific propositions. However, such information generally is not in dispute. Gathering of fuelwood and removal of crop residues or animal manures in the course of using biomass as fuel have, for instance, been argued to contribute to serious deforestation in the long run, reduce soil fertility, and expose soil to increased wind and water erosion. Biomass combustion has the potential to create indoor air pollution if wood stoves are not properly installed. It has been reported that emissions of benzo-(a)-pyrene, a known carcinogen, can be fifty times greater from wood combustion than from oil combustion.

Air and/or thermal pollution are the major potential environmental problems that are related to the production and consumption of geothermal, ocean, and waste energy. Particularly, it is the combustion of waste energy that can generate gaseous emissions and solid wastes that are comparable to those produced during coal combustion, and therefore is likely to raise the same ecological and health concerns as those of coal if operations are large scale. Meanwhile, of the renewable energy sources, wind energy conversion appears to be the most environmentally benign. It does not entail the emission of air pollutants, nor the generation of water contaminants and solid wastes. Noise pollution and the disruption of wildlife are the most serious potential ecological impacts of wind energy. Requirements for large areas of land and the possibility of affecting the Earth's heat balance if produced on a large scale worldwide are the most important ecological issues linked to the production and use of solar energy. On the whole, renewable energy clearly offers a cleaner and healthier alternative than conventional fuels, like coal and oil, and an ecologically safer option than nuclear energy.

Substitution of renewables for fossil fuels on a reasonable scale is practically possible in the future. Specifically on account of the global warming problem, its significance is that NRSE can reduce and stabilize the emissions of CO_2 from energy consumption over the long run. Biomass and solar energy are the backstop technologies that offer great potentials in permitting such fuel substitution. In developing countries, total insolation amounts to about 10,000 billion tonnes of oil equivalent energy per year (120,000 Twh), or roughly 6,500 times their annual consumption of commercial energy. Technical options for meeting commercial energy demands using solar energy include photovoltaic, thermal, and photo-electrochemical schemes. Modern photovoltaic schemes can now convert 7–20% of insolation into electrical energy depending on cell design and quality of materials used, while efficiencies for future advanced systems are projected to reach more than 30%. Similarly, solar-thermal schemes have already achieved conversion efficiencies of over 20% and with projected efficiencies of 30%.

Solar energy can be produced on a large scale with fairly small claims on land resources. That is, the land requirement to meet commercial energy demands via solar resources is small relative to the total amount of land that is available. At conversion efficiencies of 15% less than 0.1% of land area would be required theoretically to meet commercial energy needs in developing countries from solar resources. Land intensities are also low especially when compared with hydroelectricity. For example, a 100 meter head hydro scheme with favorable topography can yield 10–30 GWh/sq.km. of reservoir area when full. A solar scheme in high insolation areas with a 15% conversion and a 50% allowance for spacing can produce 150 GWh/sq.km. This is approximately five to fifteen times more than that of the hydro scheme.

The main issue concerning solar energy production is cost. For instance, costs of photovoltaic units are currently about $6,000/kwp for grid-tied systems. This represents an important economic constraint to large-scale commercial production of solar energy. However, projections done by the US Department of Energy reported costs of $2,100/kwp in year 2000, $1,500/kwp in 2010, and $1,000/kwp in the long term. In high insolation areas where conversion efficiencies are better, this would mean generation costs of 4–6 cents/kwh and thus indicate that solar schemes can be competitive with fossil fuels in the future.

A major attraction of biomass as a backstop technology is that it can serve a diverse range of energy needs (e.g., electricity generation, demands for synthetic fuels, ethanol, and methanol). Biomass therefore can play an important role in meeting long-term demands for commercial energy, should there be regulations to restrict the use of fossil fuels. But energy production from biomass is, by and large, still uneconomic. Using biomass on a large scale to substitute for oil fuels, for instance, can increase the costs of energy considerably. Ethanol programs in Brazil and the United States presently incur costs in the order of $75–100/bbl of oil equivalent energy. Advanced engineering studies show possible cost reductions to $60/bbl or less in the long run; however, this still may amount to $20–40/bbl more than the long-term ex-refinery costs of oil fuels.

For electricity generation, the costs of biomass fuels relative to fossil fuels are more favorable. In the United States, which has over 9,000 MW of biomass-fired power stations, engineering studies show that new high efficiency generation technologies using gasified biomass in combined-cycle power plants can result in generation costs of 4–6 cents/kwh. This suggests that such schemes can be competitive with fossil fuels, for which generation costs of 5 cents/kwh is typical among OECD countries.

Biomass energy production can be very land intensive – e.g., typical energy yield is 0.2–0.3% of incident sunlight (less than one-fiftieth of the conversion efficiency of solar schemes). Major expansions of biomass programs can therefore place considerable pressures on land resources and land prices. Cost factor and land requirements nonetheless illustrate that there are economic incentives to complement biomass fuels with solar energy. A gradual introduction of these backstop technologies, together with environmental taxation and standards, should represent an ideal means for dealing with the environmental problems caused by energy production and use.

Transnational and global issues

It is important to note here that environmental externalities are not limited to national boundaries, individual energy sources, or supply systems. Just as the activities of different sectors within a national economy have impacts that affect the quantity, quality, and price of energy supplied by authorities, the activities of different nations create important transnational and worldwide effects, the most important of which are acid rain and the potential for global warming.

Acid rain is a well-known phenomenon that the industrialized countries have grappled with collectively for some years. In North America, acid rain has long been a contentious issue between the governments of the United States and Canada, and progress in the United States in reducing SO_x and NO_x emissions in the mid-western states, the principal source of acid rain emissions that have had extensive impacts on the north-eastern United States and on eastern Canada, has been slow. In Europe, acid rain in Scandinavia has been associated with emissions in the UK, where tall stacks were long used as a way to avoid local impacts. Acid rain is now also emerging as a serious transnational problem in a few developing countries, most notably in Asia, where large coal users like China and India are likely to cause significant environmental externalities in the region.

Global externalities tend to be indirect and have a more collective origin. The prime example affecting the energy sector is the case of long-term global warming. Due to the accumulation of carbon dioxide, methane, nitrous oxide, chlorofluorocarbons, and other greenhouse gases in the atmosphere, the average temperature of the earth's climate is likely to increase by 1.5–4.5 degrees centigrade over the next century, with proportionally larger increases in the higher latitudes (IPCC, 1990). This phenomenon is expected to have a direct and substantial impact on the global energy budget. Climate scientists project that the major hydrological cycle (cloud formation, precipitation, runoff, evaporation) will accelerate. Because of the complexity involved, there is considerable uncertainty in currently available global climate models (see, e.g., Mintzer, 1987). Nevertheless, one estimate suggests that both precipitation and evaporation are expected to increase globally by 7–15% if the heat-trapping effect doubles over preindustrial levels (Postel, 1989). However, the distribution of these increases will not necessarily be identical, resulting in areas with markedly different hydrological regimes, and uncertain consequences for agriculture. The increase in temperatures, evapotranspiration, and CO_2 levels will also affect vegetation growth differently around the world (Falkenmark *et al.*, 1987). Another effect that is feared is a rise in the mean sea level and flooding of low lying lands, as well as an increase in storms and other catastrophic weather events.

Developing countries and mitigation efforts

Mitigating transnational and global externalities requires collective actions. Developed countries have made a number of important strides forward in domestic environmental management, some of which, such as controls on pollution emissions, will have transnational impacts. Whilst costly in the short run, in the long term these are seen to be generally economically beneficial. On a local scale, developing countries also have considerable scope for environment-improving activities that are economically attractive for them, e.g., energy conservation and ameliorating the domestic environmental consequences of energy use. Many of these actions have significant positive transnational and global environmental benefits.

However, on a larger scale, developing countries are less able to afford actions to protect the global commons. This is also an equity issue, since much of the responsibility for cumulative damage to the global environment lies firmly with the developed countries. They should take an active role in partnering the developing countries in environmental management issues. A key question here is the extent to which developing countries contribute to and are affected by global environmental problems. This is not a clear-cut issue since some countries may feel themselves highly vulnerable yet virtually non-contributory to global climate changes (such as Bangladesh and The Maldives who are very vulnerable to sea level rises, yet whose present state of industrialization and energy utilization is such that their contribution to greenhouse gases is very low), whilst others (such as China and India) clearly do account for substantial shares of global emissions but at the same time experience varying degrees of impact.

The foregoing discussion sets the context within which the developing countries are capable of participating in environmental mitigation efforts. It is quite obvious that developing countries do not have the ability to contribute financially to global environmental cleanup efforts where the measurable benefits to the national economy are too low to trigger investment. Coincidentally, many developing-country projects which do have positive measurable benefits at the more local level are being bypassed on account of capital constraints. However, the picture is not all bleak. The principle of assistance to developing countries to make local and global environmental mitigation efforts, in terms of technology transfer, financial support, and other means, is already well established. Bi-lateral donors are already emphasizing environment-oriented development programs designed to achieve greater sustainability of assisted projects. For instance, in May 1987, the Danish Parliament passed a resolution to strengthen efforts on natural resources rehabilitation and conservation for official Danish development cooperation. The Netherlands has adopted similar objectives. Some of the current multi-lateral initiatives to aid developing-country environmental management, such as the proposed Global Environmental Fund and Ozone Fund, are briefly outlined in box 7.2 along with their significance for developing countries. Developing countries clearly should take advantage of this available funding and other kinds of technical support offered by developed nations to tackle environmental management issues of both national and international significance.

Box 7.2   *Global environmental initiatives*

The Montreal Protocol, which was adopted in 1987 as a framework within which reduction in the consumption and production of certain types of chlorofluorocarbons (CFCs) is to be achieved, recognized the need for global cooperation and assistance to the developing countries. Subsequent Ministerial Conferences on various aspects of global environmental issues have reinforced the idea of protecting the global commons.

Recently, following discussions among world bodies and governments to define effective criteria and mechanisms for both generating and disbursing funds, a pilot global environmental fund facility (GEF) was set up. A larger, more permanent framework is being pursued, once the early results of the GEF can be analyzed in the context of the 1992 UN Conference on Environment and Development in Brazil. More generally, global financing issues might be analyzed and resolved through a trade-off involving several criteria: affordability/additionality, fairness/equity, and economic efficiency (Munasinghe, 1990).

First, since developing countries cannot afford to finance even their present energy supply development, to address global environmental concerns they will need financial assistance on concessionary terms that is additional to existing conventional aid. Second, as noted in the Brundtland Commission report (World Commission on Environment and Development, 1987) past growth in the industrialized countries has exhausted a disproportionately high share of global resources, suggesting that the developed countries owe an "environmental debt" to the larger global community. This approach could help to determine how the remaining finite global resources may be shared more fairly and used sustainably. Finally, the economic efficiency criterion indicates that the "polluter pays" principle may be applied to generate revenues, to the extent which global environmental costs of human activity can be quantified. For example, if total emission limits are established (e.g., for CO_2), then trading in emission permits among nations and other market mechanisms could be harnessed to increase efficiency.

The GEF is a core multilateral fund of about $1.5 billion, set up as a pilot over the next three years. This fund would finance investment, technical assistance and institutional development activities in four areas: global climate change, ozone depletion, protection of biodiversity, and energy resource degradation. A more narrowly focussed Ozone Fund of about $160-240 million has been created also to help implement measures to reduce CFC emissions under the Montreal Protocol. Both funds will be managed under a collaborative arrangement between the UNDP, UNEP, and the World Bank. In particular, they have begun to fund those investment activities that would provide cost-effective benefits to the global environment, but would, however, not be undertaken by individual countries without concessions. Thus, these funds have been specifically designed to fill the void which is created by the lack of individual national incentives for those activities which would, nonetheless, benefit us all.

To summarize, international pressures to implement environmental mitigatory measures place a severe burden on developing countries. The crucial dilemma this poses to developing countries is how to reconcile development goals and the elimination of poverty – which will require increased use of energy and raw materials – with responsible stewardship of the environment, and without overburdening economies that are already weak. It can be argued that, in view of the severe financial constraints that developing countries already face, the response of these countries in relation to environmental preservation cannot extend beyond the realm of measures that are consistent with near-term economic development goals. More specifically, the environmental policy response of developing countries in the coming decade will be limited to conventional technologies in energy efficiency improvement, conservation, and resource development.

The developed countries are ready to substitute environmental preservation for further economic expansion and should, therefore, be ready to cross the threshold, providing the financial resources that the developing countries need today and developing the technological innovations and knowledge-base to be used in the twenty-first century by all nations. The Global Environmental Fund and Ozone Fund, presently being established, will facilitate the participation of developing countries in addressing issues at the global level.

Incorporating environmental impacts into economic decision-making

Three main forms of environmental assessment (EA) are applicable to developing country work:

Environmental impact assessment (EIA): usually a specific attempt to identify the environmental costs and benefits of a particular project;

Regional environmental assessments: a more widespread approach to assessing the range of problems and influences of one or more projects within a determined region (e.g., a river basin);

Multi-objective sectoral assessment: a study of the trade-offs among a number of project alternatives within the wider context of the energy and related sectors, sometimes involving analysis of macro-economic or economy-wide linkages.

An exhaustive review of the theory and practice of any single method goes beyond the scope of this book: in any event all are evolving methodologies that are gradually being reformulated and refined by agencies as the various techniques of appraisal, implementation, and review are applied under actual project conditions. Instead, the World Bank's own broad-based, flexible approach to EA is described and the main points, applicable for use by developing country planners and decision-makers under most general circumstances, are outlined. Since this approach encompasses project-specific, regional and sectoral EAs, it provides a useful framework for introducing some of the important multi-level concepts to be adopted by planners. The information is particularly relevant to those planners who might otherwise discount EA as a luxury, rather than as a fundamental tool of project planning and implementation.

Background

In 1989 the World Bank introduced formal environmental reviews (ERs) as a mandatory part of its project appraisal process, the culmination of a gradual shift during the previous decades towards more comprehensive environmental analysis in the Bank's operations. The World Bank has made a move to "integrate environmental considerations into its work...The Bank's goal is to blur the lines between environmental activities and the rest of the Bank's work – to make them one" (World Bank, 1989a). Depending on the outcome of the ER (also known as a screening), an environmental assessment can be requested from the borrower as a mandatory requirement for the acceptance of a project proposal and the disbursement of funds.

The basic concept behind EA is that cost-effective prevention and mitigation of environmental impacts is best achieved during the project design phase, whereas if a consideration of the environment is left to the implementation phase, changes in the project become increasingly difficult and costly. EAs usually require as much time as technical feasibility studies, varying between six and eighteen months, and usually take up less than 1% of the total capital costs of a project. ERs and EAs should address three main points: (1) the identification of all important environmental issues early in the project cycle, (2) the design of environmental improvements into any basic project objectives, and (3) the avoidance, mitigation, or compensation for any adverse impacts resulting from a project.

EAs may be undertaken on a project-specific basis, as a regional planning tool, or as a sectoral review. Implementation of an EA in terms of prevention, mitigation, and compensation for project impacts usually costs between 0% and 10% of a total project budget, averaging at around 5%. This does not include possible savings resulting from the various measures.

Procedures

The World Bank project EA is normally carried out after a period of Environmental Review (ER) known as screening. The ER decides which of four categories the project falls into based on the extent to which projects are expected to have environmental impacts:

1 EA required – project may have diverse and significant environmental impacts;

2 Limited EA required – project may have specific environmental impacts;

3 EA is unnecessary – project with few or minor environmental impacts expected;

4 EA is unnecessary – environmental project designed to achieve specific environmental impacts.

EAs are the responsibility of the borrower, who must arrange for funds and appoint a multi-disciplinary team of consultants (preferably with a significant national component of specialists). The Bank can provide financial assistance for EAs through a Project Preparation Facility advance, or from the Technical Assistance Grant Program for the Environment. The Bank expects the borrower to take the views of affected groups and local NGOs fully into account in project design and implementation and in particular in the preparation of EAs. The thrust of the EA, carried out by appointees of the borrower, focusses on issues critical to deciding whether or not to proceed with a given project, in a given format and how to implement it efficiently.

In the context of Bank Operations, EA is undertaken in tandem with prefeasibility and feasibility studies, incorporated into the loan agreement negotiations with borrowers, and assessed for compliance during supervision of implementation. Evaluation of impacts and effectiveness of mitigatory methods are incorporated in the project completion report.

Prior to implementation, a Bank appraisal mission will review the EA with the borrower, resolve any remaining environmental questions, assess the capacity of country institutions to implement recommendations, and discuss environmental conditionalities to the loan agreements. The borrower is then obliged to implement measures to mitigate anticipated environmental impacts, to monitor programs, to correct unanticipated impacts, and to comply with any environmental conditionalities.

The main components of an EA include:

a baseline data synthesis;

an assessment of potential environmental impacts $(+/-)$;

a systematic analysis of alternative options;

formulation of a prevention, mitigation, and compensatory action plan;

review of environmental management and training requirements;

formulation of a monitoring plan during and after project implementation;

a summary of interagency coordination aspects and needs;

a series of consultations with affected communities and local NGOs.

Table 7.3 *Checklist of environmental factors for assessment*

The operational directives issued by the Bank request that the appointee implementing the EA consider the following broad checklist of factors when assessing the project, region, or sector environmental impacts and sensitivities:

Agrochemicals – impact on surface and ground energy by these;

Biological diversity – conservation of endangered species, critical habitats, protected areas;

Coastal and marine resources – planning and management of these; impact of activities on these;

Cultural properties – preservation of archaeological and historic sites;

Dams and reservoirs – environmental issues in planning, implementation, and operation of these;

Energysheds – protection and management of these;

Hazardous and toxic materials – safe management, use, transport, storage, and disposal of these; impact on surface and ground energy by these;

Induced development and other socio-cultural aspects – impacts of these (i.e., the boomtown effects of secondary growth of settlements and infrastructure);

Industrial hazards – prevention and management of these;

International energyways – effects of activities on quality or quantity of energy flows in these;

International treaties and agreements on the environment and natural resources – review of status and application of these;

Involuntary resettlement – issues related to this;

Land settlement – physical, biological, socio-economic, and cultural impacts of these agreements;

Natural hazards – effects on project from these;

Occupational health and safety – dangers to former and promotion of latter;

Tribal peoples – rights to land and to energy of these;

Tropical forests – issues relating to use and preservation of these;

Wetlands – conservation and management of these.

Wildlands – protection of these from adverse impacts.

Regional EAs should be used as planning tools to help devise implementation strategies which account for the combined impact of existing projects and to help prepare projects sensitive to the cumulative impacts, synergisms, iterations, and competition for natural and socio-cultural resources. Regional EAs usually comprise the following main components:

definition of the regional area in question;

the selection of sustainable development patterns from available alternatives;

the identification of cumulative impacts of different activities;

the identification of environmental interactions or conflicting demands on resources in terms of costs and benefits;

the formulation of criteria for environmentally sustainable development;

the identification of regional monitoring and data needs;

an examination of policy alternatives for achieving sustainable development.

Clearly, the regional EA fits in comfortably with the INEP approach to energy sector development (see chapter 2), and is a useful, if not prerequisite database for more effective planning.

Sector EAs are also very useful to the INEP process since their purpose is to examine the impacts of multiple projects planned in the same sector, to view alternative investment or technology strategies (e.g., the decision to adopt centralized, or decentralized waste/energy treatment), and to evaluate the effects of sector policy changes (e.g., the decision to price energy at its true cost rather than at a subsidized rate).

Sector EAs can help define guidelines and criteria for the successful design and implementation of projects in the sector and so preclude the need for multiple project-specific EAs. They help identify the major environmental issues in the sector and help develop a database, enabling project-specific EAs to proceed more quickly. Sector EAs also help evaluate the capabilities of agencies to carry our ERs and EAs and hence determine the need for institutional strengthening and support.

Limitations and implementation difficulties

One of the main limitations for effective EA is the relatively minor experience of environmental management in developing countries. Also lacking is an integrated, intersectoral framework for coordinated action in the fields of monitoring and managing various interactive activities. The World Bank consequently views interagency coordination (especially government agencies and NGOs) as crucial to effective EA because environmental issues, in their complexity and variety, are often intersectoral, regional, and even international in nature. Training and institutional support is required in environment-related issues and is usually a prime component of any World Bank initiated project ER and EA.

The effectiveness and acceptability of an environmental management program depends on the environmental policies and regulatory structure in the project country. This determines how well the recommendations of the EA can be put into effect and hence the preventive, mitigatory, and compensatory actions that can be taken. Major difficulties facing many developing countries are the weak environmental inspection, monitoring and enforcement functions.

According to Bowers (1990), EAs should attempt to bring out the distributional implications of public investment decisions. This has been lacking in past efforts, although it is common that the gainers are frequently fewer and more wealthy than the losers. A more rigorous approach to benefit-cost analysis which entails the identification of all impacts of a project on social welfare, including impacts on the environment, might be useful. Where items can be meaningfully valued, they should be so and the costs and benefits for different segments of society identified. Items for which monetary values cannot be assigned should be assessed in whatever units are appropriate to them and an informed judgment made about their significance (for instance using some kind of ranking matrix for alternative project or policy options).

Economic valuation of environmental impacts[2]

In chapter 6 we introduced the rudiments of benefit-cost analysis as providing a rational basis for the identifcation of projects and programmes. In an ideal case, the environmental consequences would be expressed in monetary terms, and the benefit-cost analysis modified accordingly. Several different approaches might apply to the valuation of environmental assets, including:

   Use value: which is determined by its contribution to current production or consumption;

   Option value: which is determined by the future value (of an unutilized asset) when the option to use it will be exercised;

   Existence value: which arises from the satisfaction of merely knowing that the asset exists, although the valuer has no intention of using it (for example, the existance of a famous spring that one has no intention of ever visiting);

   Bequest value: which is determined by the satisfaction of preserving an asset as a legacy for future generations.

Use and option values are rather direct, whereas existence and bequest values tend to be linked to more altruistic motives. Nevertheless, whatever the conceptual basis of economic value, there are several practical techniques that permit us to estimate a monetary value for environmental assets and impacts.

Directly market-based techniques
When a change in the environment affects actual production or productive capability, the value of the change in net output may be used to estimate the value of the environmental change. For example, the pollu-

---

[2] For a complete discussion, see, e.g., Munasinghe (1992).

tion of a lake by toxic industrial discharges may be valued in terms of the reduced value of fish catches. Similarly, deteriorating environmental quality may affect human health. Ideally, the monetary value should be determined by the willingness-to-pay of individuals to preserve the environment. In practice, second-best techniques are used: for example, in the case of health impacts on humans, one might use foregone earnings through premature death or sickness, or medical expenditures to recover health. Although this "value-of-health" approach is often questioned on ethical grounds, the underlying assumption of the finite worth of human life is used nevertheless in social and health care decisions. For example, in examining the cost-benefit of retrofitting existing nuclear plants with enhanced safety equipment, the United States Nuclear Regulatory Commission uses a figure of $1,000 per avoided person-rem as an indication of the benefits of retrofitting.

Surrogate market techniques

A surrogate (or indirect) market for environmental assets may be found where implicit consumer valuation of environmental effects determines the structure of prices of other goods and services. There are three variants of this approach:

Hedonic prices – property value approach (represents a subset of the more general land value approach): For instance, the effects of air pollution have been analyzed by comparing prices of houses in affected areas with the usually higher prices of houses of equal size and similar neighborhood characteristics in relatively unaffected areas of the same metropolis. The approach is based on the assumption of a competitive real estate market, and requirements of information and statistical analysis are significant; therefore, applicability to developing countries may be limited.

Hedonic wages – wage-differential approach: This is based on the assumption that higher wages are necessary to attract workers to locate and work in polluted areas, for instance.

Travel cost approach: The area surrounding a site is divided into concentric zones of increasing distance from the site. A site-user survey of this area reveals a demand curve and costs of travel to reach the site for users starting from the different zones. Thus the associated consumer surplus can be determined. This approach has been used also to value "travel time" in projects dealing with energy and fuelwood collection. However, the method provides valuation of only some aspects of direct user benefits of environmental sites, and is limited in this sense.

Shadow-project techniques
If a project leads to the destruction of a habitat or environmental asset then it can be valued at the cost of providing an offsetting or alternative environmental asset elsewhere that compensates for these losses by gains. For instance it would be possible to replant trees at another site, to compensate for a forest area flooded by a dam. If such a shadow (offsetting) project is subsequently actually carried out, no net environmental damage will occur, and valuation of the cost of creating the alternative is appropriate. Care must be exercised to determine reasonable offsetting alternatives.

Contingent valuation techniques
In the absence of preferences as revealed in markets the most commonly used approach is contingent valuation (or bidding game). People are asked what they would be willing to pay for a benefit (e.g., the prevention of the destruction of an environmental asset), and/or what they would be willing to accept by way of compensation to tolerate environmental damage. Willingness-to-pay is constrained by the income level of the respondent, whereas willingness-to-accept is not. Therefore the latter estimates tend to be higher than the former.

Because this method can capture current use value as well as bequest, option, and existence value, and because results may be generalized to the entire population, estimates tend to be rather large and may have significant impact on the cost-benefit accounts (in contrast to the other methods explained above).

An analytical framework for energy-environment interactions

The above-mentioned factors can be considered within an environmental-economic framework which considers the principal points concerning energy use, environmental impacts, and economic efficiency. In many countries today, inappropriate policies have encouraged wasteful and unproductive uses of energy. In such cases, better energy management could lead to improvements in:

Economic efficiency (higher value of net output produced);
Energy use efficiency (higher value of net output per unit of energy used);
Energy conservation (reduced absolute amount of energy used);
Environmental protection (reduced energy related environmental costs).

However, these four objectives are not always mutually consistent. For example, in some developing countries where the existing levels of per capita energy consumption are very low and certain types of energy use are uneconomically constrained, it may become necessary to promote more energy consumption in order to raise net output (thereby increasing economic efficiency). There are also instances where it may be possible to increase energy use efficiency while decreasing energy conservation.

Despite the above complications, the basic approach of maximizing economic efficiency remains valid. In other words, the economic efficiency criterion which helps us maximize the present value of net output from all available scarce resources in the economy should effectively subsume purely energy oriented objectives such as energy use efficiency and energy conservation. Furthermore, the costs arising from energy-related adverse environmental impacts may be included (to the extent possible) in the energy supply economic analytical framework to determine how much energy use and net output society would be willing to forego in order to abate or mitigate environmental damage. It must be remembered that the existence of the many other national policy objectives described in chapter 2, including social goals that are particularly relevant in the case of low-income populations, will complicate the decision-making process even further.

The foregoing discussion may be reinforced by the use of a simplified static analysis of the trade-off between energy use, environmental costs, and net output of an economic activity.

Energy efficiency
In figure 7.2 let Y represent the usual measurement of the net output of productive economic activity in a country, as a function of some resource input (say energy) and considering only the conventional internalized costs, i.e., not accounting for environmental impacts. Due to policy distortions (e.g., subsidized prices), the point of operation in many developing countries appears to be at A, where the resource is being used wastefully. Therefore, without invoking any environmental considerations, but merely by increasing economic and resource use efficiency (i.e., energy efficiency), output as usually measured could be maximized by moving from A to B. A typical example might be improving energy end-use efficiency or reducing power supply system losses (as explained in detail in chapter 8).

Quantifiable national environmental costs
Now consider the curve EC_{NQ} which represents economically quantifiable national environmental costs associated with energy use. Examples might be air pollution induced health effects (including costs of avoid-

ance or protection measures like installing desulphurization equipment or electrostatic precipitators at a coal power plant), or the costs of resettlement at a dam site. The corresponding corrected net output curve is:

$$YE_{NQ} = Y - EC_{NQ}$$

This has a maximum at C that lies to the left of B, implying lower use of (more costly) energy.

Non-quantifiable national environmental costs
Next, consider the "real" national output YE_{NT}, which is net of total environmental costs, whether quantifiable or not. The additional costs to be considered include the unquantified yet very real human health and other unmonetarized environmental costs. These total (quantifiable and non-quantifiable) costs are depicted as EC_{NT}, and once again:

$$YE_{NT} = Y - EC_{NT}$$

As shown, the real maximum of net output lies at D, to the left of C.

Transnational environmental costs
Finally, E_G represents the globally adjusted costs, where the transnational environmental costs (to other countries) of energy use within the given country, have been added to EC_{NT}. In this case:

$$YE_G = Y - EC_G$$

This is the correspondingly corrected net output which implies an even lower level of optimal energy use. For example, consider the costs imposed on other countries (such as the transborder impacts of a major dam or coal-fired power plant). If it is decided to reduce energy use within this country further, in order to achieve the internationally adjusted optimum at E, then a purely national analysis will show this up as a drop in net output, i.e., from D to E. As other countries benefit, this drop in net output may justify compensation in the form of a transfer of resources from the beneficiary countries. More generally, the transnational costs imposed by other countries on the nation in question will be a function of regional or global resource use rather than the national resource use shown on the horizontal axis.

Finally, the additional curve YT shows net output for a technologically advanced future society that has achieved a much lower energy intensity of production.

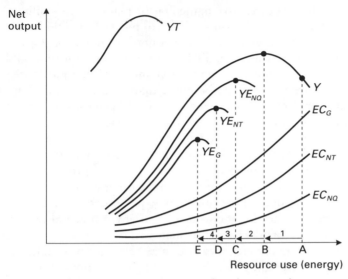

Figure 7.2   Trade-off between energy use, environmental costs, and economic output

Policy issues for developing countries

The foregoing analysis illustrates the crucial dilemma for developing countries. In figure 7.2, all nations (including the poorest) would readily adopt measures that will lead to the first shift (from A to B) which simultaneously and unambiguously provides both economic efficiency and environmental gains. Most developing countries are indicating increasing willingness to undertake the second shift (from B to C). However, implementing the third shift will definitely involve crossing a "pain threshold" for many third world nations, as other pressing socio-economic needs compete against the costs of mitigating unquantifiable adverse environmental impacts of energy use.

We note that real economic output increases with each of these three shifts, as shown by the movement upward along the curve YE_{NT} from C to D. However, these shifts are often mistakenly perceived as being upward only from A to B (energy use efficiency improvements), followed by downward movements from B through C to D. It is therefore important to correct any misconceptions that environmental protection results in reduced net output. This can be achieved through institutional development, applied research, strengthening of planning capabilities, etc. However, it is clear that the fourth shift (from D to E) would hardly appeal to resource constrained developing countries unless concessionary external financing was made available, since this movement would imply optimization of a global value function and costs that most often exceed in-country benefits. It must be noted that, in the foregoing, we have neglected considerations involving reciprocal benefits to the given country due to energy use reductions in other countries.

In other words, the developing countries can be expected to cooperate in transnational and global environmental programs only to the extent that such cooperation is consistent with their national growth objectives. The role of the developed countries, on the other hand, is to incur the risks inherent in developing innovative technological measures which are the prerequisites for the next level in environmental protection and the mitigation of adverse consequences. These risks include the possibility that the more extreme measures may turn out to be unnecessary or inapplicable after all, given the prevailing uncertainty about the future impact of current environmental developments.

We may briefly further conclude that, while the energy required for economic development will continue to grow in the developing countries, in the short to medium run there is generally considerable scope for most of them to practice better energy management, thereby increasing net output, using their energy resources more efficiently, and increasing the global availability of energy. In the medium to long run, it should be possible for the developing countries to adopt the newer and more advanced (energy efficient) technologies that are now emerging in the industrialized world. Developing countries must mobilize a greater fraction of their accessible energy supply to match the rising needs of a growing population, and the demands of newly served rural populations. This can be significantly offset by the reduction in energy losses. Consequent to a growth in population and energy use is a corresponding increase in the potential for pollution and or occurrence of other environmental externalities discussed earlier.

PART III

Subsectoral analysis

CHAPTER 8

The electricity subsector

Electricity is the first subsector to be discussed in some detail in this book. While not to suggest that other subsectors such as coal, oil, and gas are not important, there are three reasons for electricity to merit special treatment. The first is the technical complexity of the sector, which makes both investment planning and pricing rather more difficult than for the other major subsectors. The second is the fact that all countries need to deal with electrification issues, whereas a great number of countries do not have to deal with the problems of expanding oil, gas, or coal supply because they lack such resources. The third reason is the capital intensity of the subsector: in many countries the power sector accounts for the single largest fraction of public sector investment.

The developing countries have made significant gains in terms of access to, and per capita consumption of electricity over the last few decades. Other evidence also suggests that in many countries the power sector tends to be better organized and perform better than other sectors of the economy. However, during periods of high growth, power utilities have had to weather oil price increases and high inflation and have been hampered in their efforts to attain financial targets because governments have been slow in responding to changing conditions and in granting tariff increases. Thus, an urgent need has arisen to arrest deteriorating trends, given that power investments absorb as much as half of all public investments in some countries, and often are the cause of severe debt-related and macroeconomic stresses.

Despite the many indicators of deteriorating performance in the electric power sector, it is evident that access to service has increased considerably in terms of both average per capita kilowatt hour generation and percentage of population served. The results from a recent World Bank review of the power sector in developing countries (Munasinghe, Gilling, and Mason, 1988) highlight these issues. In fifty-one

137

Table 8.1 *Technical and non-technical losses, in % of net generation*

	Total	Technical	Non-technical
Sri Lanka	18	14	4
Panama	22	17	5
Sudan	31	17	14
Bangladesh	31	14	17
Liberia	35	13	22
Malaysia	28	11	17
Ivory Coast	12	8	4

Source: Munasinghe, M., J. Gilling, and M. Mason, 1988. *A Review of World Bank Lending for Electric Power*, World Bank, Washington DC, Energy Series Paper #2 p.60.

countries surveyed, generation increased at an annual average of 7%, from 196 kwh/capita in 1968 to 529 kwh/capita in 1982. Correspondingly, the average rate of per capita GDP growth was only 2%. The annual average growth rate of connections for twenty-nine power projects for which data were available was 9%. Even in countries with little or negative economic growth, the majority had more than 5% annual growth in generation and better than 3% annual growth in connections.

Such improvements in access have required sustained high rates of investment and expansion in total assets (as high as 15% annually in many countries). Because these investment needs have placed a great economic burden on the economy as a whole, many utilities have been forced to scale down their programs due to budget and other constraints. Furthermore, investments in the past decades have been predominantly weighted toward generation, with a consequent underfunding of the transmission and distribution side. Thus, many developing country power systems now suffer from unbalanced investments, with overcapacity in generation coexisting with serious underinvestment in distribution.

One consequence of this unbalanced investment is the high level of technical losses recorded in many developing country power systems (see table 8.1). High loss levels drive up supply costs and increase financial burdens. They are also indicative of a poor quality of service since substandard distribution networks which lead to losses are also responsible for voltage fluctuations and power outages. Frequently, investments on the distribution side, that are relatively small compared to supply side investments, suffice to achieve significant energy savings by reduction of technical losses. There are also considerable non-technical losses in third world electricity systems. These occur due to outright theft and inadequate metering, billing, or collection. In the developing countries, total network losses during the 1967–78 period averaged 13%, whereas a reasonable techno-economic norm would be less than 8%. It is also disconcerting to note that, in most cases, losses have either progressively increased or remained unchanged, despite the heavy power sector investments. Service quality has shown a similar adverse trend.

While an accurate assessment of supply costs is not available, it is quite apparent that tariffs have not kept up with costs even in financial terms (see box 8.1 on page 140). On average the operating ratio (i.e., total costs as a fraction of total revenue) for over 300 projects reviewed by the World Bank deteriorated from 0.65 in the 1966–73 period to 0.80 during 1980–5. Despite increasing emphasis on economic efficiency pricing placed by external agencies, only relatively modest progress has been achieved globally, even though marginal cost-based tariff structures have been implemented in several countries.

The shortfall in revenue, which is reflected by this adverse trend in the operating ratio, has largely contributed to the poor financial performance of the LDC power sector. Cost escalation has also been responsible for this decline. In addition to the operating ratio, sector financial performance has been monitored using several other key utility financial ratios, such as rate of return on assets, self-financing ratio and days receivable. Rates of return have declined progressively, from 9.2% in 1966–73 to 7.9% in 1974–9 and 6.0% in 1980–5. The trend in rate of return is shown in figure 8.1. The self-financing ratio (which measures the amount of investment requirements financed by internal cash generation) also worsened over time, starting at an average of 25% in 1966–73 but falling to 17% by 1980–5. Days receivable (which reflects the utility's ability to collect its bills and act against delinquent customers) increased from seventy-seven days during 1966–73 to 108 days in the 1970s, and to 112 days in the 1980–5 period.

From the foregoing a considerable deterioration in sector financial performance could be observed over the period starting before the first oil crisis (1966–73), through the two oil shocks (1974–9), and afterwards (1980–5). Since this decline began before 1973, there is little evidence that the two oil crises precipitated the deterioration, although they may have worsened the downward trend.

A widely prevalent phenomenon in some developing countries has been that of overoptimism in power demand forecasting. Indeed, this phenomenon has significantly contributed to the growing economic

Box 8.1 *Tariffs and financial performance in India*

The problems of inadequate revenue generation are nowhere better illustrated than in India, where in 1989 the average cost of supply was 5.5 cents/kwh, while the average revenue was 4.4 cents/kwh.

SEB	Average revenue paise/kwh	Average supply cost paise/kwh	Debt service ratio	Rate of return %
A.P.	64.5	64.3	1.0	0.2
Bihar	97.0	148.3	−0.1	−23.5
Gujarat	89.0	101.9	0.3	−11.5
Haryana	60.8	79.3	0.2	−11.7
H.P	65.9	117.3	0.1	−50.7
Jammu & Kashmir	44.7	108.4	−0.8	−26.6
Karnataka	71.8	74.5	0.6	−5.6
Kerala	53.4	67.2	0.3	−14.8
M.P.	77.7	82.6	0.9	1.1
Maharashtra	81.0	84.9	0.8	1.4
Orissa	66.6	72.3	0.6	−5.7
Punjab	48.4	94.4	−0.2	−30.3
Rajasthan	79.7	90.3	0.6	−4.6
Tamil Nadu	64.8	86.5	−0.3	−23.1
U.P.	66.4	101.5	0	−18.8
West Bengal	97.5	122.5	0.2	−24.1
all SEBs			0.3	−11.8

The practical consequences of the capital constraints and poor financial situation of the State Electricity Boards (SEBs) for construction programs are well illustrated by the recent experience of Gujarat. For the year 1989–90, the Annual Plan for Gujarat, prepared by the Gujarat Electricity Board (GEB) and submitted to the state government, called for investment outlays of Rs 66.4 billion. The state government recommended Rs 40 billion, while the Central Electricity Authority (CEA), the Federal body charged with nationwide power sector planning and coordination, accepted a plan for Rs 55 billion. The Indian Planning Commission, after discussions with all parties, recommended outlays of Rs 45.8 billion. However, in light of shortages of resources at the state level, the final authorization by the state government was Rs 34.3 billion. Even at this level, there remains an unbridged gap of Rs 7 billion, a result of operating losses incurred by GEB due to insufficiency of the tariff.

Indeed, tariffs at the State Electricity Board level are subject to abrupt changes imposed by state governments. In 1987, a fairly severe drought in Gujarat resulted in falling farm incomes even while the need for irrigation pumping increased. This in turn lowered water tables, raising still further the costs of irrigation. In an attempt to provide relief to farmers, the state decreed that the agricultural tariff be based on installed horsepower of pumpsets only, with the revenue loss to be covered by a subsidy from the state government. Only one half of such amounts due have actually been paid to the Electricity Board. Thus the typical SEB lives in a state of perpetual financial crisis.

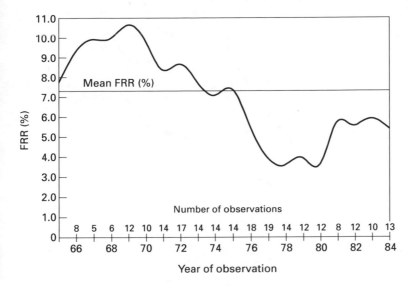

Figure 8.1   Trends in rate of return

burden. Such overoptimism can be partly attributed to the unexpected slowdown following the twin oil shocks of 1973–4 and 1979–80, where the energy price increases and recessionary conditions were more severe than anticipated. However, as shown on figure 8.2 for the case of India, such optimism has frequently predated the energy crises of the 1970s.[1]

Institutional performance, reviewed on the basis of such indicators as the number of consumers per employee, adequacy of maintenance, and general utility efficiency, has stagnated at a relatively unsatisfactory level over the past two decades.[2] Part of this can be attributed to the high growth rates in demand, frequently calling for a doubling of the plant capacity in service in seven to ten years. The requirements for maintenance and efficient operations have increased commensurately and have strained the available management and manpower resources.

[1] Of course to some extent the failure to attain forecasts is due to the inability to expand supply due to capital constraints, a problem that has long plagued India.

[2] The socio-political pressures to increase public sector employment are reflected partly in the number of consumers per employee. Excluding bulk users, a sample of third world utilities has shown that about two thirds have fewer than 100 connections per employee. This is a low figure, even in the context of an unskilled labor-surplus economy, especially since many utility workers are skilled and practically all should be at least semi-skilled. Only a small fraction (10%) of power utilities had more than 150 consumers per employee. Adequacy of maintenance is more difficult to measure quantitatively. Survey based qualitative assessments of maintenance practices indicate that almost half of the utilities surveyed fell into the poor to very poor category. Qualitative assessment of general utility efficiency has indicated similarly weak results.

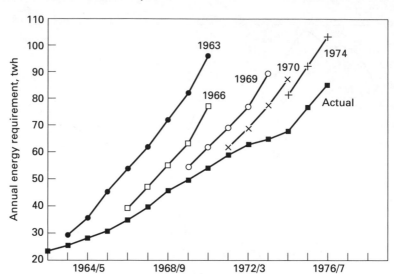

Figure 8.2   Forecasts and actual electrical energy requirements in India

Furthermore, rapidly changing external conditions, such as foreign exchange shortages and economic volatility, make the managerial task increasingly difficult.

Basic principles for efficient investment and pricing policy

From the engineering-economic viewpoint, the basic objective of modeling is to determine a set of policies that will maximize the net benefits of electricity consumption to society as a whole. This also corresponds to the most efficient use of scarce economic resources, and maximization of output or GDP. In this section, we will focus on the national economic viewpoint. As discussed in chapter 1, there are several other important objectives such as meeting the basic energy needs of poor consumers, independence from foreign sources, raising financial resources for future investments, etc., which will also influence both pricing and investment policy.

It is convenient to begin by recalling that economic efficiency requires both: (a) efficient production of electricity, by ensuring least-cost supply through optimal long-run investment planning as well as short-run power system operation and management, and (b) efficient electricity use, by providing marginal cost-based price signals that ensure optimal consumption patterns and resource allocation.

While the close relationship between optimal investment and pricing policies have been generally recognized for some time (Boiteux, 1949), theoretical work in recent decades has focussed on the optimal conditions for price and capacity levels that must be simultaneously satisfied to maximize the net social benefits of electricity consumption. Determining the optimal capacity level is equivalent to establishing the optimal level of reliability, since capacity additions do improve reliability. The link between a least-cost supply of electricity and efficient pricing is important, even from a practical point of view, since an inefficient power utility that is routinely permitted to pass on excessively high costs to consumers (under the umbrella of marginal cost pricing) will have very little incentive to reduce costs and produce more efficiently.

The investment decision has traditionally been treated within the framework of the least-cost system expansion plan. In recent times sophisticated system planning models and techniques have been developed, based on the criterion of minimizing the cost of supplying a given long-range demand forecast, at some acceptable reliability level or quality of supply (Anderson, 1972; Sullivan, 1977; Endrenyi, 1978). The optimal size, mix, and timing of new capacity additions are treated in this way, and related models also provide for optimal (least-cost) operation of the system.

The theoretical foundations of optimal electricity pricing date back as far as the pathbreaking efforts of Dupuit and, subsequently, Hotelling; Ruggles provides a comprehensive review of work in this area up to the 1940s (Dupuit, 1932; Hotelling, 1938; Ruggles, 1949). The development of the theory, especially for application in the electric power sector, received a strong impetus from the work of Boiteux and others, from the 1950s onwards (Boiteux, 1949; Steiner, 1957; Boiteux and Stasi, 1974; Williamson, 1966; Turvey, 1968). Recent work has led to more sophisticated investment models which permit determination of marginal costs, developments in peak load pricing, consideration of the effects of uncertainty, and the costs of power shortages or outage costs suffered by consumers due to unreliable power supply, and so on. Phenomena such as the "Averch-Johnson" effect have been studied in the United States, where private utilities may adopt overly capital-intensive technologies to inflate their rate bases and circumvent rate-of-return regulation (Crew and Kleindorfer, 1979).

Although the close relationship between optimal investment and pricing policies have been recognized for some time, these links were systematically analyzed only in some of the more recent studies. By explicitly incorporating effects to the stochasticity of supply and demand, and introducing the notion of shortage or outage costs in welfare maximizing models of electricity consumption, it has been shown that the optimal conditions for price and capacity levels must be simultaneously satisfied (Turvey and Anderson, 1977; Munasinghe, 1979; Crew and Kleindorfer, 1979). In this context, determining the optimal capacity level is equivalent to establishing the optimal level of reliability (or lower consumer outage costs) and vice versa. Problems relating to the dichotomy of having to choose between short- and long-run marginal costs, and the correct allocation of capacity costs among peak, shoulder, and off- peak consumers have been illuminated in recent work.

We may summarize this complex analysis in simple terms, as follows: the optimal price is the marginal cost of supply. Simultaneously, the optimal reliability (capacity) level is defined as the point at which the marginal cost of increasing reliability is exactly equal to the corresponding reduction in marginal outage costs of consumers. Furthermore, let us define the short-run marginal cost (SRMC) as the cost of meeting additional electricity consumption, with capacity fixed, while the long-run marginal cost (LRMC) is the cost of providing an increase in consumption (sustained indefinitely) into the future in a situation where optimal capacity adjustments are possible. When the system is optimally planned and operated (i.e., capacity and reliability are optimal), SRMC and LRMC coincide. However, if the system plan is suboptimal, significant deviations between SRMC and LRMC will have to be resolved within the pricing policy framework. Finally, if there are substantial outage costs outside the peak period, then the optimal marginal capacity costs may be allocated among the different rating periods (i.e., peak, intermediate, and off-peak) in proportion to the corresponding marginal outage costs.

For practical purposes, the joint optimal price and reliability conditions are used in an essentially uncoupled form. Thus the optimal price is determined at some target reliability level and optimal reliability is set assuming fixed price. By iteration, the solutions may be made mutually consistent. The optimal reliability rule is not easy to apply, especially because outage costs are difficult to estimate (Munasinghe, 1979). However, application of the marginal cost-pricing rule has been attempted in several countries (most notably, France), and, while interpretations vary among practitioners, the approach is gaining wide acceptability (Munasinghe and Warford, 1981).

A framework for power systems optimization

A framework which determines the optimal investment (or reliability) level for a power system is summarized below. It is shown that this methodology, in which the reliability level is a variable to be optimized, subsumes the traditional least-cost investment planning approach of meeting a given demand forecast at a fixed or target reliability level. The optimization of power system losses, another vital area, is also discussed.

The model presented is static (or one period), deterministic, and also has several other simplifying assumptions which improve the clarity of the presentation but do not affect the principal results to be derived. The essence of the optimizing methodology described here is that reliability of supply quality, R, should be treated as a generalized variable, that is to be optimized. The quality of supply affecting customers may be defined very broadly in terms of a set of measurements including frequency and duration of interruptions, and the extent of voltage and frequency variations.

Changes in R have several important economic consequences. First, as supply quality increases, the costs of building, operating, and maintaining the system (SC) also increase. On the other hand as R rises, the shortage costs and inconvenience suffered by consumers due to disruption in supply including outages, low voltages, etc., QC, will decrease. An improvement in supply quality will also raise the consumers' expectation regarding the future level of reliability, R^*, and is also likely to induce increased electricity demand which provides additional net benefits of consumption. Changes in R^* may also affect QC, as consumers adapt their behavior patterns to reduce their shortage costs. Thus by increasing R, it would be possible to trade-off the higher system costs against the decrease in QC and increased net benefits of induced demand.

Let the demand for electricity in the area of service of a power system be given by:

$$D = D(p, R^*, Y, Z)$$

where p is the price per unit, R^* is the reliability of service quality consumers expect to receive, Y is a variable which captures the level of economic activity (e.g., income), and Z is a vector of other relevant explanatory variables. For purposes of optimization, we assume Y and Z are exogenously given.

The net benefits (NB) of electricity consumption may be written:

$$NB(D,R) = TB(D) - SC(D,R) - QC(D,R,R^*) \tag{8.1}$$

where TB is the total benefit of consumption. TB, as well as SC and QC are functions of D, while the functional dependence of SC and QC on R and R^* has been explained earlier.

Before optimizing this model, we recognize that electricity tariffs are often not readily subject to change, and simultaneous optimization of price and capacity is a theoretical ideal. Thus, from a practical point of view, it may be appropriate (or necessary) to uncouple the joint price and reliability in the presence of fixed or given tariffs, at least on the first round. Once optimal reliability (subject to given prices as defined above) is determined, tariffs can be revised to reflect any changes in the marginal cost of supplying electricity implied by the new reliability level. Using this new level of tariffs and resulting demand, reliability can be reoptimized iteratively, as described later.

Allowing only R to vary, the first-order (necessary) condition for dmaximization of net benefits is:

$$\frac{dNB}{dR} = \left(\frac{\partial D}{\partial R^*}\right)\left(\frac{\partial R^*}{\partial R}\right) \cdot \left[\frac{\partial(TB-SC)}{\partial D}\right] - \frac{\partial(SC+QC)}{\partial R} - \left(\frac{\partial R^*}{\partial R}\right) \cdot \left(\frac{\partial QC}{\partial R}\right) = 0$$

The derivative $\partial R^*/\partial R$ represents the change in reliability expectation due to variations in R, and may appear unrealistic in the single-period static case presented here. However, it is conceptually the counterpart of terms such as $(\partial R_t^*/\partial Rt - t')$ for $t' = 1, 2, \ldots, S$; which appear in the dynamic model and indicate the influence of actual reliability level changes in previous years, on the quality of supply expected today. We may rewrite the above as:

$$\left(\frac{dSC}{dR}\right) = -\left(\frac{dQC}{dR}\right) + \left(\frac{dTB}{dR}\right) \tag{8.2}$$

where:

$$\left(\frac{dSC}{dR}\right) = \left(\frac{\partial SC}{\partial R}\right) + \left(\frac{\partial R^*}{\partial R}\right) \cdot \left(\frac{\partial D}{\partial R^*}\right) \cdot \left(\frac{\partial SC}{\partial D}\right)$$

$$\left(\frac{dQC}{dR}\right) = \left(\frac{\partial QC}{\partial R}\right) + \left(\frac{\partial R^*}{\partial R}\right) \cdot \left[\left(\frac{\partial D}{\partial R^*}\right) \cdot \left(\frac{\partial QC}{\partial D}\right) + \left(\frac{\partial QC}{\partial R^*}\right)\right]$$

and:

$$\left(\frac{dTB}{dR}\right) = \left(\frac{\partial R^*}{\partial R}\right) \cdot \left(\frac{\partial D}{\partial R^*}\right) \cdot \left(\frac{\partial TB}{\partial D}\right)$$

The term (dSC/dR) on the left-hand side of (8.2) represents the total change in supply costs due to variations in the actual supply quality, and consists of two components. The first part $(\partial SC/\partial R)$ is the direct effect of R on SC, while the second component captures the indirect effect via the chain of interactions in which R affects R^*, which, in turn, affects the demand, which finally causes a change in supply costs.

The term (dQC/dR) is the total change in shortage costs with respect to reliability, and has three components, among which the first two may be interpreted analogously to the corresponding components of (dSC/dR). The last part ($\partial R^*/\partial R$)·($\partial QC/\partial R^*$) represents the change in QC due to changes in reliability expectations R^*, which are themselves caused by variations in R.

Finally, the term (dTB/dR) denotes the change in total benefits caused by the induced demand changes arising from variations in R^*, themselves caused by changes in R. We will refer to this term as the change in total benefits due to induced demand. TB and QC must be specified carefully to avoid overlap. The effect of R on TB is based on the fact that consumers will alter their demand level D because their reliability expectation R^* has changed. In other words, their demand curve has shifted because their perception of shortage costs has altered, and this change in TB essentially reflects the long-term change in expected shortage costs. Therefore, the term QC in (8.1) should be interpreted as the remaining short-term unavoidable shortage costs, arising from the difference between the actual and expected reliability levels.

Equation (8.2) implies that to maximize the net benefits of electricity consumption, the quality of supply should be increased up to the point where the marginal increase in system costs is equal to the marginal decrease in the costs of poor supply quality, plus the increase in the benefits of induced demand. These marginal costs and benefits include both the direct effects of changes in R, and the indirect effects due to induced variations in R^* and D.

We note that (dSC/dR) > 0, since all the components such as $\partial SC/\partial R$, $\partial R^*/\partial R$, $\partial D/\partial R^*$ and $\partial SC/\partial D$ would be positive. Similarly (dTB/dR) > 0, because all its components are also positive. Finally, we might expect (dQC/dR) > 0, assuming that the dominant component ($\partial QC/\partial R$) is always negative (although the sign of some of the other components may be positive or indeterminate).

These results may be interpreted more clearly using figure 8.3, where SC and QC are shown (by solid lines) as monotonically increasing and decreasing functions of quality of supply (R), respectively. The total costs curve is defined by $TC = SC + QC$. TB is also an increasing function of R due to the effects of induced demand. As shown in the figure, the optimal value of quality of supply (R_m) where the marginality conditions in (8.2) are satisfied, occurs when the slopes of the TC and TB curves are exactly equal. At this point net benefits: ($NB = TB - TC$); are maximized. The new economic criterion for power system optimization represented by (8.2) is general enough to be

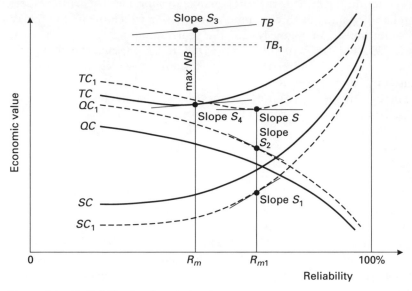

Figure 8.3   Reliability level optimization

applicable to all levels of power system planning, that is, for generation, transmission, and distribution.

It is useful to analyze the way in which the above approach relates to, and subsumes the traditional economic criteria used in power system planning. First, suppose $R = R^*$ and the effects due to induced demand are ignored, i.e., $\partial D/\partial R = 0$. Then (8.2) may be rewritten:

$$\frac{\partial SC}{\partial R} = -\frac{\partial QC}{\partial D} \tag{8.3}$$

This more restricted marginality condition may be interpreted using figure 8.3, in which the broken curves SC_1 and QC_1 are both shown slightly displaced to the right because the ignored components in (dSC/dR) and (dQC/dR) are both assumed to be positive and would tend to increase the slopes of SC_1 and QC_1, respectively. In other words (8.3) implies that the optimal reliability level R_{m1} occurs when the slope of SC_1 is equal to the negative slope of QC_1. This point is also the minimum of the (broken) total costs curve: $TC_1 = SC_1 + QC_1$. Equivalently, since TB_1 is now independent of R, from (8.1), minimizing TC_1 is equivalent to maximizing net benefits. In general, R_m and R_{m1} would not coincide.

Next, suppose that both the demand D and the target reliability level

R are assumed to be fixed. Then maximizing NB reduces to simply minimizing the costs of supply SC for exogenously given D and R, which is the conventional and most commonly encountered planning criterion, i.e., least-cost system expansion. Clearly, the least-cost rule is most appropriate for a private utility which is concerned only with its own costs. In contrast, both (8.2) and (8.3) imply that not only SC but also the costs and benefits of consumption should be included in the planning criterion. This is more comprehensive and represents the viewpoint of society as a whole. Finally, (8.2) is more general than (8.3), because the effects of induced demand have been included.

In this formulation, the reliability measure is defined in a very generalized way. Therefore, the selection of the optimal plan and the associated reliability level is made on the basis of economic cost-benefit analysis, and is quite independent of the actual index of reliability. However, from a practical point of view, it is important to develop reliability indices which not only characterize future system performance in a satisfactory manner, but are also meaningful at the consumer level, and could be easily used to determine the costs of shortages incurred by users. From this viewpoint, load-point indices of the frequency and duration type, by individual consumers on a disaggregate basis, would be the most convenient measures to use. It is also important to know the times when outages occur. Since outage costs are generally a non-linear function of outage duration, ideally, the probability distribution of duration should be computed. However, in practice, a knowledge of the mean duration at specific times may be sufficient, e.g., during the periods of peak, intermediate, and off-peak demand.

Next, let us relax the assumption regarding the original fixed price p. Consider the situation where the stream of system supply costs SC associated with the optimal expansion plan $i = m$, on the first round, necessitate significant changes in the assumptions regarding the evolution of prices p which were themselves used to determine the initial demand forecast. For example, the use of a marginal cost-pricing rule or some simple financial requirements, such as an adequate rate of return on fixed assets, may require previously unforeseen changes in future electricity tariffs, to compensate for the new supply costs. Such a shift in prices would directly affect load growth. Furthermore, the new target reliability levels implied by the first round optimal expansion path $i = m$, may themselves affect reliability expectation, and thus have a secondary impact on demand and shortage costs.

In such a situation, the impact of the new sets of prices and the expected reliability levels on the demand forecast and shortage cost

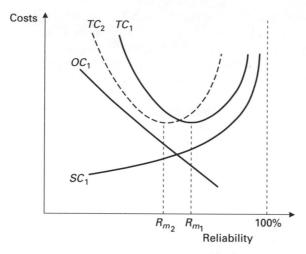

Figure 8.4   Shifts in optimal reliability levels

estimates should be considered when iterating through the model again. To clarify this result, the simplified model results (i.e., assuming $\partial D/\partial R = 0$) shown by the broken lines in figure 8.3, have been redrawn as solid lines in figure 8.4. Then the iterative changes in demand and shortage cost forecasts, would in general, shift the whole total cost (TC_2) curve as shown by the broken line in figure 8.4, leading to a new optimal reliability R_{m2}. In this fashion, the direct and indirect feedback effects of reliability on demand may be considered iteratively until a set of self-consistent price, demand, and reliability levels was determined.

Loss optimization

The worldwide scarcity of energy resources and the increasing costs of energy supply have highlighted the importance of energy conservation and elimination of waste by both producers and users of energy. Power system loss reduction is one of the principal ways for achieving this in the electricity power sector.

In the process of delivering electricity to consumers, losses are incurred at the generation, transmission, and distribution stages of a power system. Generation losses may be improved by improving the efficiency of plant and reducing station use, e.g., using new technologies like combined-cycle thermal plant, replacing old boilers, and generally uprating old thermal generators, using higher efficiency designs in new hydro installations, or replacing older turbines, etc. Leaving generation

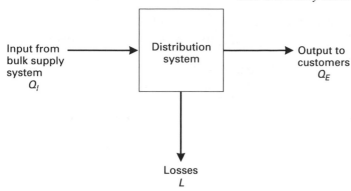

Figure 8.5   Losses in a power distribution system

aside (where acceptable norms for losses vary according to the mix of plant), recent work indicates that average energy losses in the power delivery system, i.e., transmission and distribution, should normally be below 10% of gross generation, while economically optimal loss levels may be as low as 5%.

The framework summarized below will permit technical loss levels in any part of a power system to be economically optimized (Munasinghe, 1981). We recognize that other types of loss such as theft or unmetered consumption may also be significant in some systems and should be reduced. However, these issues are not analyzed within the scope of the present model. Minimizing such unaccounted-for energy may involve steps such as replacing broken meters, disconnecting and prosecuting customers who steal electricity, establishing a system of prepayment of bills, using different individuals to do the meter reading and billing (as an anticorruption measure), and so on.

The essence of the optimization model described below is the trade-off between power system costs and the resultant decrease in the cost of losses. While system costs are relatively easy to measure in terms of the economic value of physical inputs like capital, labor, and fuels, the value of losses is more difficult to establish. Therefore, after discussing loss optimization, we establish below how physical losses in a power system may be valued in economic terms.

We develop the model in terms of optimizing distribution losses, but clearly, the same analysis is applicable to any other part of the power system. Consider the electric power distribution system shown in figure 8.5. An amount Q_I of electrical energy is supplied as input by the bulk power system of which an amount L is dissipated as losses and the remainder Q_E is delivered to consumers.

This static analysis is deliberately simplified for clarity of presentation. Thus the quantities Q_I, Q_E, and L would actually be disaggregate (e.g., peak kw, peak, shoulder, and off-peak kwh, etc.), with each component being valued separately. Similarly, the calculation would have to be performed in present value terms over a long period (e.g., twenty years) to allow for the full life cycle of components, and dynamic load growth. We also ignore quality of supply and outage costs considerations, explicitly considered in (8.1).

The net benefits (NB) of electricity consumption from the social viewpoint is given by:

$$NB = TB - SC$$

where, as defined earlier, TB is the total benefit of consumption and SC is the supply cost. TB depends on the amount of electricity consumed, i.e., $TB(Q)$. We may break SC down into two principal components:

$$SC = BSC + DSC$$

where BSC is the bulk supply cost and DSC is the distribution system cost (investment, operation, and maintenance, etc.).

If we use VQ_I, the value of input electricity (Q_I), as a measure of BSC, then:

$$SC = VQ_I + DSC$$

and:

$$NB = TB - (VQ_I + DSC)$$

Suppose we continue to supply Q_E to consumers but are able to incrementally reduce distribution losses by an amount dVL, by improving the network. But $Q = Q_E + L$, and since we have just assumed that Q_E is constant, dQ_I = dVL. Therefore, Q_I decreases by the same amount as losses L, and VQ_I also falls. TB is unchanged since Q_E is the same. The change in net benefits is given by:

$$dNB = dVQ_I - dDSC = dVL - dDSC$$

where VL is the change in value of losses which is assumed to be negative. (Note that dVL = dVQ_I, although VQ_I is much greater than VL.) In other words, the increase in net benefits equals the decrease in value of losses less the increase in distribution system costs.

Therefore, net benefits to society would increase if the reduction in value of losses exceeded the increase in the distribution costs. Thus an operational criterion which distribution planners should use is that loss reduction measures should continue up to the point where a marginal

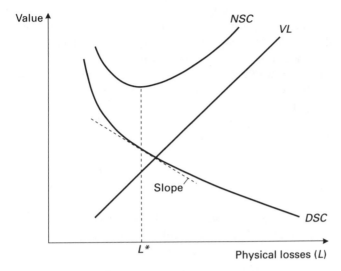

Figure 8.6   Optimizing the level of losses

increment in distribution costs will be exactly counterbalanced by the decrease in value of losses. Equivalently, we can argue that to maximize NB, net supply cost: $NSC = VL + DSC$ should be minimized.

These relationships are summarized in figure 8.6, which shows that VL increases and DSC falls as L increases, while the economically optimal loss level L^* occurs when NSC (the sum of VL and DSC), is a minimum. At L^*, the slopes of VL and DSC are equal and opposite.

The economic value of losses

In many engineering studies, emphasis has been placed on applying accounting principles to loss evaluation, rather than economic principles. Although concepts such as present worth of annual revenue requirements, levelized annual costs, and equivalent investment costs are used, there is no application of economic theory in these procedures (Nickel, 1980).

The principal point we make is that both kilowatt and kilowatt-hour distribution losses at various time periods should be correctly valued at the long-run marginal costs (LRMC) of supply from the bulk supply system. While this issue is being addressed more clearly now, it was overlooked in the work of earlier authors who often suggested lower values for these losses – especially kilowatt losses (Johnson, 1976, Baldwin *et al.*, 1961). The valuation of kilowatt-hour energy losses does not pose major problems. If distribution losses decrease at any given moment, then the bulk supply LRMC of energy at different time (e.g., peak, shoulder, off-peak, or by season of the year) provide a measure of the value of kilowatt-hours lost in the distribution system.

However, when distribution system improvements are made, the greatest change usually occurs with respect to kilowatt losses during the peak period. Although the distribution feeder peaks and the bulk system peak may not overlap, any reduction in kilowatt losses during the bulk system peak will lead to a savings in generation and transmission (G&T) capacity. Even if G&T investments are not actually deferred, the LRMC of bulk kilowatt supply may be used as a proxy for the value of kilowatt losses in the distribution system at the time of the bulk system peak as described below.

Losses and customer loads are indistinguishable as far as the bulk supply system is concerned. If, for example, losses do not impose burdens on bulk capacity, then the incremental costs of serving customers will also be negligible. Furthermore, in an optimally planned electricity supply system, the two conditions (discussed earlier) that must be satisfied are that: (a) the optimal price equals the LRMC of supply, and (b) the optimal incremental cost of system improvement equals the cost of outages avoided due to improved reliability.

When losses are reduced, it is equivalent to a reduction in demand. Thus bulk system capacity additions may be deferred yielding cost savings represented by bulk supply LRMC. Alternatively, if the generation and transmission expansion investments continue relatively unchanged (e.g., due to lumpiness), then the improved bulk supply reliability will provide cost savings (due to averted outage costs at the margin) that are equivalent to the marginal savings that could have been realized from deferred G&T investments. We note that, in the first case, the cost savings accrue to the power supplying company whereas in the second case, the customers gain. Thus from a social viewpoint both costs savings are equivalent, whereas from the power company's viewpoint the former is more desirable.

Policy implementation

The basic framework and models described in the previous section must be suitably modified and interpreted, as discussed below, to reflect real-world conditions and constraints, before they can be used for policy purposes.

Power system planning is a sophisticated and well-developed topic with an abundant literature. Therefore, the purpose of this section is to

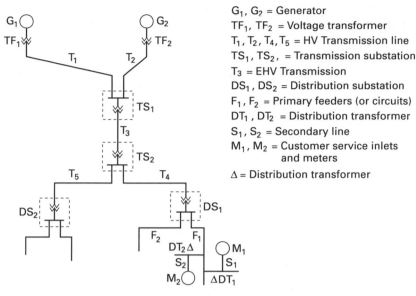

G_1, G_2 = Generator
TF_1, TF_2 = Voltage transformer
T_1, T_2, T_4, T_5 = HV Transmission line
$TS_1, TS_2,$ = Transmission substation
T_3 = EHV Transmission
DS_1, DS_2 = Distribution substation
F_1, F_2 = Primary feeders (or circuits)
DT_1, DT_2 = Distribution transformer
S_1, S_2 = Secondary line
M_1, M_2 = Customer service inlets
              and meters
Δ = Distribution transformer

Figure 8.7   Typical power system configuration

outline the engineering-economic principles underlying conventional least-cost system planning, with appropriate references to more detailed treatment of various topics, where appropriate.

Ideally, the planning of the whole power system should be integrated. To make the practical problems of system design workable, however, it is convenient to analyze the procedure in terms of the main subsystems: generation, transmission, and distribution (Sullivan, 1977; Wismer, 1971; Knight, 1972; Vardi and Avi-Itzhak, 1981). This type of hierarchical reduction is logical from several points of view.

It is useful at this stage to briefly review the basic principles underlying power systems. An electric power system must supply electricity to consumers at the power level they want and at the time and place of their choosing, while maintaining an acceptable quality of service – i.e., voltage and frequency levels must lie within specified limits. The basic parts of a power system may be analyzed in terms of their functions: generation, transmission, and distribution. The concept of a generating source or power plant is relatively unambiguous. Both transmission and distribution facilities carry the electric power from the source to the consumer. These ideas are further clarified in figure 8.7, a schematic diagram of a simple power system.

The output from two power generating plants G_1 and G_2 (hydroelectric or thermal) is increased to the high voltage (HV) level at source by the respective transformers TF_1 and TF_2 and is fed into the busbars in transmission substation TS_1 via the HV transmission links T_1 and T_2. At TS_1 the voltage is further increased to the extra high voltage (EHV) level, before the power is transmitted through the EHV line T_3 to substation TS_2. A voltage reduction occurs at TS_2, after which the electric power is fed, through HV transmission lines T_4 and T_5, into the distribution substations DS_1 and DS_2 located close to the load centers. Another voltage reduction occurs at DS_1 and DS_2, and then power flows out of the distribution substation busbars, through primary feeders such as F_1, to various distribution transformers (for example, DT_1), where the voltage is decreased further. Finally, the power is delivered to a representative consumer, through the secondary distribution line S_1, and service inlet and meter M_1.

In transporting power the general principle is that voltage level depends on distance and power flow. Transmission lines are used to carry large amounts of power over long distances, while distribution lines involve smaller power flows over shorter distances. The technical distinction between transmission and distribution facilities is usually made on the basis of their operating voltages. Although voltage standards vary greatly from country to country, broadly accepted ranges for voltage levels are as follows: EHV transmission, more than 220 kV; HV transmission, 69 to 220 kV; primary distribution, 6 to 35 kV; and secondary distribution, 110 to 480 volts. In practice, considerable overlap is likely, and facilities, operating at voltages in the range of 35 to 100 kV (often called subtransmission), may be included within the distribution or transmission category, depending on their function.

An operating power system is much more complex than the one described above and in general has many generating sources linked to many load centers via an interconnected transmission network. Transmission interconnections may be used to tie the power systems of several different utilities together to form an even larger power pool. The distribution grid at a single load center would serve thousands of consumers. Furthermore, many other components, including protective and relaying devices as well as load control and dispatching equipment, would play an important role in a large interconnected system.

As was noted in the previous section on load forecasting, various completion times are associated with projects that involve different parts of a power system, ranging from up to ten years for the design and construction of a large nuclear generating plant to one or two years for distribution schemes. Also, the problems and design philosophies associated with the different parts of the total power system are inherently dissimilar. For example, distribution system planners require detailed knowledge of localized geographic areas and must deal with many small components such as distribution transformers, switches, and reclosers. At the other extreme, generation planning is carried out on a global level and is concerned with large components such as turbines, and these generally have interaction modes that are more complex to analyze. Consequently, the models and criteria now used to design the various subsystems are also different. The following mathematical discussion is cast in the context of traditional system expansion planning, i.e., choosing the design that minimizes system cost while meeting given requirements for load and reliability. The basic ideas involved, however, may be readily adapted to the new approach in which the reliability level is treated as a variable, and the total cost to society, or sum of system and shortage costs, is minimized (Anderson, 1972).

Early approaches to system design and planning were rather intuitive and relied heavily on the designers' past experience. In contrast, the mathematical methods currently used rely on optimization models. The goal is to minimize an objective function, usually the present discounted value of system cost subject to various constraints, such as meeting targets for load and reliability, and maintaining technical and operating requirements (IEEE, 1976; Rischl, 1975).

In general, if the problem is deterministic, with a known objective function and constraints – i.e., best estimates of plant costs, load, and demand in generation planning – then some definitive nominal design may be found. With uncertainty, flexible design strategies are required. In the worst case strategy, upper and lower design limits are determined that correspond to maximum and minimum values of the objective function and constraints. Given a probabilistic distribution of values of the objective function and constraints, the statistical technique results in the average design configuration emerging from among the design variations.

The specific techniques for solving the optimization problem may be considered under three categories. Mathematical programming approaches – which include linear, non-linear, integer, mixed-integer, and dynamic programming versions – are the most useful when the objective function is simple and well defined. They rely on explicit (computerized) algorithms that are used to find the solution after a finite number of steps. Search techniques, which may be used when programming methods are difficult to apply, are generally easier to implement, but they do not guarantee convergence to the solution within a reasonable time. Special procedures are often elegant, but they are usually applicable only to particular problems (Ford and Fulkerson, 1962).

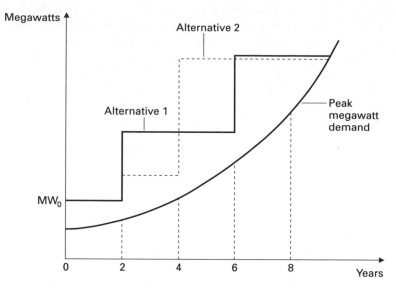

Figure 8.8   Optimal timing of generation capacity additions

Generation

The basic questions in the design of generation systems involve the size, timing, type (or mix), and location of generating plants. The economic aspects of each of the choices involved are clarified below by using a simple approach. Figure 8.8 depicts the problem of size and timing resulting from the growth of peak megawatt (MW) demand over time in a typical system with limited capacity. The installed capacity of existing generating plant MW will not be sufficient to meet the demand in two years, allowing for a suitable reserve margin. Two expansion alternatives are available that meet all the constraints. In the first, two medium-size generating plants would come on stream in the second and fourth years. In the second option, a small plant would be commissioned in the second year, followed by a large power station in the sixth year. The system planner must choose the cheaper alternative. In a real system, the expansion paths over a longer period of time would be compared. In this example, the two alternative plans have been made roughly equivalent after the sixth year to highlight the nature of the choice of size and timing of the next two generation additions. Moreover, in predominantly hydroelectric systems, energy shortages caused by limited storage space may precede any capacity constraints.

The selection of an appropriate plant mix is best discussed in the

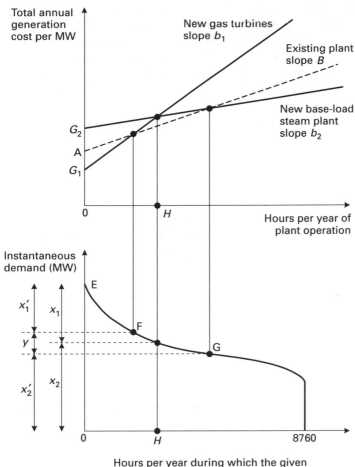

Figure 8.9   Choice of generation plant mix

context of the annual load duration (LDC) for a system. The LDC for a given year is shown in figure 8.9, in which the hourly megawatt demand of the system is plotted against the number of hours of the year during which this level of demand is equaled or exceeded. The peak demand occurs only over a short period of time. Since the average level of megawatt demand – that is, the total energy in megawatt-hours or area under the LDC curve divided by 8760 – is less than the peak demand, the load factor will be less than unity.

For simplicity, only two kinds of generating units are initially considered: gas turbines and base-load steam plants. The relevant characteristics of both these types of machines are shown by the solid lines in the upper diagram of figure 8.9, which is a linearized graph of the total average cost per megawatt of installed capacity, that is, capital cost plus operating cost, plotted as a function of the number of hours of operation. Gas turbines have lower capital costs, represented by the intercept a_1, which is the investment cost of a megawatt, averaged yearly over the lifetime of the machine. They have higher fuel costs than steam plants, however, as indicated by the slope b_1 of the operating cost curve.

First, consider the problem of determining the amounts of new gas turbine and base-load steam capacity that must be built to meet the given load, if the existing generating plant is ignored. From the economic point of view, gas turbines are more expensive than base-load units if they are to be used more than H hours a year. This essentially static picture is only illustrative, because the relevant stream of present discounted investment and the operating costs of the machines would have to be compared over many years. To pursue this further, the lower diagram indicates that it would be economical to serve the bottom X_2 megawatts (the base load) with steam units and the upper X_1 megawatts (the peak load) with gas turbines. A reserve margin may be included if necessary.

Next, the modifications required in generation expansion planning because of old or existing plants are illustrated using a simple example. Suppose that Y megawatts of generating capacity exist already. This plant has an operating cost given by slope B in figure 8.9. To clarify the representation, assume $b_1 > B > b_2$. The capacity costs of the existing plant have already been incurred, and the planner must determine the optimal point of operation for these Y megawatts on the LDC. This is done geometrically by moving the line parallel to itself up or down on the diagram until the vertical distance between the appropriate points F and G on the LDC is equal to Y megawatts.

The intercept A is the shadow value of capacity of the existing plant, that is, the equivalent saving in capacity costs for the system resulting from use of the existing generating plant. The new plan requires full use of the Y megawatts of existing capacity and X_1 and X_2 megawatts, respectively, of new gas turbines and base-load steam units to be constructed to meet the LDC. $X_1' \neq X_1$ and $X_2' \neq X_2$, the existence of old capacity has altered the optimal mix of new plants required. In more complicated cases, if some of the existing capacity is inefficient and has very high operating costs, the optimal plant mix may include only part or none of this old plant.

In practice, many kinds of generating machines of various sizes would have to be taken into account including nuclear, coal, and oil-fired steam, gas turbine, conventional and pumped-storage hydro, and, more recently, geothermal, tidal, and wind-powered units. When generation additions are being considered to meet future load growth, however, the basic principle of selecting units with lower capital but higher operating costs for peaking purposes – and the opposite for non-peaking operation – would generally hold true.

Transmission

Usually, the problem of locating the generators is closely linked with the design of the transmission system; therefore, they should be discussed in the same context. Transmission planning typically involves solving a dynamic network-type problem. The basic objective is to select the type, timing, and location of additional lines that would connect the various generating stations to the different load centers in the least expensive way. In addition, requirements involving the load, reliability level, and other constraints must be satisfied.

A commonly used network model is the dc load flow model, which may be used in either a linear or non-linear framework. In the single-step approaches that are essentially static, the design optimization is repeated at various points. When generation and load levels are specified – for example, in the last year of the planning horizon – the repetition provides instantaneous snapshots of the system's evolution. Long computing times are required in dynamic methods to handle transmission line variations in both space and time, as in the analysis of a large interconnected area during each year of the planning period. The problem of time is simplified by preselecting several expansion alternatives according to certain performance criteria. None of these techniques can guarantee a definitive solution, however, given the size of the problem and the limits on calculating times (Stott, 1974).

There are two general types of criteria for transmission system performance: steady-state and transient (CIDA, 1977). Steady-state performance of the system consists basically of verifying that line and transformer design limits are not exceeded under normal loading and operating conditions or with single contingencies, such as loss of one line, transformer, or generator. Transient performance criteria are used to test the model for stability in various situations. One group of tests involves examining how well an interconnected system would maintain steady-state stability under both normal and contingency conditions, when excited by a small disturbance such as the switching on of a minor load. Verifying the system's dynamic stability is also important. This involves the degree of damping of high-amplitude oscillations induced by a large fault, such as failure of a major line because of a three-phase fault to ground or the loss of a block of generators.

A return to the question of generator location is appropriate at this point. The analysis of combined generation and transmission system models raises formidable problems. Therefore, although the generation and transmission subsystems are intimately related, separate models are generally used for the detailed design of each subsystem.

More specifically, a typical large computerized generation planning model would yield the appropriate plant mix, size, and timing. Sometimes a limited and often inaccurate representation of the transmission network is included. The optimal locations to supply the specified load centers would be chosen from among several potential sites within the context of a more detailed transmission planning model. In practice, it would be necessary to iterate between the models to derive the best mutually consistent solution.

Distribution

Although planning generation and transmission systems is an inter-related process, the distribution grid serving a localized geographic area or load center can be designed independently. Recently, computerized methods have been developed to determine the optimal size, timing, and location of distribution substations and primary feeders. Sophisticated models and computerized algorithms, however, are not as widely used in the design of distribution systems as in generation and transmission work.

In the more conventional approach, forecast loads are imposed on the existing distribution system at various times in the future, and the network is systematically strengthened to meet these loads adequately. The location of new substations and primary feeders and the upgrading of existing ones would be determined to meet consumer demand within acceptable voltage limits under both normal and emergency conditions, as well as during peak and off-peak periods. Flexibility in the design to facilitate isolating faulted sections of feeders and to permit customers to be switched from faulted to functioning feeders would be an important consideration.

Often, because of the large numbers of customers and components, such as line sections, distribution transformers, and so on, only certain representative feeders would be analyzed in detail to establish general criteria such as maximum kilowatt-amperes for a circuit. Such criteria could then be applied to other feeders without further detailed study. In

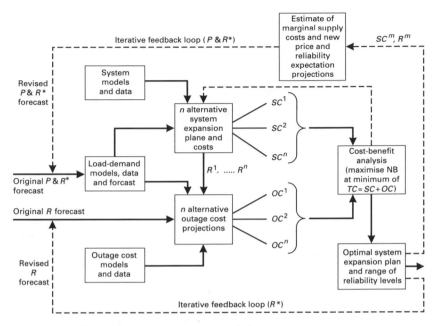

Figure 8.10   Reliability optimizing methodology

general, the larger and more complex the service area, the greater would be the advantage of using even simple computerized techniques for circuit-by-circuit analysis.

Implementing the optimal system reliability model

Figure 8.10 is a flow chart of the reliability optimizing methodology presented in this section. To begin with, a framework and set of models to analyze the economic costs incurred by different categories of consumers (e.g., residential, industrial, etc.) due to electric power shortages of varying intensity is presented. Concurrently, a disaggregate long-range (e.g., twenty years) load/demand forecast is estimated, based on a predetermined evolution of electricity prices, within the area to be served by the electric power utility. Next, several alternative (least-cost) power system plans are prepared to meet this future load, at several different levels of reliability. The expected annual frequency (i.e., the number) and duration of power failures associated with each alternative system design or plan, as well as the time of occurrence of these shortages, and the average numbers and types of consumers affected by them, is estimated for the entire forecast period.

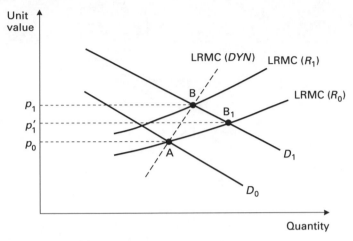

Figure 8.11   Evolution of long-run marginal cost (LRMC) as reliability changes

By substituting the estimated outage frequency and duration results in the consumer outage cost models, it is possible to determine the total future outage costs for each system plan. On the supply side, the investment and operating costs of each alternative design may also be estimated. Then a cost-benefit model is used to compare the outage costs with the corresponding power system costs attributable to each alternative plan. At this stage, some preliminary feedback of forecast frequency and duration data, as well as disaggregative outage costs and system costs from the cost-benefit model, may be used to further improve system design. Finally, the optimum long-run system expansion plan and a range of associated reliability levels are established, which maximize the net social benefits, or equivalently, minimize the total costs (i.e., system costs plus outage costs) to society.

Two further possibilities exist for including feedback effects. The principal return path is via the impact of electricity prices on the load forecast, i.e., if the new optimized system plan requires changes in the original assumptions regarding the future prices which were used to make the initial demand projection. A similar, but less important feedback effect due to the influence of changes in the reliability expectation of consumers, on both the demand and the outage costs, may also be incorporated into the analysis. Therefore, if necessary, it is possible to iterate through the model several times, to arrive at a mutually self-consistent set of price, demand, and optimum reliability levels.

Figure 8.11 illustrates the new procedure in a different way. Suppose that in the starting year the optimal price p_0 has been set equal to the LRMC(R_0), at the market clearing point A. The LRMC(R_0) curve is derived from the system plan with the optimal reliability level R_0, keeping R_0 fixed. Thus initially both price and reliability are jointly optimized.

Now if the demand curve shifts from D_0 to D_1 after some time, the optimal price is not necessarily p_1' on the same LRMC(R_0) curve; using this static LRMC corresponds to the traditional method of system planning with a fixed-target reliability level R_0. The optimal reliability may have changed to R_1 and the appropriate curve is LRMC(R_1) with optimal price p_1. Thus as demand increases, the dynamic optimal long-run marginal cost curve LRMC(DYN) lies along AB.

In practice B is unlikely to be a well-defined point because although the LRMC curve is generally known from known supply-side (technological-economic) considerations, the slope and position of the demand curve are not. Therefore, since B is a poorly defined and shifting target, a trial-and-error approach is required. As demand grows, capacity is added to expand output, while price and reliability are optimized iteratively. Thus, when reliability is optimized, price and demand growth are assumed to be fixed, and when price is optimized, reliability and demand are assumed to be fixed. Thus, through successive iterations, the mutually self-consistent set of optimal price, reliability, and demand levels would be reached at point B.

The effect of variable reliability on system expansion planning

At this stage, several important features of the reliability optimization approach presented here, should be emphasized: first, this method adds an entirely new dimension to the traditional process of system expansion planning. Usually, the power authorities examine several alternative long-range power system plans which are designed to meet a basically fixed-load forecast (although some variation in the growth of demand may be considered, for sensitivity testing), at some predetermined, desired level of reliability and subject to other political, environmental, and legal constraints. Then, the plan which has the lowest value of total costs is chosen. This cost minimization approach is equivalent to the maximization of net benefits criterion used in cost-benefit analysis, provided that the benefit streams of the alternatives being compared are identical.

In the approach described here, the reliability level is also a variable to be optimized. Therefore, the system planner must design a number of alternative systems to meet the future demand (which is initially assumed to be fixed) at each of several target reliability levels, but still subject to the other constraints mentioned above. Then these alternatives are compared, and the one which minimizes the total costs (defined as the sum of the outage costs and the system costs) is chosen as the optimum one. In other words, the conventional system planning criterion of minimizing only the system costs is subsumed within the new procedure, where the total social costs are minimized.

Second, another level of sophistication in system expansion planning is possible with the new model, by considering variations in the demand forecast. The main focus in this method is on the reliability level, which is optimized subject to an initially given forecast of load growth, i.e., assuming a fixed evolution of electricity prices. Ideally, from an economic point of view, both price and reliability should be optimized simultaneously, as discussed in greater detail earlier. However, electricity tariffs in the real world are most often fixed, and therefore it is more practical to assume a given evolution of prices when the first round of optimum reliability levels are determined. Any resulting changes in the pricing assumptions can be fed back iteratively into the model to improve the optimum.

Third, the framework for evaluating outage costs as well as system costs in this new approach, is basically economic, and more appropriate in the context of the national economy, or society, as a whole. The goods and services used as inputs to the electric power system (e.g., labor, land, physical assets, materials, etc.) are considered as scarce economic resources which could be used in alternative production, and they are valued accordingly. In particular, if markets are highly distorted, shadow prices may be used. Such an approach is particularly appropriate in the case of a publicly owned power utility, often the case in the developing countries. In contrast, the traditional system-planning approach is more compatible with the financial or accounting viewpoint of a private utility. Finally, the model may be suitably disaggregated to permit optimization of an interconnected system at various levels of aggregation ranging from the global (e.g., in terms of system-wide generation reliability), to the specific (e.g., in terms of distribution reliability for small geographic areas).

CHAPTER 9

The fuelwood subsector

Accelerating rates of deforestation in the world's tropical and semi-tropical zones have drawn increasing public attention over the past decade. While the main reason for the loss of tropical rain forest is quite evidently the need to clear land for settlement, especially in such countries as Brazil and Indonesia that face very severe population problems, in the world's semi-tropical and semi-arid zones the reasons for deforestation are generally more complex. Land clearing for permanent settlement, felling for construction timber, and exploitation of the wood resource as an energy source all play key roles.

But while there is general agreement that fuelwood (and biomass) is presently the most important energy source in many poor developing countries (see table 9.1), the degree to which fuelwood consumption is

Table 9.1 *The importance of biomass as an energy source: 1980 household energy consumption, % distribution by source*

	Sudan	Ethiopia	Niger	Senegal	Nigeria
Fuelwood, charcoal	94	46	99	95	88
Animal dung, crop residues	5	54	NA	NA	NA
Electricity	0.2	0.05	0.6	3	7
LPG, kerosene	0.5	0.15	0.4	2	5
Total	100	100	100	100	100
Household energy Consumption, 10^6 TOE	10.2	8.1	0.7	1.5	16.6
Household fuelwood Consumption, 10^6 TOE	9.6	3.7	0.7	1.4	14.6

Source: Various World Bank Energy Assessments, also Anderson and Fishwick, (1984) p. 12, plus authors' estimates.

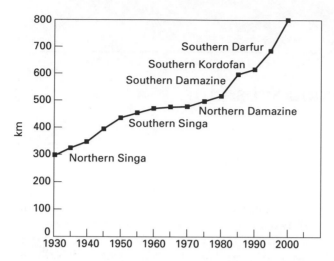

Figure 9.1   Distance of charcoal producing areas from Khartoum

itself a cause of accelerating deforestation remains open to dispute.[1] In rural areas fuelwood is generally gathered by women, with the bulk of the use in the form of twigs and branches. However, large-scale forest depletion is much more likely to result as a consequence of increasing demands for woodfuel in rapidly growing urban areas.

Certainly with respect to the Sahelian countries of Africa, the evidence that the commercialization of fuelwood markets in rapidly growing urban areas has led to a progressive deforestation around the major cities is incontestable. In the Sudan, for example, the zone of deforestation around Khartoum has progressively widened, as illustrated on figure 9.1: by the year 2000, it is anticipated that the charcoal producing areas will be some 800 km distant from Khartoum, with the tree inventory of the central region essentially depleted by the turn of the century (see figure 9.2). The situation around other urban areas in Africa – Dakar in Senegal, Niamey in Niger, and Addis Ababa in Ethiopia – is quite similar.

One might suppose that the impact of increasing fuelwood shortages falls primarily on the rural population. Yet, as shown in box 9.1, it is in

[1] For example, Shaikh and Karch (1985) argue as follows with respect to the Sahel: "agricultural settlement, herding and forest fires are important contributors to forest depletion in the Sahel, but wood energy use is probably the single most important depleting factor. However, it does not follow that fuelwood shortage is the most serious result of deforestation. Soil erosion and destruction of the agricultural production base are much more threatening to the future economic viability of the region."

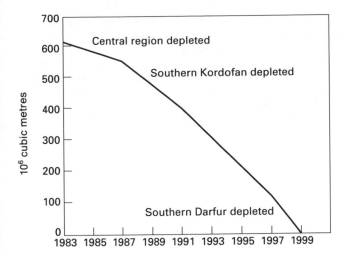

Figure 9.2 Projected tree inventory in the northern Sudan using current practices

Table 9.2 *Fuelwood consumption and mean annual increment (in 1,000m³/yr)*

	Accessible supply	Consumption	Excess of consumption over supply	%
Mauritania	97	963	866	893
Senegal, 1981	7200	4600	– 2600	– 36
Senegal, 2001	6300	7200	900	14
Niger, 1980	1400	4100	2700	193
Niger, 2000	1000	7200	6200	
Sahel, 1980	17000	22000	5000	30
Sahel, 2000	15000	34000	19000	127
Nigeria	13500	23300	9800	73
Ethiopia, 1982	13600	34000	20400	150
Sudan, 1980	44400	75800	31400	71

Source: Anderson and Fishwick (1984) p. 15 and various World Bank Energy Assessment Reports.

Box 9.1 *Fuelwood prices in the Sudan, Ethiopia, and Sri Lanka*

The evolution of charcoal prices in the Sudan exemplifies the impacts of accelerating deforestation rates. Over the past twenty-five years, market prices of charcoal in Khartoum have increased almost three times faster than production costs, with the greatest escalation occurring in the 1984–6 period. Prices in urban centers closer to the production areas are much lower, about 6Ls/sack in February 1984 as against 9.50Ls/sack in Khartoum.

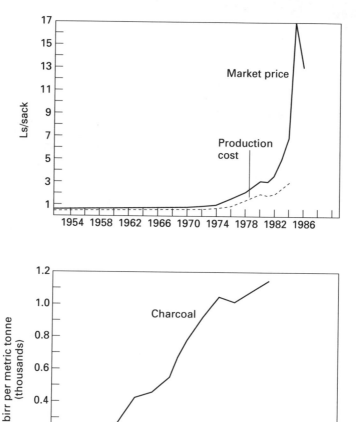

Table 9.3 *Cooking devices in the Dominican Republic*
(as percentage of households in each category)

	Wood only	Charcoal only	Charcoal and LPG	
Non-poor, large towns			40	60
Non-poor, small towns		30	50	20
Poor, large towns	3	44	33	20
Poor, small towns	12	78	7	3

Source: Meier (1985b), p. 82.

the urban areas that prices rise most steeply.[2] Moreover, there is clear evidence from a number of countries that fuelwood (and charcoal) remains the predominant fuel for the urban poor. On table 9.3, for example, we show the results of a household survey conducted in the Dominican Republic, in which urban households were classified by income group ("poor" and "non-poor") and size of urban center – note the sharp differences across income groups in the devices used for cooking.

Indeed, a typical substitution "ladder" is (1) low quality biomass fuels such as dung and crop residues, to (2) higher quality biomass fuels such as wood and charcoal, to (3) kerosene, to (4) LPG, and finally, to (5) natural gas and electricity.[3] One of the issues for policy is the income threshold at which transitions occur. In Pakistan, for example, all but the poorest can afford to switch from biofuels to kerosene stoves (costing about Rs50–70), but only middle- and upper-income groups can normally afford LPG, for which as much as Rs1,200 is required for cylinder, regulator, and simple burner (Leach, 1986).

In addition to the direct consequences of fuelwood shortages there exist a number of important externalities that are by no means limited to the energy sector. A reduction in cooking time, or a reduction in the number of cooked meals, are other likely responses to fuelwood shortages (that may stem from an inability to pay the higher prices), which in turn may reduce nutrition and health levels as a consequence of undercooked food, infrequent meals, and changes in dietary patterns. Furthermore, a whole range of deleterious agricultural, hydrological, and environ-

---

[2] There is a similar variation in fuelwood prices in Sri Lanka. In 1986, prices in the urban centers such as Colombo were about Rs120/- per cubic meter, Rs100/- in the tea-growing areas of the hill country, and Rs35/- in more thickly forested rural areas ($1 = Rs26/-).
[3] Similarly for lighting, the ladder is normally (1) candles, (2) low-output/efficiency kerosene lamps, (3) high-output/efficiency and higher-cost kerosene lamps, and (4) electricity (Leach, 1986).

mental impacts follow from the increases in soil erosion and surface runoff rates that accompany deforestation.[4] For example, soil erosion in the Ethiopian highlands is estimated to average about 20 tons per ha. per year. According to some estimates based on aerial photogrammetry, presently about 1% of Ethiopia's best soils are lost each year (World Bank, 1984). However, from a practical standpoint it is extremely difficult, and probably unproductive, to quantify these impacts in economic terms, given the inherent uncertainties of their measurement. In most cases, the readily quantifiable energy sector impacts will be sufficient to justify policy interventions.

Modeling and data issues

Of all of the subsectors examined in this book, from a strictly analytical perspective the fuelwood sector is the easiest to model, having little of the technical complexity characteristic of, say, electrical system networks, or petroleum refineries. Therefore, the requisite modeling skills are limited to the algebra of material balances. On the other hand, data problems are the most formidable.

The fundamental relationships between supply and demand, and the resultant impact on the natural forest area (or, equivalently, on the volume of the growing stock), are readily illustrated by a simple analytical model. The rate of change of the growing stock is given by the equation:

$$dS/dt = iS(t) - C$$

where

$S(t)$ is the growing stock at time t,

C is the rate of consumption,

i is the annual increment, per unit volume of growing stock.

If $i = 2\%$, $S(0) = 100$, and $C = 3$, the growing stock declines as shown on figure 9.3, at an ever increasing rate.

Suppose that consumption itself increases exponentially, an assumption consistent with a constant rate of population growth. Then the rate of change of the growing stock is given by:

$$\frac{dS}{dt} = iS(t) - D.H(0)\,(1 + g)^t$$

[4] In Senegal, the World Bank Energy Sector Assessment came to the following conclusion "in the absence of policy interventions, the situation would become similar to that already evident around Niamey in Niger and other parts of the Sahel – increasing Sahelisation, loss of topsoil through wind erosion, decline in crop yields, and total loss of potential livestock, fodder, and fuelwood supplies – all of which severely adversely affect rural incomes."

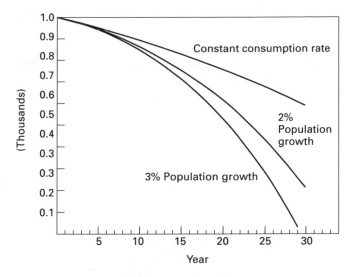

Figure 9.3   Depletion of the growing stock

where
  g is the rate of growth of population,
  $H(0)$ is the number of households at time 0,
  D is the per capita consumption of fuelwood.
  With the same initial conditions as before, and with an annual growth rate of consumption of $g = 2\%$, the growing stock inventory declines even faster, as also shown on figure 9.3. With a 3% population growth rate, depletion occurs within thirty years!
  As we have seen in box 9.1, as the growing stock declines, prices are likely to increase, which under the usual assumptions of the price responsiveness of demand would tend to reduce consumption by one of two mechanisms – a decrease in the unit consumption (say through the introduction of an higher efficiency cookstove), or by fuel substitution (fewer households using fuelwood in favor, say, of LPG stoves).
  Suppose, then, that the per capita consumption of fuelwood is given by the typical demand equation:

$$D(t) = d(0) \left(\frac{Y(y)}{Y(0)} \right)^a \left(\frac{P(t)}{P(0)} \right)^b$$

where
  $Y(t)$ is the household income at time t,
  $D(t)$ is the per household fuelwood demand at time t,
  $P(t)$ is the fuelwood price at time t,

a is the income elasticity of demand (which we can assume to be negative),

b is the price elasticity of demand (also negative).

Based on the observed patterns of price evolution (as shown on box 9.1), one might postulate that the fuelwood price varies inversely with the growing stock, for example as given by the expression:

$$\frac{P(t)}{P(0)} = \frac{S(0)}{S(t)}$$

At this point analytical solutions become fairly complex. Moreover, although such models may well provide useful insights into the nature of the problem, they prove to be of relatively little value for actual policy use, since the most important purpose of modeling in this area is to demonstrate to decision-makers the impact of specific program and policy options. That is, one needs to demonstrate to policy-makers in a fairly direct way how the dissemination of a particular improved cookstove would affect the tree inventory. Decision-makers are not likely to be swayed by the results of analytical models dependent on price elasticity assumptions that are difficult to validate. Numerical simulation with spreadsheets is much more useful, since the impact of specific cookstove, plantation, and agro-forestry initiatives can be readily incorporated.

Table 9.4 illustrates the principles upon which such spreadsheet models are based:[5] the key formulas for the growing stock equations are the recursive relationships:

$$G(t) = D(t) - S(t)$$
$$L(t) = [G(t) - A(t)y(s)]/y(c)$$
$$A(t + 1) = A(t) - L(t)$$

where

$A(t)$ is the average forest area at time t,

$L(t)$ is the loss of natural forest area in the t-th time period,

$G(t)$ is the quantity of fuelwood to be met by the natural forest,

$D(t)$ is the total fuelwood demand at time t.

$S(t)$ is the supply met from other sources (plantations, agricultural wastes, etc.),

$y(s)$ is the growth increment ("allowable cut"),

$y(c)$ is the yield from clear cutting.

Obviously there is some degree of approximation error in such dis-

---

[5] For reasons of space we show only a nine-year period. However, models used in support of policy-making in this area typically extend to as much as 30–40 years, given the long time horizons of plantation programs.

Table 9.4: *Fuelwood supply-demand balance for the northern provinces of the Sudan*

		1985	1986	1987	1988	1989	1990	1991	1992	1993
Households (10^6)	2.00% growth/yr	3.00	3.06	3.12	3.18	3.25	3.31	3.38	3.45	3.51
Fraction with new stove		0.00	0.00	0.00	0.00	0.00	0.00	0.00	0.00	0.00
Fraction using other fuels		0.00	0.00	0.00	0.00	0.00	0.00	0.12	0.23	0.33
Households using other fuels		0.0	0.0	0.0	0.0	0.0	0.0	0.4	0.8	1.2
Households with new stove		0.0	0.0	0.0	0.0	0.0	0.0	0.0	0.0	0.0
Households with old stove		3.0	3.1	3.1	3.2	3.2	3.3	3.0	2.7	2.4
Consumption in old stoves	(14.75m³/ HH)	44.3	45.1	46.0	47.0	47.9	48.9	43.9	39.1	34.8
Consumption in new stoves		0.0	0.0	0.0	0.0	0.0	0.0	0.0	0.0	0.0
Total consumption		44.3	45.1	46.0	47.0	47.9	48.9	43.9	39.1	34.8
Growing Stock	10^6 m³	617	586	554	520	485	448	409	374	343
Mean annual increment	0.022%	14	13	12	12	11	10	9	8	8
Other supplies	10^6 m³									
Consumption		44	45	46	47	48	49	44	39	35
Excess of consumption over supply	10^6 m³	31	32	34	35	37	39	35	31	27
Production cost	Ls/sack	5.73	6.25	6.87	7.61	8.52	9.64	11.07	12.72	14.61
Stumpage tax	Ls/sack	0.27	0.27	0.27	0.27	0.27	0.27	0.27	0.27	0.27
Retail price (1)	Ls/sack	6.00	6.52	7.14	7.88	8.79	9.91	11.34	12.99	14.88
Actual consumer price	Ls/sack	6	6.52	7.14	7.88	8.79	9.91	10.00	10.00	10.00

Note: The full spreadsheet extends to 2030.

crete recursive relationships, since all changes are assumed to occur at the end of time periods. However, such errors are much smaller than the uncertainties in the data. The numerical values indicated on this table correspond to the northern provinces of the Sudan.

Some illustrative results generated by such a model are shown in box 9.2. In the absence of price effects, the growing stock is depleted by the turn of the century (figure A). This corresponds to the assumptions of the Sudan National Energy Plan shown previously in figure 9.1.

Box 9.2: *Illustrative computations of the fuelwood supply-demand balance for the Northern Sudan*

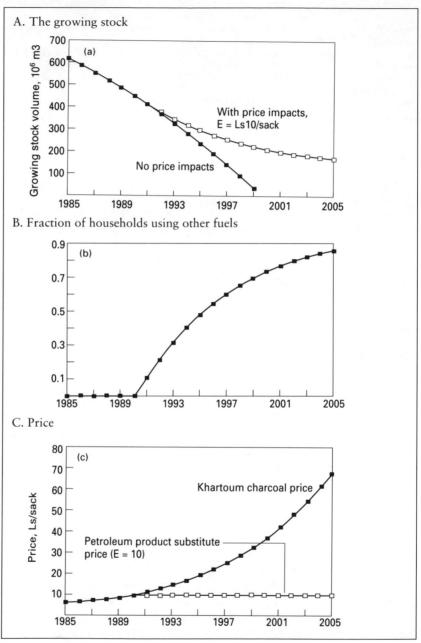

Table 9.5 *Distribution of forest cover in Senegal*

	Natural forest cover (NFC) 1,000 ha[a]	%	Stumpage volume 1,000m³ (of NFC)	Stumpage volume m³/ha m³/ha of NFC	Mean annual increment 1,000m³	Mean annual increment m³/ha
Fleuve	3269	24	3049	0.9	272	0.1
Louga	1989	15	1426	0.7	160	0.2
Diourbel	283	2	514	1.7	49	0.2
Sine Saloum	836	6	5269	6.3	296	0.4
Eastern Senegal	5406	39	68294	12.6	3873	0.8
Casamance	1879	14	60623	32.3	2561	1.4
Total	13662		139175		7211	

Note: [a] including National Parks, of which 800,000 are in eastern Senegal.
Source: Gorse (1982).

If one assumes that as the growing stock is depleted, prices begin to rise sharply (see C), the fraction of households using other fuels will rise (see B). Here we assume that the price of the petroleum product substitute is equivalent to about Ls10/sack of charcoal, and that the fraction of households using the substitute fuel is proportional to the difference between the substitute price and the charcoal price (which is shown to rise very sharply as the growing stock nears depletion). To be sure, these are merely illustrative calculations, and a variety of alternative models might be postulated as a basis for predicting the demand and supply curves.

Geographic scale proves to be a critical issue in modeling. Sharp differences in population density and climate result in substantial differences in the fuelwood supply-demand balance across relatively small distances. In Nigeria, for example, there is a growing scarcity of fuelwood in the northern areas and the main urban centers, yet transport costs prevent alleviation of such shortages from the substantial forests of central Nigeria.

In table 9.5 we quantify such regional imbalances for the case of Senegal. With the exception of the coastal dune and mangrove areas, the vegetation closely follows the major climatic zones, with mean annual wood increments closely related to annual rainfall levels. In the Sahelian zone, that accounts for some 20% of the land area, wood production is below 0.3 m³ per ha. of forest cover, and rainfall is less than 700 mm/year. In the Sudanese zone which accounts for 60% of the land area (with annual rainfall between 700 mm and 900 mm), wood production is between 0.3 m³/ha. and 1 m³/ha. of forest cover. Finally in the Guinean

Table 9.6 *Fuelwood models*

Model	Developed by	Applications
FRAP	EDI, Inc.	Morocco, Mali, Sudan.
BMASS	Sri Lankan Ministry of Energy	Sri Lanka
BIOCUT	Oak Ridge National Laboratory	Liberia
LEAP	ESRG, Inc/ Beijer Institute	Kenya

zone of the remote southern parts of Senegal (having dense wooded savannahs, with rainfall in excess of 1,200mm/year), wood yields exceed 1 m³/ha. As is evident from table 9.5, national averages hide great regional variations. For example, the productive natural forest cover in the Casamance and the east is far from the understocked and over-populated areas in the coastal areas of western Senegal. It is obvious from such data that any credible modeling effort would need to include at least this level of regional detail, with supply-demand balances calculated for each region, linked by interregional transportation cost functions.

Next, we examine how these issues are dealt with in analytical models used in the field. In table 9.6 we list some of the models developed over the past few years for use in a variety of different countries.

The Forest Resources Analysis and Planning Model (FRAP) is one of the better known fuelwood models, having been used in numerous African countries including Morocco, Gambia, Mali, and the Sudan. FRAP is a detailed simulation model, written in LOTUS 1-2-3, which projects forest resource supply and demand over a twenty-year period. Recognizing the importance of regional differences, up to twenty separate regions can be incorporated. Twenty-two input tables accept data by region based on forest classifications, annual increments, and stand volumes by forest zone, wood recovery, forest fires, herding, managed forests and plantations, and, on the demand side, rural and urban populations and growth rates, fuel mixes, energy devices and efficiencies, final energy demands by end use, industrial and commercial energy consumption, non-energy wood demands and growth rates, and demand elasticities, among others.[6]

FRAP is linked to a related model INVEST (not to be confused with the Morocco ENVEST model described in chapter 16) that allows a user to create and evaluate potential investments, including fuel substitution projects, supply measures (plantations, agro-forestry, forest manage-

---

[6] For a good example of the use of the FRAP model as an aid to the formulation of policy, see, e.g., Shaikh and Karch (1985).

ment) and device efficiency improvements (kilns, stoves, etc.). As many as 180 different combinations of investment projects by region can be created on file, and any combination assembled in portfolios and evaluated to assess their impact.

The Sri Lanka model was originally written in FORTRAN, but subsequently rewritten in LOTUS 1-2-3 for use in analyzing policy options for the National Energy Strategy. Its use is detailed as part of the case study presented in chapter 15. Both LEAP and the Sri Lanka models are ideally suited for the sort of sensitivity analysis and "what if" simulation necessary to deal with typical data problems.

Policy interventions

A broad range of policy interventions have been attempted to deal with the fuelwood problem. These fall roughly into three categories: supply augmentation (exemplified by fuelwood plantation and agro-foresty approaches), demand management (exemplified by the efforts to reduce woodfuel consumption by the introduction of improved efficiency woodstoves), and fuel substitution (primarily through pricing policy and the expansion of the petroleum product distribution system into rural areas).

The rationale for improving the efficiency of woodstoves is obvious.[7] This is illustrated on figure 9.4, in which we return to our illustrative model of the northern Sudan, and superimpose a cookstove program implemented over five years that introduces a stove with an efficiency of some 20% (as opposed to an assumed 10% efficiency of an unimproved stove).

It is of course true that the price system acts in a self-regulating way, and that higher fuelwood prices should, in principle, increase incentives to augment the supply, and induce conservation on the part of consumers. Moreover, at some point, the cost of fuelwood will exceed that of petroleum product substitutes.

This point is illustrated in figure 9.5. The impact of increasing fuelwood shortages can be represented by an upward shifting supply

---

[7] Although once again some cautions are appropriate. For example, Donovan and Bajracharya (1980), said this about some of the early efforts to improve woodstoves in Nepal: "The impetus to change appears to be enforced from the top down rather than inspired and initiated from the grass roots level. Moreover, in the implementation of the various policies the focus appears to be on the hardware, or the technological fix. Isolated from their social and environmental context, and evaluated solely on engineering merits, these new technologies always appear promising. The new Nepal Chulos is an example of this orientation ... however, it appears that the basic principles of combustion theory are poorly understood as the various improved designs are modified to suit local cultural preferences ... and improvements in efficiency remain theoretical only. To their dismay, owners of these new stoves may find themselves using more fuel than before". Over the past few years, however, these problems have begun be better understood, as we shall see in the case study of Sri Lanka presented elsewhere.

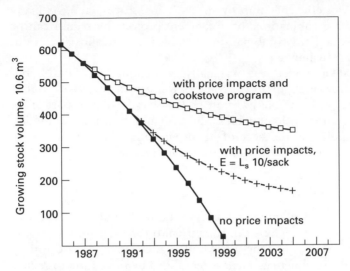

Figure 9.4   The impact of an effective cookstove program on the growing stock in the northern Sudan

curve that reflects the increasing cost of gathering and transportation from ever more distant locations from the major consumption points. Consider, for example, an initial supply curve S, intersecting the demand curve D at price P_1 (see figure 9.5). Assume the cost of the petroleum product substitute is constant at P_s. Now as the supply curve shifts upward, at some point the market clears at exactly P_s, at point X. Beyond this point, any further upward shift in the supply curve (say to S_3) does not result in further fuelwood price increases, but rather an increased market share for the petroleum product, and a decreasing share for the domestic resource (since the consumer sees the supply curve as ABXC, rather than ABE).

This is not a purely abstract analysis, because it leads to several important policy conclusions, even in the absence of precise numerical estimates of the supply and demand elasticities. Indeed, it does not really matter whether fuelwood is, or is not, a direct cause of deforestation. If the forest resource declines, then sooner or later the cost of fuelwood will increase to the point of its petroleum product substitute. This, in turn, has two highly undesirable consequences. First, the increasing cost of meeting basic energy requirements will be concentrated in the groups perhaps least able to afford it, primarily the poor.[8] Second, higher

[8] Survey data from Pakistan indicates that in 1978–79, the poorest urban income groups spent 8.6% of their income on fuels and power, while the highest urban income group spent only 2.4% of their income.

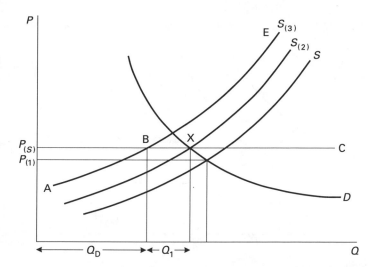

Figure 9.5   Suply and demand for fuelwood

consumption of petroleum products increases the oil import bill (or, in the case of oil exporting countries, decreases export earnings).

However, a critical question in all of this is whether prices in fact reflect the real economic costs. Before attempting any policy intervention three questions should be asked: first, to what extent do the domestic prices of the petroleum product substitutes reflect the opportunity costs to the economy – the well known and ubiquitous subsidies for kerosene and LPG often impose a first distortion? Second, to what extent do the free-market prices of fuelwood in urban areas reflect the true costs to society of the implied loss of the forest resource (such as the long-term loss in agricultural productivity due to increased soil erosion)? And third, to what extent do infrastructure and institutional barriers distort a choice made upon the basis of the true basic energy price for cooking?

The first question needs little attention here.[9] LPG and kerosene subsidies are widely advocated on the very grounds that imposing the true cost on the consumer would increase pressure on the fuelwood resource. However, the degree to which this is actually the case is open to some question.

The answer to the second question posed above, namely the degree to

[9] An excellent starting point for what has become a vast literature on petroleum product pricing is Siddayayo (1985). But it may also be noted that this same literature devotes very little attention to fuelwood pricing.

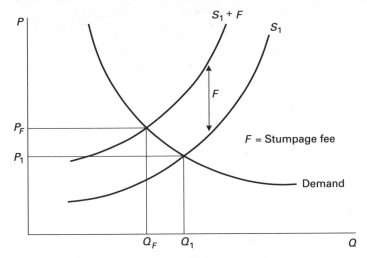

Figure 9.6   Stumpage fees.

which market prices in urban areas reflect the true economic costs to society, is invariably that the long term consequences of deforestation are not reflected in urban fuelwood prices. In theory, the appropriate policy intervention is to apply a stumpage tax, which has the effect of shifting upward the supply curve (see figure 9.6). This provides an incentive for conservation and fuel substitution, and an incentive for private tree plantings.

In figure 9.7 we return to our illustrative model of the northern Sudan. The simulation shows the impact of increasing the stumpage tax from an equivalent of Ls0.27/sack to Ls10/sack. The impact on the growing stock is dramatic, almost doubling the standing crop by 2005.

In practice, however, the administrative problems of enforcement are formidable, given the general weakness of forestry departments. The problems of stumpage fees and price controls are well illustrated by the Senegal experience (Gorse, 1982). The cost of a permit to take wood from the natural forests was a purely nominal CFAF120/stere (about $1.00/m^3). In 1978, the government raised this fee to CFAF2000/stere ($11.00/m^3) for permits to cut wood in official plantations. In Senegal professional loggers constitute a well-organized industry, with forestry cooperatives, private companies, and individuals receiving licenses from, and paying stumpage fees to, the Forestry Department under a quota system that allocates forest products in the proportion of 60% to cooperatives, 25% to companies, and 15% to individuals. However, this organized production accounts for only about 17–20% of the total

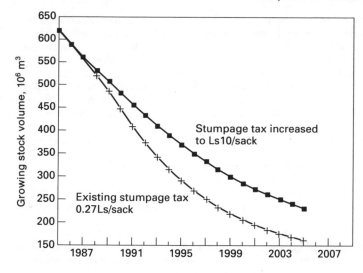

Figure 9.7   The impact of stumpage tax increases

consumption, the remainder being collected by rural inhabitants for their own use as a free good (the so-called "droit de usage") without any license fee.

Retail prices for both firewood and charcoal are controlled by the government at CFAF20/kg for firewood, and CFAF30/kg for charcoal. However, the wholesale price in Dakar frequently exceeds the official retail price, at which times retailers adjust by reducing by as much as by 50% the quantity sold at the official unit price.

Annex: Fuelwood policy analysis and implementation in Sri Lanka

Sri Lanka faces a number of very serious energy problems, among which the fuelwood question is perhaps of greatest long-term consequence because of its inherent time scale and its potentially devastating economic, environmental, and social impact. Although precise statistics are lacking (for example, detailed LANDSAT image analysis upon which to estimate recent trends appears not to have been done for Sri Lanka), there is a general consensus that the natural forest had declined from about 45% of total land area in 1950 (29,000 km²) to about 16,000 km² by the early 1980s.

As usual, identifying the reasons for this decline are much more difficult, and hence controversial. Certainly it is true that most of the deforestation has occurred in the dry zone, which is not heavily populated. The expansion of agricultural land (with felled trees being only partially utilized), the extraction of timber for commercial purposes (both legal and illegal), and the fuel requirements for agro- and rural industries are clearly important contributing factors. As noted by Pushparajah (1981), *chena* cultivation ("slash and burn") is an inefficient use of land in the modern context, providing low yields and low financial returns. Yet some forest reserves in the Hambantota and Usangoda regions in the south have been completely taken over by shifting cultivation. Some estimates of the current rate of loss of land area for *chena* clearing and agricultural development are as high as 150,000 acres/year, implying a total disappearance of forest cover by the year 2000 unless corrective action is taken.

While the degree to which trees have been felled for fuelwood purposes alone is unclear, a few relatively simple calculations indicate that current levels of fuelwood consumption using traditional cookstoves exceeds the sustainable yield of the existing biomass resource. Rubberwood and various agricultural wastes make up about 46% of the current consumption. The balance from the natural forest is about 4 million tons/year. With current forest area of 1.6 million hectares, the sustainable yield would need to be 2.5 tons/ha. This is much higher than the available estimates of the allowable cut, estimated at about 1.5 to 2.0 tons/ha. This is especially true for the dry zone, where yields are much lower.

Institutional issues The first priority to obtain a policy consensus was to address the institutional questions: until mid 1982, the institutional structure in the energy sector was extremely fragmented. Indeed, the actions to be taken in 1982 and 1983 to address these shortcomings proved to be fundamental to the achievement of the subsequent policy coordination not just in the fuelwood sector, but to other energy sectors as well, leading eventually, in 1985, to a national energy strategy (NES).

In mid 1982 the institutional structure was characterized by the existence of a number of energy institutions without an effective mechanism for policy coordination. This was rectified by the creation of an Energy Coordinating Team, organized into three task forces: (1) Energy Planning and Policy Analysis, (2) Energy Efficiency, Demand Management, and Conservation (EDMAC), and (3) New, Renewable, and Rural Sources of Energy (NERSE). The members of these task forces are senior managers from the relevant line organizations seconded to assist their activities. NERSE is the task force charged with formulating a fuelwood management program as its first priority.

Again there is much more to such reorganizations than theoretical niceties. One of the first concrete results of the new structure was the relative ease with which perhaps the most crucial decision for the cookstove program was made – who to put in charge. In many other countries, the practice has been to assign this task to one of the fledgling and usually inadequate agencies involved in renewable energy resources, not infrequently an institution closely related with some particular stove design.

In Sri Lanka, several local organizations such as SARDOVAYA, CISIR, the state timber corporation, and the Ceylon Electric Board (CEB) had made some early efforts in design and field testing of improved stoves. Experience gained by these organizations proved to be valuable for the future programs, although widespread dissemination was not achieved for the following reasons:

absence of an effective institutional framework for widespread dissemination,

little or no government support,

lack of funds for implementation of extension programs,

designs unacceptable to the intended users,

lack of women's participation in the extension programs,

lack of trained personnel,

lack of general awareness of the need for fuelwood conservation and means available to aid conservation.

Therefore, in 1983 the NERSE task force formed a working group to embrace all organizations actively involved or interested in fuelwood conservation. This step permitted proper planning and implementation of a long-run strategy and also helped to work out the machinery for management and coordination of a program of action called the National Fuelwood Conservation Program (NFCP).

It was realized at an early stage that a single organization could not be expected successfully to perform all the activities required for a mass popularization and dissemination program. Through the NFCP framework it was found to be possible to make use of the existing institutional framework of participating organizations, rather than set up a new (and redundant) organization. The existing organizations already had excellent extension services and community development programs that could be harnessed. The NFCP channeled government and donor funds to these operating organizations and also provided the crucial policy coordination, supplementary technical expertise, and other relevant assistance.

While the NFCP was launched and coordinated by the NERSE task force, the Energy Unit of the CEB, a well-established and tightly knit group, acted as the central management team and orchestrated NFCP operations nationwide. The strategy of implementation was to make use of the existing village level institutional infrastructure, primarily with the assistant government agents (AGAs) acting as local coordinators who manage a network of promoters, stove builders, and potters. Each person in the chain receives a financial incentive per stove installed. This approach not only avoided the necessity for a new organization for dissemination activities, but also permitted the use of authority, experience, and close relationship enjoyed by the AGAs to existing institutions and with the villagers. This is essential when introducing new concepts and activities. Moreover, the AGAs have access to and authority over many village level organizations that have proved valuable to the program.

The program was initially started in the five key areas on the island: Kandy, Mahaweli ("H" area), Ratnapura, Hambantota, and Badulla. It was subsequently expanded to other regions as experience was gained. Cookstove programs have floundered elsewhere not so much for inadequacies of design or inadequate attention to cultural adoption (a subject that has become endlessly stressed), but because once the program reaches a sufficiently large size (at which it may begin to make a difference), lack of management skills result in inevitable disorganization and chaos. To be sure, it is too soon to conclude definitively whether the Sri Lankan approach has been successful, but the NCFP has shown most encouraging results since 1983.

Impact analysis There is an understandable reluctance to base important policy decisions and launch major government programs on inadequate data. On the other hand, essential irreversibility of deforestation mandates early action. Indeed, a program to popularize fuelwood-efficient cookstoves was launched almost immediately after the institutional reforms without waiting for the usual studies, since a few simple calculations were sufficient to justify the need. Subsequent analytical work in support of the NES served not merely to confirm the initial analysis, but more importantly to document the robustness of the policy decisions with respect to the key uncertainties, and to substantiate some of the quantitative targets. Indeed, the major thrust of the NES analysis was to document the validity of certain program and policy initiatives over wide ranges of input assumptions.

The fuelwood sector is notorious among energy analysts for its paucity of data and Sri Lanka is no exception. The first systematic survey of fuelwood consumption was conducted only in 1983. An early field survey was that of Bialy, who studied a village in the dry zone near Anuradhapura. His results indicated a consumption of 50 kg per household per week, extrapolated on the basis of 2 million fuelwood using households to some 5 million tons/year. Basing important policy conclusions upon such meagre evidence would indeed be difficult.

Fortunately, by 1983 the results of a first comprehensive survey of 518 households in a stratified random sample were reported by Wijesinghe (1984). His results indicated a much higher figure than those suggested by the earlier estimates, with a 1981 island-wide consumption estimated at 7.3 million tons. However, Wijesinghe's study also raised a number of new issues that might ultimately prove crucial to the success of any policy of initiatives, the most important being very high variation in the composition of fuelwood among the principle climatic zones. In the rubber and coconut zones the predominant fuelwood sources are rubber wood and crop wastes, respectively. However, in the dry and tea zones these two sources play a relatively minor role. The rubber and coconut zones represent the areas of highest rural population density.

The analysis Fuelwood problems cannot be considered in isolation, but must be analyzed within the general socio-economic and energy sector matrix in which they are embedded. Such an analysis was carried out in Sri Lanka, within an integrated national energy planning framework. An ensemble of microcomputer based models installed in the Ministry of Power and Energy was used for this purpose. This ensemble of models, which included a detailed fuelwood subsector model, was used to analyze the impact of alternative programmatic options. With the NFCP already in place, the emphasis was to demonstrate the impacts of delays in yields, and actual (rather than ideal test) stove efficiencies. Also emphasized was the need to justify expanding the existing fuelwood plantation program.

Figure 9.8A shows the anticipated trends in total fuelwood consumption, including both residential and industrial demands and assuming a 2% annual growth rate of households. The key assumption is that any demand that cannot be met from rubber wood, agricultural wastes, and the sustainable yield of the standing crop will be met by cutting (although as noted above, the cutting may in fact occur for other reasons). The resulting forest loss in year t, $L(t)$, is given by:

$$L(t) = \frac{G(t) - A(t)\, y(s)}{y(c)}$$

where
  $y(c)$ is the yield from clear cutting, in tons/ha.,
  $y(s)$ is the sustainable yield ("allowable cut"), in tons/ha.,
  $A(t)$ is the average forest area in the year t, in ha.,
  $G(t)$ is the quantity of fuelwood to be met by the natural forest.
  Hence the following year, the forest area is:

$$A(t + 1) = A(t) - L(t)$$

The combination of the increased demand and cumulatively smaller natural forest area shown obviously leads to an accelerating rate of loss of forest area,

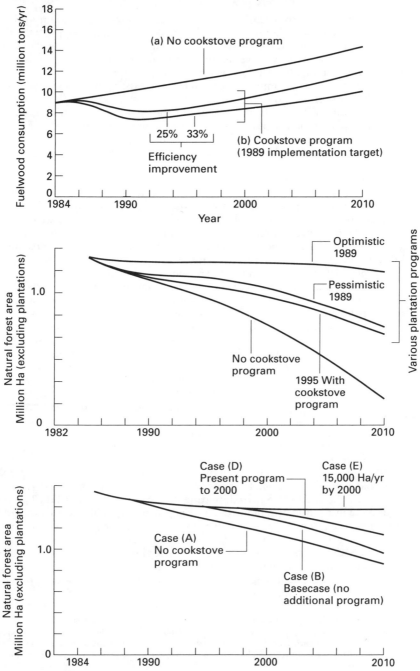

Figure 9.8   Fuelwood balances for Sri Lanka

as shown in figure 9.8B. Clearly, the absence of a cookstove program leads to entirely unacceptable consequences by the turn of the century. Figure 9.8B also shows the impact of the cookstove program, under different target dates (all households using the new stove designs) and various input assumptions (particularly the sustainable yield for the dry zone).[10]

Figure 9.8C shows the impact of expanding the existing fuelwood plantation program. These simulations underscore the relationship between the cookstove and plantation programs. In the absence of the cookstove program, even the accelerated plantation program fails to arrest the rate of deforestation. This, of course, follows from the difference in time scale, since the cookstove program has immediate impact, whereas the plantation program is subject to a growing time lag.[11]

Conclusions The analysis indicates very clearly the need for both cookstove and plantation programs, a conclusion likely to extend to other countries. If an accelerated plantation program is not initiated soon, the possibility of another relatively low cost, short-term solution is no longer present. Today we can buy time for the plantation programs by promoting stove designs whose efficiency gain per rupee is large. The next increment in efficiency gain will become more difficult and costly. In a sense, Sri Lanka faces its "last chance" to avoid a catastrophic deforestation of the type encountered elsewhere.

The NFCP was launched as an official government program in early 1983, with an ambitious goal of reaching saturation by 1989. At least in the initial stages of the program, the cost to each household would be Rs25/-, with the overall per stove cost estimated at Rs50/- (the balance being subsidized by the government). To put these costs in perspective of the typical rural household budget, one might note that the average monthly expenditure for durable goods in the largest income group (monthly income Rs1,000–1,500) is Rs27/-. This same income group spends Rs80/- per month for fuel and light. Several stove designs have been installed in the initial phases of the program: the Sarvodaya stove, with tests indicating up to 23% saving in the amount of wood required (relative to the traditional open hearth) and the CISIRLIPA stove, whose tests indicate a 21% saving relative to the semi closed open hearth and 30% relative to the three stone open hearth.

It is of course too soon to make any judgment about the ultimate success of the NFCP. By late 1985 some 23,000 of the improved cookstoves were in place, somewhat behind the original targets. Nevertheless, the institutional reforms that occurred in the 1982–5 period, putting the implementation of NFCP in the hands of an institution of demonstrated management capability (the CEB) and a strong field organization, and the policy consensus that supports the program at all levels of government, all provide grounds for a certain optimism. One can also be confident of the robustness of the policies initiated over wide ranges of uncertainties in data assumptions, including the performance of the stoves (recent testing in the field suggests actual declines in fuelwood consumption do indeed lie between 20 and 30 percent.)

---

[10] Yields vary widely, from 1.6 tons/ha. in the dry zone to 4.7 tons/ha. in the wet zone.

[11] The calculations assumed the use of Eucalyptus Camuldulensis, with which the forest department already has some experience. Its yield pattern is estimated at 110 tons/ha in the sixth year, 143 tons/ha. in the eleventh and sixteenth years, and 71 tons/ha. in the twenty-first year, at which time replanting becomes necessary.

PART IV

Sectoral integration

CHAPTER 10

Pricing

Pricing is a particularly important tool, especially to achieve long-run changes. However, energy supply systems usually require large capital investments with long lead times and lifetimes. Therefore, once the investment decision is made, usually on the basis of the conventional least-cost method of meeting demand by subsector, with due regard for inter-fuel substitution possibilities, there is a lock-in effect with respect to supply. Thus prices should be related to the long-run planning horizon. On the demand side also, many energy conversion devices (e.g., motor cars, gas stoves, electric appliances, and machines) are expensive relative to average income levels and have relatively long lifetimes, thus limiting the ability of consumers to respond in the short run to changes in relative fuel prices.

The objectives of energy pricing are closely related to the general goals of energy policy noted in chapter 1, but they are more specific. First, the economic growth objective requires that pricing policy should promote the economically efficient allocation of resources, both within the energy sector and between it and the rest of the economy. In general terms, this implies that future energy use would be at optimal levels, with the price (or the consumer's willingness to pay) for the marginal unit of energy used reflecting the incremental resource cost of supply to the national economy. Relative fuel prices should also influence the pattern of consumption in the direction of the optimal or least-cost mix of energy sources required to meet future demand. Distortions and constraints in the economy necessitate the use of shadow prices and economic second-best adjustments, as described in the next section.

Second, the social objective recognizes every citizen's basic right to be supplied with certain minimum energy needs. Given the existence of significant numbers of poor consumers and also wide disparities of income, this implies subsidized prices, at least for low-income consumers.

Third, the government may be concerned with financial objectives relating to the viability and autonomy of the energy sector. This would usually be effected by pricing policies that permit institutions (typically, government-owned) in the different energy subsectors to earn a fair rate of return on assets and to self-finance an acceptable portion of the investments required to develop future energy resources.

Fourth, energy conservation is also an objective of pricing policy. While prevention of unnecessary waste is an important goal, other reasons often underlie the desire to conserve certain fuels. These include the desire for greater independence from foreign sources (e.g., oil imports) and the need to address deforestation and erosion problems.

Fifth, we recognize a number of additional objectives, such as the need for price stability to prevent shocks to consumers from large price fluctuations, and the need for simplicity in energy pricing structures, to avoid confusing the public and to simplify metering and billing.

Sixth, the government may use taxes on energy, and petroleum in particular, as an important source of fiscal revenue and even macro-economic policy. For example, in Morocco taxes on petroleum accounted for as much as 20% of the total government revenue in the late 1980s. This is of course not unique to developing countries: many European governments, and the United Kingdom in particular, attempted to use taxes on gasoline to "fine tune" their economies in the 1950s and early 1960s.

Finally, there are other specific objectives, such as promoting regional development (e.g., rural electrification) or specific sectors (e.g., export-oriented industries), and other socio-political, legal, or environmental constraints.

We conclude by noting that from the viewpoint of economic efficiency, the price indicates the consumer's willingness to pay and the use value of energy; and to consumers, it signals the present and future opportunity costs of supply that draws on various energy sources.

Pricing policy instruments

Governments of course play a pervasive role in the pricing of commercial energy resources, and the relative neglect of issues relating to traditional forms of energy. Governments exercise direct influence over energy pricing, usually through the ownership of energy sources or price controls. Indirect influences occur through such means as taxes, import duties, subsidies, market quotas, taxes on energy-using equipment, and government-guided investments in energy resources.

In practically all developing countries, the electric utility is government owned. In oil and gas production, refining, and distribution, as well as in coal mining, both public and private organizations operate, often side by side. However, irrespective of the form of ownership, all governments exercise some form of wholesale or retail price control, usually at several levels, including during production, during refining, after transport or transmission, and so on. Income and excise taxes are also levied from both public and private energy sector companies.

Quite often certain fuels in specific uses tend to be subsidized, although leakages and abuses of subsidies by non-targeted consumer groups also occur. Thus kerosene for lighting and cooking, rural electricity for lighting and agricultural pumping, and diesel fuel for transportation commonly qualify for subsidies. Cross-subsidies exist between different fuels, user groups, and geographic regions; therefore high-priced gasoline may finance the subsidy on kerosene, industrial electricity users may subsidize household consumers, and a uniform national pricing policy usually implies subsidization of energy users in remote areas by those living in urban centers. The principal problem associated with subsidies is that the energy producer may not be able to raise sufficient revenues to finance investment to meet expanding demand, or even to maintain existing facilities, and thus shortages eventually result. Furthermore, cross-subsidies give consumers the wrong price signals, with consequent misallocation of investments.

Import and export duties, excise taxes, and sales taxes are levied, often by several levels of government, from federal to municipal, at various stages in the production, processing, distribution, and retailing chain. In many developing countries, the combined levies are several hundred percent of the original product price for some items, and negative or close to zero for others. Several less obvious methods, such as property taxes, water rights and user charges, and franchise fees are also used to influence energy use. Energy prices are also affected by the wide range of royalty charges, profit sharing schemes, and exploration agreements that are made for the development of oil and gas resources between governments and multi-national companies.

Other policy instruments are often used to reinforce pricing policies, such as quotas on imported or scarce forms of energy, coupled with high prices. Conservation regulations may affect depletion rates for oil and gas, while availability of hydro power from some multi-purpose dams may be subordinate to the use of water for irrigation or river navigation. Many special policies involving tax holidays and concessions, import subsidies, export bonuses, government loans or grants, high taxes on large automobiles, etc., are also used to affect energy use.

The traditional fuels subsector has been relatively neglected because transactions involving these forms of energy are usually of a non-commercial nature. However, there is growing acceptance of the coordinated use of indirect methods, such as displacement of fuelwood used in cooking by subsidizing kerosene and LPG, increasing the supply of fuelwood by reforestation programs and effective distribution of charcoal, enforcing more severe penalties for illegal felling of trees, and proper watershed management.

An economic framework for efficient pricing

As indicated above, energy pricing has a number of potentially conflicting objectives, and therefore a realistic integrated energy pricing structure must be flexible enough to permit trade-offs among them. To allow this flexibility, the formulation of energy pricing policy must be carried out in two stages (Munasinghe, 1980). In the first stage, a set of prices that strictly meets the economic efficiency objective is determined, based on a consistent and rigorous framework. The second stage consists of adjusting these efficient prices (established in the first step) to meet all the other objectives. The latter procedure is more *ad hoc*, with the extent of the adjustments being determined by the relative importance attached to the different objectives. In this section we first examine a rigorous framework for establishing strict economically efficient prices; in the following section we present a modeling framework that is designed to assist the process of *implementing* a practical pricing policy by adjusting the strict efficient prices to meet the other objectives.

Shadow pricing theory has been developed mainly for use in the cost-benefit analysis of projects. However, since investment decisions in the energy sector are closely related to the pricing of energy outputs, for consistency the same shadow pricing framework should be used in both instances. Shadow prices are used instead of market prices (or private financial costs) to represent the true economic opportunity costs of resources.

In the idealized world of perfect competition, the interaction of atomistic profit-maximizing producers and atomistic utility-maximizing consumers yields market prices that reflect the correct economic opportunity costs, and scarce resources including energy will be efficiently allocated. However, in the real world, distortions may result from monopoly practices, external economies and diseconomies (which are not internalized in the private market), interventions in the market process through taxes, import duties, and subsidies, etc., and these distortions cause market prices for goods and services to diverge substantially from their shadow prices or true economic opportunity costs.

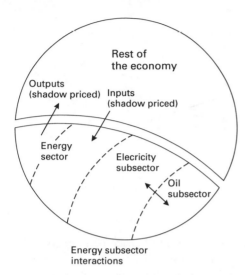

Energy subsector
interactions

Figure 10.1   Energy-economic linkages

Therefore, shadow prices must be used in investment and output pricing decisions to ensure the economically efficient use of resources. Moreover, if there are large income disparities, we will see later that even these "efficient" shadow prices must be further adjusted, especially to achieve socially equitable energy pricing policies for serving poor households.

It is important to realize right at the outset that lack of data, time, and manpower resources often precludes the analysis of a full economy-wide model. Instead, the partial approach shown in figure 10.1 may be used, where key linkages and resource flows between the energy sector and the rest of the economy, as well as interactions among different energy subsectors, are selectively identified and analyzed, using appropriate shadow prices such as the opportunity cost of capital, shadow wage rate, and the marginal opportunity cost for different fuels. In practice, surprisingly valuable results may be obtained from relatively simple models and assumptions.

Suppose that the marginal opportunity cost (MOC) of supply in a given energy subsector is the curve MOC(Q) shown in figure 10.2. For a typical non-traded item like electricity, MOC that is generally upward sloping is calculated by first shadow pricing the inputs to the power sector and then estimating both the level and structure of marginal supply costs (MSC) based on the long-run system expansion program. For tradable items like crude oil and for fuels that are substitutes for

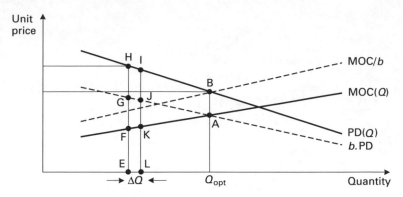

Figure 10.2   Basic concepts

tradables, the CIF price of imports, or the FOB price of exports, with adjustments for internal transport and handling costs, are appropriate indicators of MOC. For most developing countries, such import or export MOC curves will generally be flat or perfectly elastic. Other fuels such as coal and natural gas could be treated either way, depending on whether they are traded or non-traded. The MOC of non-renewable, non-traded energy sources will generally include a "user cost" or economic rent component, in addition to the marginal cost of production. The economic values of traditional fuels are the most difficult to determine, because in many cases there is no established market. However, as discussed later, they may be valued indirectly on the basis of the savings they allow on alternative fuels such as kerosene, the opportunity costs of labor for gathering firewood, and/or the external costs of deforestation erosion.

Thus, for a non-traded form of energy, MOC is the opportunity cost of inputs used to produce it plus a user cost where relevant, while for a tradable fuel or a substitute, MOC represents the marginal foreign exchange cost of imports or the marginal export earnings foregone. In each case, MOC measures the shadow-priced economic value of alternative output foregone because of increased consumption of a given form of energy. After identifying the correct supply curve, we next examine the demand-side effects, especially second best corrections that capture interactions between different energy subsectors. This second step is just as important as the first one, and therefore it will be examined in some detail.

In Figure 10.2, the market-priced demand curve for the form of energy under consideration is given by the curve PD(Q), which is the consumer's willingness to pay. Consider a small increment of consumption ΔQ at the market price level p. The traditional optimal pricing approach attempts to compare the incremental benefit of consumption due to ΔQ, (i.e. the area between the demand curve and x-axis), with the corresponding supply cost, (i.e. the area between the supply curve and x-axis). However, since MOC is shadow priced, PD must also be transformed into a shadow-priced curve to make the comparison valid. This is done by taking the increment of expenditure $p\Delta Q$, and asking what is the shadow-priced marginal cost of resources used up elsewhere in the economy, if this amount $p\Delta Q$ (in market prices) is devoted to alternative consumption (and/or investment).

Suppose that the shadow cost of this alternative pattern of expenditure is $b(p\Delta Q)$, where b is called a conversion factor. Then the transformed PD curve, which represents the shadow costs of alternative consumption foregone, is given by PD(Q); in figure 10.2, it is assumed that $b < 1$. Thus at the price p, incremental benefits EGJL exceed incremental costs EFKL. The optimal consumption level is Q_{opt}, where the MOC and b.PD curves cross, or equivalently where a new pseudo-supply curve MOC/b and the market demand curve PD intersect. The optimal or efficient selling price to be charged to consumers (because they react only along the market demand curve PD, rather than the shadow-priced curve b.PD) will be $p_e = $ MOC/b at the actual market clearing point B. At this level of consumption, the shadow costs and benefits of marginal consumption are equal, that is, MOC $=$ b.PD. Since b depends on user specific consumption patterns, different values of the efficient price p_e may be derived for various consumer categories, all based on the same value of MOC. We clarify the foregoing by considering several specific practical examples.

First, suppose that all the expenditure ($p\Delta Q$) is used to purchase a substitute fuel; that is assume complete substitution. Then the conversion factor b is the relative distortion or ratio of the shadow price to market price of this other fuel. Therefore $p_e = $ MOC/b represents a specific second-best adjustment to the MOC of the first fuel, to compensate for the distortion in the price of the substitute fuel. Next, consider a less specific case in which the amount ($p\Delta Q$) is used to buy an average basket of goods. If the consumer is residential, b would be the ratio of the shadow price to the market price of the household's market basket (here, b is also called the consumption conversion factor). The most general case would be when the consumer was unspecified, or detailed information on consumer categories was unavailable, so that b would be the ratio of the official exchange rate (OER) to the shadow exchange rate (SER), which is also called the standards conversion factor (SCF). This represents a global second-best correction for the divergence between market and shadow prices averaged throughout the economy.

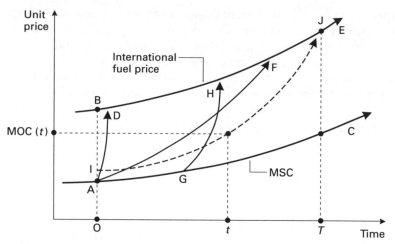

Figure 10.3   Marginal supply curve of a domestic non-renewable resource

Extensions to the basic pricing model

The analysis so far has been static. However, in many instances the situation with regard to the availability of a given energy source, interfuel substitution possibilities, and so on tends to vary over time, thus leading to disequilibrium in certain fuel markets, and divergence of the short-run price from the long-run optimal price. This aspect is illustrated below by means of an example that shows how the optimal depletion rate and time path for MOC of a domestic non-renewable resource will be affected by varying demand conditions, especially the degree to which the resource can be traded, extent of reserves, and substitution possibilities.

Suppose that the present-day marginal supply cost (MSC) (including extraction costs, and additional transport and environmental costs, etc., where appropriate) of a domestic energy source such as coal lies below the thermal equivalency price of an internationally traded fuel (e.g., petroleum or high-quality coal), as indicated by points A and B in figure 10.3. The international energy price that acts as the benchmark is assumed to rise steadily in real terms, along the path BE. Let us first examine two polar extremes based on simple, intuitively appealing arguments.

First, if the reserves are practically infinite and the use of this fuel at the margin will not affect exports or substitution for imports of traded fuels, then the MOC of the domestic energy source in the long run would continue to be based on the marginal supply cost, that is, along the path AC, which is upward sloping to allow for increases in real factor costs or extraction costs. On the other hand, suppose there is a ready export market for the indigenous resource, or substitution possibilities with respect to imported fuels. In this case the marginal use of this resource will reduce export earnings or increase the import bill for the international fuels in the short run, because the reserves are small or output capacity is limited. Then, the marginal opportunity cost would tend to follow the path AD and rise quickly toward parity with the international energy price.

The actual situation is likely to fall between these two extremes, thus yielding alternative price such as AFE or AGHE. Here, the initial use of the resource has no marginal impact on exports or import substitution, but there is gradual depletion of finite domestic reserves over time, and eventual transition to higher-priced fuels in the future. For a given volume of reserves, the rate of depletion of the domestic energy source will be greater and the time to depletion will be shorter if its price is maintained low (i.e., on the path AGHE) for as long as possible rather than when the price rises steadily (i.e., along path AFE). The macroeconomic consequences of the path AGHE are also more undesirable because of the sudden price increase at the point of transition, when the domestic resource is exhausted. In practice the price path may well be determined by non-economic factors. For example, the price of newly discovered gas or coal may have to be kept low for some years to capture the domestic market and displace the use of imported liquid fuels (which continue to be subsidized for political reasons). In general, the desire to keep energy prices low as long as possible must be balanced against the need to avoid a large price shock in the future.

More rigorous dynamic models, which maximize the net economic benefits of energy consumption over a long period, have been developed to determine the optimal price path and depletion rate; however, these models depend on factors such as the social discount rate, the size of reserves, the growth of demand, and the cost and time lag needed to develop a backstop technology (which could replace the international energy price as the upper bound on price). Uncertainties in future supply and demand – such as the possibility of discovering new energy resources or technologies – add to the complexities of dynamic analysis. The classical argument was developed by Hotelling in 1931. This approach indicates that the rate of increase in the optimal rent (or difference between price and marginal extraction cost) for the resource should equal the rate of return on capital (r). This implies that the optimal path MOC would be IJE in figure 10.3, defined at any time t by

$$MOC(t) = MSC(t) + JL/(1 + r)^{T-t}$$

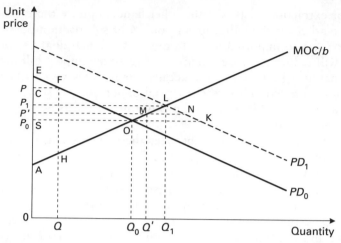

Figure 10.4   Demand growth

where JL is the rent at the time of depletion T. Thus MOC consists of the current marginal costs of extraction, transport, environmental degradation, and so on (MSC), plus the appropriately discounted "user cost" or foregone surplus benefits of future consumption (JL). As T approaches infinity, IJ would tend toward AC, which is the infinite reserve case, while as T falls to zero, IJ would approximate AD more closely, corresponding to the case of very small reserves and rapid transition to the expensive fuel.

We now consider another type of dynamic effect due to the growth of demand from year 0 to year 1, which leads to an outward shift in the market demand curve from PD_0 to PD_1 as shown in figure 10.4. Assuming that the correct market clearing price P_0 was prevailing in year 0, excess demand equal OK will occur in year 1. Ideally, the supply should be increased to Q_1, and the new optimal market clearing price established at P_1. However, the available information concerning the demand curve PD_1 may be incomplete, making it difficult to locate the point L.

Fortunately, the technical-economic relationships underlying the production function or known international prices usually permit the marginal opportunity cost curve to be determined more accurately. Therefore, as a first step, the supply may be increased to an immediate level Q', at the price p'. Observation of the excess demand MN indicates that both the supply and, if necessary, also the marginal cost price should be further increased. Conversely, if we overshoot L and end up in a situation of excess supply, then it may be necessary to wait until the growth of demand catches up with the oversupply. In this interactive

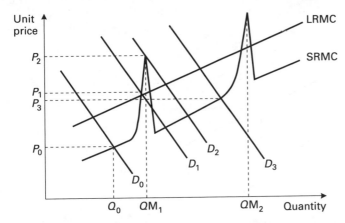

Figure 10.5   Long- and short-run marginal costs (LRMC, SRMC)

manner, it is possible to move along the MOC curve toward the optimal market clearing point. As we approach it, note that the optimum is also shifting with demand growth, and therefore we may never hit this moving target. However, the basic guideline of pegging the price to the marginal opportunity cost of supply and expanding output until the market clears is still valid.

Next, we examine the practical complications raised by price feedback effects. Typically, a long-range demand forecast is made assuming some given future evolution of prices, a least-cost investment program is determined to meet this demand, and optimal prices are computed on the basis of the latter. However, if the estimated optimal price that is to be imposed on consumers is significantly different from the original assumption regarding the evolution of prices, then the first-round price estimates must be fed back into the model to revise the demand forecast and repeat the calculation.

In theory, this iterative procedure could be repeated until future demand, prices, and MOC estimates become mutually self-consistent. In practice, uncertainties in price elasticities of demand and other data may dictate a more pragmatic approach in which the MOC would be used to devise prices after only one iteration. The behavior of demand is then observed over some time period and the first round prices are revised to move closer to the optimum, which may itself have shifted as described earlier.

When MOC is based on marginal production costs, the effect of capital indivisibilities or lumpiness of investments causes difficulties in many energy subsectors. Thus, owing to economies of scale, investments for electric power systems, gas production and transport, oil refining,

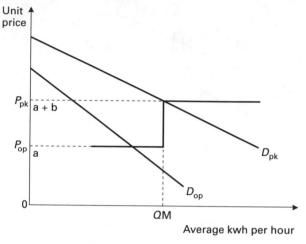

Figure 10.6   Peak load pricing

coal mining, reforestation, and so on tend to be large and long lived. As shown in figure 10.5, suppose that in year 0 the maximum supply capacity is QM_1, while the optimal price and output combination (p_0, Q_0) prevails, corresponding to demand curve D_0 and the short-run marginal cost curve SRMC (e.g., variable, operating, and maintenance costs).

As demand grows form D_0 to D_1 over time and the limit of existing capacity is reached, the price must be increased to p_1 to clear the market – that is, "pricing rationing" occurs. When the demand curve has shifted to D_2 and the price is p_2, capacity is increased to QM_2. However, as soon as the capacity increment is completed and becomes a sunk cost, price should fall to the old trend of SRMC – for example, p_3 is the optimum price corresponding to demand D_3. Generally, the large price fluctuations during this process will be disruptive and unacceptable to consumers. This practical problem may be avoided by adopting a long-run marginal cost (LRMC) approach, which provides the required price stability while retaining the basic principle of matching willingness to pay and incremental supply costs. Essentially, the future capital costs of a single project or an investment program are distributed over the stream of output expected during the lifetime of this plant. This average investment cost per unit of incremental output is added to variable cost (SRMC), to yield LRMC, as shown in figure 10.5.

Another method of allocating capacity costs, known as peak load pricing, is particularly relevant for electricity and also natural gas. The basic peak load pricing model shown in figure 10.6 has two demand curves; for example, D_{pk} could represent the peak demand during the *x* daylight and evening hours of the day when electric loads are large, while D_{op} would indicate the off-peak demand during the remaining $(24 - x)$ hours when loads are light. The marginal cost curve is simplified assuming a single type of plant with the fuel, operating, and maintenance costs given by the constant a, and the incremental cost of capacity given by the constant b. The static diagram has been drawn to indicate that the pressure on capacity arises due to peak demand D_{pk}, while the off-peak demand D_{op} does not infringe on the capacity Q. The optimal pricing rule now has two parts corresponding to two distinct rating periods (i.e., differentiated by the time of day):

peak period price p_{pk} $\quad = a + b$
off-peak period price p_{op} $\quad = a.$

The logic of this simple result is that peak period users, who are the cause of capacity additions, should bear full responsibility for the capacity costs as well as fuel, operating, and maintenance costs, while off-peak consumers pay only the latter costs. Peak load pricing can also be applied in different seasons of the year.

Related problems of allocating joint costs arise in other energy sub-sectors as well – an example is the allocation of capacity costs of natural gas, or of refinery costs among different petroleum products. The former may be treated like the electricity case. For oil products, the light refinery cuts that are tradable, such as kerosene, gasoline, and diesel, have benchmark international prices. However, other items like heavy residual oils may have to be treated like non-tradables. Furthermore, associated gas that may be flared at the refinery is often assumed to have a low MOC, although subsequent storage and handling for use as LPG will add to the costs. A more rigorous approach would be to use a linear programming model of a refinery to solve the dual problem as a means of determining shadow prices of distillates, as discussed in chapter 6.

A more general aspect of the capacity constraint, which encompasses peak load pricing, is that energy prices have to be structured. For example, the MOC shown in figure 10.2 may vary by the type of consumer, geographic location, time and level of consumption, voltage level (for electricity), and so on. These values of MOC then have to be modified to reflect demand-side considerations (as discussed earlier). Therefore, the economically efficient prices in a given energy subsector may exhibit considerable structuring.

The interrelated issues of supply and demand uncertainty, safety margins, and shortage costs also raise complications. In the case of electricity the least-cost system expansion plan to meet an electricity demand forecast is generally determined assuming some (arbitrary) target level of system reliability for the loss-of-load probability (LOLP) or reserve margin. Therefore, marginal costs depend on the target reliability level, when in fact economic theory suggests that reliability should also be treated as a variable to be optimized, and both price and capacity (or equivalently, reliability) levels should be optimized simultaneously. The optimal price is the marginal cost price as described earlier, while the optimal reliability level is achieved when the marginal cost of capacity additions (to improve the reserve margin) are equal to the expected value of economic cost savings to consumers due to electricity supply shortages averted by those capacity increments. These considerations lead to a more generalized approach to system expansion planning, in which we seek to minimize total costs consisting of the sum of system costs as well as shortage costs suffered by consumers – by optimizing the reliability level as described above. This total cost minimizing criterion effectively subsumes the traditional system planning rule of minimizing only the system costs. The underlying model is explained in some detail in chapter 8.

This approach may be generalized for application in other energy subsectors. Thus while sophisticated measures of reliability like LOLP do not exist outside the power subsector, the concept of minimizing total costs to society is still relevant. For example, in oil and gas investment planning, the cost of shortages due to gasoline queues, lack of furnace oil, or gas for domestic and industrial use may be traded off against the supply costs of increased storage capacity and greater delivery capability incurred by augmenting surface transport or pipeline systems. Clearly, these additional considerations would modify the marginal costs of energy supply and thus effect optimal pricing policies.

Finally, externalities, especially environmental considerations, have to be included as far as possible in the determination of efficient energy prices. For example, if the building of a new hydroelectric dam results in the flooding of land that had recreational or agricultural value, or if urban transportation growth leads to congestion and air pollution, these costs should be reflected in MOC. While such externality costs may, in certain cases, be quite difficult to quantify, they may already be included (at least partially) on the supply side, in terms of measures taken to avoid environmental degradation, for example, the cost of pollution control equipment at an oil refinery or coal-burning electricity plant, or the cost of landscaping strip-mined land. Estimation of environmental costs is most problematic in the case of non-commercial or traditional energy sources such as fuelwood, where marginal opportunity costs could be based (when appropriate) on the externality costs of deforestation, erosion, loss of watershed, and so on. Other measures of the economic value of traditional fuel would include the opportunity cost of labor required to collect fuelwood, or the cost savings from displaced substitute fuels such as kerosene and LPG.

Adjustments to efficient prices to meet other objectives

Once efficient energy prices have been determined, the second stage of pricing must be carried out to meet social, financial, political, and other constraints. We note that efficient energy prices deviate from the prices calculated on the basis of financial costs, because shadow prices are used instead of the market prices. This is done to correct for distortions in the economy. Therefore, the constraints that force further departures from efficient prices (in the second stage of the pricing procedure) may also be considered as distortions that impose their own shadow values on the calculation.

Subsidized prices and lifeline rates
Socio-political or equity arguments are often advanced in favor of subsidized prices or "lifeline" rates for energy, especially where the costs of energy consumption are high relative to the incomes of poor households. Economic reasoning based on externality effects may also be used to support subsidies, for example cheap kerosene to reduce excessive firewood use and prevent deforestation, erosion, and so on. To prevent leakages and abuse of such subsidies, energy suppliers must act as discriminating monopolists. Targeting specific consumer classes (for example, poor households) and limiting the cheap price only to a minimum block of consumption are easiest to achieve, in practice, for metered forms of energy like gas or electricity. Other means of discrimination, such as rationing, licensing, etc., may also be required. All these complex and interrelated issues require detailed analysis.

The concept of a subsidized "social" block, or "lifeline" rate, for low-income consumers has another important economic rationale, based on the income redistribution argument. We clarify this point with the aid of figure 10.7 which shows the respective demand curves for energy AB and GH of low (I_1) and average (I_2) income domestic users, the social tariff p_s over the minimum consumption block 0 to Q_{min}, and the efficient price level p_e. All tariff levels are in domestic market prices. If the actual price $p = p_e$, the average household will be consuming at the "optimal" level Q_2, but the poor household will not be able to afford the service.

If increased benefits accruing to the poor have a high social value, then, although in nominal domestic prices the point A lies below p_e, the consumer surplus portion ABF multiplied by an appropriate social

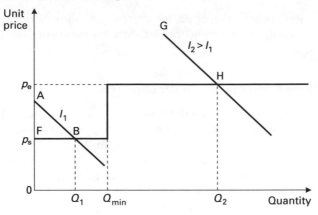

Figure 10.7   Lifeline rates

weight w could be greater than the shadow price of supply (see the appendix for details). The adoption of the block tariff shown in figure 10.7, consisting of the lifeline rate p_s, followed by the full tariff p_e, helps capture the consumer surplus of the poor user but does not affect the optimum consumption pattern of the average consumer.

In practice, the magnitude Q_{min} has to carefully determined, to avoid subsidizing relatively well-off consumers; it should be based on acceptable criteria for identifying "low-income" groups and reasonable estimates of their minimum consumption levels (e.g., sufficient to supply basic energy requirements for the household). The level of p_s relative to the efficient price may be determined on the basis of the poor consumer's income level relative to some critical consumption level, as shown in the appendix. The financial requirements of the energy sector would also be considered in determining p_s and Q_{min}. This approach may be reinforced by an appropriate supply policy (e.g., subsidized house connections for electricity and special supply points for kerosene).

Financial viability
The financial constraints most often encountered relate to meeting the revenue requirements of the sector, and are often embodied in criteria such as some target financial rate of return on assets, or an acceptable rate of contribution toward the future investment program. In principle, for state-owned energy suppliers, the most efficient solution would be to set the price at the efficient level, and to rely on government to subsidize losses or tax surpluses exceeding sector financial needs. In practice, some measure of financial autonomy and self-sufficiency is an important goal for the sector. Because of the premium that is placed on public

funds, a pricing policy that results in failure to achieve minimum financial targets for continued operation of the sector would rarely be acceptable. The converse and more typical case, where efficient pricing would result in financial surpluses well in excess of traditional revenue targets, may be politically unpopular, especially for an electric utility. Therefore in either case, changes in revenues have to be achieved by adjusting the efficient prices.

It is intuitively clear that discriminating between the various consumer categories, so that the greatest divergence from the marginal opportunity cost-based price occurs for the consumer group with the lowest price elasticity of demand, and vice versa, will result in the smallest deviations from the "optimal" levels of consumption consistent with a strict efficiency pricing regime. In many countries the necessary data for the analysis of demand by consumer categories is rarely available, so rule-of-thumb methods of determining the appropriate tariff structure have to be adopted. However, if the energy subsector exhibits increasing costs (i.e., if marginal costs are greater than average costs), the fiscal implications should be exploited to the full. Thus, for example, electric power tariffs (especially in a developing country) constitute a practical means of raising public revenues in a manner that is generally consistent with the economic efficiency objective, at least for the bulk of the consumers who are not subsidized; at the same time they help supply basic energy needs to low-income groups. Similar arguments may be made in the petroleum subsector, where high prices for gasoline, based on efficiency, externality, and conservation arguments, may be used to cross-subsidize the "poor man's" fuel – kerosene, or diesel used for transportation.

Other considerations
There are several additional economic, political, and social considerations that may be adequate justification for departing from a strict efficient pricing policy. The decision to provide commercial energy like kerosene or electricity in a remote rural area (which often also entails subsidies because the beneficiaries are not able to pay the full price based on high unit costs), could be made on completely non-economic grounds, e.g., for general socio-political reasons, such as maintaining a viable regional industrial or agricultural base, stemming rural to urban migration, or alleviating local political discontent. Similarly, uniform nationwide energy prices are a political necessity in many countries, although this policy may, for example, imply subsidization of consumers in remote rural areas (where energy transport costs are high) by energy users in urban centers. However, the full economic benefits of

such a course of action may be greater than the apparent efficiency costs that arise from any divergence between actual and efficient price levels. Again this possibility is likely to be much more significant in a developing country than in a developed one, not only because of the high cost of energy relative to incomes in the former, but also because the available administrative or fiscal machinery to redistribute incomes (or to achieve regional or industrial development objectives by other means) is frequently ineffective.

The conservation objective (to reduce dependence on imported energy, improve the trade balance, and so on) usually runs counter to subsidy arguments. Therefore, it may be necessary to restrict cheap energy to productive economic sectors that need to be strengthened, while in the case of the basic energy needs of households, the energy price could be sharply increased for consumption beyond appropriate minimum levels. In other cases, conservation and subsidized energy prices may be consistent. For example, cheap kerosene might be required, especially in rural areas, to reduce excessive woodfuel consumption and thus prevent deforestation and erosion.

It is particularly difficult to raise prices to anywhere near the efficient levels where low income and a tradition of subsidized energy have increased consumer resistance. In practice, price changes have to be gradual, in view of the costs that may be imposed on those who have already incurred expenditures on energy-using equipment and made other decisions, while expecting little or no change in traditional energy pricing policies. At the same time, a steady price rise will prepare consumers for high future energy prices. The ·efficiency costs of a gradual price increase can be seen as an implicit shadow value placed on the social benefits that result from this policy.

Finally, owing to the practical difficulties of metering, price discrimination, and billing, and the need to avoid confusing consumers, the pricing structure may have to be simplified. Thus, the number of customer categories, rating periods, consumption blocks, and so on, will have to be limited. Electricity and gas offer the greatest possibilities for structuring. The degree of sophistication of metering depends, among other things, on the net benefits of metering and on problems of installation and maintenance. In general, various forms of peak electricity pricing (i.e., using maximum demand or time-of-day metering) would be particularly applicable to large-, medium-, and high-voltage industrial and commercial consumers. However, for very poor consumers receiving a subsidized rate of electricity, a simple current limiting device may suffice, because the cost of even simple kwh metering may exceed the net benefit (which equals the savings in supply costs due to reduced consumption, less the decrease in consumption benefits). For electricity or gas, different charges for various consumption blocks may be effectively applied with conventional metering. However, for liquid fuels like kerosene, subsidized or discriminatory pricing would usually require schemes involving rationing and coupons, and could lead to leakage and abuses.

Pricing policy in practice: adjusting to lower world oil prices

With the sharp decline in the world oil price since 1986, governments have been faced with a new set of challenges for domestic energy pricing policy. To what extent should the windfall be passed to consumers? Should domestic prices be adjusted uniformly, or should the cuts be selective? How quickly should any adjustments be made? And to what extent should the pricing system itself be reformed to better cope with more volatile prices?

As might be expected, the response of governments to the sharp drop in oil prices in 1986 shows wide variations. At one extreme, perhaps, is India which increased domestic prices for some petroleum products in Spring of 1986. Morocco has elected essentially to maintain 1985 price levels, with the foreign exchange windfall accruing to the government. Pakistan has adopted an intermediate position, with selected price cuts, whilst Thailand made cuts across all products on three occasions in 1986.

Nevertheless such price adjustments were generally taken on the basis of *ad hoc*, short-term political considerations rather than as a consequence of a more comprehensive, longer term policy to deal with the new price environment that is likely to be characterized by substantial price fluctuations, both up and down, for the foreseeable future. Indeed, there are very good reasons for governments to try to smooth out some of the more violent fluctuations in the interests of maintaining some consistency in the signals given to consumers (in the third quarter of 1986, for example, Morocco was able to buy substantial quantities of spot crude at below $9.00, a situation that was quickly reversed with prices settling in the $15–18/bbl region in early 1987).

Beyond the already noted need to take a broader perspective than to look merely at the oil import bill, there are numerous issues that must be examined in the process of defining an appropriate response to the new price environment, of which the most difficult to deal with is the balance between short-term and long-term considerations in a price environment characterized by great uncertainty and volatility. Since the conclusion of the Gulf War, prices have returned to the $15–25/bbl range, and there are strong economic efficiency arguments for passing through the price decrease to consumers, especially to maintain the competitiveness of energy-intensive exporters.

On the other hand, if, as some analysts expect, oil prices will again rise sharply in the mid to late 1990s, then the short-term benefits of passing through the windfall may be offset by the high costs of restarting programs built up over the past decade. This applies to both demand management programs (where many programs were beginning to show substantial progress by the early 1980s in overcoming non-market barriers to energy efficiency investments), as well as resource development programs to replace imported oil.

Indeed, one of the arguments advanced in India in Spring of 1986 to maintain (and in some cases even increase) domestic prices was to maintain investment incentives for domestic oil development. For example, the debate over whether or not to proceed with the secondary recovery program for the Bombay High oil field, aimed at keeping production at the 300,000 bbl/day level for another five years, typified such concerns; while the Ministry of Petroleum asked for production cuts, this was opposed by the Oil and Natural Gas Commission (ONGC), concerned that cutting production would aggravate water encroachment.

There are similar concerns in many other developing countries that had started to be successful in developing their own domestic hydrocarbon resources. Yet even aside from any irreversible physical impacts that follow from such production cutbacks, the experience of the 1970s indicates clearly that there are substantial lags in getting new programs started even when prices are increasing sharply, with substantial negative impacts in the interim.

The problems of adjustment to lower oil prices are even more difficult in countries where substantial investments for domestic oil, gas, and coal resource development were made over the past decade, or planned for the immediate future, on the basis of high oil prices. Natural gas pricing in particular has been difficult for countries such as Pakistan and Thailand. And many projects planned for the near future, such as the expansion of the Jerada anthracite mine complex in Morocco, for which the decision was made prior to the 1986 drop in world oil prices, need to be reevaluated.

Yet in the absence of a comprehensive pricing framework for the entire sector, such decisions will be particularly hard to make. Where multi-national oil companies are active in resource development, as in Thailand, they were quick to scale down their exploration programs as international oil prices fell in the mid 1980s. However, the state-owned entities typically responsible for coal and natural gas development in developing countries are subject to broader political pressures, and are generally reluctant, and much slower, to change investment plans.

In general, the energy pricing systems currently in place in developing countries reflect the legacy of the problems of adjustment to increasing oil prices over the past decade. Subsidies became widespread as governments attempted to shield consumers from price increases. In many cases, unrealistic exchange rate policies led to domestic energy prices that were far below international price levels. And some countries introduced complex tariff structures and cross subsidization mechanisms (such as the Oil Fund in Thailand, the Caisse de Compensation in Morocco, the Stabilization Fund in Senegal) that tended to cause new distortions and administrative problems. Indeed, many of the problems characteristic of administered pricing systems (such as the diversion of residentially priced LPG to automotive and industrial use to avoid the higher tariffs for these latter categories, or the use of subsidized kerosene to dilute non-subsidized fuels) might have been avoided in a deregulated environment.

A framework for policy impact analysis

The point that the primary role of energy modeling is quantitative impact assessment of policy options is nowhere better illustrated than in the area of pricing. There are countless examples of situations where there is general agreement that one needs to move from some current situation, often characterized by substantial administrative complexity and significant distortions, to one based upon economic rationality along the lines elaborated above. But the difficulties arise in implementation, of moving toward some goal in such a way that the impacts on affected parties can be managed and mitigated if necessary.

Proposals to change the energy pricing structure will invariably encounter very close scrutiny, if not strong opposition, from powerful institutions. Because of the importance of the energy sector as a revenue source to the government, Ministries of Finance, and especially Customs in the case of oil-importing countries, will examine proposed changes from their particular viewpoint of revenue maximization. Sector institutions, especially refineries, national oil companies and the electric utility, are often very powerful politically; they will examine any proposed changes from the standpoint of the impact on their financial statements, and their ability to finance investment proposals. Finally, it is not at all uncommon for changes in the consumer price to require approval by the office of the Prime Minister or the President, whose concern will be the impact upon consumers, and upon low-income consumers in particular.

TUNISIA

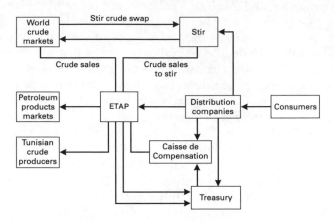

SENEGAL

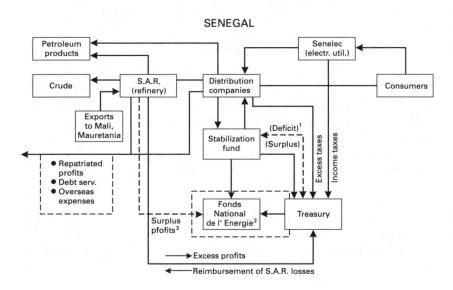

[1] Fund is currently in deficit.

[2] Fonds Natl. D'Energie is a treasury account.

[3] S.A.R. has yet to contribute to the Fonds National.

Figure 10.8   Flow of petroleum related funds in Tunisia and Senegal

To ignore these practicalities simply courts failure. Proponents of pricing policy changes must therefore come to the political negotiating table with appropriate information about the specific and detailed impacts upon the affected parties. In order to do this it is necessary to have a comprehensive understanding of the role of prices in the flow of funds between the individual participants in the energy system. This requires, in fact, the ability to simultaneously simulate the financial statements of all of the major energy sector institutions, the flow of funds among them, and between them and the treasury, consumers, the Central Bank, and overseas entities from whom energy is bought and sold. It is a task ideally suited to spreadsheet modeling.

The flow of funds can in fact be extremely complex, as suggested by the examples on figure 10.8. In Senegal, for example, there is a Stabilization fund whose purpose is to cross-subsidize petroleum product prices. Any surplus from this fund, as well as any excess profits from the refinery, are remitted to the National Energy Fund, whose purpose is to finance energy studies and projects. Indeed, it is often quite difficult to model accurately the complex administered pricing systems, particularly in the case of institutions whose operating deficits may be covered by treasury subsidies, or where complex royalty and/or production sharing agreements exist with multi-national oil companies that may be active in oil exploration and development.

Analytically, such models typically consist of a set of non-linear equations. As an illustrative, albeit highly simplified, example, consider the following equation set that links price, investment, and consumption:

$$Q = a\lambda^\beta$$
$$I = \gamma(Q - Q_0)^\delta$$
$$\lambda = \sigma\frac{I}{Q} + \pi$$

where
λ = price,
Q = consumption,
I = investment,
and where a, β, γ, δ, σ, π, and Q_0 are constants. The first equation is a demand function, that hypothesizes that demand is some function of price, raised to the power of some constant (the price elasticity). The second equation says that the investment requirement is a function of the growth in demand, subject to scale economies; and the third equation defines price as the sum of the import price (π) and a markup to cover investment costs.

Box 10.1 *Convergence properties of iterative replacement algorithms*

To illustrate the convergence properties, assume the following numerical structure:

$$Q = 1.0\lambda^{-0.2}$$
$$I = 10Q^{0.5}$$
$$\lambda = 0.1\left(\frac{I}{Q}\right) + 32$$

where $\pi = 32$ represents the world oil price in \$/bbl, λ is the retail oil price in \$/bbl (ignoring any distinction between crude and products), Q is consumption in million bbl/yr, and $\beta = -0.2$ is the price elasticity of demand. To solve this system we choose some trial value of λ, say $\lambda_o = 40$, and then recalculate each equation *seriatim*:

$$\lambda_0 = 40$$
$$Q_1 = 0.478 \ (= 40^{-0.2})$$
$$I_1 \ = 6.91 \ \ (= 10(0.478)^{0.5})$$
$$\lambda_1 \ = 33.44 \ (= 0.1)6.91(0.478) + 32)$$
$$Q_2 = 0.4956(= 33.44^{-0.2})$$
$$I_2 \ = 7.04 \ \ (= 10(0.4956)^{0.5})$$
$$\lambda_2 \ = 33.42 \ (= 0.1(7.04/0.4956) + 32)$$
$$Q_3 = 0.4956(= 33.43^{-0.2})$$

Already we see that successive values of Q are to within three decimal places: evidently this model converges very rapidly indeed.

We thus have three simultaneous equations in three unknowns; because of the price elasticity and scale economy representations they are in fact non-linear. For such systems a variety of methods are possible for solution: a very efficient one is known as Newton's Method, which provides very good convergence performance. Unfortunately it requires the evaluation of the first derivatives of the equation set, which makes programming in a spreadsheet environment somewhat difficult. However, simple iterative replacement works for most such representations of pricing systems, and especially well in spreadsheet models even when there are several thousand equations (although convergence may well have to be established on a case by case basis). In box 10.1 we illustrate the principles of this method, and the convergence properties of our simple model.

On figure 10.9 we illustrate the actual results of such a model, in which we show the value of the price and demand variables through successive iterations of a such a model of Costa Rica. Note that the simulation converges to the same equilibrium price regardless of the first trial value for price. Obviously this is a most important characteristic for the procedure to have practical value!

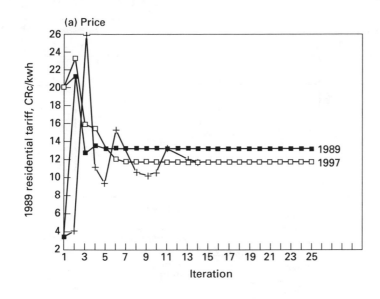

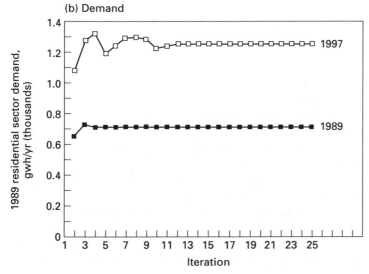

Figure 10.9   Convergence performance of an electricity model simulation of Costa Rica

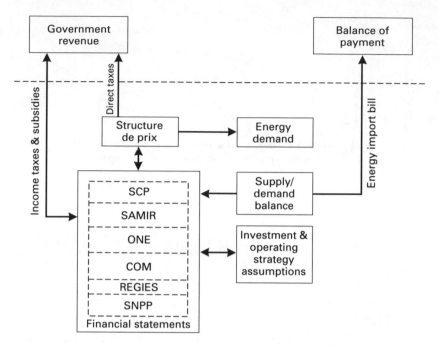

Figure 10.10   The Morocco pricing model

Such models have been built for a number of countries over the past decade, including Sri Lanka, Tunisia, Thailand, and Morocco. The implementation for Morocco is depicted on figure 10.10. Programmed in the new Version 3 of LOTUS 1-2-3, separate spreadsheets are used for each institution, the energy balance, and the cashflow analysis: although they are simultaneously loaded into memory together with a macro library for full model simulations, each of the individual financial models can also be run in a stand-alone mode. (SCP and SAMIR are the two refineries, ONE is the electric utility: not shown are the additional spreadsheets for the petroleum product distribution company SNPP, the "Regies," that distribute electricity (and water), and CDM the national coal company that operates the Jerada Anthracite complex.) There are several thousand active rows in the model, which occupies over 4Mb of RAM. A full iterative solution requires about one minute on a 25Mhz 386-based microcomputer (see IDEA, 1990 for a detailed documentation of the model).

Version 3 of LOTUS is particularly suited to pricing models because it permits three-dimensional structures. On figure 10.11 we show the layout

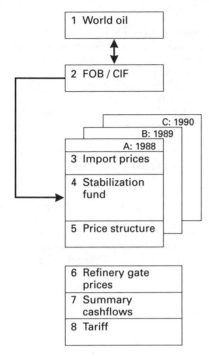

Figure 10.11   Spreadsheet design for the Morocco model

of the spreadsheet that models the price structure and the flow of funds in the petroleum system. As in the energy balance, the columns of such a three-dimensional spreadsheet represent different fuels, the rows the individual line items of the price structure (see figure 10.11), and the third dimension represents time.

Annex: Electricity pricing

As mentioned earlier the relevant MOC for the electric power sector is the long-run marginal cost (LRMC) of supply. Thus the first stage of the LRMC approach is the calculation of pure or strict LRMC that reflects the economic efficiency criterion. If price was set strictly equal to LRMC, consumers could indicate their willingness to pay for more consumption, thus signaling the justification of further investment to expand capacity. In the second stage of tariff setting, ways are sought in which the strict LRMC may be adjusted to meet the other objectives, among which the financial requirement is most important. If prices were set equal to strict LRMC, it is likely that there will be a financial surplus. This is because marginal costs tend to be higher than average costs when the unit costs of supply are increasing. In principle, financial surpluses of the utility may be taxed away by the state, but in practice the use of power price pricing as a tool for raising central government revenues is usually politically unpopular and rarely applied. Such surplus revenues can also be utilized in a way that is consistent with the other objectives. For example, the connection charges can be subsidized without violating the LRMC price, or low-income consumers could be provided with a subsidized block of electricity to meet their basic requirement, thus satisfying socio-political objectives. Conversely, if marginal costs are below average costs – typically as a result of economies of scale – then pricing at the strict LRMC will lead to a financial deficit. This will have to be made up, for example, by higher lump sum connection charges, flat-rate charges, or even government subsidies.

Another reason for deviating from the strict LRMC arises because of second-best considerations. When prices elsewhere in the economy do not reflect marginal costs, especially for electric power substitutes and complements, then departures from the strict marginal costs pricing rule for electricity services would be justified. For example, in rural areas, inexpensive alternative energy may be available in the form of subsidized kerosene and/or gas. In this case, pricing electricity below the LRMC may be justified, to prevent excessive use of the alternative forms of energy. Similarly, if incentives are provided to import private generators and their fuel is also subsidized, then charging the full marginal cost to industrial consumers may encourage them to purchase their own or captive power plant. This is economically less efficient from a national perspectives. Since the computation of strict LRMC is based on the power utilities' least-cost expansion program, LRMC may also need to be modified by short-term considerations if previously unforeseen events make the long-run system plan suboptimal in the short run. Typical examples include a sudden reduction in demand growth and a large excess of installed capacity that may justify somewhat reduced capacity charges, or a rapid increase in fuel prices, which could warrant a short-term fuel surcharge.

The LRMC approach permits a high degree of tariff structuring. However, data constraints and the objective of simplifying metering and billing procedures usually requires that there should be practical limit to differentiation of tariffs by : (a) major customer categories – residential, industrial, commercial, special, rural, and so on; (b) voltage levels (high, medium, and low); (c) time of day (peak, off-peak); and (d) geographic region. Finally, various other constraints also may be incorporated into the LRMC based tariffs, such as the political requirement of having a uniform national tariff, subsidizing rural electrification, and so on. In each case, however, such deviations from LRMC will impose an efficiency cost on the economy.

Thus, the LRMC approach provides an explicit framework for analyzing system costs and setting tariffs. If departures from the strict LRMC are required for non-economic reasons, then the economic efficiency cost of these deviations may be estimated roughly by comparing the impact of the modified tariff relative to (benchmark) strict LRMC. Since the cost structure may be studied in considerable detail during the LRMC calculations, this analysis also helps to pinpoint weaknesses and inefficiencies in the various parts of the power system – for example, overinvestment, unbalanced investment, or excessive losses at the generation, transmission, and distribution levels, in different geographic areas, and so on. This aspect is particularly useful in improving system expansion planning.

Finally, any LRMC-based tariff is a compromise between many different objectives. Therefore, there is no "ideal" tariff. By using the LRMC approach, it is possible to revise and improve the tariff on a consistent and ongoing basis, and thereby approach the optimum price over a period of several years, without subjecting long-standing consumers to "unfair" shocks, in the form of large abrupt price changes.

Calculating the strict LRMC

Strict LRMC may be defined practically as the incremental cost of optimum adjustments in the system expansion plan and system operations attributable to a small increment of demand which is sustained into the future. The term long-run incremental cost may also be used interchangeably with LRMC, because the changes refer to small but finite variations. LRMC must be structured within a disaggregated framework, based chiefly on technical grounds. This structuring may include: differentiation of marginal costs by time of day, voltage level, geographic area, season of the year, and so on. The degree of structuring and sophistication of the LRMC calculation depends on data constraints and the usefulness of the results, given the practical problems of computing and applying a complex tariff; e.g., in theory, the LRMC of each individual consumer at each moment of time, may be estimated. The basic concepts for calculating strict LRMC are summarized below while details of theory and illustrative case studies may be found in Munasinghe and Warford (1981), and Turvey and Anderson (1977).

Cost categories and rating periods

The three broad categories of marginal costs are: capacity costs, energy costs, and consumer costs. Marginal capacity costs are basically the investment costs of generation, transmission, and distribution facilities associated with supplying additional kilowatts. Marginal energy costs are the fuel and operating costs of providing additional kilowatt-hours. Marginal customer costs are the incremental costs directly attributable to consumers including costs of hook-up, metering, and billing. Relevant operation and maintenance costs (O&M), as well as administrative and general costs (A&G) must also be allocated to these basic cost categories. Furthermore, where appropriate, these elements of LRMC must be structured by time of use, voltage level, and so on.

The first step in structuring is the selection of appropriate rating periods. The system load duration curves and generation schedules, should be examined to determine periods during which demand presses on capacity and supply costs are highest. These cyclical critical periods may be due to daily demand variations (e.g., evening lighting load), or seasonal variations in both demand (e.g., summer air conditioning peak load), and supply (e.g., dry season for hydro systems). To illustrate the principles of structuring and calculating strict LRMC, we begin with an all thermal system that does not exhibit marked seasonability of demand, choosing only two rating periods by time of day, i.e., peak and off-peak. Seasonal variations in LRMC and the analysis of hydro-electric systems are discussed later.

Marginal capacity costs

Consider in figure 10.12, the typical system annual load duration curve (LDC) ABEF for the starting year 0, divided into two rating periods: peak and

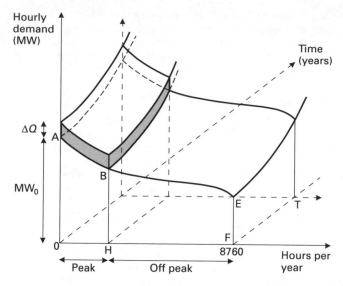

Figure 10.12   Typical annual load duration curve (LDC)

off-peak. As demand grows over time, the LDC increases in magnitude, and the resultant forecast of peak demand is given by the curve D in figure 10.13, starting from the initial value MW. The LRMC of capacity may be determined by asking the following question: what is the change in system capacity costs ΔC associated with a sustained increment ΔD in the long-run peak demand (as shown by the shaded area of figure 10.12 and the broken line $D + \Delta D$ in figure 10.13? Consequently, the LRMC of generation would be $(\Delta C/\Delta D)$, where the increment of demand ΔD is marginal both in time, and in terms of MW. In theory, ΔD can be either positive or negative, and generally the ratio $(\Delta C/\Delta D)$ will vary with the sign as well as the magnitude of ΔD. If many such values of $(\Delta C/\Delta D)$ are computed, it is possible to average them to obtain LRMC.

In an optimally planned system, the new incremental load would normally be met by advancing future plant or inserting new units such as gas turbines or peaking hydro plant. Using a computerized generation planning model, it is easy to determine the change in capacity costs ΔC by simulating the expansion path and system operation, with and without the demand increment ΔD. If a more sophisticated tariff structure having many rating periods is used, then the LRMC in any rating period may be estimated by running the computerized system expansion model with a sustained load increment added to the LDC during that particular period. This method that stimulates the optimal system planning process is based on the dynamic LRMC concept.

When constraints due to time, data, and facilities preclude this ideal approach, more approximate methods may be used. Simple considerations based on a more static interpretation of LRMC often yield very good results. Suppose that gas turbines are used for peaking; then the required LRMC of generating capacity $(\mathrm{LRMC_{Gen.Cap.}})$ may be approximated by the cost per kw

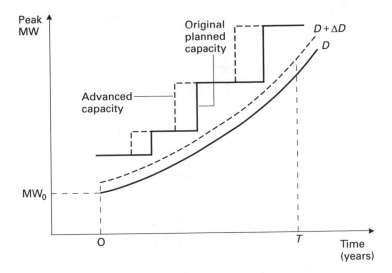

Figure 10.13 Forecast of peak power demand

installed, annuitized over the expected lifetime. This figure must be adjusted for the reserve margin (RM%) and losses due to station use (L_{su}%). Thus a typical expression would be:

$$LRMC_{Gen.Cap.} = (\text{Annuitized cost per kW})(1 + RM\%)/(1 - L_{su}\%).$$

In our basic model, all capacity costs are to be charged to peak period consumers. Therefore, if the capacity costs of base load generating units are included in the calculations, it is very important to net out potential fuel savings due to displacement of less efficient plant by these new base load units. Even intuitively, it would not be sensible to incorrectly charge peak consumers the high-capacity costs of expensive base load units (e.g., nuclear), thus encouraging them, for example to install their own captive gas turbine plant.

Next, the LRMC of transmission and distribution (T&D) are calculated. Generally, all T&D investment costs (except customer costs – discussed later) are allocated to incremental capacity, because the designs of these facilities are determined principally by the peak kilowatt that they carry rather than the kwh. However, particularly at the distribution level, the size of a given feeder may depend on local peak demand which may not occur within the system peak period and this could complicate the problem of allocating distribution capacity costs among the various rating periods (Boiteux and Stasi, 1964). The concept of structuring by voltage level may be introduced at this stage. Consider three supply voltage categories: high, medium, and low (HV, MV, LV). Since consumers at each voltage level are charged only upstream costs, capacity costs at each voltage level must be identified.

The simplest approach is to use the average incremental cost (AIC) method to estimate the LRMC of T&D. Suppose that in year i, ΔMw_i, and I_i are the increase in demand served (relative to the previous year), and the investment cost respectively. Then, the AIC of capacity is given by:

$$AIC = \frac{\displaystyle\sum_{t=0}^{T} \frac{I^t}{(1+r)^t}}{\displaystyle\sum_{i=L}^{T+L} \frac{\Delta MW_i}{(1+r)^t}}$$

where r is the discount rate (e.g., the opportunity cost of capital), T is the planning horizon (e.g., ten years), and L is the average time delay between the investment and commissioning dates for new facilities. We note that in the AIC method the actual additional increments of demand are considered as they occur, rather than the hypothetical fixed demand increment ΔD used (more rigorously) in calculating generation LRMC. However, because there is no problem of plant mix with T&D investments, AIC and the hypothetical increment method will yield similar results, while AIC is also usually much easier to calculate using readily available planning data. An alternative method of determining marginal T&D costs at several different voltage levels would be to use historical data to fit regression equations such as:

(Transmission costs) $= a + b$. (Peak demand).

However there is no guarantee that such past relationships would hold true in the future, as the system expands. Assume that the AIC of EHV and HV transmission has been computed and annuitized over the lifetime of the plant (e.g., thirty years) to yield the marginal costs $\Delta LRMC_{HV}$. Then, the total LRMC of capacity during the peak period, at the HV level would be:

$$LRMC_{HVCap.} = LRMC_{Gen.Cap.}/(1 - L_{HV}\%) + \Delta LRMC_{HV}$$

where $L_{HV}\%$ is the percentage of incoming peak power that is lost in the EHV and HV network. This procedure may be repeated at the MV and LV levels. The LRMC of T&D calculated in this way is based on actual growth of future demand, and averaged over many consumers. However, facilities associated with given generating sites or loads should be specifically allocated to these uses rather than averaged out, e.g., transmission spur line, exceptionally low or high distribution costs for one or more given customers.

Marginal energy costs and treatment of losses
The system lamda concept is useful in calculating marginal energy costs. The LRMC of peak period energy will be the running costs of the machines to be used last in the merit order, to meet the incremental peak kilowatt-hour represented by ΔD. In our model, this would be the fuel and operating costs of gas turbines, adjusted by the appropriate peak loss factors at each voltage level. Similarly, the LRMC of off-peak energy would usually be the running costs of the least efficient base load or cycling plant used during this period. Exceptions occur when the marginal plant used during a rating period was not necessarily the least efficient machine that could have been used. For example, less efficient plants, which have long start-up times and are required in the next rating period, may be operated earlier in the loading order than more efficient plant. This would correspond to minimization of operating costs over several rating

periods rather than on an hourly basis. Again since the heat rate of the plants could vary with output level, the simple linear relationship usually assumed between generation costs and kilowatt-hours may need to be replaced by a more realistic non-linear model. We note that the loss factors for adjusting off-peak costs will be smaller than the peak period loss factors when current flows are greatest (Cichetti *et al.*, 1977).

The treatment of losses raises several important issues. While total normal technical losses (including station use) vary from system to system, if these are significantly greater than about 15% of gross generation, then loss reduction should have a high priority. When engineering losses in excess of acceptable levels are routinely passed on to the customer, this may act as a disincentive to improvements in technical or administrative efficiency. Losses due to theft and unpaid bills are also often loaded on to paying customers. Here again, the issue is whether these non-technical losses could be reduced by appropriate measures, or if incremental consumption always has an avoidable component of such losses associated with it. Theft in US systems has been estimated to average about 2% of gross generation, but norms in developing countries may have to be set somewhat higher (Donziger, 1979; Boiteux and Stasi, 1964). The LRMC analysis at the generation, transmission, and distribution levels helps to establish whether these incremental costs are excessive because of overinvestment, high losses, or both.

Consumer costs

It has proved difficult to allocate part of the distribution system investment costs to customer costs, on the basis of a skeleton system required to serve a hypothetical minimum load. Similarly a regression analysis of past data to fit equations such as:

(Distribution costs) $= a + b$ (Peak demand) $+ c$ (Number of customers)

has not been too successful because peak demand and the number of customers are usually highly correlated. Therefore, general distribution network costs may be considered as capacity costs, while customer costs are defined as those which can be readily allocated to users. Initial customer costs consist of non-current expenses attributable to items such as service drop lines, meters, and labor for installation. These costs may be charged to the customer as a lump sum or distributed in payments over several years.

Recurrent customer costs that occur due to meter reading, billing, administrative, and other expenses, could be imposed as a recurring flat charge, in addition to kilowatt and kilowatt-hour charges. In general, the allocation of incremental (non-fuel operation, maintenance, and administrative) costs among the categories: capacity, energy, and customer costs, varies from system to system and requires specific analysis. However, these costs are usually small and their allocation will not greatly affect the results.

Analysis of hydro generation

Several issues arise in the analysis of hydro systems, particularly when seasonal variations in LRMC are important. Generally, in an all hydro system the LRMC of generating capacity would be based on the cost of increasing peaking capability (i.e., additional turbines, penstocks, expansion of powerhouse, etc.), while incremental energy costs would be the costs of expanding reservoir storage. When there is significant spilling of water (e.g., during the wet season), incremental energy costs would be very small (e.g., O&M costs only), and at times when demand does not press on capacity, incremental capacity costs may be ignored. However if the system is likely to be energy constrained and all incremental capacity is needed primarily to generate more energy because the energy shortage precedes the capacity constraint for many years in the future, then the distinction between peak and off-peak costs, and between capacity and energy costs, tends to blur. In an extreme case, because hydro energy consumed during any period (except when spilling) usually leads to an equivalent draw-down of the reservoirs, it may be sufficient only to levy a simple kilowatt-hour charge at all times, e.g., by applying the AIC method to total incremental system costs.

In a mixed hydro thermal system, an important general guideline is that if the hydro is used to displace thermal plant during a rating period then the running cost of the latter is the relevant incremental energy cost. If pumped storage is involved, the marginal energy cost or value of water used would be the cost of pumping net of appropriate losses. Also, if the pattern of operation is likely to change rapidly in the future (e.g., shift from gas turbines to peaking hydro as the marginal peaking plant, or vice versa), then the value of the LRMC would have be calculated as a weighted average, with the weights depending on the share of future generation by the different types of plant used.

Types of tariff structures

Over the last fifty years price structures have become increasingly complex as both the techniques for analyzing the structure of supply costs and the metering hardware available to apply these tariffs have become progressively more sophisticated. Since the quantity, quality, and price of electricity supplied to each consumer can be, if necessary, individually controlled or at least monitored, a high degree of discrimination and structuring is possible with electricity prices. In theory, a separate tariff could be devised for each customer. In practice, however, as discussed in the previous section, the complexity of the tariff would be limited by the metering capabilities, the problems of billing, and the ability of electricity users to comprehend and react to the price signals provided by the power utility.

The structuring of LRMC with respect to voltage level, geographic area, and customer type have been discussed earlier. This section focusses on how tariffs may be devised and implemented, that vary in relation to the following principal aspects: (a) energy or kilowatt-hour consumption, (b) power demand based on kilowatt or kilovolt-ampere consumption, and (c) fixed charges, including both non-recurring and recurring charges. Structuring of aspects (a) and (b) by time of use and usage level will also be reviewed, as well as interruptible rates, the use of tariff adjustment clauses to correct for power factor, fuel surcharges, and so on. These basic building blocks may be combined in various ways to yield literally hundreds of tariff structures differing in their finer details.

The most common form of tariff is the energy charge based on the customer kilowatt-hour consumption over a given period of time, typically one month. Kilowatt-hour meters that record consumption continuously over shorter periods – for example, fifteen-minute intervals or during two different periods of the day – may be used to implement electricity prices that vary by time of use (TOU). During the peak period, typically, the capacity charge is converted into an equivalent kilowatt-hour charge and added to the energy charge.

Unit charges may also be varied according to the number of kilowatt-hours consumed, yielding two basic types of block tariff structures. Block structures may also be used with kilowatt or capacity charges but this is not a common practice. In the increasing or inverted block tariff, the kilowatt price increases as consumption rises. Incorporation of the increasing block structure in applying the LRMC-based methodology has already been discussed, particularly in the section on social or subsidized prices.

The decreasing block tariff, in which the initial slab of consumption has the highest price followed by successively cheaper blocks, has been widely used especially for households and small consumers with only kilowatt-hour metering, where more complex metering would be economically justified (see the section on metering and billing). The rationale for this policy included arguments that: (a) the utility could recover some of the fixed customer costs through the high-priced initial block even though kilowatt-hour consumption was low; (b) the first block corresponded to the high cost of supplying the customers' peak period load, whereas additional consumption was mainly caused by off-peak appliance use that could be supplied at relatively low cost; (c) the utility should encourage increased consumption to realize economies of scale in production; (d) price discrimination could be used to extract the maximum revenue from smaller users who had low price elasticities of demand while also encouraging consumption of larger users who were more sensitive to high prices; and (e) if temporary excess capacity existed – for example, when a new hydro site was developed – the new energy could be supplied "costlessly" and, therefore, higher consumption should be encouraged to collect the maximum potential revenues.

All of these arguments ignore the fact that, if any slab of the decreasing block tariff is significantly below LRMC, it signals the consumer that electricity is much cheaper than it really is, thus encouraging wasteful consumption. First, if customer costs must be recovered then single or recurring fixed charges should be used. Second, unless there is clear evidence that customers with greater consumption have a higher user load factor and consume relatively more off-peak energy at the margin, any additional kilowatt-hours consumed by all consumers will be equally costly to supply. Therefore, there would be little basis for price discrimination according to consumption level. Third, even if economies of scale exist at the aggregate level of the utility, they do not apply in the case of the variable costs to individual customers. In fact, few utilities currently exhibit any economies of scale, and real unit costs of supply in the long run are rising. Fourth, it cannot be generally assumed that the consumption of larger users would be more sensitive to price. Fifth, using up any short-run excess capacity is not costless in the long run, because, if demand growth is unduly stimulated, future investments must be advanced. Finally, the decreasing block rate is highly regressive and "unfair," because it penalizes poorer consumers who generally use less electricity but must pay higher prices per unit purchased (see also, earlier discussion of lifeline tariffs).

As explained earlier, the purpose of structuring tariffs by TOU, voltage level, geographic area, and so on, is to convey the LRMC of supply to consumers as accurately as possible. Although peak load or TOU tariffs may also be determined on the basis of accounting costs, the allocation of system capacity costs to different pricing periods in this case is usually quite arbitrary. For example, one method attempts to identify peaking, intermediate, and base load generation plant and then allocates the costs of these units to the peak, shoulder, and off-peak periods. Another procedure uses the probability of contribution to the peak based on the number of hours in each rating period in which demand exceeds some arbitrary threshold level, divided by the total number of such hours in the year, as the allocation criterion. None of these methods satisfy the economic efficiency objective, and therefore, references to peak load and TOU rates in the subsequent discussions imply that these are based on LRMC.

TOU metering (when this is justified) is the best way to apply an LRMC-based pricing structure. The Hopkinson or two-part tariff with separate energy and peak demand charges is used widely, but if the consumer's maximum kilowatt or kilovolt-ampere demand is not measured at the time of the system peak, then he or she could be unfairly penalized. If only kilowatt-hour metering is available, the capacity charge may be levied on the customer's connected kilovolt-amperes; for example, with a current limiting breaker or fuse to limit the maximum load. But this is even more questionable, since it requires that the relationship between the consumer's peak demand and connected kilovolt-amperes be accurately known. Interruptible tariffs are an extreme form of peak load pricing in which the customer agrees to be disconnected or shed at short notice when there is a power shortage. These prices have to be low because there is no burden on system capacity. Sometimes the interruptible customer is offered the option of remaining on the system at a time of shortage provided he pays a much higher price. In either case, when demand presses on supply the interruptible tariff increases rapidly either to a high value or to infinity – if the customer is automatically shed.

Fixed charges are most often related to consumer costs as described earlier. A lump-sum payment may be levied to cover the initial cost of providing the service connection, or the repayment period may be spread over several years to provide relief to customers. Recurrent fixed costs are charged to meet the costs of meter reading, billing, and other repetitive expenses. In some cases, the charge based on a consumer's connected kilovolt-amperes is also called a "fixed" charge, but this is really a proxy for the capacity or kilowatt cost which is a variable charge.

In general, the conversion of strict LRMC into applicable kilowatt, kilovolt-ampere, or equivalent kilowatt-hour charges during different pricing periods requires knowledge of customer characteristics, such as the load factor, diversity or coincidence factor, ratio of connected kilovolt-amperes to maximum demand, and so on (Munasinghe and Warford, 1981).

Tariffs contain power factor (PF) penalty surcharges in excess of the regular price to encourage consumers whose PF drops below some acceptable limit to install capacitative correction. Fuel surcharge or fuel adjustment clauses are also becoming increasingly common. This permits the utility to quickly pass on to the consumer any unforeseen increases in fuel costs, especially of liquid fuels. Ideally, any changes in relative input prices would require reestimation of strict LRMC followed by changes in the tariff structure, but the legislative procedure to achieve the latter may take a long time. A convenient short-run fuel adjustment clause can, meanwhile, provide much needed financial relief.

Recent advances in low-cost metering and switching equipment have made it possible to consider (where appropriate), more sophisticated approaches to supply/demand balancing such as spot pricing and load control. Spot pricing of electric power is an effort to exploit the full potential of the marginal cost pricing framework by the use of modern communication and computation capabilities (Schweppe *et al.*, 1988; Berrie, 1987). This scheme calls for the variation of electricity price at frequent intervals in real time (for instance, each hour) in keeping with the marginal cost changes in the system. These prices are communicated to the consumer who is then expected to respond by load adjustment. While the implementation of spot pricing schemes entails an added cost in communication, metering, and computation, the potential savings to both the power producer and the consumer can often be significant. Producers benefit by achieving some of their demand management objectives such as peak shaving and load shifting. Consumers benefit by being able to select service levels according to their individual needs and by a reduction in total cost.

There may be significant potential for the application of spot pricing in the more sophisticated developing countries, in which utilities are subject to high variations in supply availability. Spot pricing is an efficient means of rationing power supplies. Also, the rapid growth of power systems in developing countries provides opportunities for incorporating system design innovations and new approaches to producer/consumer interaction.

CHAPTER 11

Energy–macroeconomic linkages

As noted in the introduction, the evolution of energy planning in developing countries had as one of its main roots the need to deal with the macroeconomic impact of the sharp oil price increases that occurred in the mid-1970s. For the typical small oil-importing developing country, the most immediate point of impact whenever a change occurs in the world oil price is the balance of payments. How developing countries should adjust to such changes is one of the major problems faced by energy and macroeconomic planners: as we shall see in this chapter, however, modeling such impacts, and quantifying the impacts of the policies that might be appropriate to mitigate the macroeconomic consequences, proves to be exceptionally difficult.

Certainly what one might call "first-order, short-run" impacts on the merchandise trade balance are simple enough to quantify: Expressed as percentages of both imports and exports, we noted in chapter 1 (see table 1.1) the stress that increasing oil import bills have placed upon the merchandise trade balance of developing countries. Indeed, since in the short run structural adjustments are unlikely, a given change in the oil price is very likely to result in a proportional change in the oil import bill.

In 1986 the world oil price collapsed, with prices as low as $10/bbl at their most extreme. This price decline obviously afforded substantial relief to oil-importing countries. Since then, prices have gradually risen, and by the end of the 1980s stabilized in the $18–22/bbl range. Yet the Iraqi invasion of Kuwait in August 1990 illustrated all too well the volatility of world oil markets, with spot prices staying well above $30/bbl for extended periods in late 1990. Obviously if there is major damage to production facilities as a result of any war in the Persian Gulf, and damage to Saudi Arabian fields in particular, oil prices will soar to dizzy heights. At present the majority of observers expect the oil price to return to its pre-invasion price, then climb gradually over the

228

next decade, primarily as a result of increasing demand on OPEC production as many major non-OPEC fields (and the North Sea and Alaska in particular) reach exhaustion. However, the conventional wisdom on oil prices has been shown to be quite unreliable, and even at $20–25/bbl over the next decade, the oil import bill will continue to represent a substantial burden for many of the world's poor countries.

The macroeconomic impact of increasing oil prices

The question of how the sharp increases in the real oil price in the 1970s affected economic performance remains controversial. One fairly common view of the adjustment process to higher oil prices is one that involves three phases. As expressed by Fried and Schultze (1975), in the first stage the large increase in the price of oil raises the general price level and simultaneously transfers income from consumers to producers of energy, who in turn accumulate a large fraction of their suddenly swollen incomes in unspent financial surpluses. In a second, transition phase, oil-exporting countries begin to increase purchases from oil-importing countries. Energy producers in the consuming countries begin expand their production facilities, or begin an active search for fossil fuels themselves, in response to the higher prices of their products. In the final phase, energy consumers are fully paying for the higher prices through a transfer of real resources – as reflected in higher exports to foreign producers of energy and higher resource costs for domestic production of primary sources of energy.

While such views seem unarguable, there is much controversy over the extent to which the energy price shock had a deleterious impact on the economies of the industrialized countries. The general consensus as far as the United States was concerned was that the sharp increases in the world oil price were indeed a prime cause of the recession of the mid-1970s and the accompanying inflation. In a typical opinion, Mork and Hall (1980) conceded the presence of other factors, such as the removal of the last price controls of the Economic Stabilization program, but concluded that such factors were substantially less important than the oil price shock itself.[1]

Of course, one of the reasons for the political popularity of such arguments in the industrialized countries is that the blame for the declining economic performance could be placed rather conveniently on OPEC.[2]

---

[1] Typical estimates of the United States' GNP loss due to higher energy prices lie in the range of 3–5% – see, e.g., Mork and Hall (1980), Hudson and Jorgenson (1978), Bopp and Lady (1982).

[2] Of course this was matched by OPEC's own rhetoric: Amuzegar, the former Iranian Representative to the IMF, wrote in 1978: "Again, not withstanding repeated rebuttals by OPEC leaders and spokesmen – and despite corroborative analyses by some courageous Western Observers – the

However, there is also the view, expressed well by Pindyck (1979), that the macroeconomic impact of the first oil shock was made more severe than it would otherwise have been by inappropriate policy responses because the strongly contractionary monetary and fiscal policies that were followed, that might have worked well against the ordinary demand-pull inflation that governments had become used to, could not possibly have had an impact on the kind of exogenously generated inflation that was experienced in 1974.

Moreover, the argument has also been made that the magnitude of the second oil price increase in the 1979–80 period was significantly affected by the energy policy responses (or, perhaps more accurately, the *lack* of any coordinated policy response) on the part of the consuming countries. Thus, the frenzied panic on the spot market, the lack of a strategic petroleum reserve, and the inability of the International Energy Agency to function effectively all contributed to the ability of OPEC to increase official prices in the October 1978 to February 1979 period, as prices, particularly on the Rotterdam spot market, soared to the $38–40/bbl range.

There are few detailed studies of the impact of oil prices on the economies of developing countries. There are some analyses at the aggregate level, particularly in the periodic reviews by such bodies as the World Bank and the IMF. However, because of the diversity of the countries involved, even within the usual group of low-income, oil-importing countries, such aggregate analyses often have little relevance to policy-making at the country level. By the mid 1970s, after the first oil price shock, the conventional wisdom ran something along the following lines, as expressed by Fried and Schultze (1975):[3]

In the case of non-oil developing countries the problems of higher oil prices center chiefly around their impact on foreign exchange earnings and reserves, rather than on aggregate demand. Economic growth in these countries is heavily

accusations, innuendos, and half-baked cliches continue to appear in newspaper columns and consultants' newsletters. The clamor is usually a bit louder just before each semi-annual meeting of OPEC Oil Ministers. But holding OPEC responsible for all global woes is an integral part of business luncheon speeches on the state of the world economy, and provides a convenient whipping boy for up and coming business leaders and waning politicians."

[3] Two other typical views of this period are worth recalling. Tims (1975), commenting on the adjustments to the first oil price increase in 1973–4 notes: "Higher oil prices have had a substantial adverse impact on the economic prospects of the developing countries. They contributed heavily to a reduction in the terms of trade of these countries, and to a long lasting impairment of their capacity to import. These consequences have been aggravated recently by the effect of the recession in the industrial countries, which put downward pressures on both the volume and the prices of the exports of the developing countries." Willrich *et al.* (1975) made the following assertions: "Faced with a quadrupled price, an oil-importing LDC has three basic options. First, it may simply absorb curtailed imports through a reduction in its gross national product (GNP). Second, it may attempt to offset the increase in its oil import bill with an increase in the prices for its exports. And third, it may seek increased development assistance from foreign sources. In the context of any of these options, an LDC may redesign its development plans specifically to emphasize energy conservation."

Box 11.1 *The role of concessional aid*

There is general agreement that increased development assistance played a major role in the adjustment to higher oil prices. Even when expressed in constant dollars, official development assistance from all OECD countries has increased significantly over the period in question. This overall increase, however, obscures the relative contribution of individual countries: Japan, France, and the United Kingdom being the most generous, Switzerland and the US the least so, when expressed as % of GNP.

Official development assistance from OECD and OPEC as % of GNP

	1960	1970	1977	1983
OECD				
US	0.53	0.31	0.22	0.24
Switzerland	0.04	0.15	0.19	0.24
Sweden	0.05	0.38	0.99	0.88
UK	0.56	0.36	0.37	0.36
Germany	0.31	0.32	0.27	0.48
OPEC				
Saudi Arabia			4.8	2.82
Kuwait			10.1	4.86
United Arab Emirate			10.9	3.80

Source: World Bank Development Reports, 1978, 1979, 1984.

To what extent did OPEC itself contribute to such aid flows? In terms of share of GNP, contributions from the Persian Gulf countries have been substantial, as shown above, although contributions have shown significant declines since 1980, as oil revenues in these countries have slipped. Data on OPEC Official Development Assistance are not very reliable, but some countries such as Kuwait appear to have contributed as much as 10% of GNP. However, the geographical distribution of much of this OPEC assistance is highly uneven, with a large proportion going to other Islamic countries such as Tunisia, Jordan, and the Sudan.

dependent on the availability of foreign exchange, which in turn is a major factor determining their capacity to import capital goods, to support investment, and to generate economic growth. They have been, and will continue to be affected by higher oil prices in four principal ways. First, the oil induced recession in the industrial countries shrinks their export markets and thereby reduces their ability to import. Second, out of their reduced foreign earnings, a larger fraction has to be devoted to paying for oil, leaving a smaller amount available for the other imports needed to meet development plans. Third, adverse changes in their trade balances can impair the ability of developing countries to borrow in private capital markets. And fourth, the transfer of

Table 11.1 *Importance of the oil price shock,
1974–8 (% of total external shock attributable
to higher import prices of fuels)*

Morocco	20.0
Kenya	30.6
Thailand	32.0
Philippines	31.9
Jamaica	34.1
Peru	15.6
Tanzania	20.0
Ivory Coast	19.2

Source: Adapted from Balassa (1981b).

income from OECD countries to members of OPEC can affect the flow of concessional aid to the developing countries.

A series of detailed studies were conducted in support of the World Bank's 1981 World Development Report, of which two are of special interest here. Liebenthal (1981) reviews the experience of low-income Africa in the 1974–8 period, with special attention to four countries: Sudan, Senegal, Tanzania, and Kenya. Although the impact of higher oil prices is not addressed in any great detail, the importance of other contributing factors in the generally poor economic performance emerges clearly. Liebenthal concludes:

For the most part, neither exports nor import-substitution increased after the first oil price shock. Adjustment therefore took the form of reduced domestic output, offset in part by increased external assistance and in part by compensating terms-of-trade movements. This failure of the productive sectors to respond reflects in part the unfavorable initial conditions which Africa faced, and which would have constrained progress even if external circumstances had been better – a limited or under-exploited resource base, weak institutions, limited skills, a lack of infrastructure – in short, the structure of poverty itself.[4]

Balassa (1981b) examined the policy response of twelve LDCs in the period 1973–8, as shown in table 11.1. He found that higher oil prices account for between 15% and 35% of the total external shock attributable

[4] With respect to investment, Liebenthal concludes "Sudan, Senegal and, to a lesser extent, Kenya embarked upon or expanded public sector investment programs during the 1970s. It is clear that in several cases these programs, whatever the virtues of the individual projects taken piecemeal, were over-ambitious in relation to available technical and managerial capacity. In addition, the Sudanese and Senegalese programs subsequently fell victim to financial stringency, caused in part by international economic problems but more significantly by unperceived or inadequately anticipated inefficiencies in the functioning of existing facilities, especially in the public sector. The reaction to financial stringency was then to try to defend these programs by continuing to allocate increasingly scarce resources to them."

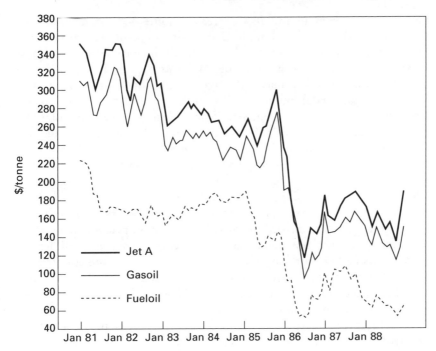

Figure 11.1   Monthly prices on the Rotterdam spot market

to higher import prices. Thus although higher oil prices are important, in the context of the overall deterioration of the terms of trade, they represent a relatively small share.[5]

The impact of falling world oil prices

Since 1980, the real price of oil has fallen. In the period 1980–5 the nominal price was roughly constant, the real dollar price therefore fell. Then in 1986 both nominal and real prices fell sharply, more recently showing a gradual rise in nominal terms but staying roughly constant in real, dollar terms. However, in a period of falling oil prices and increasing value of the dollar, the principal beneficiary of the falling oil price was the US. Elsewhere, the decline in the crude oil price was offset by the dollar appreciation; indeed, according to the IEA, the weighted average of crude oil prices in the 1981–5 period incurred by the

[5] In Balassa's words: "in both periods (1974 and 1977), the rise in oil imports accounted for only a part of the rise in total imports – 37% in 1973/4 and 28% in 1977/8. Other non-oil factors were clearly involved in the very sharp increase in imports."

European members of the IEA increased some 30%, whereas when expressed in dollars they remained roughly constant. However, since early 1985, at which time the value of the dollar peaked, precisely the reverse has occurred, with the crude oil prices paid by European countries, when expressed in national currencies, falling more sharply than in the US. Again according to the IEA, in the period April 1985–January 1986 the European IEA members experienced a price drop of some 25.7% (expressed in their national currencies), whereas the average cost of crude oil imports to the US (expressed in $) fell only 11.2%. Since the dollar appreciated even more sharply since January 1986, this effect was even more pronounced in the first eight months of 1986, during which time the crude oil price collapsed.

Clearly this effect applies to developing countries as well, although the magnitude of the distortion caused by crude oil prices being quoted in dollars (rather than in some market basket of currencies) will depend on a number of country-specific factors. For example, the countries in Africa that are part of currency unions tied directly to the French franc, or other francophone countries whose trade is dominated by transactions in French francs, obviously have an experience similar to France. In others, sharp increases in the domestic price may result from periodic devaluations, even in times when the world price is stable.[6]

Worker remittances and exports to oil-exporting countries
The direct impact on the current account attributable to the sharp drop in world oil prices can be expected to be offset by declines in two other sources of foreign exchange whose relationship to the world oil price seems intuitive: remittances from workers in oil-exporting countries and exports to the oil-exporting countries, both of which would be expected to decrease as the economies in the Persian Gulf countries contract. Worker remittances have become very important to the economies of some of the countries in the Asian region. In Pakistan, for example, remittances which flow through the banking system alone accounted for as much as 8% of GNP in 1985. Yet even before the sharp drop in oil prices in 1986, worker remittances had begun to decline. For example, in the period 1983–5, exports to oil-exporting countries fell 17.1% in Korea, 23.4% in Bangladesh, and 10.6% in India, but increased 32.8% in Thailand. Worker remittances fell 37% in Korea, 20% in Bangladesh, 1.8% in Thailand. Indeed, in the case of a country that imports little oil,

[6] For example, domestic prices in Thailand, say for fueloil, fell from 45 baht/hl in early 1982 to 38 baht/hl by mid 1983, reflecting the concomitant drop in world prices. In late 1985 the bhat was devalued, and the domestic fueloil price rose to 47 baht/hl even as fueloil prices on world markets began to drift downward.

such factors might well cause a worsening of the current account balance even as the oil price falls. In any event, these factors are likely to be country specific, and generalizations are difficult.

In the same vein, it should be noted that, in the countries of North Africa and Turkey, worker remittances are largely a function of economic activity in the European countries rather than the Persian Gulf, and would therefore not be expected to show a sharp drop as oil prices fall. However, increasing unemployment in these European countries, and mounting social resentment (especially against the North African community in France, and the Turkish community in Germany) make the outlook even here somewhat doubtful.

Finally, it should be noted that in many countries a substantial fraction of worker remittances is channeled into the black market rather than into the official banking system. In others, a large part of the remittances takes the form of imported consumer goods, brought in by workers returning from temporary overseas employment. For example, in Pakistan, where such imports are estimated by the Customs, and recorded as imports in the balance of payments statistics, this category was estimated to account for some \$150 million annually in the mid-1980s.[7]

Quantifying the impacts of oil price shocks

Some very simple models go a long way in illustrating the magnitude of the impacts caused by changes in the world oil price. A first step in such an analysis would be a simple accounting model of all of the transactions in the balance of payments that are related to the world oil price – changes resulting from the change in the price of oil, changes resulting from increases (or decreases) in worker remittances from oil-exporting countries, changes in net financing and concessional aid from oil-exporting countries (see box 11.1), and changes in exports to the oil-importing countries.

First define the oil-related payments gap, G, as:

$$G = I - W - Y - L \qquad (11.1)$$

where
I = net oil imports,
W = worker remittances from oil-exporting countries,
Y = exports to oil-exporting countries,
L = net financing from oil-exporting countries.

[7] However, even here the impact is likely to be highly country specific. For example, in 1983-5, at a time when Sri Lanka's US garment quotas were not filled, Hong Kong and Singapore manufacturers moved in, providing a welcome boost to private investment. However, today, Sri Lanka's quotas are

Thus G represents the oil import bill adjusted for worker remittances, exports, and net financing. Since the focus of interest is how these terms adjust in response to changes in the oil price, let us capture the change in the payments gap from one year to the next (or over any period of interest), as:

$$\Delta G = \Delta I - \Delta W - \Delta Y - \Delta L \tag{11.2}$$

In turn, the change in the oil import bill can be attributed to three factors: a change in the oil price, GDP growth, and structural adjustments that tend to reduce oil imports per unit of GDP (shifts to less energy-intensive activities, fuel substitution, conservation, increases in domestic oil production). The change in the oil import bill itself is given by:

$$\Delta I = Q_1 P_1 - Q_0 P_0 \tag{11.3}$$

where

Q_t is the oil import volume at time t,

P_t is the oil import price (at CIF) at time t.

The change in the oil import bill can be decomposed into a term that reflects just the impact of the price change (the "price shock") and a term that accounts for changes in the physical quantity of imports (the "volume adjustment"):

$$\Delta I = \underset{\text{(price shock)}}{Q_0 \Delta P} + \underset{\text{(volume adjustment)}}{\Delta Q P_1} \tag{11.4}$$

The growth in oil imports can be expressed as a function of the growth in the economy as:

$$Q_1 = Q_0 (1 + g)^a \tag{11.5}$$

where g is the actual GDP growth rate experienced over the period of interest, and a is the actual oil/GDP elasticity.

Therefore the actual change in the volume of oil imports is given by:

$$\Delta Q = Q_1 - Q_0 = Q_0(1 + g)^a - Q_0 = Q_0 g^a \tag{11.6}$$

Now define as *trend* oil imports the imports at the end of the period that would have been required as a result of the *trend* GDP growth rate $\hat{g}$, and at the trend elasticity $\hat{a}$. This is the level of oil imports that would have occurred if there had been no structural adjustment (the oil/GDP elasticity stays at trend) and no change in the GDP growth rate:

filled, and the government is not permitting the establishment of new factories from overseas. Instead, Sri Lanka moved into the manufacture of higher-priced goods (and has begun to supply trendy, and higher priced, American clothing outlets).

$$Q_1 = Q_0(1 + g)^{\hat{a}} \tag{11.7}$$

from which follows that the expected change in oil imports at the trend rates of GDP growth and oil/GDP elasticity is:

$$\Delta \hat{Q} = Q_0 \hat{g}^{\hat{a}} \tag{11.8}$$

Finally define as *hypothetical* imports, those required at the actual growth rate but without structural adjustment, i.e., at trend elasticity:

$$V_1 = V_0(1 + g)^{\hat{a}} \tag{11.9}$$

from which follows the expected change at actual growth rate but at trend elasticity:

$$\Delta Q^* = Q_0 \hat{g}^{\hat{a}} \tag{11.10}$$

Thus the volume adjustment term decomposes into three parts: changes due to GDP growth (at trend), ΔS; changes due to changes in the GDP growth rate, ΔX, and changes due to structural adjustments, ΔZ:

$$\Delta Q = \underset{(\Delta S)}{Q_0 \hat{g}^{\hat{a}}} \quad + \underset{(\Delta X)}{(Q_0 \hat{g}^a - Q_0 \hat{g}^{\hat{a}})} \quad + \underset{(\Delta Z)}{(Q_0 \hat{g}^a - Q_0 \hat{g}^{\hat{a}})} \tag{11.11}$$

We can now substitute all of these terms into (11.2):

$$\Delta G = (\Delta P + \Delta S + \Delta Y + \Delta Z) - \Delta W - \Delta Y - \Delta L \tag{11.12}$$

or, rearranging terms:

$$\Delta P = (W + \Delta Y + \Delta L - \Delta S - \Delta Y - \Delta Z) + \Delta G \tag{11.13}$$

In which the response to the oil price shock ΔP is decomposed into:
   ΔW increased worker remittances,
   ΔY increased exports to oil-exporting countries,
   ΔL increased finances from oil-exporting countries,
   ΔS structural adjustments,
   ΔX increased GDP growth,
   ΔA changes in GDP growth,
leaving the net impact ΔG.

The impact of oil price changes in Pakistan

The relationships between oil prices and worker remittances is well illustrated in the case of Pakistan, a country whose oil import bill increased from some $380 million in 1975 to $1.4 billion by 1983–4. However, over the same period, worker remittances from the Persian Gulf increased from $334 million to a peak of $2.8 billion in 1983!

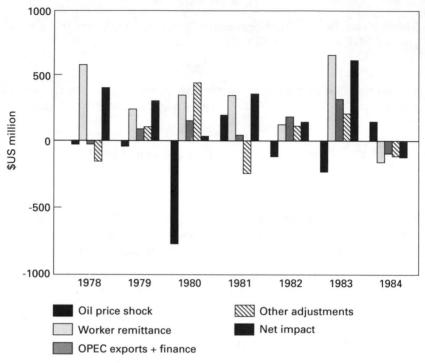

Figure 11.2   The impact of oil price shocks in Pakistan

Figure 11.2 shows the adjustment process in graphical terms. Using the above methodology, we portray all of the transactions in Pakistan's external accounts that are demonstrably linked to the world oil price: the first bar represents the impact of the oil bill itself, the second bar the change in worker remittances, the third the increase in exports to Persian Gulf countries, and increased finance from them, the fourth structural adjustments in the domestic economy (that change the amount of oil imported, a category that includes the development of indigenous energy supplies), and the fifth the net impact.

Even in 1980, when the oil price shock to Pakistan was particularly severe, the overall impact is a net improvement in the foreign exchange position. Indeed, the only year in the period examined for which the net impact is negative is for 1984, a year in which the oil price to Pakistan decreased (which might normally be expected to result in a positive impact!); but declines in exports, worker remittances, and decreased finance from OPEC sources made the net balance negative. Moreover one should note that this analysis includes only worker remittances through the official banking system.

Model linkages

While the sort of simple accounting framework presented above assists in the understanding of how countries have adjusted to oil price shocks in the past, they are of little use in providing policy guidance for the future. This requires a much more sophisticated treatment of the interactions between the domestic macroeconomy and the external accounts. Of course it is true that one very simple way of financing an increased oil import bill is to borrow; and indeed many oil-importing developing countries did precisely that as a short-term response to the oil price shocks of the 1970s, thereby insulating the domestic economy from such shocks in the short run. However, sooner or later such borrowings must be repaid, and thus these same countries experienced major problems in their debt service obligations in the early 1980s. Perhaps the question that is most often asked by decision-makers concerns the impact of passing through world oil price changes to domestic prices.

Some of these impacts are relatively easy to predict: certainly in the medium to long term the price elasticity of demand will ensure that increases in energy prices will induce some level of conservation, and reduce oil imports. More difficult to answer are questions concerning the impact on domestic inflation, and losses in output. And the most difficult of all is the ability to predict if, and how, such negative impacts might be mitigated by government policies. Will an expansionary government expenditure policy to increase aggregate demand and stimulate the economy be effective? To what extent are the impacts of price increases concentrated on the poor, and what forms of subsidies, if any, should be extended to these groups?

Energy is linked to economic activity in so many complex ways that it is difficult to unravel the overall puzzle, isolate the individual elements, and construct a logical model of energy-economic interactions. Clearly one has to start somewhere, and the usual starting point is some view of the future growth of GDP. Given this starting point, it is conceptually a relatively straightforward matter to estimate the associated energy demands. As discussed in chapter 5, for example, the typical econometric energy model may be driven by overall GDP growth rates, supplemented by more disaggregate sectoral value added. From these demand estimates energy supply, investment, and prices are in turn derived, upon which are based estimates of the levels of foreign investment, foreign debt service, and current account impact associated with

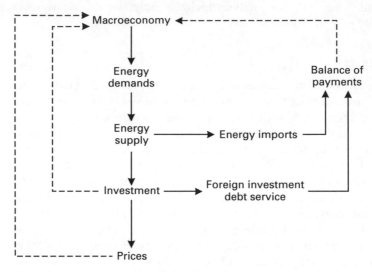

Figure 11.3   Energy-economic linkages

energy imports. These linkages (i.e., macroeconomic impacts on the energy sector), depicted in figure 11.3 with the solid arrows, can be referred to as *forward* linkages.

In contrast, it is much more difficult to quantify the impacts of the energy sector on the national economy – which we here term *backward* linkages – indicated in figure 11.3 with the broken arrows. Questions such as the inflationary impact of a doubling of energy prices, or the degree to which energy sector investment detracts from investment elsewhere in the economy, are difficult to measure with any precision. In smaller countries, where skilled manpower may be the most constrained resource, quantifying the opportunity costs of diverting such resources from other sectors to the energy sector may be equally elusive.

Forward linkages: linking demand models to economic projections

Even despite the relatively straightforward nature of the forward linkages, a major problem of energy demand forecasting is internal consistency. A frequently encountered approach is to project value added of each of the major sectors separately, with overall GDP growth obtained by aggregation. Often these sectoral growth rates are aligned with the official projections of the government. While it may well be the case that for some base case such official projections are indeed internally consistent, as soon as individual growth rates in individual sectors are changed, internal consistency may be lost. For example, if the growth rate of the construction sector is increased, how is consistency with that of the cement sector achieved? Similar problems are encountered when using the Reference Energy System approach, where energy end-uses are driven by individual sectoral activities.

The input-output table has long been used by economists to achieve consistency among the economic sectors. Using the conventional notation:

y = vector of final demands (assumed known) of dimensions $(n \times 1)$,
A = matrix of interindustry coefficients $(n \times n)$,
x = vector of gross outputs $(n \times 1)$

then the product $A\,x$ represents outputs needed to satisfy intermediate demands, from which total output follows as:

$$Ax + y = x \qquad (11.14)$$

which has the well-known solution for gross output of each sector:

$$x = (I - A)^{-1} \atop (n \times 1) \qquad (11.15)$$

where I is the identity matrix.

With a consistently specified picture of the overall economy, a consistent forecast of energy demands follows. These can be broken down into two main categories: those associated with the producing sectors of the economy, which can readily be linked with the sectoral output vector x. Thus, if there are m energy products, and E is an $(m \times n)$ matrix of energy coefficients, say denominated in Btu per \$ of value added, then the resultant vector of energy demands , e, is given by:

$$
\begin{array}{llll}
e & = E & x & \\
(m \times 1) & (m \times n) & (n \times 1) & (11.16) \\
[\text{Btu}] & [\text{Btu/\$}] & [\$] &
\end{array}
$$

As already noted in chapter 5, in the ideal case the energy coefficients are specified in useful energy terms, rather than as fuel consumption; ideally one would wish to know how many Btu of process heat are required per unit of output in a given industry, so as to be able to separate useful energy from the efficiency of the device being used, and which fuel is used.

The second component of energy use is associated with final rather than intermediate demand, and comprises the energy use in households and government. Again it is not too difficult to derive some consistent

	Energy supply	Energy product	Non-energy
Energy supply	A_{ss} [Btu/Btu]	A_{sp} [Btu/Btu]	0
Energy product	A_{ps} [Btu/Btu]	0	A_{pi} [Btu/$]
Non-energy	A_{is} [$/Btu]	0	A_{ii} [$/$]

Figure 11.4   Decomposition of the extended input-output table

specification of such energy demands as a function of an appropriate set of variables.

An extended input-output model

The standard input-output approach can be extended to include a treatment of energy in such a way that not all cells have monetary units. First, we introduce the notation:

x_s = output vector for energy supply,
x_p = output vector for energy products,
x_i = output vector for non-energy sectors,
y_s = final demand for energy supply,
y_p = final demand for energy product,
y_i final demand for non-energy sectors,

with which we then rewrite the standard form (11.14) as

$$
\begin{aligned}
A_{ss}x_s + A_{sp}x_p \qquad\qquad\; + y_s &= x_s \\
A_{ps}x_s \qquad\quad + A_{pi}x_i + y_p &= x_p \\
A_{is}x_s \qquad\quad + A_{ii}x_i + y_i &= x_i
\end{aligned}
\qquad (11.17)
$$

The coefficient submatrices are identified on figure 11.4, denominated in accordance with table 11.2. Note that the A_{is} block assumes that non-energy sector output (in $ terms) remains consistent with energy sector output (that we have removed from the monetary denominated sector). Similarly, the A_{ps} block assures that the energy inputs to energy supply (e.g., energy inputs to refineries, coal mines, etc.) are accounted

Table 11.2: *The A-matrix coefficients*

A_{ss}	=	input-output coefficients describing sales of the output of one energy/supply conversion sector to another energy conversion sector and conversion losses incurred in producing or distributing energy. Conversion losses may be excluded if all coefficients are calculated on the basis of delivered energy.
A_{sp}	=	input-output coefficients describing how distributed energy products are converted to end-use forms. They contain the end-use conversion efficiencies embodied in the Reference Energy System described later in this chapter.
A_{si}	=	0 implying that energy supplies are not used by non-energy producing sectors; energy is distributed to the non-energy producing sectors via energy product sectors.
A_{ps}	=	input-output coefficients describing how energy products – final energy forms – are used by the energy supplying industries. For example, electricity use for lighting a refinery would be included here.
A_{pp}	=	0 implying that energy products are not used to produce energy products.
A_{pi}	=	input-output coefficients describing how energy products – final energy forms – are used by non-energy producing sectors. This submatrix describes the ways end-use energy forms are used in the non-energy producing sectors.
A_{is}	=	input-output coefficients describing the uses of non-energy materials and services by the energy industry. An example of this would be requirements for machinery for oil drilling or coal mining.
A_{ip}	=	0 implying that energy product-sectors equipment require no material or service inputs. This is because they are pseudo sectors and not real producing sectors.
A_{ii}	=	input-output coefficients describing how non-energy products are used in the non-energy producing sectors. Coefficients in this submatrix are enumerated in purely monetary terms, A_{ii} is equivalent to the A matrix of the conventional input-output framework.

for. Clearly all of the information in the top six blocks of the partitioned A-matrix is also contained in the RES.

At this point, then, we have a system driven essentially by a composite vector of final demands: non-energy final demands in monetary units for non-energy sectors (y_i) and final demands for energy products (y_p). The latter depicts solely the energy demands of consumers and government since energy products neither represent investment goods nor are they usually exported. Any exports of energy supplies (coal, oil, etc.) would appear in the y_s vector.

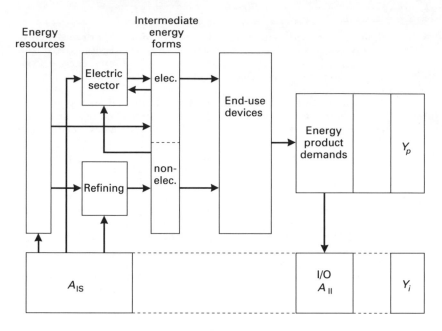

Figure 11.5   The structure of the TEESE model

Application to India: the TEESE model

The TEESE model (for TERI Energy Economic Simulation and Evaluation), developed by the Tata Energy Research Institute in Delhi, India, is a good example of a model that applies these concepts to a developing country situation. Indeed, the model embodies a number of recent hardware and software developments: it uses LOTUS-Symphony for data entry and matrix generation, and the commercially available SUNSET LP83 package for linear programming optimization; it is designed for use on the IBM AT fitted with a 80287 math coprocessor that permits quite large LP systems to be solved in a matter of minutes, and it is the first Brookhaven-type model in which the input-output model is embedded in the LP as a constraint set along the lines suggested above:[8] the general structure is depicted on figure 11.5. The LOTUS input format makes the model both flexible and user friendly; the previous reliance on special matrix generation languages (such as the PDS/MAGEN code used in earlier mainframe BNL models) is therefore eliminated.

[8] The equation structure of the model is described in Meier and Mubayi (1981).

The TEESE model has been used not just for analysis of the aggregate India energy system at TERI by Pachauri and Srivastava (1988), but also of individual states at the Indian Institute of Management at Ahmedabad, where the model was applied to the states of Gujarat, Kerala, and Rajasthan. Obviously applying the model at the state level requires state-specific input-output tables, for which data problems are perhaps even more formidable than at the national level. In India, however, regional I/O tables have been available for certain states for some time, and the TEESE model studies were able to use I/O tables constructed in the years 1979–81, as opposed to the current national table which is based on 1984–5 data.

It should be noted that these modeling exercises are not purely academic, but have played an important role in redirecting energy policy. In India, the Planning Commission plays an important role in coordinating the investment plans across the various energy subsectors, but prior to 1983 these plans had a supply-side orientation, without much attention given to demand management (Pachauri and Srivastava, 1988). In 1983 the government established a new, high-powered Advisory Board on Energy to provide new directions to the country's energy policy. This Board has sponsored the development and application of the TEESE model, and the studies have attempted to address a number of urgent policy issues in a comprehensive way. Some of the problems and issues to which the model has been directed include:

1 The problems of captive generation: in some industries close to 25% of their electricity requirements are met by costly, oil-based captive generation units as a result of demand curtailments in the grid.
2 The question of fertilizer feedstocks: model results suggest that they should be imported rather than produced domestically because of the differential between domestic production cost and the naphtha export price.
3 The question of whether crude oil should be imported and refined in domestic refineries, or whether products should be imported directly: model results indicate that even in the presence of excess refinery capacity, under current market conditions products rather than crude should be imported.

Backward linkages: a model for Colombia

The model for Colombia by Carroll (1983) was one of the first energy-economic models to be written in LOTUS 1-2-3, and was developed for the energy planning agency of Colombia (Estudio Nacional de Energia,

ENE). Colombia is one of the previously mentioned Latin American countries where energy sector investment has had an increasing impact on the balance of payments: from only 6% of national investment in the early 1970s, energy sector investment rose to more than 15% by the early 1980s. The model was developed largely in response to the need to analyze energy sector issues, and energy investment in particular, within a broad macroeconomic framework.

The structure of the model is similar to the minimum standards model of the World Bank, but tailored to the specific analytical and institutional needs of energy planning. The basic concept is that the system of national accounts is balanced consistent with economic growth policy and the *explicit* recognition of energy sector requirements. Gross domestic product in year t is the sum of value added in the three sectors of the economy used in the model: agriculture, manufacturing, and other:

$$GDP_t = YA_t + YM_t + YO_t$$

where
   GDP_t is the GDP in year t,
   YA_t is the value added in the agricultural sector,
   YM_t is the value added in the manufacturing sector,
   YO_t is the value added in other sectors of the economy.

These levels of economic activity are also the drivers for the detailed energy demand forecasting analyses done by ENE. YA_t and YM_t are exogenous variables, assumed to be target levels for value added in these two sectors, established by national policy. YO_t is an endogenous variable, defined as a function of YA_t and YM_t by the econometrically estimated equation:

$$YO_t = -42.229 + 1.234 \, [YA_t + YMt]; \, R = 0.99$$

Investment is disaggregated into non-energy (I) and energy sector investment (IE). Non-energy investment is determined by applying simple capital/output coefficients to GDP, again estimated econometrically:

$$I = 17289 + 0.10129 \, GDP_t + 0.020339 \, (GDP_t - GDP_{t-1}); \, R = 0.95$$

The estimation of even such a simple relationship is subject to significant data problems. Historical energy sector data, which needed to be subtracted from total investment to obtain non-energy sector investment, proved to be very difficult to determine. Annual reports of the electric utilities were available for the period 1978–82, and this was assumed to constitute 70% of total energy sector investment. Only aggregate investment for five-year periods was available as a basis for the early 1970s.

Total imports are disaggregated into capital goods, intermediate plus consumer goods, foods, and energy imports:

$$M_t = MK_t + MG_t + MF_t + ME_t$$

where

M_t is total imports,

MK_t is capital goods imports,

MG_t is intermediate plus consumer goods imports,

MF_t is food imports,

ME_t is energy imports,

Capital goods imports are related to investment, and intermediate plus consumer good imports are related to economic activity by the econometrically estimated relationships:

$$MK = -7324.5 + 0.42927\ I;\ R = 0.77$$
$$MG = -4934 + 0.257\ GDP - 1.3054\ YM;\ R = 0.94$$

Food imports are related to per capita *GDP*, population, and agricultural value added by the equation:

$$MF = 7005 + 2126\ GDP/POP - 1.3054\ POP - 0.065545\ YA;\ R = 0.48$$

where the last term represents the effects of import substitution, and where *POP* is the population, an exogenously defined variable.

The level of energy imports is again exogenous to the macroeconomic model, being based on the detailed ENE energy sector balance; total exports (*X*) are disaggregated into non-energy goods and services (*XO*), and energy exports (*XE*):

$$X = XO + XE$$

Finally, the system of accounts is closed with the income identity, wherein consumption follows as:

$$C = GDP - I + M - X$$

The resulting model has nine equations and nine endogenous variables, and was implemented in LOTUS 1-2-3. Obviously this is a very simple model indeed, and cannot capture all of the important economic interactions between the energy sector and the economy in Colombia. Yet it is quite typical of the sort of model that has been used in many developing countries as a starting point for analysis of these linkages: see, e.g., Hill (1984) for a comparable model of Liberia, or Rogers *et al.* (1988) for a model of Costa Rica.

CHAPTER 12

Energy sector models

The most elementary "model" of the energy sector, the energy balance, was introduced in chapter 4. Such balances, as noted, can be assembled without the benefit of computers, although the use of modern spreadsheets now greatly facilitates the process. In the discussion of chapter 4 we were mainly concerned with the preparation of historical balances, the main methodological issues, and with the rules of sound spreadsheet practice. Reference Energy Systems, the network equivalent of the tabular balance, were also introduced earlier, particularly as a device for the preparation of demand scenarios (in chapter 5).

When preparing energy balances for future years, two very important technical issues arise: the first concerns the electric sector generation mix, the second the refining sector. If one starts, say, with the demand projection (i.e., at the bottom of the energy balance table), a projection for electricity consumption is readily derived; by applying an aggregate T&D loss rate, the generation requirement follows, say G. To derive the fuel inputs into generation, the simplest formulation, readily programmed in a spreadsheet, is an assumption of the form:

$$G_j = a_j G$$

where G_j is the generation from the j-th generation type (hydro, coal, etc.), and a_j is the fractional composition of total generation. The fuel input F_j follows from:

$$F_j = h_j G_j$$

where h_j is the heat rate, expressed in an appropriate set of units (see discussion in chapter 4).

While such a formulation is very easily programmed into an energy balance spreadsheet, it proves not to be very useful. Suppose in a second scenario one postulates some form of demand management, resulting in a reduced electricity demand. Applying the same set of a_j coefficients to the generation requirement is not likely to give very realistic results (except in all-hydro systems, in which case the calculation is trivial anyway), because in reality generation units are dispatched in merit order, which means that when peak demand is reduced, it is only the least efficient units whose output gets reduced, while the output of the most efficient units remains unchanged. Clearly, to be realistic, one must incorporate some form of merit order dispatch, and that is quite difficult to do within an energy balance spreadsheet.

Similar problems arise with petroleum products and assumptions made for the refinery. Because of the inherent flexibility of refinery operations, not just in terms of the product mix, but also in terms of the crude slate that might be used for any given situation, the use of fixed "yield" coefficients that relate crude throughput to refined product output may lead to quite unrealistic estimates of product imports and exports needed to balance domestic demand. Incorporating even a few heuristic rules about how refinery outputs might adjust with changes in the product mix proves to be quite difficult in a simple spreadsheet model.

In sum, while spreadsheets are very useful to *display* the results of future energy balances, modeling future energy balances solely in a spreadsheet environment is very difficult if the results are to withstand scrutiny.

All of this, of course, is just another way of pointing to the difficulties of managing the interface between levels of the hierarchy. What is really required are energy balance models that can directly incorporate the results of detailed subsectoral models that are typically operated not by the energy planning agency, but by the implementing agencies. In the case of the electric sector, for example, the energy balance model needs to be able to accept the results of a generation expansion planning model such as WASP or EGEAS; in all but the largest countries, this means an ability to deal with a list of individual units in generation merit order, and include even a simple merit order dispatch calculation to deal with the problem of how the electric sector responds to demand management. How some representative energy models deal with these problems is examined below in our overview of software packages.

Linear programming models of the energy system

The use of optimization tools to guide energy policy has fascinated planners from the very early days of national energy planning that followed the first energy crisis in the early 1970s. The United States Department of Energy in particular made a huge investment in models

Table 12.1 *LP models for developing countries*

Country	Model	Reference (see bibliography for full citation)
China		Tsinghua University (1984).
India	TEESE	Pachauri and Srivastava (1988). This model is reviewed in detail in chapter 11.
Indonesia	MARKAL[b]	Developed for the Indonesia Atomic Energy Commission.
Israel		Breiner and Karni (1981)
Mexico	ENERGETICOS	Goreux and Manne (1973)
Nigeria	MESSAGE[a]	Adegbulugbe, Dayo, and Gurtler (1989)
Pakistan		Riaz (1980)
Thailand	Master Plan Model	Thailand (1982)
Tunisia	BNL/BESOM derivative	Gordian Associates (1981).

Notes: [a] Model for Energy Supply System Alternatives and their Environmental Impacts, developed at IIASA.
[b] Developed by Brookhaven National Laboratory and the Kernforschungsanlage Julich, Germany, for the IEA.

in the mid 1970s in an attempt to rationalize the basis for national energy planning, many of which had their genesis in the Brookhaven Energy Systems Optimization Model (BESOM). The first version of BESOM was a simple linear programming optimization of the United States Energy System, which was followed by a series of increasingly sophisticated models that were linked to a national input/output table and the Hudson-Jorgenson Macroeconomic model (Hoffman and Jorgenson, 1977. Indeed, many of today's best-known energy models are derivatives of BESOM. For example, the MARKAL model, developed under the sponsorship of the International Energy Agency (IEA) in 1979–81 as a collaborative project between a German Research Institute and Brookhaven National Laboratory, is a multi-period linear programming optimization model that can be driven by a number of alternative objective functions beyond the conventional minimization of total system cost. Conceptually similar is the ensemble of models developed for the EEC, that draws on work at the Institut Economique et Juridique de L'Energie at the University of Grenoble.[1] Well-known models such as MEDEE and EFOM have been adapted by Systems Europe SA, a Belgian Company, into a variety of medium- and long-term national and multi-national models used by the EEC and other European energy planning agencies (Systems Europe, 1986).

[1] For a good description of the early work in energy systems modeling in France, see, e.g., Laponche (1978). Some of the more recent models are discussed in Criqui *et al.* (1985).

Linear Programming (LP) models have been formulated for many developing countries as well. BESOM itself has been applied in Tunisia, South Korea, Yugoslavia, and Greece. MARKAL has been used in a number of developing countries' energy planning projects sponsored by the German technical assistance agency, including Brazil and Indonesia. LPs have also been written for China, India, Pakistan, and Thailand, among others. But in fact the first energy system LP written for a developing country appears to go back to the late 1960s to the ENER-GETICOS model of Mexico (Goreux and Manne, 1973). Table 12.1 lists some of these LP models for developing countries.

One can visualize an energy system LP as a network optimization problem, in which the objective is to route energy flows in network in such a way that some objective function is optimized, and subject to the requirement that all end-use demands are met. Assume, for the moment, an objective function of the type:

$$
\begin{array}{ccc}
\min S & = & c & x \\
(1 \times 1) & (1 \times n) & (n \times 1) \\
[\$] & [\$/\text{Btu}] & [\text{Btu}]
\end{array}
$$

where c is a vector of unit costs, and x is a vector of activities that represent the energy flows in particular segments of the network. This minimization is subject to a set of linear constraints that can be written as:

$$
\begin{array}{ll}
G_1 x & = d \\
G_2 x & \leq s \\
G_3 x & = 0
\end{array}
$$

where d is a vector of end-use demands (which correspond to the right-hand side of the Reference Energy System), s is a vector of supply constraints, and where the third equation represents all other equations required to specify the network. The G_js represent the corresponding coefficient matrices.

This LP formulation, which is in essence that of the early versions of BESOM, suffers from a number of deficiencies. First, for the model to have any operational value, one must distinguish between energy flows and capital stocks; not to do so implies that all facilities are always used at some constant capacity or utilization factor, obviously a somewhat questionable assumption where an important question concerns which items of old, oil-fired capital stock should be retired in favor of new, non-oil and renewable energy utilizing capital stock. One thus needs the additional constraint:

$$G_4x - G_5w \leq W$$

where w is a vector of capital stock additions (denominated in capacity units, such as bbls/day, MW, and so forth), and W is a vector of existing capital stocks. In addition, we need to add a term to the objective function to reflect the cost of capital stock additions, namely:

$$\text{Min } S = cx + \text{CRF } p\, w$$

where p is a vector of capacity costs (e.g., \$ per MW of capacity), and CRF is the appropriate capital recovery factor.

A further refinement is the addition of a capital constraint, namely:

$$p\, w \leq R$$

where R is the capital constraint. Obviously it is relatively simple to add other constraints, say on the total import energy import bill, or on the foreign debt service component of the investment cost.

How useful is such a single-period LP? Suppose the vector of energy demands represents the projected energy demands in the year 2000, and W represents the vector of existing capital stock. Then the LP as formulated optimizes the energy system under the objective that the annual system cost in the year 2000 is to be minimized, under some assumption of world energy prices (some subset of the x vector of activities represents energy imports). The capital stock additions are those that are needed between now and the year 2000.

Of particular interest are the values of the dual variables, or shadow prices, associated with binding constraints (see chapter 6 for an introductory discussion of dual variables and their interpretation). The dual variables associated with the energy supply constraints represent the value of an additional unit of that energy to the energy system as a whole, and should therefore be equal to its price. The value of the dual variables associated with the energy demands provide information on the cost to the energy system as a whole of an additional unit of demand; these therefore provide guidance on where conservation efforts need to be focussed.

It is worth adding a certain note of caution about the entire notion of "optimality." The "optimal" solution provided by a run of such an LP model is really applicable only to the very specific scenario of exogenous variables used. Thus the optimum solution for a year 2000 oil price of \$20/bbl will look very different to that obtained when the real oil price is \$40/bbl. Indeed, much of the investment in capital-intensive hydroelectric facilities in Latin America (and elsewhere) was justified on the basis of "optimal" capacity expansion models run in the late 1970s when

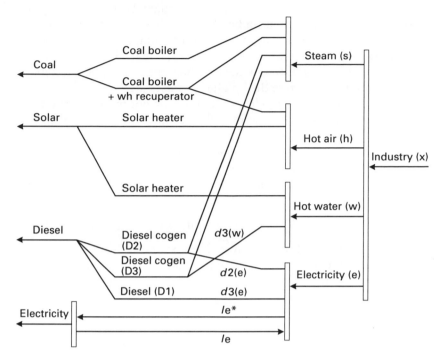

Figure 12.1   Representation of industrial end uses

real oil prices were seen as increasing almost *ad infinitum*; yet in light of current oil prices, and the problems of servicing foreign debt, the "optimality" of these investments is questionable. LP models should thus be viewed not as devices to provide decision-makers with "optimum" solutions, but as a computational convenience that facilitates intelligent analysis in general, and sensitivity analysis in particular. Thus what is of interest is an understanding of how the least-cost solution changes with changes in the underlying assumptions that are beyond the control of the policy-maker.

End-use devices

The treatment of end-use devices, and of the linkages between fuel consumption and useful energy, are perhaps best treated by example. Consider for this discussion the treatment of industrial process heat. Clearly different industries have very different profiles for temperature and pressure distributions of their process heat requirements: even for a first-order assessment of how such needs might be met in an optimal fashion requires differentiation between, say, steam, hot water, and hot air. What makes the situation even more complex is the increasing importance of cogeneration, which requires that electricity needs be integrated into the industrial analysis. Once again we turn to a network representation to illustrate the linkages, as indicated on figure 12.1.

Whatever the type of model, simulation or optimization, the key is proper formulation of the energy balance equations. Thus each of the different end-use devices (such as boilers, generators, cogeneration, solar heaters) contribute to one (or in the case of cogeneration, more than one) energy balance. For example, a simple diesel generator (D_1) on figure 12.1, consumes d_1 units of diesel fuel, and produces $d_1(e)$ units of electricity, such that

$$d_1(e) = \epsilon_{1e}d_1$$

where ϵ_{1e} is the first law efficiency. Now suppose that a simple waste heat boiler is fitted, say as the cogeneration set D_2: this produces both steam in the amount $d_2(s)$ and electricity $d_2(e)$, such that:

$$d_2(e) = \epsilon_{2e}d_2$$
$$d_2(s) = \epsilon_{2s}d_2$$

clearly the point of cogeneration being that $\epsilon_{2e} + \epsilon_{2s} > \epsilon_{1e}$. Suppose further that a waste heat recuperator is fitted to the steam boiler, to produce, in addition, hot water. This defines a third technology D_3, that produces electricity $d_3(e)$, steam $d_3(s)$ and hot water $d_3(w)$, such that:

$$d_3(e) = \epsilon_{3e}d_3$$
$$d_3(s) = \epsilon_{3s}d_3$$
$$d_3(w) = \epsilon_{3w}d_3$$

The resulting energy balances are then straightforward: in the case of electricity, for example, we have:

$$\Sigma d_j(e) + I_e - I_e^* = E$$

where I_e is electricity supplied from the grid, and I_e^* is surplus energy sold by the industry from self generation back to the grid. Note that in a linear programming model these two variables cannot be combined into a single variable *net* generation (which could be either negative or positive), since in an LP framework the non-negativity requirement precludes negative values of any variable.[2]

---

[2] The same is true, for example, of the treatment of petroleum product imports and exports: for each product there must be a single variable for imports, and for exports, in place of a single variable "net imports" (which might be negative in the case of an export).

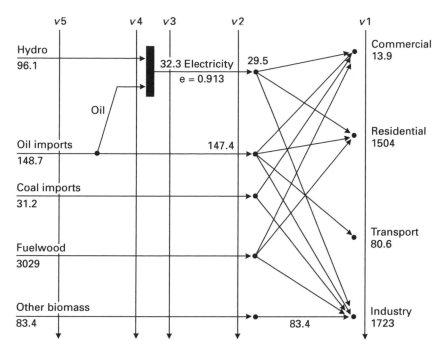

Figure 12.2   The RESGEN concept

Software packages for energy sector integration

With microcomputers in use throughout the world in energy planning activities, a comprehensive review of the software currently in use for energy sector integration has become a virtually impossible task. For purely illustrative purposes we therefore discuss here only some of the better-known software packages: the intent is to give the prospective user of energy planning software some assistance in evaluating the strengths and limitations of alternative approaches.

It should be noted that advances in hardware, and in the development of general purpose commercial software (such as LOTUS 1-2-3) continue to occur at a rapid pace. Therefore energy models, too, are changing at a rapid pace, with models developed as little as five years ago being replaced by new and more powerful packages that exploit the hardware advances. Thus in the seven years that have elapsed since the 1985 UNDP workshop on Microcomputer Applications for Energy Planning in Developing Countries, many new models have been developed, and some of the models presented in the conference proceedings have since been replaced (United Nations, 1985).

Box 12.1 *RESGEN matrix algebra*

Recall the RES of figure 12.1. If we start from the extreme right-hand side with total sectoral demand, then the sequence of vectors v_1, v_2, ... can be defined as indicated below:

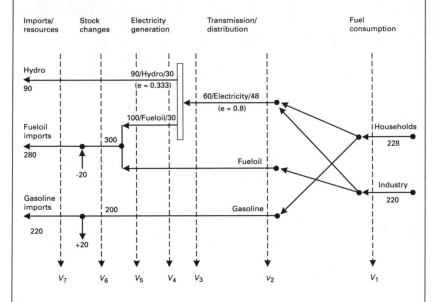

The first transition, from V_1 to V_2, is therefore given by:

$$\begin{vmatrix} 48 \\ 200 \\ 200 \end{vmatrix} = \begin{vmatrix} 0.1228 & 0.0909 \\ 0 & 0.909 \\ 0.8771 & 0.0 \end{vmatrix} \begin{vmatrix} 228 \\ 220 \end{vmatrix}$$

The second transition, from V_2 to V_3, follows as:

$$\begin{vmatrix} 60 \\ 200 \\ 200 \end{vmatrix} = \begin{vmatrix} 1/0.8 & 0 & 0.0 \\ 0 & 1.0 & 0.0 \\ 0 & 0 & 1.0 \end{vmatrix} \begin{vmatrix} 48 \\ 200 \\ 200 \end{vmatrix}$$

RESGEN

This is one of the more widely used software packages for energy planning in developing countries, having been used by national energy planning agencies in Indonesia, Thailand, Sri Lanka, Haiti, the Dominican Republic, Uruguay, Pakistan, and Morocco, among others. As in the case of a number of other models, RESGEN is more accurately described as a software package to generate models, than as a model *per se*.

The basic computational concept is illustrated on figure 12.2: this is the Malawi RES presented earlier in chapter 4 (see figure 4.4). The RES network is sliced vertically into vectors (or arrays); as one moves from right to left (from demand to supply), each successive vector $v(n)$ is calculated from its predecessor, $v(n-1)$, by a matrix transformation of the general form:

$$\underset{(n \times 1)}{v(n)} = \underset{(n \times m)}{T} \times \underset{(m \times 1)}{v(n-1)}$$

where T is a transformation matrix (see box 12.1).

Mathematically, then, RESGEN is just a series of matrix algebraic equations. Special operations, such as the electric sector dispatch, and the incorporation of project level information, require of course some special operators. However, in the software package itself the user does not deal at all with matrix algebra.

RESGEN is designed to be used as part of hierarchical modeling systems, and therefore requires some sort of macroeconomic driver: in the case study we review the macroeconomic accounting framework used for this purpose in Sri Lanka. The unique feature of RESGEN is that it permits three different types of demand structure to be used simultaneously: (i) econometric specifications (as discussed in chapter 5, and similar to those used in ENERPLAN, as discussed below); (ii) industry and/or project specific demands (that allows the user to modify demands according to the specific fuel inputs (or outputs or fuel substitutions or fuel use reductions from conservation); and (iii) process models (in which fuel demands are built up from a projection of end-use devices, again as discussed in chapter 5).

The basis for the electric sector calculations is a plant specific dispatch into a linearized load duration curve. The dispatch algorithm dispatches individual plants into the vertical blocks of the load duration curve based on capacity availability. Again with the institutional considerations in mind, the base case plant list takes the form of alternative capacity expansion plans as might be generated by a more detailed capacity expansion model, such as WASP.

The three-block linearization proves to be sufficient for a fairly good replication of actual system dispatching: in the Dominican Republic, validation of the model against known 1985 data showed deviations in the 0–5% range at the level of specific plants. In the Pakistan version of RESGEN plants are dispatched on a monthly basis, taking into account anticipated maintenance schedules, and the month-to-month changes in hydro availability. Because the shape of the load curve and the input assumptions regarding forced outage rates and the like are fully under the user's control, the model has been successfully used to examine the impacts of demand management programs, drought conditions, and system rehabilitation on electric utility fuel use and investment requirements.

RESGEN is a model of great flexibility, but as such it imposes rather severe requirements on the user. Familiarity with Reference Energy Systems is highly desirable (and indeed the program user manual devotes much space to discussion of basic energy analysis concepts). Compared for example to ENERPLAN, the user requires considerably more in the way of up-front training before he can successfully implement a model. Indeed, experience with the early FORTRAN versions of RESGEN pointed to the shortcomings of any compiled program, and led to the development of a spreadsheet based version as successfully used by the Energy Wing of the Ministry of Planning in Pakistan.

ENERPLAN

The ENERPLAN software package was developed by the Tokyo Energy Analysis Group for the UNDP in 1984–5. The package provides the user with both macroeconomic and energy sector models, with the former designed as a driver for the input side of the energy model. The two models can also be exercised independently. In fact, since the user is free to build whatever equation structure deemed appropriate, ENERPLAN is again best described as a software package to build models, rather than a model *per se*.

The analytical approach for both macroeconomic and energy sector modules can be summarized as follows:

Postulate an econometric model.

Enter the historical data for the variables in the program database.

Conduct an econometric analysis to determine the model coefficients.

Run the simulation model using the coefficients estimated in step 3.

Obviously, such an approach is extremely flexible, leaving it to the user to determine the level of detail at which he wishes to work. Indeed, as noted by the authors: "the main strength of ENERPLAN is its programmability. Thus the program can handle models reflecting a whole range of schools of economic thought" (p. 155). Moreover, the general programming environment is extremely user friendly. New models can be implemented rather easily, which has particular advantages for assistance agencies that may need to implement many country models.

Another important feature is that the model is written around an existing econometric package. The user enters the database, specifies the equations, and in a first step one can estimate the coefficients of the equations in question. Since this is perhaps a particularly suitable approach for estimating the coefficients of a macroeconomic model, we see this as the main strength of ENERPLAN. As we shall note below, however, it is also one of the weaknesses with respect to the technical relationships in the energy sector.

From the standpoint of potential application to developing countries generally, the key shortcoming is the absence of a project level capability. Consequently there is also no relationship between energy project investment and output: for example, in an application to Thailand, the output of coal + lignite fired electric generation plants is given by the equation:

$$\text{HCEL} = (.02203 - .00806*\text{PCL/PCR} + .97929*\text{HCEL}(-1)/$$
$$\text{ELEL}(-1) - 0.3*\text{HDEL}(-1) + .14238*\text{DUM79})*(\text{ELEL} - 3*\text{HDEL})$$

where
  HCEL = coal and lignite generation,
  HDEL = hydropower generation,
  (-1) = denotes time lag of one period,
  ELEL = total electricity,
  DUM79 = exogneously specified dummy variable,
  PCL = coal import price,
  PCR = crude import price.
Such formulations are of course typical of econometrically specified models: but the degree to which econometric formulation is appropriate to smaller countries, characterized by extreme lumpiness of electric sector investment, remains doubtful. Only in very large countries, such as India and China, where the sheer magnitude of the electric sector investment program tends to smooth out at the national scale, will such an econometric approach prove useful.

The Energy Toolbox
The Energy Toolbox is an advanced microcomputer package for energy planning developed in the UK (Heaps and Tomkins, 1990). It includes a number of established modeling tools, including Reference Energy Systems, LP, energy balance tables, and econometric demand analysis, integrated through a common database. What distinguishes the package is the state-of-the-art user interface that incorporates menu systems, full-screen editing, pop-up windows, context sensitive help, and advanced graphical displays.

One of the problems with such a package lies exactly in its excellent user friendliness and ease of use. For example, one of the features of the

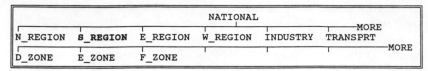

```
                              NATIONAL
┌──────────┬──────────┬──────────┬──────────┬──────────┬──────────MORE
 N_REGION   S_REGION   E_REGION   W_REGION   INDUSTRY   TRANSPRT
├──────────┼──────────┼──────────┴──────────┴──────────┴──────────MORE
 D_ZONE     E_ZONE     F_ZONE
```

```
┌─Viewing  model equations - press <RET> to edit.═══════════════════
 INCHEAD=INCOMEPC*1.15       "regional per capita income
 REGPOP     =POPULATN*0.2       "regional population

 WOODFUEL  =REGPOP*0.45         "tonnes of biomass fuels pro
 FIREWOOD  =REGPOP*0.11         "rata to population
 STALKS    =REGPOP*0.2
 RESIDUES  =REGPOP*0.1 + STALKS
 CHARCOAL  =REGPOP*0.25
 DUNG      =REGPOP*0.01
 BIOMASS   =WOODFUEL+FIREWOOD+STALKS+RESIDUES+CHARCOAL+DUNG

                                                        ┌─────────┐
                                                        │ VIEWING │
                                                        └─────────┘
└─Path: NATIONAL\S REGION═══════════════════════════════════════════
```

```
┌─────────────────────────────────────────────────────────────────┐
│                                                                   │
│    L P - E S P S                                                  │
│                                                                   │
│    D A T A P I C K    M A I N    M E N U                          │
│                                                                   │
│    MODEL:SUPC                                                     │
│                                                                   │
│    ESC/F10. Quit                                                  │
│                                                                   │
│    A.    Establish dictionaries from RES for LP model             │
│    B.    Edit main dictionary                                     │
│    C.    Edit auxiliary dictionary                                │
│    D.    Edit constraints dictionary                              │
│    E.    Generate LP objective function (base year)               │
│    F.    Generate LP constraints (base year)                      │
│    G.    Generate LP bounds (base year)                           │
│    H.    Edit time feature tables                                 │
│                                                                   │
│                                                                   │
│    Authors: R.Tomkins & C.H.Guei  Imperial College               │
│    Ver.1.10 Jan 1989                                             │
└─────────────────────────────────────────────────────────────────┘
```

Figure 12.3   Sample screens from the energy toolbox

model is that the RES can be converted into its LP analog from a simple menu (see figure 12.3B). Yet the user manual points to the dangers involved "because of this feature [the automatic conversion], a planner using this system can apply the LP approach without being an expert in the technique." Whether it is really desirable for a planner to use LP without a full comprehension of, say, the many limitations of the technique, and of the interpretation of the solution including the dual variables and reduced costs, is of course a matter for conjecture. There are those who would argue that it is probably preferable for the user to have to explicitly formulate each equation in the LP constraint matrix (which can also be done in a user friendly way in a LOTUS spreadsheet, without having to be a computer programmer), in the interests of understanding *why* the model provides the results it does.

PART V

Implementation

CHAPTER 13

Institutional arrangements

There are two fundamental institutional issues that need to be addressed in any discussion of INEP and its implementation. The first relates to the organization of the energy planning activity itself: what kind of an institution should be created for sector wide planning, where and how is policy analysis conducted within such an institution, and how does one ensure that the outputs of such an activity are properly utilized? There are countless examples of national energy planning agencies being created in developing countries that are completely ineffective, not because they lack policy analysis tools, or appropriately trained staff, or even direction from senior officials and assistance from the International Assistance Community (although in some cases these factors are lacking as well), but more often than not as a result of a poor institutional concept. Indeed, it is a theme that we have no hesitation in belaboring: if the modeling and policy analysis activity does not match the established institutional framework, it will ultimately be of little value.

The second set of issues deals with broader, but equally important questions about the organization of the energy sector, and about the relationship of the central government to energy sector activities. Moreover, in some cases the failure of the existing arrangements between national governments, energy producers, and consumers, is not due to shortcomings of the policy criteria themselves, but to the imprecise interpretation and application of these objectives. Thus, the desire for growth and modernization has resulted in unquestioned funding of energy needs, continuous central government subsidies to the sector, non-optimal or unbalanced investments, and lack of productive efficiency and incentives to maintain technical and financial discipline. Social equity and employment objectives have led to excessive subsidies to consumers, inefficient pricing, and inadequate resource mobilization. Attempts to tax sector surpluses have created highly skewed price structures, cross subsidies, and incorrect price signals. Altogether, this

environment has encouraged a casual attitude toward official interference, resulting in excessive and counterproductive government intervention in nearly every aspect of energy producers' activities.

The foregoing considerations and the desperate circumstances of
many developing country energy supply companies have generated
pressures for new approaches. In particular, there appears to be considerable interest in the scope for more decentralization and greater
private participation as one way of improving energy sector performance and relieving developing country governments of the crippling
economic burden of financing the chronic deficits of state-owned energy
enterprises. The history of the energy sector in industrialized countries
indicates periods of fierce internal debate and introspection, followed by
significant policy reforms to adapt to changing external circumstances.
The rapidly evolving environment faced by developing countries today
suggests that it would be both appropriate and healthy to carry out such
self-examination, rather than adhering rigidly to an outdated
framework.

Enhanced private participation in the energy sector is likely to be
more successful when it is one element in a broader economic package
involving policy reforms in the trading, industrial, and financial sectors
– as well as deregulation and liberalization of the energy business. Such
private participation has to do with the infusion of private capital and
the transfer of ownership to private hands as well as with the introduction of private sector management methods in order to improve
efficiency of energy supply enterprises. However, it is naive to expect
either the transfer of ownership or management or both to private
hands, to solve all the problems of the sector. Thus, in many countries it
has become one of several methods aimed at restructuring public sector
enterprises.

A new outlook for the energy sector should take three key factors into
account. First, conditions within the companies must provide incentives
for technical, financial and managerial efficiency. Remedial measures
must address a number of problems that have plagued these institutions,
including: weak planning, inefficient operation and inadequate maintenance, high technical and non-technical losses, low quality of supply
and frequent shortages, inability to raise prices to meet revenue requirements, poor management, excessive staffing and low salaries, poor staff
morale and performance, undue government interference, and so on.
For many companies these problems have persisted over time despite
efforts to identify and correct the causes through consultant studies and
institutional development programs.

Second, the national environment within which the energy supplier functions might be restructured to improve performance. Key aspects to be considered include clear-cut government policy guidelines for company management, delegation of authority to implement agreed policies and corresponding accountability, a rational regulatory framework, government non-interference in daily sector activities, and reforms in the financial climate and access to capital.[1]

Third, dealing with exogenous factors outside the policy-makers' control requires that decisions be made with due allowance for uncertainty. Thus, unpredictable changes in demand forecasts, inflation, exchange rates, interest rates, and fuel prices, require a new mindset and scenario-oriented approach to decision making, that is quite different from the deterministic methods that were more useful in the past. It also calls for a greater emphasis on flexible investments and the use of technologies that can adapt with reasonable speed to the changing environment. Planners and decision-makers would also need to consider strategies of hedging the risk brought about by volatility in international markets. Furthermore, it is becoming increasingly evident that effective policy must be determined by using a holistic framework that fully accounts for key macroeconomic and intersectoral linkages – an approach that is more comprehensive than the narrower, intrasector analysis used earlier.

Indeed, the current situation in the LDC energy sector will be difficult to sustain in the long run and continued sector growth in many countries will hasten the deterioration rather than lead to improvements. Unless there is an improvement in the quality of service to accompany the expansion of service to new customers, there will be increasing difficulties in persuading customers to pay higher energy prices. Governments are very sensitive to the objections of customers (generally the politically influential urban minorities) who resist paying higher prices for poor quality service which shows little sign of improvement. Inability to generate higher revenues results in the underfunding of all activities and deterioration of service levels, thus reinforcing the vicious cycle.

It seems apparent from the above that there is a strong argument in favor of putting greater emphasis on efficiency and restructuring issues rather than concentrating solely on continued energy sector expansion. Especially in the case of electricity, more attention needs to be given to improving the quality of service and reducing losses through rehabilitation and reinforcement of power systems. Given the present state of many power utilities, it may not be possible to achieve rehabilitation

---

[1] For an interesting comparison of a successful institutional environment (South Korea) and a relatively unsuccessful environment (Nigeria) see Schramm (1990).

and service improvements simultaneously with full system expansion. Furthermore, in many countries there is a backlog of maintenance requirements in addition to the need to improve operations. Finally, environmental protection measures may also increase the future costs of energy supply. These needs already place a burden on institutions which do not have sufficient qualified manpower to adequately meet the requirements for both expanding the system and operating existing systems.

Enterprise efficiency, greater autonomy, and management reforms

Although many difficulties have plagued developing country energy producers, probably the most pervasive has been excessive government interference in organizational and operational matters. Such interference has adversely affected least-cost procurement and investment decisions, hampered attempts to raise prices to efficient levels, mandated low salaries tied to civil service levels, and promoted excessive staffing. This in turn has resulted in inadequate management, the loss of experienced staff due to uncompetitive employment conditions and poor job satisfaction, weak planning and demand forecasting, inefficient operation and maintenance, high losses, and poor financial monitoring, controls, and revenue collection.

In order to address these difficulties, an important principle must be recognized – that, given the complexity of energy problems and the scarcity of resources and managerial talent in developing countries, each set of issues should be dealt with by that level of decision-making and management best suited to analyzing the difficulty and implementing the solution. This hierarchical approach corresponds closely to the INEP concept; political decision-makers, senior government officials, and ministry level staff should focus on critical macroeconomic and energy sector strategy and policy in order to determine global expectations of power utility performance. The senior management of an energy company, appropriately guided and buffered by an independent board of directors, would then conduct their daily operations free from government interference, to meet the overall national policy objectives and targets within regulatory guidelines. As far as possible, the management should be assured of continuity at the top, even in the face of political changes. While the enterprise is provided wider autonomy, it would now become more accountable in terms of performance measured against an agreed set of specific objectives and monitored indicators. The increased responsibility of senior management would require more consultation with government and especially consumer representatives (which rarely occurs in many developing countries). Major changes in enterprise management may be required to mirror changes in the company's external environment, discussed above. The enterprise's organizational structure and procedures may be inadequate. Once again, the fundamental principle that will help to address these problems is delegation of authority. In many developing country energy companies, the senior management attempts to deal with all problems, and trivial issues often get more attention than critical ones.

Provided that middle managers could be adequately trained, senior managers could (by appropriate delegation of tasks) free themselves to deal with higher-level policy. The middle management would account for their performance through an agreed set of performance indicators, while obtaining greater responsibility and latitude to make decisions. This process would then be repeated down to the lowest working levels. Obviously, staff training and education at all levels and stages of a career-path would play a critical role in ensuring the success of such an approach.

Restructuring, private participation, and decentralization

The natural monopoly characteristics of some energy enterprise functions, as well as the willingness to manipulate these enterprises for general policy purposes, are in many countries accepted as sufficient reasons for maintaining large centralized public sector organizations. Nevertheless, given the observed problems inherent in stimulating management of developing country state enterprises to be cost conscious, innovative, and responsive to consumer needs, there may be a need for more fundamental change. It could be worthwhile to trade off some of the perceived economies of scale in energy enterprises for other organizational structures which provide greater built-in incentives for management efficiency and responsiveness to consumers. In particular, varying the forms of ownership and regulation in the energy sector, and the power sector, should be considered.

Options for private and cooperative ownership of energy enterprises could include both local and foreign participation as well as joint ventures. As long as a given regulatory framework prevails, it can be argued that the form of ownership (private and public) would not by itself affect operating efficiency. The main point is that, to the extent possible, the introduction of competitive market forces should be encouraged. Governments may wish to divest themselves of either all or part of some government owned enterprises, or organizational structures. Thus, they might provide an environment in which governments, enterprise managements, and energy consumers are all better off. A first step toward decentralization could be for government-owned energy enterprises to competitively contract out activities or functions better handled by others. Many companies already subcontract various construction related activities. Some portions of the billing and collection process, or routine maintenance, can also be subcontracted. Among the advantages of such arrangements have been lower costs and greater programming flexibility.

While several potential opportunities for private participation in the LDC energy sector have been identified and are being developed around the world, these have not been without significant impediments. Frequently, these projects are hindered at the outset by a policy and institutional framework that discourages private sector involvement. Since the energy sector occupies a central position, changing the public ownership framework in a manner conducive to private participation may prove to be extremely difficult. Furthermore, LDC energy companies often operate in a climate which is economically weak and politically unstable. This increases the risk of expropriation and frequent disruptions. Furthermore, even in circumstances where the private enterprise was initially encouraged and approved, the likelihood of subsequent adverse regulatory changes and other contractual breaches would be greatly enhanced. Finally, the LDC energy sector is characterized by extraordinary technical uncertainties such as fuel shortages, lack of skilled personnel, and a weak supporting infrastructure.

Especially in the case of electricity, there are also opportunities for decentralization on a spatial basis. For example, larger countries may have independent regional power grids. Power distribution companies could be separated by municipality, with perhaps limited overlap in some fringe franchise areas, and have the right to purchase from various suppliers, when feasible. If private participation were allowed, one advantage might be that at least the large power consumers could also be legitimate shareholders who would be concerned not only with service efficiency but also with the financial viability of the company.

Power generation also has potential for efficiency improvements through divestiture. While the bulk power transmission and distribution functions might be regarded as having more natural monopoly common carrier type characteristics, this is not so with generation. In fact, there is substantial scope for competition in power generation with independent (perhaps foreign-owned enclave) producers selling to a central grid, as in the case of large industrial cogeneration. The first such major private power project is the 2×350MW Shajiao B station in the People's

Republic of China located in the Shenzhen Special Economic Zone, immediately adjacent to Hong Kong.[2]

There are a number of legislative models potentially appropriate to developing countries.[3] For example, in the United States the Public Utilities Regulatory Policies Act of 1978 (PURPA) specifically encourages small privately owned suppliers to generate electricity in various ways for sale to the public grid. As a result there are now a large number of small companies producing electricity presumably at costs below those incurred by traditional large utilities. Similar laws are beginning to be passed in developing countries as well: Costa Rica, Pakistan, Turkey, and India are among countries that have recently passed legislation to facilitate the development of private power.[4]

In fact, with innovative legislation and contractual arrangements, and strengthened utility capability to manage these new schemes, greater scope for cogeneration and free-standing generation might be possible. Larger countries might find small entrepreneurs ready to invest in small hydro or similar generation facilities. The advantage to the power company would be a deemphasis on large lumpy capital-intensive projects; moreover, it would be such newly established private enterprises that would put up all or part of the capital and be paid only out of revenues from power sold at guaranteed prices. For larger enclave generation facilities (perhaps peat, coal, or nuclear), the concept would be that a foreign investor finance and build the plant, operate and maintain it for an agreed period, and be repaid out of power sold at guaranteed prices convertible into foreign currency.

Finally, with the proper institutional structure, developing countries could take advantage of many technological innovations that could lead to increased power sector efficiency. Cogeneration – i.e. the simultaneous production of power and heat – has substantial potential in developing countries, as yet largely unrealized. On the generation side, several advancements in gas turbines have been developed in recent years (see, e.g., Williams, 1990) and the conversion of simple steam cycle plants to combined cycle operation is being adopted by some developing

---

[2] The bulk of the financing came from a Japanese equipment supplier backed by the Import-Export Bank of Japan, and by a syndicate of banks led by Citicorp of Hong Kong. The major equity holder is Hopewell Holdings limited, a Hong Kong development company. For further discussion, see, e.g., Dykes (1988) or Sullivan (1990).

[3] The United Kingdom model, in which the entire nationalized power industry (with the exception of nuclear generation facilities) was privatized in a single share offering in December 1990, is not generally regarded as a particularly appropriate model for developing countries: a gradual approach to an increasing role for the private sector is viewed as being much more likely and more politically acceptable.

[4] For a concise review of developments to facilitate private power in developing countries (and specifically recent developments in Thailand, Chile, Indonesia, Pakistan, Turkey, the Philippines, India, Malaysia, Costa Rica, and the Dominican Republic, see, e.g., Sullivan (1990).

countries with great success, with overall conversion efficiencies nearing 45%. In energy conversion too, several advances have been reported (such as innovative coal combustion technologies) with superior environmental and technical characteristics. In India, the privately owned Ahmedabad Electric Company in Gujarat was the first to order a utility scale fluidized bed combustion unit from the major Indian Manufacturer (BHEL). All of these technological options have imminent application potential in developing countries, but the institutional structure must be appropriate: experience shows that smaller, privately owned entities are much more willing to take the risks (and of course also reap the rewards) associated with new technology than large government-owned entities.

Many of the same points can be made for the petroleum subsector as well. Refineries that are wholly owned by the government, and operate under financial arrangements that guarantee a specific rate of return regardless of actual technical and financial performance have few if any incentives to reduce technical losses, or to reduce crude runs and import products directly when market conditions make the direct importation of products profitable in foreign exchange terms. While it is true that a few developing country refineries have been shut down over the past decade (such as in Liberia and Zimbabwe), most continue to operate in an institutional environment that offers few incentives to maximizing financial and technical efficiency.

Annex: Implementing an institutional framework for energy planning: the case of Sri Lanka

In late 1982, the President of Sri Lanka appointed a Senior Energy Advisor (SEA) to accomplish the following broad tasks:

Establish an effective organizational framework for overall energy coordination and integrated national energy policy analysis and planning.

Create a database, analytical procedures, and support systems.

Train and develop a team of energy specialists.

These objectives were largely achieved during the subsequent three years. In the process of carrying out this longer-run overall program, a number of urgently needed (and beneficial) specific activities were also carried out, such as the preparation of the national energy strategy (NES), the national energy demand management and conservation program (NEDMCP), and the national fuelwood conservation program (NFCP).

The upper part of figure 13.1 shows the energy sector institutional framework in mid 1982. One major drawback was the large and varied number of ministries and line agencies involved in the different energy subsectors, with inadequate coordination among them:

Electricity (Ministry of Power and Energy/Ceylon Electricity Board – CEB; Mahaweli Ministry/Mahaweli Authority – MA);

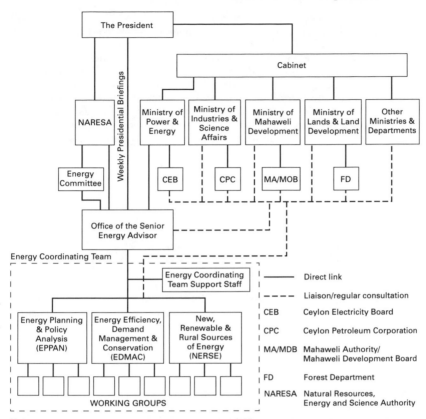

Figure 13.1   Energy sector institutional framework

Petroleum (Ministry of Industries and Scientific Affairs/Ceylon Petroleum
    Corporation – CPC);
Fuelwood (Ministry of Lands and Land Development/Forestry Department –
    FD);
Overall science and energy policy, and research and development (Natural
    Resources, Energy and Science Authority – NARESA).
In general, energy policy up to 1982 tended to be subsector focussed, somewhat *ad hoc*, and supply oriented, with insufficient emphasis on demand
management. In November 1982, President Jayewardene approved the setting
up of an Energy Coordinating Team (ECT) to help remedy this situation. The
initial organization of the Energy Coordination Framework is shown on the
lower part of figure 13.1. A special effort was made to ensure policy coherence in

the commercial energy subsectors (oil and power), by improving links among ECT, CEB, CPC, and MA. A similar strengthening of coordination in the fuelwood subsector (through the FD) was also pursued.

The rationale underlying the ECT concept was that the new framework, in the first instance, was not intended to be another bureaucracy that would seek to control the energy sector. The objective was to coordinate and facilitate the work of relevant ministries and existing line agencies, prevent duplication of effort and policy conflicts, supplement weak or neglected areas in the energy sector, and provide direct advisory inputs to the President. In any case, major structural changes in the organization of the energy sector could not be undertaken in the short run. The ECT framework was the most practical method of initiating and carrying out urgently needed tasks in the sector, without undue disruption of existing activities. As the ECT matured and experience was gained in energy coordination, some further organizational changes in the energy sector were gradually implemented, as described in the next section.

The ECT consisted primarily of three coordinating task forces (CTFs) that covered the following areas:

Energy Planning and Policy Analysis (EPPAN);

Energy Efficiency, Demand Management, and Conservation (EDMAC);

New, Renewable, and Rural Sources of Energy (NERSE).

The principal activities of the task forces were as follows:

Energy Planning and Policy Analysis (EPPAN): EPPAN sought to meaningfully integrate all energy sector activities, and its time perspective was also basically medium- to long-term in nature. One of EPPAN's most important goals was to identify the overall objectives of national energy policy, and then attempt to define a national energy strategy (NES) that met these objectives (see main text for details). A comprehensive computerized energy database was also set up. EPPAN reviewed the disaggregate supply and demand projections for oil, electricity, and fuelwood, provided by other organizations.

Energy Demand Management and Conservation (EDMAC): EDMAC included a number of short- to medium-term activities aimed at increasing energy efficiency and eliminating waste in both the energy supplying and consuming sectors. The National Energy Demand Management and Conservation Program (NEDMCP) focussed on industry, commerce, transport, households, agriculture, and energy-supplying institutions. Coordinated application of policy tools, including rational energy pricing, was stressed.

New, Renewable, and Rural Sources of Energy (NERSE): The principal focus of NERSE was to:

> Coordinate R&D activities in this area that are now being carried out by a large number of research organizations and universities;
>
> Carry out technical, economic, and financial reviews of these technologies, in order to identify the ones which would be most promising from the actual energy viewpoint;
>
> Promote, finance, and encourage commercialization of these selected technologies.

The highest priority of NERSE was quickly identified as the National Fuelwood Conservation Program (NFCP), involving the speedy dissemination of improved cooking stoves to about 2.6 million Sri Lankan homes. Chapter 9 has already discussed the quantitative analyses undertaken in support of this program.

Each coordinating task force (CTF) had as members six to eight senior managers from the relevant organizations, who were seconded to help in ECT activities. The CTFs were chaired by the SEA, and initially met once a month. Major policy decisions agreed on at CTF meetings would normally be conveyed to the President through the SEA, and, if necessary, reach the appropriate line agency through the Cabinet. Agreed policy was also conveyed directly to concerned line agencies through the relevant members. This facilitated speedy and accurate implementation of policy, and practically eliminated potential conflicts between the ECT and operating energy institutions. CTF members were also obligated to carry out studies and/or provide data as requested at meetings. Meanwhile, the CTFs could draw upon a Secretariat or Support Staff, and also had a number of associated working groups (WGs) on specific topics.

Finally, a number of important institutional changes were undertaken. Until 1982, the Ceylon Petroleum Corporation (the state oil company) was a part of the Ministry of Industries. After considerable debate, this key institution was shifted into the Ministry of Power and Energy in early 1985: at the time the Ministry was directly under the President. The Lanka Electricity Company (LECO), established as a private company, its shares held initially by the CEB and the Ministry of Local Government and Housing, was created in 1984 to gradually take over independent electricity distribution networks hitherto operated very inefficiently by local authorities and municipalities. Some of these systems had loss rates in excess of 40%, and most had loss rates over 30%! In the several years that LECO has been in operation, it has been most effective in reducing these loss rates by comprehensive programs of system rehabilitation financed by loans from the Asian Development Bank. By 1988 LECO's losses had fallen to 14%. The new government in 1990 further strengthened the role of the Ministry of Power and Energy by creating within it a special Ministry for Energy Conservation, which took over the functions of the former EDMAC Task Force.

CHAPTER 14

Implementing the analytical process

Energy Planning is an on-going process, not a one-time exercise that will provide a permanent policy framework. As such, energy sector planning is no different to planning conducted at the levels above and below it: most implementing institutions in the energy sector – electric utilities, refineries, etc., conduct planning in a regular cycle, with demand forecasts and investment plans typically updated annually. And at the macroeconomic level, many developing countries have five-year planning cycles: but even here policies and investment plans are typically reviewed and updated on an annual basis.

Yet the notion that sector-wide energy planning also needs to be cast as an on-going activity is one that many countries have yet to embrace. Very often the only regular activity is the compilation of historical energy statistics in the form of the ubiquitous Energy Databook. Indeed, in our experience one of the first items on the agenda to establish an on-going energy planning activity is to define a structured staff work program that focusses on the notion of a planning cycle, rather than on aperiodic planning efforts. And only by integrating the work program of the energy planning entity with those of its counterparts can one expect to achieve meaningful progress.

In this chapter we focus on three issues that are central to the implementation of the planning process. The first is the overriding need for consistency, which is perhaps more a matter of dialog with counterpart institutions than a modeling exercise as such. The second is how to deal with uncertainties: indeed, the constantly changing conditions in the global economy, in global energy markets, and in domestic economic development is the most important reason not just for the formulation of robust investment plans, but for regular updates of the energy strategy. This is a topic of considerable importance, and we discuss it in some detail. And the third deals with how microcomputers themselves are used: experience indicates a number of pitfalls, ranging

276

from inappropriate organization (the "big room" philosophy in which microcomputers are all put together in a single location, ostensibly for all kinds of spurious technical reasons, rather than where they belong, distributed among analysts' desks) to confusion about how they should be used.

Attaining consistency

Almost always the first order of business in a newly launched planning activity, or even at the beginning of the regular planning cycle, is an attempt to attain consistency across all levels of the hierarchy, so that the assumptions used by macroeconomic planners at the top level are fully consistent, with, say, the demand projections used by the individual subsectors. In modeling jargon, the first task is to create a "base case," that represents some set of business-as-usual conditions. Unless a consistent set of assumptions in imposed across the hierarchy on both domestic and world prices, economic growth and its sectoral decomposition, and so forth, no useful analysis of policy and investment options can be conducted.

Indeed, experience indicates that if the base case created by an energy sector planning agency can replicate the essential results of the subsector institutions and the macroeconomic planners, subsequent policy discussion of alternatives is greatly facilitated because debate can be directed toward the substantive issues rather than on the quality and contents of models. And, to the extent that consensus about a base case cannot be reached, it is pointless to proceed with any modeling effort until any fundamental consistency issues are resolved. Obviously, the process of creating such a base case will require the close participation of these other agencies: in chapter 15 we outline how this was done in the case of Sri Lanka.

How does such an exercise proceed in practice? As we have noted earlier, the key is to recognize that bottom-up and top-down approaches must be imposed simultaneously. While no rigid formula exists for such a process, questions of the following type arise almost everywhere:

1 What are the assumptions for economic growth, and income elasticity of demand used by the electric utility and national oil company for their demand projections? Are these consistent with those used in the latest macroeconomic plan? Can one reconcile the assumptions for the level of oil imports postulated in the macroeconomic plan with those from a bottom-up analysis?
2 Are the assumptions across subsectors consistent? For example, how does the oil company project the oil demands of the electric utility?

3 Can the assumptions used by the macroeconomic plan for investment and foreign debt service be reconciled with the expansion plans of energy subsectors? (It is quite common to discover that the "needs" of the electric utility for capital investment would consume a totally unreasonable share of total investment in the economy: if in the past the electric sector has accounted for, say, 20% of total public investment, a plan that implies an increase to 30% needs to be scrutinized rather carefully.)

While questions of this type are largely a matter of common sense, experience shows there is always great temptation to avoid discussion of such inconsistencies because they are often difficult to resolve. Indeed, without an appropriate institution to discuss such issues, the energy planner alone can make little progress: hence the importance we ascribe to the creation of an effective forum right at the outset. And to proceed to any energy sector modeling, and optimization models in particular, without full agreement over a base case is simply futile. It is a point worth endless repetition, because it is so often ignored.

Dealing with uncertainty

The problem of how to deal with the impact of uncertainty is characteristic of most aspects of national development planning, but in few sectors is the pervasive influence of uncertainty as serious as in the energy sector. The volatility of world energy markets, the uncertainty surrounding a potential resource base, the unknown performance of new technologies, the lack of data on traditional energy uses, and variations in critical economic parameters, such as costs of resources and technologies, fuel prices, foreign exchange rates, interest rates, etc., all pose unique problems to the planner. Experience shows that energy investment programs that are unable to respond flexibly to rapidly changing external forces end up as costly failures; the search for policies and programs robust under such uncertainties is a central theme of energy planning and analysis.

The extent of the problem faced by energy and economic planners is well illustrated by the experience with the projection of world oil prices. On figure 14.1 we show a comparison of the World Bank's official projections over the period 1978–88, with actual prices (all expressed in constant dollars): as is fairly evident, these forecasts have not proven to be very successful. Nor is the forecasting track record of other institutions much better.[1]

---

[1] For example, the projections made by the United States Department of Energy in 1978, as embodied in its annual Report to Congress, forecast the 1980 price at $13/bbl, and the 1990 price at $15/bbl.

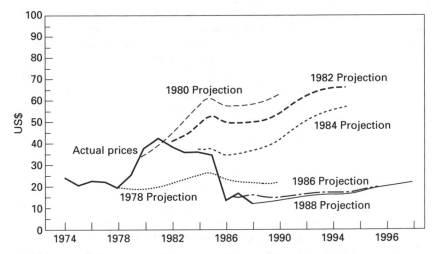

Figure 14.1   World Bank projections of the world oil price, in constant 1987 $/bbl
Source: Crousillat (1988).

While decision theorists make distinctions between risk and uncertainty based on the degree to which the probability distribution of the outcomes are known, in practice a more useful categorization of uncertainty is one based on the ability of the planner (and decision-maker) to identify and/or control the variance of an assumption. For example, the price trajectory of the OPEC marker crude is clearly critical to the definition of planning assumption, and to the ability to identify cost-effective policies and programs. Yet there is essentially nothing that the planner can do (in a typical oil-importing country) to forecast the price trajectory, much less derive a useful probability distribution for estimating the variance of a forecast.

A useful classification of uncertainty distinguishes between the following four types: (1) exogenous uncertainties, defined as those over which the planner has little if any control (such as the world price of oil); (2) the uncertainty over natural phenomena (rainfall, distribution of fossil resources, fluctuations in wind intensity, etc.); (3) economic uncertainties, attributable to our still very incomplete understanding of the functioning of modern economies and human behavior; and (4) project and data uncertainties that can be controlled by the planner through judicious application of surveys, experiments, and demonstration.

There is a well established body of analytical techniques that deal with the second type of uncertainty, usually referred to as "decision analysis"; and indeed these techniques are widely used in subsectoral energy models for petroleum exploration, probabilistic simulation of electric generating systems, and the management of multi-purpose water resource systems. The successful application of such techniques depends on the ability to define the underlying probability distributions, which in turn demands an adequate database. Despite the usual problems of data in developing countries, however, experience shows it to be much easier to extrapolate probability distributions for natural systems (from other countries, or similar climate and geologic regimes) than to extrapolate socio-economic phenomena.

Application of such decision analysis techniques to the features of the international economic system are much more difficult, because the laws of physics do not apply to political, economic, and social behavior, and hence a derivation of the necessary probability distributions becomes an almost impossible task. For example, all manner of game-theoretical models were developed in the late 1970s to model OPEC behavior and the future trajectory of the world oil price. Yet few, if any, came even close to projecting the oil price downturn in the 1981–3 period, much less the sudden decline in 1986. Indeed, such models have not been used successfully anywhere in developing countries as a basis for decision-making.

In response to these difficulties, the standard technique has been the use of scenario simulation, in which values of such exogenous factors are hypothesized without any initial judgment on the likelihood of occurrence. In effect, the judgment about uncertainty is shifted from the analyst to the decision-maker, since it is the latter who must make the trade-offs between scenario and policy response on the basis of the projected impact.

Dealing with exogenous uncertainties

Consider the example where a primary objective of the national energy strategy is to optimize net present value of benefits (benefits less costs) of various oil substitution options. Included in the optimal program would be all those measures whose present value of benefits exceeds the present value of cost – as depicted on figure 14.2. On the far left are measures that require no investment whatsoever, but that typically produce large foreign exchange savings. For example, under current market conditions, some old refineries in Africa would be best shut down in favor of refined product imports (or, in the interest of maintaining access to suppliers, drastically reduce the crude run). Savings here typically run

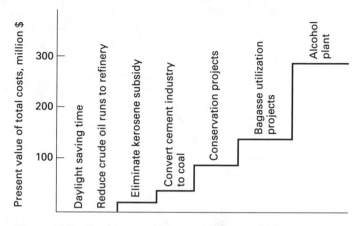

Figure 14.2   Ranking energy management and investment programs

into the tens of millions of dollars at essentially zero foreign investment cost. As we move to the right on this curve, measures require increasing amounts of investment (per unit of oil saved). The hypothetical alcohol plant on the far right incurs higher costs than it produces in oil import savings (as a consequence of high investment costs), and would, therefore, be excluded from an optimal program under this particular criterion.

If we generalize the discrete impacts of particular projects as a smooth curve (figure 14.3), then the point of optimality in the energy program, which corresponds to the minimum of the total cost curve, occurs at point X. The gradient of the curve at this point is exactly unity.

If world oil prices decrease, then the curve of figure 14.3 will shift to the left, as the value of the oil savings per unit cost decreases. On the other hand, if the price of oil increases, then the curve will shift to the right. Accordingly, the optimal level of energy related investment will vary with the oil price in the manner indicated in figure 14.4. Since in general the future oil price is highly uncertain, it follows that the investment decision problem must also be made in the face of uncertainty.

In practice, exogenous uncertainty is most frequently analyzed by the use of scenarios: the impacts of the different options available to the decision-maker are displayed – in the example at hand – as a function of the different price trajectories. It is then the decision-maker who must balance the probability of each price scenario against the impacts of each case: and it is foolish to suppose that more analysis, or more modeling, will reduce the uncertainty. Nor would the advice of even the

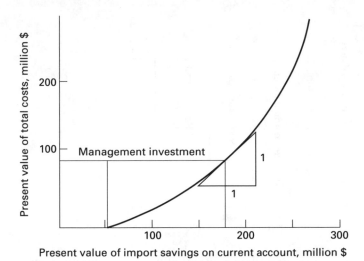

Figure 14.3   Total foreign exchange requirements

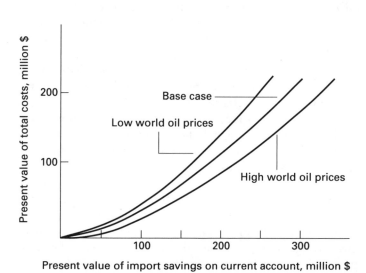

Figure 14.4   Uncertainty and investment effectiveness

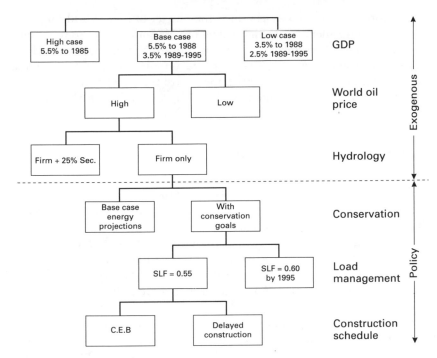

Figure 14.5   Scenario design for the Sri Lankan national energy strategy

most widely respected expert on world oil markets be of great value when it comes to forecasting such items over five and ten year intervals. It is extremely unlikely that even a most sophisticated model of the global oil market could have projected the actual trajectory of oil prices over the past twenty years shown on figure 14.1.

Scenario analysis, however, if it is to be practical, imposes some rather severe limitations on a prospective modeling system. First, since there may be several exogenous scenarios for each of several parameters, the possible permutations of scenarios quickly proliferate. The analyst must be able to quickly test out a multitude of scenarios, discard those with duplicative or uninteresting outcomes, and focus on a more manageable subset. Too many scenarios will simply overwhelm the typical decision-maker. Figure 14.5 illustrates the scenario design used to analyze policy options for the preparation of the Sri Lanka national energy strategy.

It could of course be argued that decision-makers do in fact have at least some degree of explicit control over the border price as a result of bilateral negotiations. There is no question that in the past many oil-importing LDCs have cushioned the impact of high world oil prices by finding agreement with neighboring (and friendly) oil exporters, such as the San Jose Agreement (under which oil-importing countries of the Caribbean were granted special terms to import oil from Mexico and Venezuela. However, such arrangements are the exception rather than the rule: and favors so granted can be withdrawn as quickly as they are offered.

Uncertainty in natural phenomena

The second category of uncertainty relates to those natural phenomena that fall within the domain of concern for the energy planner. Typical examples include the quantity of rainfall in the catchment areas of hydroelectric reservoirs, or the likelihood of finding hydrocarbon reserve of given size in a given geological context. For example, in contrast to the world oil price it usually is possible to define probability distributions for rainfall with sufficient precision to be useful for analysis. The most common analytical problem here concerns the length of the available historical record, which in many countries is relatively short. Although in theory additional data points would provide better characterization of the probability distributions involved, in practice the planner is faced with a given number of years of hydrological data which, over the short run, necessarily represent the database. Unfortunately, definition of the tails of such distributions is the most difficult, although these are precisely the events of most concern. Monsoon failures in successive years or droughts of given years of duration are the sorts of outcome that might have a serious impact on the energy system.

Box 14.1 illustrates the consequences of drought, and of a lack of diversification in the sources of electricity supply in Ghana. In other countries, that faced similar droughts in the early 1980s – such as Sri Lanka and Morocco – thermal generation capacity prevented a complete disaster, even though some load shedding was necessary: but here the consequence is a sharp increase in the foreign exchange bill.

In practice, analysis of this kind of uncertainty is again best handled by a scenario approach, in which the evaluation is conducted in terms of a series of extreme events – as indicated on figure 14.5, that outlines the scenario design for the Sri Lankan national energy strategy analysis. In contrast to oil price uncertainties, however, much more information can be given to the decision-maker concerning the probability of the extreme events. Indeed, the scenario itself might be posed in terms of the event that occurs once in ten or once in fifty years.

Box 14.1 *The consequences of hydro dependence in Ghana*

Of Ghana's total installed capacity of 1100MW, 1072MW is at the Akosombo hydroelectric facility, owned and operated by the Volta River Authority (VRA). VRA is also responsible for transmission and bulk distribution, with a separate government corporation, the Electricity Corporation of Ghana (ECG), being responsible for distribution to customers (and generation at small diesels in isolated centers in the north and east of Ghana.) The Volta Aluminium Company (VALCO), which operates a large aluminium smelter at Tema some eighty miles to the south, is VRA's main customer. VRA also exports electricity to Benin, and is permitted to keep the foreign exchange earnings to finance its debt service and pay for equipment. VRA is generally regarded as a well-run utility, that has maintained high standards of technical management.

In the early 1980s the catchment area of the Volta river suffered a severe drought, and generation at Akosombo fell from 5340GWh in 1981 to 1798GWh in 1984 (see graph below). Even though the brunt of the impact was felt by VALCO, consumption by ECG's customers fell from 1115GWh in 1981 to 799GWh in 1984, necessitating severe load shedding throughout Ghana. The drought of course also affected export earnings (particularly of Cocoa), and coupled with other stresses on the economy, including the return of several hundred thousand expatriate workers from Nigeria after the fall in international oil prices, the economy went into deep decline.

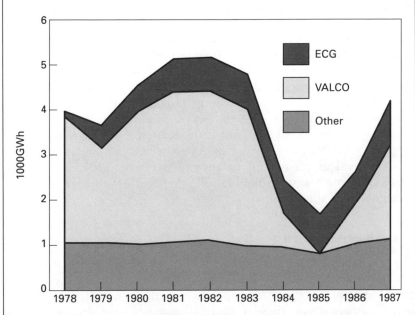

Source: Volta River Authority Annual Reports; Ghana Energy Sector Assessment.

Economic uncertainties

The third type of uncertainty relates to the linkage between energy and the economy. For the typical developing country, there are two major issues here. The first relates to the ability to quantify the linkage between energy demand and the state of the domestic economy. The second relates to fundamental uncertainties about human socio-economic behavior, important primarily in demand projection, and also energy supply responses to changes in relative input prices.

Even in the absence of any sophisticated energy-economic model, the minimum requirement is a projection of the balance of payments over a ten to twenty year time horizon, against which the impact of alternative energy strategies can be gauged. Such projections are frequently available to the energy planner from the local Ministry of Economic Development, Central bank, or from multi-lateral financing institutions such as the IMF or the World Bank. Indeed, there are few developing countries from which a recent economic memorandum is not available. The difficulty in using such projections, however, is that the assumptions concerning the link between economic activity and energy consumption (and therefore energy imports) is frequently obscure. Petroleum imports are generally projected on the basis of some gross income elasticity.

Such uncertainties are again best treated in a manner analogous to world oil prices. Given the current state of the art of modeling energy economic linkages, one should be under no illusions as to the ability to forecast with any reasonable degree of precision the domestic macro-economic impacts of alternative energy policies. Thus a range of scenarios, each postulating a different set of assumptions concerning the evolution of the world and domestic economy and exchange rates (important for setting domestic prices to which consumers react) are typically used as a basis for balance of payments projections. Upon these, in turn, are superimposed the impacts of alternative energy strategies.

Project uncertainty

The final type of uncertainty relates to the individual projects that make up the portfolio of an energy sector investment plan. In chapter 6 we made the point that the criteria applied to evaluation of sectoral options were no different from those traditionally applied to project evaluation: NPV, benefit-cost, and IRR.

The calculation of the cost and benefit streams that go into such

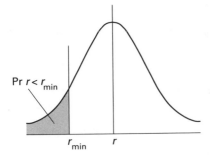

Figure 14.6 Probability distribution of IRR

calculations is of course subject to uncertainty with respect to the technical and economic data. Thus the result, whether expressed in terms of NPV or IRR, will also be subject to uncertainty. The central concept here is the probabilistic interpretation of the rate of return, in which we state the IRR not as a single number, but in terms of a probability distribution, with some mean r and variance σ.

For the investment to be sound, r should be above the cost of capital of the entity making the investment, for example, r_{min}. Moreover, the area under the curve to the left of r_{min} represents the probability that r is less than r_{min}, that is, the probability that the investment is unsound (see figure 14.6).

From the perspective of the financing institution, the shaded area is a measure of the risk involved, since whenever r_{min} is greater than r, the investment becomes unprofitable to the borrower, and hence the borrower's ability to maintain debt service payments becomes compromised. Simply stated, micro-analysis would provide a process of narrowing the variance of IRR calculations for specific investment proposals, by using field surveys and/or field demonstrations to narrow the range of uncertainty in the specific parameters that go into the definition of the cashflow calculations.

Figure 14.7 depicts a general framework for analyzing such uncertainties at the project level. Step 1 helps to specify the context of some general strategy (say solar hot water heating in the commercial/institutional sector). The analysis begins with the identification of a menu of potential technology-market combinations, specifying each to much greater detail than is possible at the macro scale – solar flat plate collectors in medium sized hotels; thermo siphons for rural schools, and so on (step 2). Each of these combinations is next subjected to a first-order rate of return calculation – which at this stage may involve

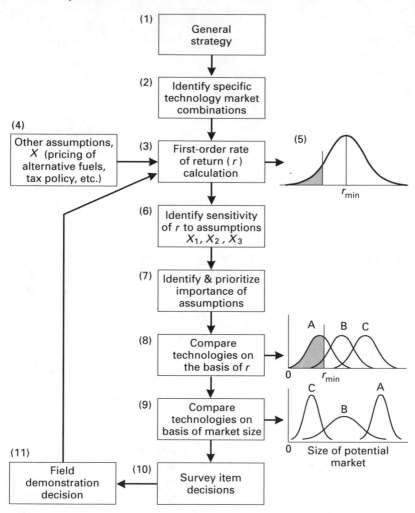

Figure 14.7   The general framework

considerable uncertainty. Thus the resulting rate of return can be viewed as a probabilistic function, of mean r (step 5). If we again denote r_{min} as the minimum acceptable rate of return on investment (more of which below), then the shaded area represents the probability of making an unsound investment. The idea of the analytical process is to reduce the variance of this probability distribution, and hence minimize the probability of making an unsound decision. By repeating the rate of return calculation for ranges or assumptions one can generate the

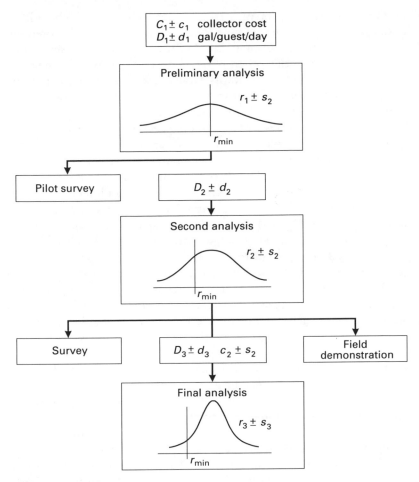

Figure 14.8   Field testing and survey decisions

desired probability distribution for r. Whenever possible, the sensitivity to each assumption should be established (step 6).

The next step is to prioritize the importance of each assumption according to its relative influence on the rate of return calculations (step 7), and to rank the technology/market pairs on the basis of candidate rate of return (step 8) *and* market size (step 9). Given the existing information, there may also be considerable uncertainty over the potential market, since particular technologies may be suited only to very limited housing types (or specific industrial processes), whose occurrence may or may not be well established.

At this point the results of steps 8 and 9 must be combined. A technology may have a very high rate of return r, but small potential market (e.g., technology C of figure 14.7), and may not deserve any further attention. On the other hand, a technology with somewhat lower rate of return, but a potentially large market – such as technology B – may merit both a field demonstration to establish local costs, and a further survey to identify market size more carefully.

Figure 14.8 demonstrates this in a more specific way, for illustrative purposes using the example of solar hot water heating for luxury hotel application. Assume that the two most important parameters subject to uncertainty are the collector cost C (per m^2 of locally manufactured flat plate collector), and the hot water consumption (in gallons/room/day). The first analysis might be done with American data for flat plate collector costs, (say $C_1 \pm c_1$) and some very sparse hotel data from a cursory initial survey, (say $D_1 \pm d_1$); and the mean of $r_1 + s_1$ is less than r_{min}. This would be sufficient to warrant a pilot survey (say of the ten major hotels) to establish hot water consumption with greater precision – say $D_2 \pm d_2$, where d_2 is less than d_1. A second rate of return analysis might yield $r_2 \pm s_2$ (with s_2 again less than s_1), upon which one may now make a decision to field test (to reduce the variance of collector costs, Y_1), as well as a further data survey (the next twenty hotels, with more details on consumption patterns). The point of this procedure is to identify data collection and field demonstration activities that are directly in support of some specific analysis: and to improve the quality of any decision taken (be it to drop the option, or to examine it further) by reducing the bounds of uncertainty.

Of course the calculations of IRR are critically dependent on the ability to accurately forecast project costs. Again the track record in the energy sector is not very good. On figure 14.9 we show the distribution of cost overruns on World Bank financed projects in the period 1967–84: in real terms, the average cost overrun was 19%. In the most extreme cases, the main cause was found to be unanticipated inflation in projects that were approved before the 1973 oil crisis but built afterwards during the years of the high worldwide inflation of the mid to late 1970s.

Implementing a microcomputer-based modeling process

Microcomputers have been introduced into energy planning over the past five years at a rate that has matched their introduction into most other fields, such as health, finance, business, and agriculture. Today microcomputers are a part of energy planning in almost all developing countries. Indeed, over the past few years microcomputers have become

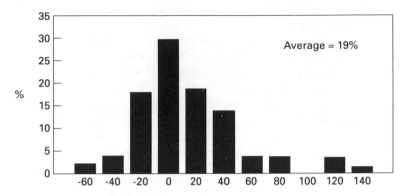

Figure 14.9   Cost overruns in World Bank projects.
Source: Crousillat (1989).

a central part of many technical assistance projects in the energy sectors. Whether or not the results have met the expectations, however, is still open to debate.

The reasons for the acquisition of microcomputers on such a near-universal scale follow in large part directly from the shortcomings of the earlier mainframe models introduced in the late 1970s (see box 3.1). Mainframes were too expensive for energy planning agencies; micro-computers are very cheap (especially when compared to the labor costs of technical assistance). Mainframes were in other buildings, at other institutions; microcomputers sat on the desks of energy planning agency staff. Furthermore, even if mainframe models were accessible, most routine calculations still needed to be done by hand with calculators; microcomputers enabled routine calculations (and other tasks, such as word processing) to be done more efficiently.

In fact, a number of reasons make microcomputers ideally suited for energy planning. First is the issue of data. The type and quantity of data useful for energy planning is well suited to the capacity of low-cost storage media associated with the current generation of microcom-puters. Moreover, microcomputer database software such as LOTUS and dBase prove to be very capable of manipulating typical energy and economic data sets. Energy planning requires neither databases in the gigabyte size range, nor the much more sophisticated software typical of mainframes that are needed to manage such databases. Indeed the computational power of the current generation of microcomputers (based on Intel 80386 or the 80486 microprocessors) is sufficient to handle any model likely to be useful for planning; even fairly large linear programs and very large spreadsheets can be solved easily with the software now available.[2]

The second reason concerns the natural match between many typical energy analysis tasks and a spreadsheet-based programming environment. Demand forecasting, macroeconomic modeling, project analysis, and the preparation of energy balances are all functions ideally suited to spreadsheet calculation. To be sure, there is no reason why spreadsheets cannot be run on mainframes, but sophisticated spreadsheets are uniquely matched to the capabilities of microcomputers and their users.

In a similar vein, even though it is true that mainframe computers could be as user-friendly as modern micros, and offer the user similar (if not superior) graphics capabilities, the fact remains that from the very start microcomputer software was developed with the layman user, rather than the highly trained programmer or engineer, in mind. Indeed, the mass market for microcomputers (and hence their low cost) would not have been possible without user-friendly software designed for general purpose application. This means that the type of staff typical of developing country energy planning agencies, who often lack advanced degrees in computer-related fields, are perfectly capable of learning how to use both the hardware and software within a modest time period. This enhanced ability to train individuals to use microcomputers is an advantage of a much more fundamental nature than the mere low cost, accessibility and desk-top scale. Indeed, microcomputers have reversed the traditional decision-making and resource allocation priorities associated with computing. In the mainframe era, the order of priorities, and costs, was (1) hardware acquisition, (2) software, and (3) training, an order that corresponded to the relative costs. Today, the order of priorities, and costs, has been reversed, with training the most expensive, and hardware the least expensive. Indeed, the cost of microcomputers is currently so low that it should be viewed not as a capital expense, but as an operating expense. Indeed, with the pace of technological change as rapid as it is, one must expect to replace such machines every few years.

Another quite fundamental impact of microcomputers has been the associated developments in software. Even in the case of the minicomputers of the late 1970s, which typically sold for $100,000–200,000, software was expensive, and in most cases needed to be custom-designed, involving expensive computer programming time. For example, a FORTRAN 77 compiler for the PRIME minicomputer was priced at about $7,000. Yet today, similar FORTRAN compilers for

---

[2] For example, the Morocco version of the Energy Finance Assessment Model (EFAM) implemented in Lotus has some 2,000 rows and requires two megabytes of RAM: it recalculates in about 30 seconds on a 12 Hz 80286 based machine with an 80287 math coprocessor.

microcomputers can be acquired for $200–300. Even more importantly, one can purchase at comparable prices readily available commercial software for most analytical tasks, ranging from linear programming and project analysis to presentation-quality color graphics. Microcomputers enable an energy planning agency to perform a range of analytical functions by simply buying low-cost commercial software, that in the mainframe era was not possible because of cost. Thus the initiation of microcomputer-based energy planning, and indeed its success, is largely a matter of the design of training programs, since the hardware and software costs themselves have become increasingly small.

But if microcomputers have made easier the task of energy analysis, and extended its range, to what extent has the quality of decisions actually improved? For all of the much advertised emphasis on presentation quality graphics, to what extent has the communication between analyst and decision-maker improved? Indeed, to what extent have decision-makers themselves used microcomputers? These are the most important questions to answer, because if the only impact of microcomputers has been to do analysis quicker, or do more analysis within the same resource limitations, then microcomputers will not have proven to be very important.

Unfortunately these are also the hardest questions to answer. In part this is because the widespread use of microcomputers is so recent that it is hard to come to firm conclusions at the present time. It is certainly true that to date, senior officials themselves have made relatively little use of microcomputers for actual decision-making. To be sure, heads of planning agencies, and perhaps even one or two ministers, may have a microcomputer at their desks, but they are most likely to be used to retrieve data, and for writing tasks, not for substantive analytical tasks. In fact, almost everywhere decisions are still made on the basis of technical analyses prepared by technical staff. Early expectations that decision-makers would themselves run models have not been fulfilled (nor indeed is it clear that this would be desirable). However, one might note that this is not unique to developing country energy planners; few, if any, Chief Executive officers of major US corporations would make decisions on the basis of their own microcomputer simulations.

Purchase and maintenance issues

In most countries of the eastern hemisphere, power supply is 220volt, 50Hz, as opposed to the western hemisphere standard of 110volt, 60Hz. In Africa and Asia, therefore, local rather than US purchase is often advocated on grounds of power supply suitability. However, it must be noted that many machines now have built-in dual voltage capability. And in cases where a large number of machines are bought in the United States, the costs of separate wiring at 110 volts with a single central power supply unit may be warranted. In any event, with most electro-mechanical devices such as disk drives operating on direct current, the only potential problem with simple (and cheap) step-down transformers is the degree to which 60Hz computer power unit transformers themselves function reliably at 50Hz.[3]

Voltage stabilization equipment is recommended in almost all situations, irrespective of whether the machines are bought locally or in the US. In some cases, uninterruptible power supply units also may be warranted where outages are frequent and prolonged. However, these are substantially more expensive than voltage stabilization equipment, and may become less important as portable and lap-top microcomputers with several hours of battery life capture a larger share of the market.

A second argument for local purchase is maintenance. Machines bought locally can be serviced locally. In particular, it is sometimes said that there is no incentive for a local company to provide maintenance on machines that were brought in by someone else. This may have been valid in 1983–5, in the early phases of the rapid introduction of micros into developing countries. Today, however, it is our experience that even machines bought in the US can be adequately serviced in most places. In any event, with the cost of hardware continuing to decline, maintenance becomes less and less of an issue – broken parts are simply discarded and replaced by new units.

Such issues, however, are relatively minor compared to the actual hardware cost. Dealer markups are very high in most developing countries, with costs typically twice US prices for premium IBM equipment, and three times the cost of US discounted "clones." This is illustrated on table 14.1, which shows a price comparison of local dealer quotes in Rabat, Morocco with US prices (as of early 1986). It should be noted that this price comparison is exclusive of import duties, which are not levied in the case of most technical assistance projects involving government agencies. Over the last few years, such price differentials have all but vanished in southeast Asia, but in Africa they remain.

Rational government policies in the computer and trade sectors can have a beneficial effect. Thus, in Sri Lanka, the Computer and Infor-

[3] Fifty percent of the power supply transformers of equipment placed in the Morocco Ministry of Energy and Mines for Energy Planning, that were purchased in the US, required replacement in the first year of the project. At first it was thought that these difficulties stemmed from 50Hz rather than 60Hz supply, but the manufacturers insisted that this would not be a source of trouble. The cause was finally traced to over-voltages resulting from incorrect transformer settings in the uninterruptible power supply unit.

Table 14.1 *Price comparisons* (1986) (in US$)

	Rabat price	US prices		
		ATT 6300 Plus	IBM XT	PC Compatible
IBM XT, 10 Hb Disk, 1 360k floppy	3915			
Memory Extension to 512 K	491	2595[a]	2395	1595[e]
DOS 2.1	498			
Keyboard AZERTY	69			
Monochrome Screen	268			
256 to 640K Memory Extension	269	—	259.95[c]	259.95
Graphics Board	359	—	130[d]	130[d]
8087 Coprocessor	314	129	129	129
Epson Printer [b]	753	369	369	369
Printer Cable	59	30	30	30
Total Costs	6995	3123	3312	2512

Notes: [a] Comes with 640K installed.
[b] Assumed to be the FX-85.
[c] AST [6]-pack plus 348K.
[d] Hercules compatible.
[e] Equivalent to IBM XT, but of non-IBM origin.

mation Technology Council (established in 1984), while establishing a national computer policy, moved swiftly to reduce import duties on computers to a nominal 5%. This reduced vendor prices significantly and has promoted the wider use of microcomputers – especially in energy planning (Munasinghe, 1986).

It is clear from the recent experience that the hardware acquisition decision needs to be carefully examined on a country-by-country basis. Even if it is true that hardware costs are now quite low, an inappropriate decision at the outset of the process of implementing microcomputer-based planning may have serious consequences later on. Therefore an expert with wide experience should make, in the case of a technical assistance project perhaps as part of an inception mission, a careful assessment of the advantages and disadvantages of each option. A comprehensive discussion on the subject, and a detailed checklist of aspects to be considered before acquiring computer hardware, is provided in Meier (1985a).

Potential problems

While microcomputers inherently address many of the problems encountered in the application of mainframes and minis to energy planning problems, and bring to energy planning agencies a potentially very powerful analytical capability, a number of cautions must be noted. Gifford (1977) identifies four main issues: the black box syndrome, infinite accuracy, data/software integrity, and instant expertise. While these issues are to some extent characteristic of all computers, mainframes as well as micros, and are by no means unique to energy planning, the ready availability of microcomputers in developing countries poses certain dangers to young institutions that have no established history of computerized operations.

As software packages become more complex, the black box problem becomes more acute. Indeed, with the rapid advances in microcomputer hardware, the potential for models becoming needlessly complex (taking advantage of higher computational speeds and larger memory) also increases. In the late 1970s, large-scale energy system models became ever larger as hardware manufacturers developed proprietary software that could solve models containing thousands of constraints and variables. For example the MARKAL model implementation for the IEA had several thousand variables and rows, yet could be solved on large mainframes in a few minutes.[4] Indeed, one of the major advantages of the spreadsheet approach to energy modeling is its complete openness – all assumptions and formulae are readily available to the user, and can be verified rather easily. Because of their relative transparency, LOTUS models can be described as "glass boxes" rather than "black boxes."

The infinite accuracy problem is illustrated by a recent discussion concerning the error introduced by a six-block linearization of a (continuous) annual load duration curve for electricity. Electric utility engineers pointed to the danger that the approximation errors would distort a subsequent fuel consumption calculation. Yet such approximation errors are of at least one order of magnitude smaller than the uncertainties that underlie the electricity demand projection itself (which defines the total area under the load duration curve).

The "garbage in, garbage out" phenomenon that has long plagued computerization has perhaps become less of an issue with microcomputers given the user-friendliness and the ease with which data-input screens can be provided with built-in error checking. At the same time,

---

[4] Obviously, what matters here is the effective turn-around time, not the CPU seconds on a mainframe actually required for the computation.

however, new difficulties have arisen with respect to the verification of spreadsheets. There are many microcomputer experts who claim that any spreadsheet of any size is likely to contain at least one error. The need for adequate documentation and verification of spreadsheets cannot be overemphasized.[5]

The instant expertise problem is well stated by Orenstein (1984), who puts the problem this way:

Anyone having the purchase price can now acquire advanced capabilities and instant expertise. The great danger is not that bad software will be acquired: the danger is that the engineer who purchases the software will not know the difference. The danger is that good and powerful software in the hands of an inexperienced engineer may become life-threatening, and the danger is also that a good and competent engineer will be too easily tempted to step into unfamiliar and dangerous waters.

While this was written in the context of software suitable for design of civil engineering structures (hence the reference to "life-threatening" consequences), the general admonition remains entirely valid to the use of microcomputers in developing countries for planning purposes. One of the biggest dangers concerns the ability to differentiate between model results that are counter-intuitive but correct, and those that are counter-intuitive because of mistakes in either the data input, or in the specification of equations. Only an individual who is well trained, and has significant technical experience, is in a position to make such judgment calls, particularly when dealing with complex models, or models with substantial technical content. Yet the shortage of experienced, well-trained individuals in developing country energy planning entities is the binding constraint on energy planning activity in general.

Case study: microcomputers in energy planning in the Sudan

Energy Sector Planning in the Sudan is the responsibility of the National Energy Administration (NEA), which acquired its first microcomputer in early 1982. Unlike the Sri Lanka and Morocco examples, where microcomputers were introduced as part of technical assistance projects in support of very specific analysis and decision-making needs, in the Sudan the introduction of microcomputers evolved almost spontaneously

---

[5] An illustration of a different sort of issue concerned the computerization of a petroleum sector report, that was previously published by hand, but which was now to be produced by LOTUS. In the case of the pricing system for petroleum products, discrepancies were encountered in the last decimal place between LOTUS generated arithmetic and that contained in the law, which had presumably been calculated by hand. Before publication, the LOTUS spreadsheets had to be edited by hand to ensure consistency with published documents. It was fortunate that an adequate verification process prevented considerable embarrassment.

Table 14.2 *Microcomputer hardware in the Sudan*

Hardware	Configuration	Introduced
Ohio Scientific	64k, 2DD	early 1982
Osborn Portable	256k, 2DD	late 1982
Hyperion Portable	256k, 2DD	early 1983
IBM PC	512k, 2DD, Monochrome	early 1984
IBM XT	640K, 10Mb Hard Disk, Color	early 1985
Compaq Portable	640k, 10Mb Hard Disk	early 1986
IBM XT 286	2Mb RAM, 20Mb Hard Disk	1987

in the appearance of a 64k Ohio Scientific machine in late 1982, left in the Sudan following an unrelated project.[6]

The Ohio scientific machine quickly became inadequate as the analytical demands increased. During the evening hours, NEA began to use Northstar microcomputers owned by the Ministry of Agriculture, and the University of Khartoum's mainframe, but the need for dedicated equipment at NEA became pressing. At this time the Georgia Institute of Technology was using an Osborne for evaluation of renewable energy projects (running Supercalc software), and thus NEA, too, acquired an Osborne portable in early 1983. This was followed in July by the first IBM PC. However, the General Petroleum Corporation (the State Oil Company) was the first to use an IBM PC-XT in the energy sector, purchased under a Chevron grant in late 1982.

Statistics show that only 1% of total possible machine hours were lost due to breakdowns and power cuts. The patterns of use by the different sections of NEA, a fairly good proxy for the type of technical work undertaken, are indicated on table 14.4. The high proportion of use by the computer section reflects its involvement in training NEA staff as a whole, some 85% of whom received instruction by the unit in 1986.

Most of the models used by NEA were developed in-house, with the occasional assistance of experts provided under the auspices of a USAID sponsored technical assistance project. A petroleum transportation model was developed in 1985 in dBase II, and an energy supply-demand model, and petroleum pricing model were developed in 1986 using LOTUS 1-2-3. The FRAP model is being used to analyze fuelwood issues. Occasional use is also made of the ENERSTAT petroleum balance model, a Pascal program developed in 1985 by Canadian consultants for the GPC (the State Petroleum Corporation).

---

[6] We are indebted to Ibrahim Mohamed, head of the NEA computer unit, for the details of the history of microcomputer use in NEA.

Table 14.3 *Commercial software used by NEA*

Software	Acquired	Function
123, dBase	1984	general
Multimate	1986	word processing
STATPLAN	1986	statistical analysis
RESGEN	1988	integrated energy planning
Quickbasic	1986	BASIC programming
LINDO	1985	linear programming
FRAP	1985	fuelwood analysis
ENERSTAT	1983	petroleum sector data analysis
Norton Utilities	1985	file management
Easywriter	1983	word processing

Table 14.4 *Utilization of NEA computers*

Activity	Use %
Biomass Project	1.7%
Pricing Study	6.7%
Project Analysis	29%
Regional Planning	0.9%
Computer Group	42%
Evenings	1.8%
Energy Planning Project	3.9%
National Energy Plan	6.7%

The Sudan experience shows that a formal energy planning package is not necessarily essential to a successful application of microcomputers to energy planning. Indeed, an analytical system developed by the local staff has a number of advantages, not least of which is the high likelihood that it will in fact be used. To be sure, as staff capabilities improve, a more formal system might prove useful, but for the moment the present approach seems well matched to the capabilities of the NEA staff.

The climate and power supply environment in Khartoum must be viewed as extremely hostile, with extremely high temperatures (albeit under low humidity), strong ambient temperature variations, high dust levels, frequent power outages, abnormal voltage and frequency transients being commonplace. Moreover, given the generally difficult economic conditions, maintenance problems might be expected to be severe. Yet the experience has shown that proper attention to the physical operating environment, and standardization on IBM and name brand IBM compatibles, can successfully overcome such potential difficulties.[7]

[7] One of the interesting features of this hardware history is how many of the first brands of microcomputers have all but disappeared from today's marketplace. Northstar and Ohio Scientific have all but vanished, and both Osborne and Hyperion went bankrupt!

CHAPTER 15

Energy issues and policy options in Sri Lanka

Sri Lanka is in many ways typical of a great number of smaller developing countries. Lacking indigenous fossil resources, oil imports have come to represent an increasing burden on the balance of payments. Its natural forests, that once covered much of the land area, have become dangerously depleted as a result of the needs for agriculture, and of increasing demand for fuelwood. With an economy that despite efforts to diversify its export base is still largely dependent upon a few major commodity crops, namely tea and rubber, its balance of payments remains precarious. And the outlook for mobilizing the significant foreign investment necessary for expansion of the capital-intensive energy sector remains a major problem.

In some respects, however, Sri Lanka is not at all typical. Sri Lanka's social indicators – health, education, general social welfare – are much higher than suggested by standard per capita income comparisons. Macroeconomic reforms initiated in the late 1970s resulted in a sustained period of real economic growth, that has slowed recently only as a result of the increasing level of civil disturbances.

Sri Lanka therefore makes for an excellent case study. Much progress was made in the mid 1980s towards the formulation of a coherent National Energy Strategy, which is currently being implemented with some success. It was also one of the first countries in which the writers were able to implement a hierarchial modeling and analysis system in direct support of policy-making, an experience that permits many useful lessons to be drawn.

Macroeconomic background

Sri Lanka's economy has undergone a remarkable transition in the past decade. In 1977–8 the incoming Jayewardene administration removed most of the import and exchange rate controls of previous administrations, and instituted a liberalized policy that actively promoted exports and foreign investment. The economy responded well, with GDP growth rates in the 1978–84 period averaging over 5% per year, after a decade of growth in the 2–3% range. That this was accomplished in a period of quite unfavorable international conditions (the second oil price shock, high interest rates, and inflation) is testimony to the efficacy of a more market oriented macroeconomic policy. However, the degree to which this can be maintained in the medium term is unclear. Falling tea prices, protectionist moves in the US against garment imports, and an increasing foreign debt service burden loom somewhat ominously on the horizon.

Despite much lower world oil prices since early 1986, the oil import bill continues to be a major burden on the current account: at $20/bbl, the oil import still represents 25% of export earnings. Equally serious is the question of energy sector debt service over the medium term: in Sri Lanka, for example, the energy sector is expected to account for some 30% of total national debt service by the late 1990s, primarily as a result of massive investments in the electric sector. Indeed, over the next ten years the electric sector is expected to account for 30% of all public sector investment, a circumstance by no means unique in oil-importing LDCs.

The impact of the first oil shock of 1973–4 was somewhat cushioned in the Sri Lankan economy due to a combination of factors. From 1970–7 the economy was highly protected from external shocks by the closed economic policies that prevailed. The strict exchange control regulations coupled with slow economic growth ensured that the burden of oil imports was manageable during the next few years. Due to the prevailing economic climate the volume of oil imports actually fell between 1970 and 1977, although the oil import bill remained a significant factor in the balance of payments. The turning points in the economy occurred in 1970 and 1977 with the change of governments and the economic policies adopted by them. As shown on table 15.1, from 1970–7 the petroleum demand fell for all products except autodiesel. This could be interpreted as a general response to the doubling of the petroleum price in a difficult economic period.

The second oil shock of 1979–80 had much more severe repercussions than the first. Table 15.3 gives a clear picture of the impact of these two oil shocks. The periods are demarcated as follows. First is 1970–3, the pre-embargo period; then the 1973–7 adjustment period for the first oil shock. 1977–80 includes the period of liberalization of the economy and the second oil shock; 1980–2 is the short-run adjustment period after the second oil shock; and 1982–6 the period of long-run adjustment.

Table 15.1 *Consumption trends for major petroleum products (in 1,000 tons)*

	1970	1977	1980	1983	1986	1970–7 %growth	1977–80 %growth	1980–6 %growth
Gasoline	148.4	111.6	107.7	117.5	130.6	− 4.0	− 1.2	21.3
Kerosene	272.5	213.1	188.7	159.1	154.2	− 3.5	− 4.0	− 18.3
Autodiesel	254.5	261.4	399.5	464.3	487.3	4.0	15.2	22.0
Industrial Diesel	87.9	46.3	61.0	295.9	36.0	− 8.8	9.6	—
Fueloil[a]	208.8	134.7	247.2	253.1	129.0	− 6.1	22.4	—
Power Sector Consumption	133.0	7.0	58.5	—	—	− 34.3	102.9	—
Fuel Oil	133.0	7.0	45.0	—	—	—	—	—
Diesel	—	—	13.5	—	—	—	—	—

Notes: [a] Excludes reexport and bunker sales.
Source: Ceylon Petroleum Corporation.

With the liberalization of the economy in 1977, the growth rate of GDP from 1977–80 averaged 6.8%. The rapidly improving economic growth during this period resulted in an accelerated demand for electricity (which previously, during 1973–7, grew at an average rate of 4.7%), due to the low tariff structure and untapped potential markets. The demand was met totally by hydropower. During 1977–80, without taking into consideration the power cuts that prevailed, electricity growth averaged 10.2%; this had a significant impact on the economy since the supply had to be supplemented by thermal generation. During the same period, demand for petroleum products grew at 7.2% compared with − 5.2% in 1973–7. In the short-run adjustment period (1980–2) after the second oil shock, demand growth for both electricity and petroleum stayed high, at an annual 10.1% and 14.7% respectively,

Table 15.2 *Petroleum import bill ($US millions)*

	1970	1977	1980	1983	1986
(A) Petroleum imports	10	160	489	468	197
(B) Petroleum reexports	5	64	181	106	84
(C) Net petroleum imports	5	96	308	362	113
(D) Non-petroleum exports	337	667	864	953	1132
(E) (C) as percentage of (D)	1.5	14.2	35.6	38.0	10.0
(F) Exchange rate, Rs per $US	5.2	15.6	18.0	25.0	28.5

Source: Sri Lanka Customs.

Table 15.3 *Evolution of GDP, energy demand and prices for the period 1970–1986*

	Pre-embargo 1970–3	Adjustment period for the first oil shock, 1973–7	Intermediate period, 1977–80	Adjustment period for the second oil shock, 1980–2	Adjustment period for the second oil shock, 1982–6
GDP growth rate [a]	2.2%	3.4%	6.8%	5.4%	4.8%
Growth rate of total energy demand [b]	—	2.8%	2.3%	2.5%	—
Electricity demand [c]	7.6%	4.7%	10.2%	10.1%	7.3%
Non-electricity demand [d]					
Demand for petroleum production	0.9%	− 5.2%	7.2%	14.7%	− 6.7%
Demand for non-fuelwood energy [e]	—	6.2%	0.4%	− 0.2%	—
Changes in energy prices					
Electricity prices [f]	− 3.12%	− 3.64%	32.6%	37.8%	—
Petroleum product prices [g]	11.2%	14.2%	30.0%	− 3.0%	7.1%

Notes: [a] Annual average rate of change of real GDP for each specified period.
[b] Annual average rate of change of total energy demand (commercial and non-commercial energy).
[c] Annual average growth rate of electricity demand.
[d] Annual average growth rate of demand for each specified period.
[e] Includes all non-commercial energy sources such as firewood, crop residues, cow dung, etc., converted into a common unit (Mtoe).
[f] Changes in weighted average prices (or price index of all commercial energy sources).
[g] Weighted average of petroleum products prices.

as the economy continued to expand. Since then growth rates have dropped significantly, particularly for petroleum (− 6.7% in 1982–6) as domestic rupee prices followed the international price decline.

The marginal increases in the demand for commercial energy in Sri Lanka up to 1985 were directly linked to the size of petroleum imports, regardless of whether these increases took the form of higher electricity consumption or direct consumption of petroleum products. Thus after 1977, the combination of increased consumption and a doubling of oil prices resulted in a rapidly growing oil import bill. By 1981, the net oil import bill more than tripled and the proportion of export earnings devoted to importing oil rose from 15% to 39%.

It is noteworthy that the first international oil crisis had no severe repercussions on the Sri Lankan economy due to the stagnant state of the domestic economy. The second oil crisis, however, not only affected the balance of payments, but also the terms of trade, which declined by over 30% between 1977 and 1980. This was due primarily to the increase in import prices of oil, and the decline in export prices of the tree crop sector.

Though investments rose from 14% to 30% of GDP from 1977–80, this was not accompanied by an increase in domestic savings. Increased investments have been financed by drawing down international reserves and commercial borrowing. As a result, table 15.2 shows that up to 1977 the cost of oil imports was not a source of serious concern to Sri Lanka. Additions to international reserves declined from an inflow of 3% of GDP in 1978 to an outflow of 6% of GDP in 1980, while net use of commercial financing rose from −1% to 6% of GDP for the same period.

The rupee, which was pegged to the dollar by a floating exchange rate, depreciated in value from Rs15.60 in 1978 to Rs23.53 in 1983. The manifestation of these financial difficulties, along with international price increases, has been a high inflation rate. Before reducing significantly to an average of 4.7% between 1984 and 1986, inflation accelerated sharply from 1978 to 1980. The recent decline in world oil prices had little effect on energy demand since this dollar price decrease was offset by the decline of the rupee value against the dollar, thus keeping domestic oil product prices relatively stable.

In brief, Sri Lanka's chief macroeconomic problems continue to be the high capital formation requirement in relation to national savings, the slow growth of exports relative to imports resulting in severe balance of payments deficits and depletion of external reserves, and a tendency toward higher than desirable inflation and unemployment rates.

The energy situation

Nature has not endowed Sri Lanka with fossil energy resources. Solar energy and hydro electricity, harnessed from the rivers which spring up from the central hilly region (the most important of which is the Mahaweli Ganga), are the main indigenous resources, together with the island's forests. Unfortunately, the natural forest area has declined rapidly over the past few decades, falling from about 44% of total land area in 1955 to about 24% in 1980. Conversion to agricultural use and increasing fuelwood consumption are the main reasons for this decline. It has been estimated that the natural forest will vanish within another twenty years at current rates of deforestation.

Gross energy supply (1983)   **Useful or net supply (1983)**

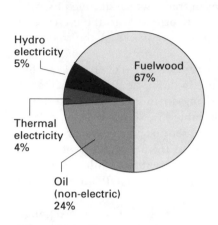

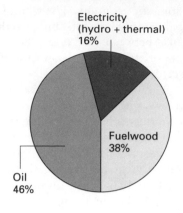

Figure 15.1   Energy supply

Though reliable data on fuelwood supply is difficult to obtain, the estimates clearly indicate its precarious and unsustainable nature. Over the past two decades, incremental wood production – from the natural regeneration of forests, agricultural residues, and rubber replanting, etc. – has fallen far behind consumption and today accounts for less than half the estimated annual consumption of around 5 million tons.

Figure 15.1 shows the typical Sri Lankan energy supply pattern. Fuelwood (67%) dominates gross energy supply, with oil at 24%, thermal-based electricity at 4% and hydro electricity supplying 5%. Oil is the most important source in supplying useful energy or net supply (46%), with fuelwood at 38% and electricity at 16% (supplied by both hydro and oil).

Since 1978 there has been a substantial increase in the demand for all forms of commercial energy, which rose in aggregate at 8.8% per annum in the 1978–80 period, as opposed to a slight decline in the preceding seven years. Petroleum consumption has grown even more rapidly since the increase in demand for electricity and has had to be met by increased thermal generation.

Sri Lanka has access to a variety of economically viable, non-conventional renewable energy resources – solar, wind, biomass, and mini-hydro – which could be utilized to meet some of the country's energy demand in the medium term. Sri Lanka's location assures it of a relatively high and uniform level of insolation which could be harnessed

**Commercial energy
electricity & oil (1983)**

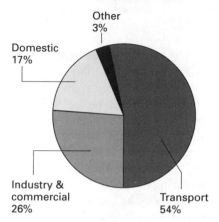

Other
3%

Domestic
17%

Industry &
commercial
26%

Transport
54%

**All energy
electricity, oil & fuelwood (1983)**

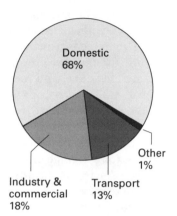

Domestic
68%

Other
1%

Industry &
commercial
18%

Transport
13%

Figure 15.2   Energy consumption patterns

for both water heating and crop drying. A very few households currently use hot water; the main market for these heaters will initially lie in the commercial and tourist sectors. The use of solar energy for crop drying is an important alternative to be developed since tea and other crop processing industries consume over one million tons of fuelwood (20% of total fuelwood consumption according to World Bank data) per year.

While the emphasis in Sri Lanka has traditionally been on large hydropower schemes, about 10 MW of small schemes (5 kw to 250 kw range) have been operating in the tea estates of the central region since 1925. However, these have been abandoned because of the availability of cheap and reliable electricity from the national grid. In addition to the rehabilitation of these existing plants, potential sites for mini-hydro schemes exist in the central hilly areas and in irrigation systems in the north central part of the island.

The typical energy consumption pattern is illustrated in figure 15.2. For commercial energy consumption (oil and electricity), transport (54%), and industry and commerce (26%) are the main users, with domestic demand amounting to 17% and other use 3%. These shares change dramatically when fuelwood is included in the analysis; domestic consumption then accounts for the major share of 68%, industry and commerce 18%, transport 13%, and others 1%.

From 1970 to 1977, the consumption of all petroleum products fell, with the exception of LPG (used mainly for cooking) and auto diesel. This has been in part due to the virtual elimination of petroleum based electricity generation that followed the addition of new hydroelectric capacity, and in part due to the response of demand to the doubling of prices in a difficult economic period. Since 1977, most products have shown increased growth in an improved economic climate. The oil demand for thermal power generation has shown more than average increases for diesel and fueloil, dropping only with the recent addition of Mahaweli hydro capacity. Only the consumption of gasoline and kerosene has continued to fall after the post-1977 period. This is a reflection of the price sensitivity of demand for both these goods.

In contrast to petroleum consumption, electricity demand continued to grow at an average annual rate of 7% during the 1970–7 period. This has been due to: (a) the attractiveness of electricity as a source of energy since there were no tariff increases during this period, while petroleum prices rose by more than 50% with the world energy crisis, and (b) the existence of a potentially untapped market for electricity. Consequently, the demand for electricity has shown less responsiveness to price and changes in the overall economic performance than petroleum products. Since 1977 electricity demand accelerated – electricity sales grew at an average of 9.6% annually until 1980. This value does not include the 3% reduction in demand due to prolonged power cuts in 1980 which resulted from the high growth rate of consumption and an unexpected and severe drought. The liberalized import of electric appliances for domestic use has also contributed to the increase in electricity consumption. The impact on the economy has been significant since this demand had to be met with increased import of petroleum products for thermal power generation.

The national energy strategy

It is against this background that a national energy strategy (NES) for Sri Lanka was developed during the period 1984–5 (Munasinghe and Meier, 1985). The important point about the NES is not the preparation of a document *per se*, as much as the process that led to a policy consensus among the key institutions and decision-makers. Obtaining a policy consensus for the energy sector is rarely easy, given the usual institutional tensions between, on the one hand, electric utilities and oil companies who are often committed to system expansion, and, on the other hand, energy sector and macroeconomic planners who must deal with the broader issues of resource allocation in the economy.

Fortunately, as a result of reforms that occurred in 1982–4, the Sri Lankan institutional setting is perhaps more conducive than elsewhere to achieving this consensus. The Energy Planning and Policy Analysis Task Force, established in 1984, is an inter-agency body charged with developing an overall national energy strategy. This task force coordinates energy policy across the various subsectors, and includes senior officials from the Ministries of Power and Energy, and Finance and Planning (the entity responsible for overall macroeconomic policy), as well as from the main energy institutions. Nevertheless, even given this relatively favorable institutional climate, the substantive issues of policy, and the search for implementable options, remain difficult.

Given Sri Lanka's precarious balance of payments position, its absence of fossil fuels, and the critical fuelwood situation, the basic directions of policy are clear. In contrast to many other countries in South Asia that nature has endowed with significant fossil resources (natural gas in Pakistan and Bangladesh; coal, oil, and gas in India), the prospects for discovering similar resources in Sri Lanka remain poor. In such a situation, not only are the energy options more limited, but also the failure to adopt a comprehensive, long-term strategy are much more severe. Otherwise, the ever increasing oil import needs will result in severe foreign exchange difficulties, having the effect of dampening economic growth. The NES is based on five main objectives, namely:

1 **Increasing the efficiency of energy use** Increasing energy efficiency is not merely for short-term benefit, but must be pursued consistently over the longer term. Lacking its own fossil resources, for the next thirty to forty years the bulk of Sri Lanka's energy must come from imported fossil fuels, until sometime in the twenty-first century when they will be replaced by newer energy technologies. Without a sustained effort to maximize the efficiency of fossil fuel utilization, development objectives will inevitably be compromised.

2 **Efficient pricing** Recent changes in electricity and oil prices have brought average commercial fuel prices close to economically efficient levels (i.e., border prices). These favorable trends must be maintained to ensure good demand management. While average prices are reasonable, the detailed structure of electricity and petroleum product prices need to be further revised – especially prices of kerosene and diesel relative to gasoline.

3 **Reducing the vulnerability to external shocks** Over the past decade Sri Lanka has experienced numerous external shocks affecting both the energy sector and the economy as a whole, particularly the two oil price shocks of the 1970s, and the 1983–4 drought. In order to reduce this vulnerability, diversification of both the type and source of energy

is important, e.g., increasing coal use for power generation and industrial energy, purchasing petroleum products and crude from a variety of sources, including the spot market, all decrease vulnerability as well as cost.

4 **Optimizing the use of indigenous resources** Hydro electricity and fuelwood represent the country's two main indigenous fuels. Even if commercial oil deposits are found in the next few years, and even if the efforts to commercialize other renewable energy technologies – small hydro, producer gas, wind, solar heating, etc. – are successful, conventional hydro and fuelwood will be the main sources of domestic energy until the year 2000.

5 **Rationalizing the institutional framework** Prior to 1983, the institutional framework was fragmented with the various energy sector line institutions like CEB, CPC, Forest Department, NARESA, Mahaweli Development Authority, etc., all reporting to different Ministries. As described in chapter 12, several reforms were made in late 1982. An Energy Coordinating Team was set up to formulate and coordinate policy. This mechanism is working well with each of the three task forces EPPAN, EDMAC, and NERSE responsible for one major programme (NES, NEDMCP, and NFCP respectively), and many smaller initiatives. This framework should be maintained and strengthened.

More recently, the Lanka Electricity Company was created as a subsidiary of the CEB to gradually take over electricity distribution and the CEB was absorbed within the Ministry of Power and Energy – further consolidating policy coordination and implementation in the commercial fuels sector. The NES should be implemented using the framework of the ECT for overall coordination, and the line agencies for implementation.

The specific policy initiatives necessary to implement these broad directions were classified by the NES into two major categories: (1) short-term options, that provide measurable results within one to three years; and (2) medium to long-term options, whose gestation period is such that implementation measures needed to be undertaken in the short run even though results would require five to ten years.

Options for the short term

The National Energy Demand Management and Conservation Programme (NEDMCP) encompassing electricity as well as petroleum products, especially in the transportation and industrial sectors, is of high priority, and was seen to have long-term as well as short-term benefits. If the goals of the NRDMCP were met, the savings on the aggregate oil import bill by 1990 were estimated to lie in the range of $US49–50million, depending on the rate of GDP growth actually attained.

The conservation program was therefore seen to provide substantial benefits independent of the state of the world oil market. It also served to cushion the impact of droughts; under the current capacity expansion plan of the CEB, attainment of the electricity conservation targets reduces oil consumption to very low levels even in drought years. Moreover, the fact that the conservation program may permit unit deferrals is of utmost importance, given the difficulties of obtaining external finance.

The National Fuelwood Conservation Programme (NFCP)
The NFCP seeks to address fuelwood and deforestation issues by improved management of both fuelwood supply and demand. The computer analysis confirmed the urgency of the problem, and the potential impact of failure to pursue the program as soon as possible. The estimates indicate that from fuelwood consumption alone (i.e., ignoring such factors as construction timber demands), the natural forest cover will decline from about 1.6m ha. to 0.3 to 0.5m ha. by 2010, depending on assumptions about the sustainable yield. Obviously, at these levels of resource depletion, sharp price increases for fuelwood can be expected, leading in turn to possible substitution by expensive, imported petroleum products. Moreover, the environmental consequences of almost complete denudation of forest cover are equally severe.

However, this program, while clearly yielding short-term benefits, is essentially of a one-time nature. It will reduce fuelwood consumption over the short to medium run, but cannot arrest the longer-term trends as development proceeds and the economy and population increase. As shown in figure 15.3, even if all households were to have adopted the improved stoves by 1989, total consumption again begins to increase after 1990, and will be at or above pre-1989 levels by the turn of the century.

Oil acquisition and pricing strategy
Given the volatility of the world oil market, the principal priority is for a more flexible acquisition strategy that can respond quickly to relative price changes. The analysis indicated that, whilst the current operation of the refinery is near optimal, small changes in relative prices have a

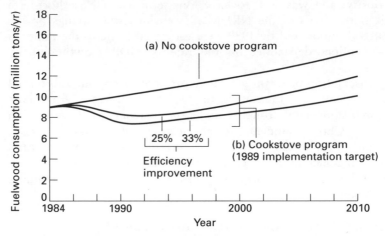

Figure 15.3   Fuelwood consumption

significant impact, particularly when crude prices are in imbalance with those of refined products. A start toward more flexible operation had already been made by allowing the Ceylon Petroleum Corporation (CPC), owner of the refinery, to purchase a higher fraction of crude on spot markets, and the refinery optimization model, originally developed by the ECT, is being used to assist oil purchasing strategy. The Single Point Buoy Mooring project will also serve to lower the total crude cost by about $6/ton (and have the additional benefit of reducing congestion in Colombo harbor). However, there remain some areas where lack of flexibility hinders optimal management, such as the long time lag involved in adjusting foreign bunker prices.

Continued attention to the oil acquisition strategy is especially warranted in light of the significant changes in the regional oil market anticipated as a result of the large additions of refinery capacity in the Persian Gulf countries that are now coming on line. Whilst the precise impact is subject to uncertainty, in light of the worldwide excess refining capacity, the low crude acquisition cost for these refineries will undoubtedly allow them to increase their market share of refined products at the expense of older, smaller refineries.

Finally, the importance of maintaining a petroleum product pricing system based on the foreign exchange cost to the country was examined by simulating the energy system under alternative price elasticity assumptions. The results indicated that failure to maintain domestic prices at their border price equivalent would have a foreign exchange impact of as much as $30million by 1995.

Options for the medium and long term

A second set of options can be expected to become effective over the medium to long term. Due to their long-term impact, however, even if they are implemented aggressively it will take at least five years before they will have any measurable impact on the overall energy situation. However, this long gestation period is the very reason why it is important that these programs begin to be pursued vigorously at the present time.

While the NFCP is clearly essential, it must be recognized that even an aggressively promoted cookstove program does not address the long-term problem, as already noted. Indeed, a detailed analysis indicates that the breathing space afforded by NFCP over the next few years must be used to put in place a plantation program of at least 1,000 ha./year, in addition to the programs already underway (that provide for about 5,000 ha./year). The long-term foreign exchange consequences of a depleted forest resource are extremely serious, quite aside from the impact on rural families whose household budgets would then face the cost of commercial fuels. In 1985, fuelwood is estimated to have provided some 4.3 million tons of oil equivalent energy; even when one takes into account the much higher efficiencies at which petroleum utilizing devices operate, this still represents an avoided exchange cost of $200million.

While a substantial expansion of the plantation program has been recommended, even if higher planting densities prove feasible, questions of land availability will arise. Moreover, the ability to mount an expanded program will also depend upon the managerial, personnel, and resource capabilities of the relevant institutions. Indeed, further technical assistance to strengthen the forestry sector may be necessary to lay the groundwork for an expanded program.

A second medium-term option is the development of renewable energy. The NERSE task force has been established to coordinate the development of a variety of renewable energy sources. Whilst some of these technologies appear promising, a concerted effort will be necessary to establish coherent implementation. To examine the scope of the impact of such efforts, we have postulated an optimistic scenario for the penetration of these technologies into the economy, as shown on table 15.4

Even under these rather optimistic assumptions, our analysis indicates that these technologies would displace only 2% of CEB's 1995 generation. The corresponding reduction in the oil import bill amounts to only 1% by 1995. Beyond this time frame, a recent detailed study of

Table 15.4 *The maximum renewables case*

Option	Basis	1995 GWh
Small hydro	15 Mw by 1995	39
Wind	5 Mw by 1995	26
Producer gas	one 150 Kw unit per year	5
Solar water heaters	30000 panels in place (6 Kw equivalent/day)	21
Biogas	5000 systems, 1.8 Kwh/day	8
Photovoltaics	10000 panels in place (1.8 Kwh/day)	3

electricity supply has identified about 240 GWh per year (or about 55 MW) of small hydro plants (all around or under 10 MW), that will be economically competitive with oil at $40 per barrel.

Nuclear power
As in many other small developing countries that lack fossil resources, the possibility of nuclear power generation has been raised from time to time. However, until the electric system load reaches at least 2,000–2,500 MW, nuclear power plants are not viable on the basis of present data, from a technical, systems, and economic standpoint. Since a 2,000 MW demand can be expected at the earliest by the turn of the century, nuclear power would be an option only beyond the year 2000. However, it should be noted that, unlike other South Asian countries, whose longer-term power generation prospects are expected to rely heavily on domestic resources (lignite, coal, and natural gas), the long-term prospects for power generation in Sri Lanka are unclear. Even if all the remaining hydro power is exploited, including small hydro, at some point substantial thermal generation for baseload is inevitable. Therefore, whilst nuclear energy is not an option of any immediacy, the situation needs periodic review, especially if technical innovations make smaller units in the 300–500 MW range economical. Training of manpower and monitoring of nuclear technological developments abroad should be pursued to maintain readiness.

Energy modeling

Energy modeling was introduced to Sri Lanka in a very cautious and deliberate fashion. As the energy planning activity commenced in support of the national energy strategy formulation, only the very

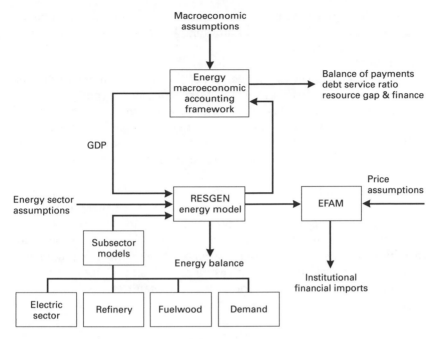

Figure 15.4   The Sri Lankan modeling system

simplest modeling activities were introduced – spreadsheets for tabulation of historical energy balances and demand projection, and the RESGEN software for projection of future energy balances. Only about a year later, as data and staff capabilities improved, were more sophisticated models introduced (such as the refinery LP). Indeed, it is one of the most important lessons of the energy planning experience of the last decade that the key to any successful modeling activity is to match the level of modeling detail and sophistication to the training and experience of the technical staff.

A second criterion for the design of a modeling framework for Sri Lanka was to match it with the institutional structure. The hierarchical nature of the planning process itself (see figure 2.1 in chapter 2), therefore demanded a corresponding hierarchial approach to the modeling effort. Thus the modeling framework had the same three levels as the planning process itself. At the first level were the subsectoral models corresponding to the line agencies such as the CPC and CEB responsible for execution of policy and day-to-day operations. At the second level were the models for energy sector integration, the focus of the ECT. Finally, at the third level was the model for integration of the energy sector with the other sectors of the economy, institutionally the domain of the Ministry of Finance and Planning. The modeling system, whose main elements are shown on figure 15.4, thus fully reflects the institutional structure.

The process begins with an analysis of the macroeconomy in the first of three modules of the ENMAC macroeconomic accounting framework. The output of this step includes projections of the sectoral decomposition of GDP and non-energy merchandise trade. The RESGEN energy model is run next. The demand equations in this model are driven by the GDP estimates passed from the macromodel. Other inputs are passed from the more detailed sectoral models: the refinery configuration and yield coefficients from the refinery optimization model and the estimates of fuelwood demand from the fuelwood model.

As part of obtaining the energy supply-demand balance, RESGEN estimates which energy facilities must be built to meet the demand, thereby providing a year-by-year estimate of investment requirements. The basis for the electric sector investments, which account for the bulk of total energy investment, is the generation plan of the CEB. Because different demand scenarios result in changes in the future electric load growth, the analysis includes an examination of the timing of capacity increments. An optimal dispatch model built into RESGEN also provides detailed estimates of CEB fuel consumption as a function of plant availabilities, hydroenergy limitations, and the system load factor.

The investment outlays, and their concomitant debt service obligations, are passed back to the macromodel together with the oil import bill (and the smaller earnings from bunkers and petroleum product exports). These energy sector transactions are merged with the non-energy transactions in a second module of the macroeconomic model. Finally the third module provides overall estimates of the balance of payments, the financing necessary to cover the external resource gap, the debt service ratio, and other macroeconomic impacts.

The RESGEN energy model passes the domestic energy transactions (e.g., sales from the CPC to the distributors, or CEB sales to consumers) to the EFAM Energy Finance Assessment Model, which assembles a picture of the energy sector financial flows among the key institutions and consumers in the sector. EFAM also provides estimates of the government revenue from the sector (from petroleum product taxes, the Business Turnover Tax on energy institutions, customs duties, etc.). The financial flows are obtained by multiplying the physical energy flows (from RESGEN) by the appropriate set of prices and taxes. EFAM can therefore be used to assess the implications of alternative energy pricing and taxation schemes.

The basis for the electric sector calculations is a plant-specific dispatch into a linearized load duration curve. The dispatch algorithm maps individual plants into the vertical blocks of the load duration curve based on the respective capacity availabilities. Again, with the institutional considerations in mind, the plant list takes the form of alternative capacity expansion plans as might be generated by a more detailed capacity expansion model, such as WASP. There is explicit consideration of the energy constraints of hydro plants, and the algorithm can be shown to provide the optimum dispatch in mixed hydro-thermal systems.

Scenarios and the analysis of uncertainty

Since one of the most important aspects of the energy planning process is the treatment of uncertainties, an initial distinction is made between the policy options that lie under the control of the Sri Lankan government, and those external factors over which the decision-maker has no control. Among the most important of these external factors are the world oil price, the overall state of the world economy that determines the external trade environment, and such factors as the level of interest rates on external debt. Because of the dependence of the electric sector on hydro electricity, rainfall variations represent another important source of uncertainty.

Economic growth

Ideally, one would wish to project the domestic economic growth rate as a function of domestic policy and the external environment. However, the present state of the art of macroeconomic modeling is such that great difficulties are still encountered in quantifying some of the key relationships. Indeed, the experience of Sri Lanka since the economic liberalization of 1977–8 disproves much of the common wisdom concerning the short-term impact of external shocks, and oil price increases in particular, on the rate of economic growth.

Due to these reasons, the domestic growth rate was used as one of the exogenous assumptions of the analysis: three scenarios of GDP growth were posited over the period 1986–95 ranging from a high case of 5.5% GDP growth through 1995, to a low case with 3.5% growth to 1990, and 2.5% thereafter.

The base case assumes a 5.5% growth from 1986 to 1989, which is consistent with the projection of the Ministry of Finance and Planning (MFP) in its last annual report on public investment available at the time this study was carried out. From 1989 to 1995 it is assumed that the rate falls to 4% per year. This scenario implies a continuation of the growth trend over the seven years since the economic reforms were introduced by the incoming administration in 1978. Even though this trend was maintained during a period of severe external shocks – the oil price increase of 1979–80, sharp increases in the price of imported goods due to worldwide inflation, as well as falling world market shares of the international tea and rubber trades – growth rates in the late 1980s in excess of this trend seemed most improbable. However, a case in which the 5.5% rate is maintained through the mid 1990s was also examined.

There were, on the other hand, a number of reasons for the GDP growth rate to be substantially lower. There was no guarantee that Sri Lanka's significant growth in manufactured exports would continue, which together with the increasing external payments burden may have begun to cause dislocations in the economy. The low scenario therefore posited a GDP growth rate of 3.5% through 1989, falling to 2.5% in the period 1990–5. It should, of course, be noted that these scenarios are not forecasts or predictions – they were used in this study for the sole purpose of examining the robustness of energy policy options under different sets of conditions.

Oil price

The future condition of the world oil market is extremely difficult to forecast. Moreover, the complexity of the market, with the intricate interactions between the prices of different crudes and petroleum products, further complicates the situation for a small importing country such as Sri Lanka. Even without some cataclysmic disruption to the world oil supply situation, significant near-term changes could occur in the petroleum product market in southeast Asia as the new refineries in the Persian Gulf come on stream. Therefore, although the landed price of crude was used as the index of the world oil price, it was shown that the interplay of petroleum product prices around this level has implications for Sri Lanka of the order of millions of dollars per year.

In the high world oil price (WOP) case, constant real prices were assumed until 1988, followed by an annual increase of 4% thereafter (again in real terms). This brings the 1995 price to about the levels experienced at the very peak of the oil crisis in the early 1980s.

The low WOP case assumed constant real prices until 1989, with a 1% per annum real price increase thereafter. Again it should be stressed that these scenarios were used (and are reported here) for indicative purposes only, rather than to imply a judgment as to the likely path of the world oil price. Indeed, the entire thrust of the national energy strategy is the identification of policy initiatives that are robust under the expected uncertainties.

In constructing the overall scenarios, one obvious issue is the degree to which the world oil price and GDP assumptions are correlated. Increases in the oil price is only one of several types of external shocks that Sri Lanka has experienced (and will experience in the future), and the adjustment mechanisms to these external shocks can be quite complex. Thus, it is not possible to forecast a direct impact on GDP from a given oil price shock (as the experience of Sri Lanka in the years 1977–82 reflects very well). Indeed, the impact of the relative ease with which Sri Lanka was able to adjust to the shocks of the 1970s, of which additional external financing was a major part, will only now be felt as the debt service obligations become due. For the same reason, the fact that oil prices are currently falling in real terms does not necessarily imply a faster domestic growth rate.

Hydrological uncertainties
A national energy strategy must be concerned with short-term as well as long-term issues, of which temporary disruptions to the supply are among the most important. As Sri Lanka becomes more dependent on hydro electricity, the ability of the Ceylon Electricity Board to cope with drought years also becomes more important since most of the major impoundments are concentrated in a relatively small area of the hill country. The impact of a failure, delay, or abnormal monsoon can be potentially quite serious, as evidenced by the situation in 1983. Two cases of hydrological outcomes were examined: the current planning basis of the CEB that is based on firm plus 25% of secondary hydro energy, and a case based on firm hydro only (that corresponds roughly to a one in fifty-year hydrological event).

The basic modeling design was thus structured around the four possible combinations of oil price and GDP growth. In the case of the electric sector analysis, we also include the hydroenergy uncertainties. On to these basic scenarios, which capture the exogenously determined factors, were superimposed a series of cases that reflected the policy interventions under consideration. These included initiatives for energy conservation, electric sector demand management, pricing, fuelwood plantation and cookstove programs, refinery management and oil import strategies, fuel substitutions, and others.

Lessons of the Sri Lankan modeling experience
There are two major lessons to be drawn from the Sri Lankan experience. The first concerns the necessary level of detail. In the energy models,

information needs to go to the project level in all subsectors on the supply side, and in the industrial sector on the demand side. In the energy-macroeconomic model, the sectoral disaggregation is quite detailed, and the output tables of the model replicate the accounts structure of the Central Bank. In contrast, many of the models recently published are based on highly aggregated parameters.

The second lesson concerns the need for the modeling framework to be policy oriented and to replicate the official government planning process. The starting point must be the official projection of the government, whatever its shortcomings. Failure of the energy sector model to replicate this projection will simply divert resources into endless, and ultimately unfruitful, debate over the model's intrinsic merits. The reason for adopting the macroeconomic projection of the Ministry of Finance and Planning as the starting point, rather than some other more formalized model incorporating our own judgments about the macroeconomic future, is to move quickly to a consensus on the starting assumptions and conditions for the modeling by the interested parties within the government, and then be able to move on to the analysis.

Annex: The macroeconomic accounting framework

A number of possible approaches for the macroeconomic analysis were considered. The first was to have used one of the generally available macroeconomic models – such as the World Bank Minimum Standards Model – and adapt it to the particular requirements of the project. However, it was quickly apparent that the level of aggregation provided by such a model was totally inconsistent with the needs of the overall analysis. Whilst perhaps useful for general policy guidance, the energy planning process in Sri Lanka has long advanced from matters of general policy direction to a more specific consideration of alternative investment programs, resulting in a level of information about investment outlays and debt service obligations difficult to reconcile with the aggregate parameters (incremental capital-output ratios and the like) that is the staple of such highly aggregated macromodels. In any event, such a model would also have been very difficult to align to the macroeconomic planning process used by the Ministry of Finance and Planning.

A second approach was to have used a more sophisticated econometric model, either taken from another source, or developed specifically for the project. A review of the many economic models that have been developed for Sri Lanka, however, revealed that none was suitable for our purposes.[1] In fact,

---

[1] The Central Bank of Ceylon publishes two excellent series that contain many quantitative studies: the Staff Studies and the Occasional Research Studies. Many of the latter are theses prepared at UK and American universities by Central Bank staff members. However, the Central Bank itself does not have a macroeconomic forecasting model, since the macroeconomic planning function lies with the Ministry of Finance and Planning. The closest thing to an economy-wide macroeconomic model at a sufficient level of detail is Sirisena (1976). However, this model is based on work done in 1972, and its estimated parameters were no longer considered valid in light of the dramatic structural adjustments that the economy has experienced since 1977.

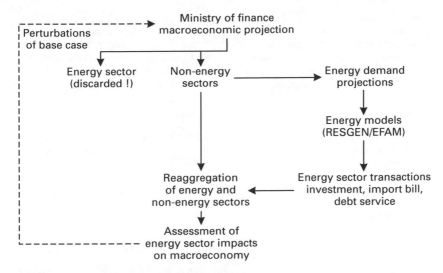

Figure 15.5   Linkages between macroeconomic and energy models

no econometrically estimated macromodel suitable for policy planning is available for Sri Lanka: the Ministry of Finance and Planning itself is only in the early stages of developing one.

The overall approach to linking the macroeconomic and energy models is illustrated in figure 15.5. The baseline for the model is the macroeconomic projection of the Ministry of Finance and Planning, which covers the immediate five-year planning horizon. The estimates of GDP are passed down to the energy models where they are used as a basis for energy demand projections.

However, the Ministry of Finance and Planning projections (hereafter MFP projections) must first be disaggregated into energy and non-energy transactions: this involves subtracting out the MFP estimates of energy imports, energy investment, etc., since the energy models of course provide a much more detailed basis for these transactions, which are added back at a later stage.

Of necessity the energy sector analysis requires a longer planning horizon than the five-year period used by MFP: this is due to the long lead times for major energy sector investments in the power (and fuelwood) sectors. Therefore, both the energy models and the macroeconomic accounting framework were extended to 1995 (with the fuelwood model run to 2010!). Of course we recognize the uncertainties inherent in macroeconomic projections over such long time horizons, concerns that are addressed through a series of sensitivity analyses simulating various long term economic trends.

In addition to general energy related data series, two major data sources are used as the basis for the macroeconomic accounting framework. The basic source for the macroeconomic projections is the Ministry of Finance and Planning Public Investment Plan of May 1985, covering the period 1985–90. The main source for historical data, and the 1984 baseline, is the Annual Review of the Economy published by the Central Bank of Ceylon. Unfortunately there are a number of differences in the sectoral disaggregation of GDP between these two sources. Because the primary focus in the macroeconomic accounting framework is the future development of the economy, rather than its historical evolution, we have adopted the MFP disaggregation scheme with ten rather than the twenty-two sectors of the Central Bank presentation: however, for our purposes this disaggregation level remains perfectly suitable.

Methodological issues

Since the energy sector models (RESGEN/EFAM) provide estimates of the aggregate energy sector impacts based on detailed project analysis and energy flows, the first task is to disaggregate the existing macroeconomic projections into energy and non-energy components. In some areas this proves to be relatively straightforward, since the MFP projections include specific line items for certain transactions such as energy imports and exports. In other cases this proves to be more difficult.

Investment goods imports

Since the Sri Lanka electric sector accounts for the bulk of the total energy sector investment, the treatment of the electric utility capital outlays is of central importance. The major questions concern the fraction of the total capital cost that will ultimately appear in the external accounts as "investment goods imports." A first approximation is to assume that the foreign aid component, the foreign exchange requirement, and the capital goods imports are all numerically equal. Clearly some part of the foreign exchange component will in fact be for services (foreign experts, A/E services, etc.): but this is usually only a small percentage of the construction cost, and would in any event not affect the overall estimate of the current account deficit. The Ceylon Electric Board (CEB) estimates that the foreign exchange requirement for the hydro plants to be built over the next few years is about 65–75%, the balance being self-financed.

One might note that the MFP projection for the foreign aid component of public sector capital expenditure is some Rs3,840 million for 1988, of which the power sector accounts for some Rs1,933 million, or 50% of the total. At the same time, the MFP projection for capital goods imports is Rs14,950 million: the power sector therefore accounts for some 13% of this broader category.

We therefore divide the MFP aggregate estimate for investment goods imports into energy and non-energy categories. The non-energy category equals the MFP projection for aggregate capital goods imports minus MFP's estimates for the foreign aid component of the power sector capital investment program (taken from the MFP Public Investment Report for 1984–8). These estimates of energy sector investment are subsequently replaced by the much more detailed, project by project analysis derived in the RESGEN energy model.

Macroeconomically consistent growth rate adjustments

While the MFP projection serves as the immediate five-year planning horizon, an important component of the energy sector analysis is to examine the implications of both faster and slower rates of economic growth. As noted earlier, GDP growth in the next few years may be slowed by declines in the tea and export manufacturing sectors. However, since neither is particularly energy intensive, the trends in overall oil consumption may be little affected (and hence result in increasing energy to GDP ratios). Some way had therefore to be found to make a consistent set of adjustments relative to the overall GDP growth rate that is the main target of public policy.

The GDP adjustments could, of course, be made on the basis of a historically estimated econometric model: but, as noted earlier, a suitable model was not available. We have therefore elected to base the sectoral growth changes associated with overall GDP targets on the MFP estimates themselves. Since the MFP projection involves a careful sector by sector analysis, this is in any event likely to be a better approach than one based on historically estimated elasticities (unless done in the context of a very sophisticated model environment). The sectoral elasticities are calculated from the identity

$$Y(t) = Y(0)(1 + g_j)^t = Y(0)(1 + G)^{a_jt}$$

where g_j is the MFP estimate of the j-th sectoral growth rate, G is the MFP estimate of the aggregate GDP growth rate, a_j is the growth elasticity of the j-th sector with respect to the overall GDP growth rate, and $Y(t)$ is the income of the j-th sector at time t. From this identity the elasticities follow as:

$$a_j = \frac{\log (1 + g_j)}{\log (1 + G)}$$

Imports and exports are adjusted in a similar fashion, by linking each import (or export) category either to overall GDP, or to some sector. For example, fertilizer imports are tied to the growth estimate for the agricultural sector. Obviously there are import categories that are not subject to such adjustments; for example, the phasing out of rice imports by 1988 is taken as independent of GDP.

Some of the other adjustments must be made in a more *ad hoc* fashion. For example, over the long term, growth in private transfers (remittances from Sri Lankan national overseas) is very likely to be highly correlated with economic conditions in the oil producing countries of the middle east, which in turn is related to the world oil price. Obviously, while such relationships are logically plausible, they are not amenable to statistical estimation. Therefore such adjustments must be made on a judgmental basis for each scenario under consideration.

The energy sector in GDP

The direct contribution of the energy sector to GDP is small, and not disaggregated in most statistics. Electricity, for example, is part of the sector "electricity, gas, water and sanitary services." The total contribution to 1983 GDP was only some 1.3% (Rs1,244 million in a total of Rs91,643 million). Although an explicit estimate could be made for domestic value added in the important energy institutions as part of the cashflow analysis in the EFAM model, the requisite effort is not judged worthwhile in view of the relative magnitudes involved, and therefore ignored in our model. This is in sharp contrast, of course, to the importance of the sector to investment and the trade balance.

The same is true for the petroleum sector. Although petroleum product exports are a significant source of foreign exchange earnings, they in fact merely offset part of the crude import cost, and the contribution to value added in the industrial sector (into which category the refinery is assigned) is small.

Results

With this macroeconomic accounting framework as the top level model a series of policy simulations were run for the entire modeling system, using the scenario design discussed previously. The key conclusions of this analysis were as follows:

1 Increasing energy efficiency of both consumption and production has a high priority, in the short and long term. Due to the lack of fossil fuel resources, reducing the import burden on the economy becomes crucial. Similarly, the rapid deforestation rates of the past must be quickly reversed, by a phased program of rapidly disseminating efficient cookstoves, and expanding existing fuelwood plantation projects.

2 The favorable trends in energy prices, where these have been raised close to efficient levels in the last few years, must be maintained. While overall levels of commercial fuel prices (oil products and electricity) support energy demand management efforts, the structuring of prices could be further rationalized (especially the relative prices of gasoline, kerosene, and diesel; electricity demand versus energy charges; and power prices paid by the various consumer categories).

3 Reducing the vulnerability to external shocks (especially world oil price changes, and reductions in rainfall), must be pursued by increasing reliance on coal use for future power generation and diversifying the supply sources for crude oil and refined products.

4 The continuing optimization of the two principal domestic energy resources – hydro electricity and fuelwood, and flexibility in investment planning under rapidly varying external conditions, is a priority. The commercialization of selected small new energy technologies, including small hydro, wind, producer gas, solar heating, etc., could help to displace up to 10% of imported energy by the year 2010.

CHAPTER 16

Energy modeling in Morocco

In this second case study we present a review of the major energy sector problems of Morocco, and examine the contribution of modeling to the study and the subsequent implementation of a number of policy reforms. The individual models that were used in Morocco have already been discussed (linear programming models for refineries at the subsectoral level, in chapter 6, and a sector-wide pricing model using LOTUS 1-2-3, in chapter 10); the emphasis in this chapter is on how they were used in the policy analysis process, and the institutional problems that needed to be addressed for a modeling effort to become useful. Moreover, Morocco was one of the first countries to introduce microcomputers for comprehensive energy planning, and the experience of the past decade illuminates both the problems, and the opportunities and potential of energy policy modeling.

A brief institutional history

As in so many places, energy modeling was introduced as a component of a bilateral technical assistance project to a Ministry of Energy. Furthermore, as also common to a number of other countries, the successes and failures of energy modeling are closely linked to the resolution of institutional problems.

The technical assistance in question was provided under the auspices of the United States Agency for International Development (USAID). The project was launched in the early 1980s, and had as one of its central features the establishment of an independent Planning and Documentation Service (SPD) within the Ministry of Energy and Mines (MEM); indeed, the creation of this unit was one of the conditions posed by USAID for the Technical Assistance project to go forward. A comprehensive energy model was to be built for this unit to assist sector-wide investment planning, particularly in connection with the five-year planning cycle, for which the Ministry has a number of statutory review functions in coordinating investment proposals from the energy sector parastatals.

What made this plan unique was the proposal that the model would be developed *de novo* on Apple-II microcomputers, rather than simply be adapted from some mainframe model – which at the time was the usual approach.[1] Microcomputers were still in their early years, compilers for FORTRAN were still rather limited, and spreadsheets had yet to advance beyond early versions of VISICALC. Indeed, the proposition that microcomputers could be successfully deployed in developing countries was one that was still questioned by many.

The first version of the model was written in FORTRAN, given the name ENVEST (for Energy Investment Planning Model), and by 1983 ran on a 128k Apple II with a Corvus hard disk. The model was of considerable complexity, and included a demand projection driven by an input-output model. Its most important feature, however, was the ability to examine the impact of specific energy projects on the future energy balance, which tied in directly with the Ministry's institutional role. Moreover, the project analysis module included a Monte Carlo simulation capability that permitted a probabilistic calculation of the internal rate of return – based on probabilistic specifications of project costs, benefits, and such parameters as construction time.

By 1985 the model had been rewritten in PASCAL, and consisted of some 50,000 lines of Pascal code. Despite a recommendation of USAID's own internal project evaluation, the hardware had not been upgraded. The result was that the model was beyond the limits of the capability of the hardware, which was now obsolete. A new phase of the project began in 1986, that did provide appropriate resources for hardware renewal, and the model was rewritten in LOTUS 1-2-3 to run on IBM ATs. Yet despite a now fully operational and documented model, its contribution to the five-year planning process review conducted by MEM in 1987 was minimal.

There were two main reasons for the relatively limited contribution of this model to energy planning. The first, as we have already noted in the preceding chapters, was the fact that the model was developed completely independently of any energy planning activity. Indeed, it was believed that the model itself was the core of the planning activity; as already noted, that was almost a guarantee that the model would see little use.

[1] For example, the USAID energy planning project in Tunisia, started at about the same time, was focussed around an energy optimization model based on the Brookhaven Linear Programming models of the late 1970s, and implemented on mainframes.

The second related to the appropriateness of the institutional setup. As a new entity that was created outside the mainstream of long-established relationships between the technical services of MEM and the parastatals, and weakly staffed, SPD had little chance of success. Space problems in the main ministry building led to the SPD being moved into a separate building some miles away, adding a physical dimension to its institutional isolation. In this environment, contacts between SPD and both the technical services of the Ministry, and its parastatals, were practically non-existent.

In 1987 the situation changed dramatically for the better. As part of the conditions for the disbursement of a second tranche of a World Bank financed Public Enterprise Restructuring Loan, the government was asked to conduct a study of ex-refinery pricing. It was soon obvious that no serious work could be undertaken without the close cooperation of the refineries themselves, and the MEM Technical Service de Raffinage (Meier and Dutkiewicz, 1989). It was also clear that the existing energy planning model was inappropriate to the analysis of pricing and taxation issues. Thus, the first time that MEM began to address fundamental energy policy issues in a systematic and quantitative way, it was discovered that the existing energy planning model could not make any contribution when the actual and very specific questions began to be posed by the policy-makers.

Moreover, right from the very beginning of this activity it was clear that one could not just examine ex-refinery prices in isolation of everything else, whatever may have been the rather limited set of questions initially posed by the World Bank. Because of the substantially different tax treatment of heavy fueloil and coal, it was quickly realized that one would need to examine the pricing structure of all fuels. Moreover, since the largest consumer of both fueloil and coal is the electric utility, any fundamental change in the price structure of heavy fuels would obviously have potentially significant impacts for the cost of electricity as well. Thus, very quickly, what started out as a rather limited examination of ex-refinery prices grew into a fundamental discussion of energy pricing policy for the sector as a whole.

Finally, recognizing the importance of location, in 1989 the SPD was moved back into the main Ministry building under new leadership. The prospects for meeting its role as a sector-wide planning entity were thus considerably enhanced.

The economics of refining in developing countries

Some general background on the economics of refining is necessary to set the stage for the analysis of the situation in Morocco. Over the past

Table 16.1 *Distillation capacity in western Europe, 1975–85*

Country	1975	1985	% change
Belgium	46.5	31.2	−33
Denmark	11.1	8.3	−25
Germany	150.1	104.1	−31
France	168.6	114.6	−32
United Kingdom	151.0	98.8	−35
Ireland	2.7	2.9	+7
Italy	207.2	134.0	−36
Netherlands	99.3	71.4	−28
Other	124.0	173.0	+31
Total	960.5	738.3	−23

decade, persistent financial losses in refining have led to widespread closure of refineries in the United States and Europe. For example, as shown in table 16.1, over the ten-year period 1975–85 western Europe lost some 23% of its total distillation capacity, with several countries losing over a third of their 1975 capacity. For a number of reasons, refining was highly profitable in the first two quarters of 1986; but netback pricing of crude, which was quite widespread at this time and which in effect guaranteed a refining profit, has fallen from favor.[2] By 1988 the rate of decline in capacity had steadied, and some refineries had reopened: nevertheless, utilization rates of available capacity in Europe remained below 70%.[3] A surge in US demand for unleaded premium gasoline again made refining profitable in late 1988, but simple hydroskimming refineries without upgrade capability were in a much less strong position. The general consensus is that refining losses, especially for hydroskimming refineries (see the glossary in box 6.1, p. 79 for definitions) without upgrade capability, will persist for some years.

Given this general outlook for the international refining industry, the continued operation of relatively small third-world refineries has come under increasing question by the International Financial Institutions (IFIs) such as the IMF and the World Bank. This is especially true in the case of many small oil-importing countries that are in severe balance-of-payments difficulties, and where assistance from the IFIs is more and

[2] For a complete discussion of Netback pricing, and other recent developments in crude oil pricing, such as spot-related contracts, see Razavi (1989).
[3] *Oil and Gas Journal*, July 1988, p. 31.

more subject to specific conditions and economic policy reforms.[4] Yet many third-world governments continue to grant large subsidies to their domestic refineries, justifying them on a variety of "supply security" grounds. Moreover, such subsidies are rarely explicit: most often they are disguised through complex administered pricing systems. Nevertheless, as with many other subsidies typical of developing countries, the IFIs argue that considerable foreign exchange savings would result from refinery closure. Finally, it is argued, the granting of hidden subsidies to refineries as part of complex, administered pricing systems also results in a complete lack of competitive efficiency in the petroleum sector as a whole. A frequently recommended prescription is the complete deregulation of the sector.

The most common justification for subsidies on the part of developing country governments is "supply security." Complete control of the pricing system, including pump prices, is also justified on grounds that the level of consumer prices should be the prerogative of sovereign nations, not that of the multi-national oil industry.[5] In any event, it is often argued that the infrastructure for product imports does not exist, and relaxation of the usual oil import monopoly of national refineries would no longer enable the refineries to meet the national petroleum product requirement in an "orderly" manner. Finally, it is asserted, especially in some of the larger developing countries, that product spot markets are too small to permit greater (and especially exclusive) reliance on product imports. Indeed, despite numerous refinery closures over the past five years in the US and Europe, only in a very few cases, such as Liberia and Zimbabwe, have developing country refineries been shut down.[6]

On both sides of this discussion much is generally held to be self evident, and opposing arguments are rarely addressed. For example, precisely what is meant by "supply security" is poorly elaborated. Suggestions that greater security might be achieved by investing savings from refinery closure in a strategic petroleum reserve are usually dismissed as impractical. Yet we know of only one case where a third-

---

[4] However, entities like the World Bank do not necessarily have any official policy on this subject. For example, refinery specialists in the Bank's technical departments often hold quite different views to those generally held by country economists.

[5] Indeed, the ability to sustain losses in refineries over long periods is cited as evidence that open market product prices are manipulated by the multi-nationals to the detriment of independent refiners.

[6] Another argument sometimes encountered, albeit of no merit whatsoever, is the need to keep refineries in operation in order to raise revenues to satisfy debt service obligations on past investments, since if the refinery is closed, any debt service obligations would need to be met directly from the government treasury! It is testimony to the distortions and misperceptions that result from administered pricing systems (wherein subsidies are hidden and shouldered by consumers) that such arguments would be raised in serious negotiations!

Table 16.2 *Product shares in selected countries* (*in* %)

	Thailand 1980	Thailand 1984	Indonesia	Ethiopia	Kenya	Ghana	Philippines 1980	Philippines 1984	Zambia
LPG	3	7		1	1	1	3	4	
Gasoline	18	16	23	24	19	33	15	15	18
Kerosene + jet	10	11	2	12	27	20	8	9	14
Gasoil	32	41	60	49	31	43	24	30	42
Fueloil	37	24	16	13	17	4	50	42	26

world country has been subject to an oil embargo, namely the Sudan, whose crude oil supply to the Port Sudan refinery was cut off by Iraq after ex-President Numeiry supported the Camp David Accord: yet in this case it was the reliance on refining, not reliance on imported products, that caused the problem.

By the same token, the economic efficiency benefits of a complete deregulation of the petroleum sector are taken to be self evident by the advocates of such reform. The circumstance that many of the preconditions for the efficient functioning of competitive markets are absent in developing countries, most notably the requirement for participation of many buyers and many sellers, is conveniently forgotten. Yet the reality is that it is very unlikely that an efficient domestic wholesale market might evolve for products whose total annual requirement might be satisfied by one or two tanker shipments.

Relative product prices
One of the most important factors affecting the economics of refining is the difference between the composition of the typical product barrel in developing countries and that of the major markets in the developed countries (especially Europe, the US, and Japan). These differences are shown in figure 16.1, which shows the total fueloil and gasoline shares of the petroleum product demand. The United States is seen to have a unique product mix, with a very large gasoline share, and small fueloil (and gasoil shares). Developing countries are seen to have a very wide range of demand shares: very often, low fueloil shares reflect low use of fueloil for electricity generation where hydro electricity is abundant (as for example in Ghana). Moreover, as indicated on table 16.2, the composition of petroleum product demand often shows sharp changes over time; in the 1978–84 period those countries that converted fueloil burning electricity plants and cement industries to coal experienced sharp changes in product shares. In Thailand, for example, the fueloil share dropped from 37% of the product barrel in 1980 to 24% in 1984.

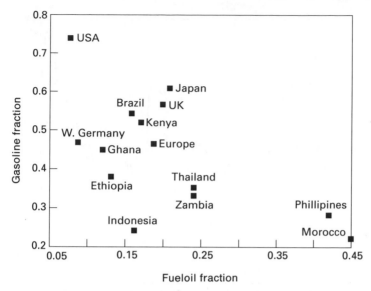

Figure 16.1   Petroleum product ratios

The differences in product slate are relevant to the economics of refining because open market crude and product prices are based on the supply-demand balance of the main markets, which means those of the US, Japan, and Europe. Fueloil therefore sells at prices substantially below that of crude, while gasoline sells at prices substantially higher than that of crude. If there were no options to convert heavy products to light products, then the differences would be more extreme. In reality, however, there is a limit to how low the price of fueloil can go (relative to light products), since at some point investments in conversion facilities (through cracking) become economic. Most importantly, however, if one values the output of a developing country refinery at international market prices, a large fueloil fraction often depresses the value of the output barrel to below that of crude, meaning that refining is uneconomic, and products would be better imported. Hydroskimming refineries are therefore often unprofitable. However, as we shall see in the discussion of refinery modeling below, transportation differences may make a big difference. An unprofitable operation in Rotterdam may be profitable in Africa because freight costs must be added to product prices, whereas crude can often be purchased at prices close to FOB, particularly under current market conditions.

As indicated in table 6.2 simple distillation of medium to heavier grade crudes will yield between 30% and 50% fueloil. It follows that a refinery has one of three options to match its products with markets

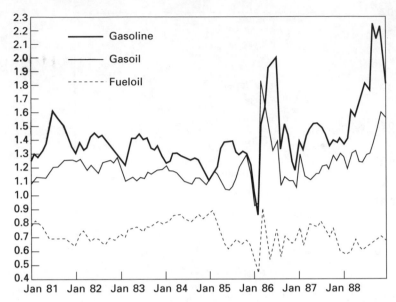

Figure 16.2   Relative prices in Rotterdam (expressed as a fraction of the Arab light crudeoil price)

that require little fueloil: it can run lighter crudes (such as Nigerian Light or Murban), it can export its surplus of fueloil, or it can add upgrading facilities to convert heavy products to light products. In western Europe and the US the latter strategy is the only way to remain competitive: for example, the recently upgraded Mongstad refinery in Norway produces not a drop of fueloil as a result of having both a fluidized catalytic cracker and a coker.

Figure 16.2 illustrates a number of important characteristics of international markets. First, gasoline and diesel prices are seen to have strong seasonal fluctuations, reflecting peak gasoline demands in summer, and peak home heating oil demands in winter. These seasonal variations are not generally encountered in developing countries. Second, note the range of variability: in late 1982 fueloil sold at about 65% of the crude price, whereas by January 1985, this had risen to near 90%. It is also interesting to note how the sharp decline in the fueloil price in 1985 (prompted by excess supply) preceded the crude price collapse in 1986.

The issues in Morocco

Morocco is in many ways typical of oil-importing developing countries. It has no substantial oil resources, and the hopes for large natural gas

Table 16.3 *Comparison of the Morocco refineries with those of Rotterdam* (*Capacities in 1,000 bbls/day*)

	Atmospheric distillation	Vacuum distillation	Cracking	Reforming
BP	400	72	50	28
Shell	348	148	99	52
Texaco	200	28	—	29
Esso	160	70	32	28
Total	110	55	35	18
Kuwait Petroleum	795	34	—	9
SCP	24	8	6	2.5
SAMIR	138			20

Source: Petroleum Economist, May 1987

reserves in the off-shore Meskala field have not been fulfilled. Imported petroleum accounts for 85% of commercial energy. There is a commercial anthracite field in Jerada in the north, but it suffers from very high production costs (over $100/ton) and has difficulties in meeting quality specifications.[7] Imported coal accounts for an increasing share, as heavy industry and the power sector have moved away from fueloil.

Morocco has two refineries: SAMIR, located on the coast at Mohammedia, south of Casablanca, and SCP, located inland at Sidi Kacem, supplied by a crude pipeline from the Port of Casablanca. SCP also runs small amounts of domestic crude. As shown on table 16.3, SAMIR is a hydroskimming refinery without upgrade capability, while SCP has some 6,000 bbl/day cracking capacity.

SAMIR is in fact a fairly large refinery by developing country standards, although it presently runs at about 50% of its capacity; as indicated on table 16.3, it is about the size of the Esso and Total refineries in Rotterdam. However, in sharp contrast to these European refineries, it lacks cracking capability. Given Morocco's domestic demand structure which has been close to 50% fueloil, this is not a major shortcoming from Morocco's domestic perspective. However, as soon as international prices are imposed on Morocco, the SAMIR refinery is at a substantial competitive disadvantage relative to its European counterparts.

---

[7] This is partly a consequence of the unfavorable geology – the main seam is only about 2 ft thick, and is highly fractured. However, the mine employs some 5,000 in a region otherwise devoid of large-scale industry, and the government is strongly committed to maintaining operations.

Historically, the overall strategy has been to meet the domestic demand for gasoil and fueloil from domestically refined products, entailing the exportation of surplus naphtha.[8] Over the past few years, the only product directly imported is LPG, whose annual demand growth has been in the 6–9% range.[9] Moreover, since 1985 the fueloil demand has dropped sharply as the electric utility and industry have converted to coal, and the expectations are that, unless the crude run is reduced, fueloil will have to be exported as well.[10]

The refineries run under a "regularization" system, under which they are assured of a return on equity. At the end of each year, any deviation from this return is offset by a transaction with the Caisse de Compensation, an arm of the Finance Ministry.[11] This process is extremely tedious and time-consuming, and the equalization payment has typically been subject to delays of several years, with consequent carrying costs.

Ex-refinery prices are currently still at the levels established in 1985, since the government decided not to adjust domestic prices in response to the world price decrease in 1986. The windfall therefore accumulated in the refineries, but the revenue involved was too much to be left to the regularization process. A series of *ad hoc* taxes was therefore imposed on crude imports to bring the windfall directly to the treasury.

In this environment the following points of contention arose: (1) there are no incentives for the refiners to be efficient because returns are guaranteed; (2) the long delays in the regularization process lead to additional financial burdens on the refiners; (3) significant foreign exchange savings could be achieved if more products were imported; and (4) price distortions between fuels and lack of effective competition constrained the optimization of resources.

Pricing and tax distortions

The administered pricing system is of Byzantine complexity, characterized further by frequent changes and *ad hoc* levies (such as the "taxe speciale" introduced in 1987 as a way to capture the windfall from

---

[8] With the exception of about 12 thousand tons a year of domestic crude run at the SCP refinery, all crude is imported. In 1987 the crude slate at SAMIR included 24% Kirkuk, 27% Kuwait, 15% Soviet Export Blend, and 12.8% Um Shaif.

[9] LPG accounts for about 8% of the domestic market, compared to present refinery yields of about 4%. The balance is directly imported by the state-owned distribution companies.

[10] Electric utility fueloil demand fell from 1,180,000 tons in 1985 to 850,000 tons in 1987. Industrial fueloil demand over the same period fell from 887,000 to 792,000 tons.

[11] For the last decade, the procedure was to estimate the level of ex-refinery prices necessary for financial equilibrium of the refineries at the beginning of each year, with any deviations from expectations adjusted through the year-end regularization procedure. Prices are set for individual products by "hierarchial coefficients" relative to fueloil – these have traditionally reflected political compromises rather than relative prices on the international markets. However, as noted, since late 1985 ex-refinery prices have remained essentially unchanged.

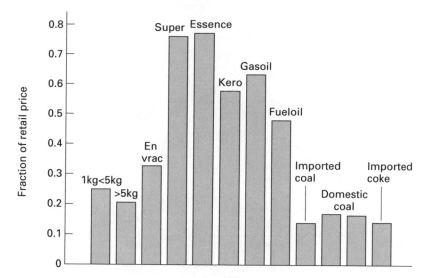

Figure 16.3   Tax burden as a fraction of the consumer price

the world oil price decrease), and non-compliance in response to payment lags. As is typical of such systems, the subsidies to refining are not explicit, and are borne exclusively by the consumer.

There are also substantial distortions at the retail price level, the most important of which concern the relative rates of tax on coal and fueloil. As shown in figure 16.3, fueloil is taxed at over three times the rate of coal, resulting in a domestic retail fueloil price (which applies to the electric utility as well as industrial users) that on a Btu basis is almost twice that of coal.[12]

Indeed, although the electric utility station at Mohammedia had dual fuel capability in 1986, it continued to burn coal during periods when CIF fueloil prices were lower than that for coal (on a Btu basis). This is illustrated in figure 16.4, which shows a comparison of oil and fueloil prices, at the burner tip in Mohammedia: fueloil, rather than coal, should have been used in early 1986 and again in late 1987. By contrast, comparable dual fuel plants in Florida, many of which had been converted to coal over the past decade, switched quickly back to fueloil in the first half of 1986.

---

[12] This is true despite the fact that direct taxes on fueloil account for only 3% of government petroleum tax revenue, comparable to the 4% on direct taxes on coal. However, since fueloil accounts for almost 50% of the refined barrel, and the bulk of tax revenue (67%) is on crude, this tax must also be allocated to fueloil.

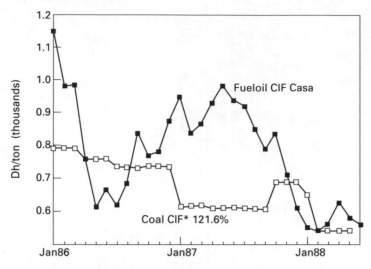

Figure 16.4   Coal/fueloil price comparison at Mohammedia

Technical and operating efficiency

A first component of competitiveness is the technical and operating efficiency of the Morocco refineries. The raw data on operating costs show figures as high as 480 dh/ton (1983, SCP), about $5/bbl at the prevailing exchange rate (figure 16.5). However, when financial charges (LIBOR-plus financing and the associated exchange rate losses during the period of dollar appreciation) are eliminated, operating costs are about 100 dh/ton for SAMIR, 210 dh/ton for SCP. These are within the range of costs at US refineries of comparable complexity.

There is considerable evidence that the refinery managements, despite state ownership, have responded efficiently to the financial incentives that are in fact in place (even though these incentives may not be economically optimal). For example, SCP has moved aggressively into the LPG bottling business and other corporate diversifications, and SAMIR has exploited to the full the regulatory inefficiencies that permit lube oil plant losses to be covered by government subsidy to the refinery (by transfer prices for lube oil feed stocks and returns that are in fact quite arbitrary).[13] At least in the case of the Moroccan refineries, there is no case that inefficient technical and financial management warrants closure.

---

[13] The point here is not that the accounting manipulations used in this scheme are efficient (which of course they are not), but that the financial management does respond to whatever regulatory environment it is faced with.

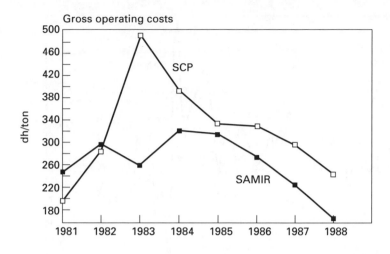

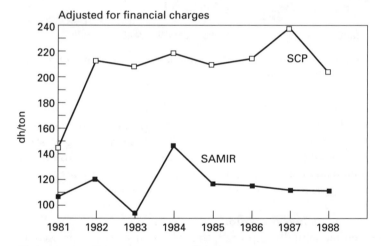

Figure 16.5 Operating costs in dh/ton

Financial costs

Financial costs are the only item of the overall operating cost substantially higher than in Europe and the US, the major components of
which in the 1981–5 period were overseas financing of crude purchases
because of balance of payments problems, and foreign exchange losses
due to the rising dollar. For example, in 1985, total SAMIR operating
costs (exclusive of crude costs) were about 1 billion dirhams (about
$100million), of which 687million dh were associated with crude finan-
cing and exchange losses.

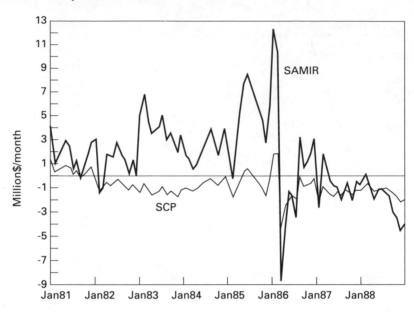

Figure 16.6   Foreign exchange savings resulting from importation of products into Morocco in $million/month

By comparison, the SAMIR regularization deficit reached 617 million in 1983, and 513 million in 1984: the carrying costs of these shortfalls were therefore considerably smaller than the crude financing costs.[14] After the 1986 oil collapse, however, and the gradual depreciation of the dollar, the financial costs have fallen dramatically, and at least for the moment do not pose a major problem to refinery finances.

Foreign exchange savings from product imports
If one uses either actually reported (from CIF invoices expressed in local currency) or Platt's quotations for crude prices, Platt's Rotterdam and/or Italian spot rates for products, and published tanker rates, one does indeed confirm substantial foreign exchange savings by refinery closure over most of the last seven years, as indicated by table 16.4. However, as is evident from figure 16.4, even in years where on an annual average basis refining is unprofitable, there are periods (as for example in Spring 1986), when refining is profitable.

As one might expect, when evaluated at international prices, the refinery at SCP is more profitable than SAMIR. However, as indicated

---

[14] In 1986 and 1987, these deficits were replaced by large surpluses, as the windfall from lower crude oil prices accumulated in the refineries.

Table 16.4 *Foreign exchange savings resulting from refinery closure (in $USmillion/year[a])*

Year	SCP	SAMIR	As % of crude import bill[b]
1981	6.4	21.7	3.09%
1982	− 9.9	13.1	1.84%
1983	− 15.8	48.0	6.99%
1984	− 8.6	27.0	3.74%
1985	− 6.3	59.0	9.02%
1986	− 10.8	14.1	4.29%
1987	− 16.4	− 8.5	− 2.5%
1988	− 14.8	− 23.0	− 10.5%

Notes: [a] negative values indicate refining is profitable.
[b] adjusted for naphtha exports.

on figure 16.6, over the past two years the difference has narrowed somewhat, as a result of a declining fueloil production at SAMIR.

LP refinery optimization, however, shows that even greater savings are possible by a flexible operating strategy, in which varying numbers of Morocco's four topping units are periodically closed in response to European market swings. The reasons are complex, but are related to: (1) differences in seasonality between European and Moroccan markets, (2) losses in naphtha and fueloil exports which are eliminated by a general strategy of meeting the national gasoline, rather than gasoil demand, from local refining, (3) the high cost of LPG imports, and (4) the ability of an LP optimized operating strategy to dynamically optimize crude slates, which is difficult to illustrate in simple calculations. Indeed, these results are consistent with studies conducted in other countries in a similar situation (such as Sri Lanka, the Sudan, and Senegal), which suggests that the traditional strategy of running national refineries to meet local gasoil demands requires reexamination. However, even though such flexible strategies can be shown to save foreign exchange, when the local currency component of operating costs is taken into account, a subsidy is still necessary.

Deregulation options
For a variety of reasons, the pressures for reform of the present system are mounting. The refineries themselves are unhappy about the degree of regulation imposed upon them by the government. The World Bank seeks reforms under the terms of its Public Enterprise Reform Loan (PERL). The Ministry of Finance recognizes that the current tax

structure requires revision (not the least reason for which is that revenues are dependent on crude imports, with tax rates on product imports currently at much lower rates). Consumers are complaining about the consequences of the domestic coal/fueloil price ratio, and the Ministry of Energy recognizes that although the refineries should not be closed, a higher level of product imports may produce substantial foreign exchange savings.

There exist, of course, a multitude of possible options for reform and deregulation. However, it is fairly obvious that only a few of the possible choices have any chance of political acceptance; there is no chance whatsoever that complete deregulation, and decontrol of consumer prices in particular, could be implemented in the near future.

On economic efficiency grounds, our preference for refinery protection is through a tolling system, on grounds that it is most easily controlled. Under such an arrangement, the refinery receives a processing fee per barrel of oil refined; this is the system used in a number of other African countries. That is, to the extent that the purpose of protection is to maintain the refineries in the long-run national interest, then a tolling arrangement ensures this objective. All other schemes of indirect protection (such as tariffs) may or may not have the desired outcome. However, for the same reason that the tolling system is desirable because it makes explicit any subsidy, it is absolutely unacceptable to the refineries, because it requires payments *from* the government *to* the refineries. Indeed, the experience with delays in the regularization payments in the past makes timely payment of the toll highly unlikely.

There is no strong reason to advocate deregulation of the retail price – in any event, the tax power can be used by government to determine the retail price level. Prices of gasoline and diesel are comparable to those of Morocco's European trading partners. Much more important is a realignment of the fueloil and coal prices, which is really a question of tax policy, not of whether retail prices are decontrolled.

The feasibility of product imports

Whatever may have been the conclusions of the simulations about the need for greater product imports, one objection that was raised was whether large quantities of products could in fact be purchased on spot product markets. Total domestic consumption of products in 1988 was about 5 million tons, of which all but some 270,000 tons of butane were domestically refined. There is no doubt that if a sudden attempt were made to acquire this quantity on the open markets, difficulties would occur. Nevertheless, when compared with currently traded volumes in the North Atlantic, the additional quantities that would need to be purchased as part of a gradual phasing in of product imports would be quite small. Indeed, it is over this larger market, including the US Gulf Coast, and not just Rotterdam, that such product imports would be spread. At present Morocco accounts for less than 1% of crude imports into the North Atlantic area, and even if all Moroccan petroleum demand were to be satisfied by imports, they would still account for only 2.3% of total product movements in the Atlantic area.

In the worst case, relying solely on export refineries in Europe, the Morocco product demands would amount to 20% of the current level of exports from such refineries. But while this appears to be significant, it represents less than 0.6% of European refining capacity. With overall European capacity utilization rates still in the 70–80% range, such incremental demands are hardly significant.

Another point of comparison is the trading volume of the NYMEX and IPC futures markets. Moroccan gasoil demand represents about 0.4% of current IPC gasoil trading volume, and 0.1% of open interest. Similarly, Moroccan gasoline demand represents 0.1% of the NYMEX gasoline trading volume, and less than 0.1% of NYMEX gasoline open interest. To be sure, the fraction of actual deliveries is a relatively small portion of the futures trading volume: but the comparisons do suggest that the potential impact of Moroccan demands on product prices would be very small.[15]

The indexation system

The reform option for which a consensus may appear possible is the indexation system of ex-refinery pricing, in which such prices would be based on Rotterdam spot prices augmented by some multiplier (the "coefficient of modulation").[16] Depending on the modality of calculation (and the degree to which taxes on crude and products are equalized) this index would need to be at around 20% for present crude runs.[17] The existing regularization scheme would be abolished, and the index would be in force for at least three- to five-year periods before renegotiation. One of the merits of the scheme is that relative prices at the ex-refinery level are comparable to international levels, and there-

---

[15] One might add that the refineries are presently prohibited by Moroccan law from hedging in the futures markets.

[16] The ex-refinery price for Month N would be promulgated by the Ministry of Energy on the basis of the average of the daily Platt's high and low quotations for both Rotterdam and Italy from day 20 of month N-2 through day 19 of month N-1.

[17] One of the still controversial details, albeit important, concerns the assumptions to be made about freight rates – the lower the freight rate, the lower the necessary value of the index.

fore provide proper signals to refiners on the crude/product import decision, investments for upgrading, and efficiency improvements.

Another feature of the system is that the refiners would keep their import monopoly. There are two reasons for this. The first is that the down-side risk to the refiners under a fixed index scheme is limited if refining losses can simply be eliminated by importing products. The second is that it is far from clear that an orderly supply of products would be ensured if products could be imported by all (a perhaps somewhat self-serving argument advanced most often by the refiners). However, it is clear that benefits from a more competitive import process (which are in any event uncertain given the small size of the Moroccan domestic market for most fuels except fueloil), are small compared with the overall benefits of reducing crude runs. What is certain is that once any given level of the index has been fixed, there are powerful incentives for the refineries to import products if it is in fact profitable to do so.

Tax reform

A major stumbling block to the adoption of the indexation system is petroleum tax reform. Under the existing tax structure, direct government revenues will fall sharply as crude runs are reduced under indexation. As a consequence the Ministry of Finance initially opposed the system. However, that is true even of the existing pricing system, and equalization of the tax structure to provide neutrality of revenues to the crude run/product import decision was hotly debated in an inter-ministerial Commission. One of the options under study is to reduce the miscellany of taxes on products[18] by a calorific energy tax imposed on all energy products, including coal, at a rate of about 500dh/ton oil equivalent.

The modeling approach

The modeling effort in support of the various studies and policy discussions that occurred in the 1987–9 period exemplifies the principal themes of this book. First, relatively little can be accomplished without a very focussed database. Thus the initial step when the World Bank first asked for the study of ex-refinery pricing was to establish a comprehensive database of energy prices covering the period 1978–86 (and

---

[18] The "structure de prix" includes a value added tax (at 7%), a "droit interieur," a "credit de droit," and a transaction with the Caisse de Compensation originally intended as a cross-subsidization mechanism, but that currently yields a net tax revenue of about 250million dh/year. Stamp duty was abolished as part of the structure de prix in early 1988.

subsequently updated regularly). A complete monthly time series for this interval was established for the prices of thirteen representative crudes, tanker rates, Rotterdam and Italian spot market prices for all of the principal petroleum products, world coal prices, and retail prices in a sample of OECD countries. Platt's Oilgram and IEA were the main data sources used.

Inevitably one of the first issues to arise when such a mass of data are to be assembled is the software to be used. For a number of reasons LOTUS 1-2-3, rather than a database program such as DBASE was used for this effort. First, many of the Platt's data series are available in LOTUS format. Second, since the models that would use the data were also written in LOTUS, interface problems were eased. Third, since the personnel that would ultimately use both models and the databases were already familiar with LOTUS, in the absence of some compeling reason to introduce a formal database software, the use of LOTUS enabled the training effort to be focussed on substantive modeling questions rather than on software familiarization. Fourth, where a database type organization of data was required, use was made of the @BASE program, a Lotus add-in that permits large amounts of data to be stored outside the spreadsheet itself. Finally, whatever the validity of the criticism recently voiced about the poor quality of LOTUS graphics for formal presentation purposes, as a means of quickly communicating the essential problems and issues to decision-makers in graphical form LOTUS is extremely powerful.

Once the data issues had been addressed, attention was next focussed on what questions would benefit from a formal modeling effort. It was clear at a very early stage that highly aggregated, long-term "energy planning models" had limited applicability to the questions at hand, even though the effort to develop the ENVEST models (described earlier in the chapter) had consumed substantial resources. What was needed was the ability to simulate the impact of pricing policy changes on the financial condition of the refineries and the distribution companies, and on government revenues. Clearly if the indexation system were to be adopted, the impact on all of the institutions would be substantial. Moreover, the resolution of many practical problems needed to be demonstrated in order to gain institutional support for the reforms. For example, it was necessary to demonstrate that the month-to-month fluctuations in product prices, which would serve as the ex-refinery price, could be absorbed by a stabilization fund, such that prices to consumers could be kept more stable – perhaps changed only quarterly or biannually, if necessary.

It should come as no surprise to the reader at this point that a

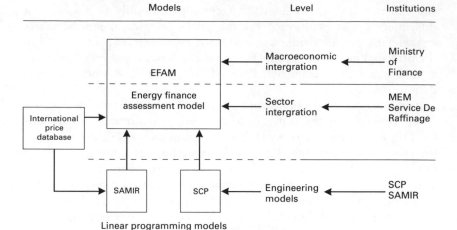

Figure 16.7   Overview of the Moroccan modeling system

hierarchial modeling system was adopted, with each level tied closely to specific institutions. Linear programming models were built with the close assistance and cooperation of the refineries, and implemented in the refinery planning departments. And a sector-wide integration model ▸ (MEFAM) was designed for use by the Service de Raffinage and the Ministry of Finance. This was written in Version 3 of LOTUS 1-2-3, and follows the design of the EFAM model described in chapter 10. This provided annual simulations (through the year 2000) of the complete energy system of Morocco, with complete financial statement models for all sector institutions, and a complete representation of the flow of funds in the sector. Thus the impact of alternative pricing system options on the flow of government revenues from the sector, and on the financial condition of sector institutions, could be examined in some detail. Figure 16.7 shows an overview of the modeling system used in these pricing and energy policy studies.

To supplement these annual simulations a series of other spreadsheet models, that shared the common database, were constructed for analysis of the short-term impacts. One model was designed to take daily oil price quotations from Platt's Oilgram to generate, in real time, a simulation of the ex-refinery price under the indexation scheme: this was used in 1989 during the test of the indexation system. This LOTUS model uses the @BASE add-in to access the Platts data that was stored in DBASE format. Since under the indexation system prices would be adjusted monthly, a further set of financial models were constructed to provide monthly simulations of the pricing system.

Lessons

At the time of writing the prospects for substantive policy reforms in Morocco appear good. The indexation system is undergoing a formal test, and the need for tax reforms is generally recognized. Efforts are now underway to define an appropriate set of legislative initiatives to facilitate such changes. All modeling activities have returned to the main MEM building, as has the SPD, where they are now integrated into the technical services. SPD has been invigorated by new leadership that reports directly to the highest levels of MEM.

Beyond these institutional issues, there are a number of further lessons here that relate to the implementation of microcomputer-based planning. First, with the dramatic decrease in the cost of hardware relative to software and training, outlays for microcomputers must be viewed as items in the normal operating budget. Second, those who wish to be innovative must also be vigilant. It is all too easy to become overconfident, whilst others catch up and even overtake with new generations of hardware and software. Thus while Morocco was the innovator in the period 1981–2, by 1985–6 the pace of technological innovation had made the original hardware and software obsolete.

But perhaps the most important lesson concerns the role of modeling in the policy-making process, and the relationship between modeling and the discussion of policy options by the decision-makers. Only at the point at which senior policy-makers began to grapple with specific issues, and began to formulate options for which political consensus might be achieved, could a set of specific questions for quantitative analysis be framed. The role of the models was to illustrate the impacts of such options. As the discussions took their course, and as technical experts were brought in to analyze other possible options, the range of options under consideration did become larger. But throughout this process, a close dialog occurred between senior officials at MEM, the management of the refineries and the electric utility, the World Bank, the technical experts, and those who actually built and operated the models. That progress toward implementation of reforms has been slow should not detract from the value of forcing, for the first time in a number of years in Morocco, open discussion of key energy sector issues and options, supported by quantitative analysis of the impacts of these options.

Bibliography

Adegbulugbe, A., F. Dayo, and T. Gurtler (1989), "Optimal Structure of the Nigerian Energy Supply Mix," *Energy Journal*, 10 (2): 165–76.

Alam, M., J. Dunkerly, K. Gopi, W. Ramsey, and E. Davis (1985), *Fuelwood in Urban Markets: A Case Study of Hyderabad*, New Delhi: Concept Publishing Company.

Amagai, H. and P. Leung (1991), "The Trade-off between Economic and Environmental Objectives in Japan's Power Sector," *Energy Journal*, 13 (3): 95–104.

Amuzegar, A. (1978), "World Economic Cooperation – Not Enough," *OPEC Review*, 2 (4): 8–15.

Anderson, D. (1972), "Models for Determining Least-cost Investments in Electricity Supply," *Bell Journal of Economics*, 3: 267–301.

Anderson, D. and R. Fishwick (1984), "Fuelwood Consumption and Deforestation in African Countries," World Bank Staff Working Papers 704, Washington, DC.

Balassa, B. (1981a), "Structural Adjustment Policies in Developing Economies," World Bank Staff Working Paper 464, Washington, DC.

(1981b), "The Policy Experience of Twelve Less Developed Countries, 1973-1978," World Bank Staff Working Paper 449, Washington, DC.

Baldwin, C. J., C. Hoffman, and P. H. Jeynes (1961), "A Further Look at Cost of Losses," *AIEE Transactions* (Power Apparatus and Systems), Vol. 80.

Baum, W. (1978), "The Project Cycle," *Finance and Development*, 15.

Baumol, W. and W. Oates (1988), *The Theory of Environmental Policy*, 2nd edition, Cambridge University Press.

Berrie, T. W. (1987), "Power System Planning Under Electricity Spot Pricing," *IEEE Transactions on Power Systems*, Vol. PWRS-2, No.3.

Bhatia, R. (1974), "A Spatial Programming Model for India's Petroleum and Petrochemical Industries," Ph.D. Thesis, University of Delhi, Department of Economics.

Boiteux, M. (1949), "La Tarification des Demandes en Pointe," *Rev. Generale de l'Electricite*, 58: 321–40.

Boiteux, M. and P. Stasi (1974), "The Determination of Costs of Expansion of an Interconnected System of Production and Distribution of Electricity," in J. Nelson (ed.), *Marginal Cost Pricing in Practice*, Englewood Cliffs, NJ: Prentice Hall.

Bopp, A. and G. M. Lady (1982), "On Measuring the Effects of Higher Energy Prices," *Energy Economics*, 4 (4): 218–24.

Bowers, J. (1990), "Economics of the Environment – The Conservationists' Response to the Pearce Report," British Association of Nature Conservationists.

Breiner, A. and R. Karni (1981), *Energy and the Israeli Economy*, Haifa: Technion.

Canadian International Development Agency (1977), "Proceedings of the Regional Power Systems Engineering Seminar," Kathmandu, Nepal.

Carroll, T. O. (1983), "Energy Sector Development, Economic Growth and Balance of Payments in Colombia," Report to Estudio Nacional de Energia/DNP, Bogota, Colombia.

Cecelski, E., J. Dunkerly, and W. Ramsay (1979), "Household Energy and the Poor in the Third World," Resources for the Future, Research Paper R-15, Washington, DC.

Chankong, V. and Y. Haimes (1983), *Multiobjective Decision-Making*, New York: North-Holland.

Cichetti, C. J., W. J. Gillen, and P. Smolensky (1977), *The Marginal Cost and Pricing of Electricity*, Cambridge, MA: Ballinger.

Cocklin, C. (1989), "Mathematical Programming and Resource Planning: The Limitations of Traditional Optimization," *Journal of Environmental Management*, 28: 127–41.

Crew, M. A. and P. R. Kleindorfer (1978), "Reliability and Public Utility Pricing," *American Economic Review* (68).

(1979), *Public Utility Economics*, New York: St. Martins Press.

Criqui, P., M. Quidoz, and I. Hajjar (1985), "Construction du Modele SIBELIN," CRNS-IEJE, Grenoble, France.

Crousillat, E. (1989), "Incorporating Risk and Uncertainty in Power System Planning," World Bank Energy Studies Paper 17, Washington, DC.

Crousillat, E. and H. Merril (1992), "The Trade-off/Risk Method: A Strategic Approach to Power Planning," World Bank Industry and Energy Department, Washington, DC.

D'Acierno, J. and A. Hermelee (1979), "Physical Aspects of the United States Oil and Gas Systems," Report BNL51076, Brookhaven National Laboratory.

deLucia, R. and H. Jacoby (1982), *Energy Planning for Developing Countries: A Case Study for Bangladesh*, Baltimore, MD: Johns Hopkins University Press.

Dixon, J. A., L. M. Talbot, and G. Le Moigne (1989), "Dams and the Environment: Considerations in World Bank Projects," World Bank Technical Paper No. 110, Washington, DC.

Donovan, D. and D. Bajracharya (1980), "Energy Research in Rural Nepal: Past Experience and Future Focus," *Energy Analysis in Rural Regions: Studies in Indonesia, Nepal and the Philippines*, East West Center, Honolulu, Hawaii, Report PR-80-2.

Donziger, A. (1979), "The Underground Economy and the Theft of Utility Services," *Public Utilities Fortnightly*, November 22: 23–7.

Down, S. (1983), "Household Energy Consumption in West Sumatra: Implications for Policy Makers," *Energy*, 8 (11): 821–33.

Dunkerly, J. and S. Steinfeld (1980), "Adjustment to Higher Prices in Oil Importing Developing Countries," *The Journal of Energy and Development*, 5 (2): 194–206.

Dupuit, P. (1932), "De l'utilite et de sa Mesure," *La Reforma Soziale*, Turin, Italy.

Dykes, W. (1988), "The Banker's Perspective," Proceedings of the Symposium on Private Power through Build-Operate-Transfer, USAID Office of Energy, Washington, DC.

Eckholm, E. (1975), "The Other Energy Crisis: Fuelwood," Worldwatch Institute Paper 10, Washington, DC.

Endrenyi, J. (1978), *Reliability Modeling in Electric Power Systems*, New York: Wiley.

Falkenmark, M. *et al.* (1987), "Water Related Limitations to Local Developments," *Ambio*, 16 (4).

Fiering, M. B. and C. S. Holling (1974), "Management and Standards for Perturbed Ecosystems," *Agro-Ecosystem*, 1 (4): 301–21.

Finger, J. (1981), "Industrial Country Policy and Adjustment to Imports from Developing Countries," World Bank Working Paper 470, Washington, DC.

Flavin, C. (1989), "Slowing Global Warming: A Worldwide Strategy," Worldwatch Institute Paper 91, Washington, DC.

Foell, W. K. and C. Green (1991), "Acid Rain in Asia: An Economic Energy and Emissions Overview," Resource Managmenet Associates, Madison, WI.

Foley, G. (1986), "The Evolution of Woodfuel Demand in a Sahelian Context," Earthscan International Institute for Environment and Development, London.

Ford, L. R. and D. R. Fulkerson (1962), *Flows in Networks*, Princeton, NJ: Princeton University Press.

Fried, E. (1985), *Economic and Security Implications of a Collapse in Oil Prices*, Washington, DC: Brookings Institute.

Fried, E. and C. Schultze (1975), *Higher World Oil Prices and the World Economy*, Washington, DC: Brookings Institute.

Gary, J. and G. Handwerk (1975), *Petroleum Refining: Technology and Economics*, New York: Dekker Publishers.

Gelb, A. (1981), "Capital Importing Oil Exporters; Adjustment Issues and Policy Choices," World Bank Staff Working Paper 474, Washington, DC.

Gifford, J. (1987), "Microcomputers in Civil Engineering: Use and Misuse," *Journal of Computing in Civil Engineering*, 1 (1).

Glakpe, E. and G. Fazzolare (1985), "Economic Demand Analysis for Electricity in West Africa," *Energy Journal*, 6 (1): 127.

Gleick, P. H. (1988), "Climate Change and California : Past, Present and Future Vulnerabilities," in M. H. Glantz (ed.), *Societal Responses to Regional Climate Change : Forecasting by Analogy*, Boulder, CO: Westview Press.

Goodland, R. (1990), "The World Bank's New Environmental Policy for Dams and Reservoirs," *Water Resources Development*, Vol. 6, December: 226–39.

Gordian Consulting Services (1981), "An LP Model of the Tunisian Energy System," Report to the Tunisian State Oil Company (ETAP), Tunis.

Goreux, L. and A. Manne (1973), *Multi-level planning: Case Studies in Mexico*, Amsterdam: North-Holland.

Gorse, J. (1982), "Senegal Energy Assessment: Woodfuels," World Bank, Washington, DC.

Hanchen, W. and Z. Dianwu (1988), "Air Pollution Control and Energy Use in China," Proceedings of the Chinese American Symposium, Najing, China, Report LBL 26260, Lawrence Berkeley Laboratory, Berkeley, CA.

Heaps C. and R. Tomkins (1990), "Energy Planning Models for Developing Countries: The Energy Toolbox Approach," Management School, Imperial College of Science, London.

Hill, L. (1984), "The Liberian Macroeconomy and Simulation of Sectoral Energy Demand: 1981–2000," Oak Ridge National Laboratory, Report ORNL/TM-9065, Oak Ridge, TN.

Hobbs, B. (1979), "Analytical Multiobjective Decision-making Methods for Power Plant Siting: A Review of Theory and Applications," Brookhaven National Laboratory, NUREG/CR 1687, New York.

Hoffman, L. and L. Jarass (1980), "The Scope for Adjustment," in P. Tempest (ed.), *International Energy Markets*, Cambridge, MA: Oelgeshlager, Gunn and Hain.

Hoffman, K. and D. Jorgenson (1977), "Economic and Technological Models for Evaluation of Energy Policy," *Bell Journal of Economics*, 8: 444–66.

Hotelling, H. (1931), "The Economics of Exhaustible Resources," *Journal of Political Economy*, 39: 131–75.

(1938), "The General Welfare in Relation to Problems of Railway and Utility Rates," *Econometrica*, 6: 242–69.

Hudson, E. and D. Jorgenson (1978), "Energy Policy and the U.S. Economy," *Natural Resources Forum*, 18: 877.

IDEA (1990), "Energy Finance Assessment Model (EFAM)," Report to the Ministry of Energy and Mines, Rabat, Morocco.

(1991), "ELECTROPLAN: A Spreadsheet Model for Least Cost Planning in Developing Countries," Report to the Office of Energy, United States Agency for International Development, Washington, DC.

IEEE Tutorial Course, No. 76CH1107-2-PWR (1976), "Application of Optimization Methods in Power System Engineering," New York: IEEE.

International Energy Agency (1985), "Energy Prices and Taxes," Fourth Quarter 1985, p. 39 and First Quarter 1986, p. 45.

Johnson, B. F. (1976), "Evaluation of the Costs of Losses in Power Systems," Consumers Power Company, Technical Report.

Knight, U. G. (1972), *Power System Engineering and Mathematics*, New York: Pergamon.

Krugmann, H. (1987), "Review of Issues and Research Relating to Improved Cookstoves," International Development Research Center, Ottowa, Canada, Report MR152e.

Laponche, B. (1978), "Previsions et Preparation aux Decisions en Mateiere Energetique," Commissariat a l'Energie Atomique, Department des Programmes, Paris.

Le Moigne, G., S. Barghouti, and H. Plusquellec (eds.) (1990), "Dam Safety and the Environment," World Bank Technical Paper No 115, Washington, DC.

Leach, G. (1986), "Preliminary Household Sector Assessment," Energy Wing, Ministry of Planning, Islamabad, Pakistan.

Leffler, W. (1979), *Petroleum Refining for the Non-Technical Person*, Tulsa, OK: Petroleum Publishing Company.

Liebenthal, R. (1981), "Adjustment in Low Income Africa, 1974–8," World Bank Staff Working Paper 486, Washington, DC.

Liebman, J. (1976), "Some Simple-minded Observations on the Role of Optimization in Public Decision Systems Decision-making," *Interfaces* (6): 102–8.

Maler, K. G. and R. E. Wyzga (1976), "La Mesure Economique des Dommages dans le Domaine de l'environnement," OECD, Paris.

Meier, P. (1985a), "Energy Planning in Developing Countries: The Role of Microcomputers," *Natural Resources Forum*, 9 (1): 41–52.

(1985b), "Energy Systems Analysis for Developing Countries," *Lecture Notes in Mathematical Systems*, 222, New York: Springer-Verlag.

(1986), *Energy Planning in Developing Countries: An Introduction to Analytical Methods*, Boulder, CO: Westview Press.

Meier, P. and B. Dutkiewicz (1987), "Petroleum Pricing in Morocco: Issues and Options," Report to the Ministry of Energy and Mines, Morocco, by IDEA, Inc.

Meier, P. and V. Mubayi (1981), "A Linear Programming Framework for Analysis of Energy-economic Interactions in Developing Countries," *European Journal of Operations Research*, 13 (1): 41–9.

Meier, P. and M. Munasinghe (1984), "Policy Analysis and Effects of Uncertainties in the Sri Lanka Energy System," Proceedings of the 2nd IMACS Symposium on Energy Modelling and Simulation.

(1987), "Implementing a Practical Fuelwood Conservation Policy: The Case of Sri Lanka," *Energy Policy*, 15 (2): 125–34.

(1992), "Incorporating Environmental Concerns into Power Sector Decision-making," World Bank Environment Department, Washington, DC.

Mintzer, I. M. (1987), "A Matter of Degrees: The Potential For Controlling the Greenhouse Effect," Research Report 5, World Resources Institute, Washington, DC.

Mork, K. and R. Hall (1980), "Energy Prices, Inflation and Recession," *Energy Journal*, 1 (3): 31–63.

Mukherjee, S. K. (1981), "Energy Policy and Planning in India," *Energy*, 6 (8): 823–51.

Munasinghe, M. (1979), *The Economics of Power System Reliability and Planning*, Baltimore, MD: Johns Hopkins University Press.

(1980), "Integrated National Energy Planning in Developing Countries," *Natural Resources Forum*, 4 (6): 359–73.

(1981), "Principles of Modern Electricity Pricing," Proc. IEEE 69: 332–48.

(1986), "Practical Application of Integrated Natural Energy Planning (INEP) Using Microcomputers," *Natural Resources Forum*, 10 (1): 17–38.

(1988), "Integrated National Energy Planning and Management: Methodology and Application to Sri Lanka," World Bank Technical Paper 86, Washington, DC.

(1990), "The Challenge Facing the Developing World," *EPA Journal*, March.

(1992), "Environmental Economics and Valuation in Development Decision-making," World Bank Environment Department Working Paper 51, Washington, DC.

Munasinghe, M., J. Gilling, and M. Mason (1988), "A Review of World Bank Lending for Electric Power," World Bank Energy Series Paper 2, Washington, DC.

Munasinghe, M. and P. Meier (1985a), "Hierarchical Modelling for Integrated National Energy Planning: Microcomputer Implementation," in M. Munasinghe, M. Dow, and J. Fritz (eds.), *Microcomputers for Development: Issues and Policy*, CINTEC and National Academy of Sciences, Colombo and Washington, DC.

(1985b), "A National Energy Strategy for Sri Lanka," Ministry of Power and Energy, Colombo.

Munasinghe, M. and W. Scott (1978), "Long Range Distribution System Planning Based on Optimum Economic Reliability Levels," Paper A78576-1 in Proc. IEEE, PES, Summer meeting, Los Angeles.

Munasinghe, M. and J. J. Warford (1981), *Electricity Pricing*, Baltimore, MD: Johns Hopkins University Press.

Murtagh, B. (1981), *Advanced Linear Programming: Computation and Practice*, New York: McGraw-Hill.

National Academy of Sciences (1980), "Firewood Crops: Shrub and Tree Species for Energy Production," Washington, DC.

Nickel, D. L. (1980), "Distribution Transformer Loss Evaluation: Proposed Techniques," IEEE Proceedings, PES Winter Meeting, New York.

Orenstein, J. (1984), "Instant Expertise: A Danger of Small Computers," Proceedings of the Third Conference on Computing in Civil Engineering, ASCE, pp. 578–82.

Organization for Economic Cooperation and Development (1985a), "Management of Water Projects: Decision-Making and Investment Appraisal," Paris: OECD.

(1985b), "Environmental Effects of Electricity Generation," Paris: OECD.

Pachauri, R. K. and L. Srivastava (1988), "Integrated Energy Planning in India: A Modelling Approach," *Energy Journal*, 9 (4): 35–48.

Pindyck, R. (1979), *The Structure of World Energy Demand*, Cambridge, MA: MIT Press.

Postel, S. (1989), "Water for Agriculture," Worldwatch Paper 93, The Worldwatch Institute, Washington, DC.

Pushparajah, M. (1981), "Management of Forest Resources," *The Sri Lanka Forester*, 15, January: 21–4.

Ramsey, W. (1979), *Unpaid Costs of Electrical Energy*, Baltimore, MD: Johns Hopkins University Press.

Razavi, H. (1989), "The New Era of Petroleum Trading: Spot Oil, Spot Related Contracts, and Futures Markets," World Bank Technical Paper 96, Washington, DC.

Riaz, T. (1980), "Long Range Energy Options: Some Policy Implications for the Pakistan Economy," *Economics of Planning*, 16 (1): 14–33.

Rischl, R. (1975), "Optimal System Expansion Planning: A Critical Review," Proceedings of the USERDA Conference, *Systems Engineering for Power: Status and Prospects*, Henniker, NH, available from NTIS Conf-750867, pp. 233–60.

Rogers, P., E. Doryan-Garron, and A. Umana (1988), "Energy-Economy Interactions: The Case of Costa Rica," Report of the Environmental Systems Program, Harvard University, Cambridge, MA.

Ruggles, N. (1949a), "The Welfare Basis of the Marginal Cost Pricing Principle," *Reveiw of Economic Studies*, 17: 29–46.

(1949b), "Recent Developments in the Theory of Marginal Cost Pricing," *Reveiw of Economic Studies*, 17: 107–26.

Schramm, G. (1990), "Electric Power in Developing Countries: Status, Problems, Prospects," *Annual Review of Energy*, 15: 307–33.

Schramm, G. and J. Warford, (eds.) (1989), *Environmental Management and Economic Development*, Baltimore, MD: Johns Hopkins University Press.

Schweppe, F. C., M. Caramanis, R. Tabors, and R. Bohn (1988), *Spot Pricing of Electricity*, New York: Kluwer Publishing.

Shaikh, A. and F. Karch (1985), "The Future of Wood Energy in the West African Sahel," Paper Presented at the Ninth World Forestry Congress, Mexico City, Mexico.

Sherman, R. and M. Visscher (1978), "Second Best Pricing with Stochastic Demand," *American Economic Review*, 24: 41–53.

Shihata, I. (1979), "OPEC Aid, the OPEC Fund, and Cooperation and Development with Commercial Development Finance Sources," *The Journal of Energy and Development*, 4 (2): 291–303.

Siddayao, C. (1985), *Criteria for Energy Pricing Policy*, London: Graham and Trottman.

Sirisena, N. L. (1976), "A Multi-Sectoral Model of Production for Sri Lanka," Central Bank of Ceylon, Colombo.

Siwatibau, S. (1981), "Rural Energy in Fiji: a Survey of Domestic Rural Energy Use and Potential," Report IDRC-157e, International Development Research Center, Ottawa, Canada.

 (1987), "Urban Energy in Fiji," Technical Report 59e, International Development Research Center, Ottowa, Canada.

Soares, S., D. Lyra, and H. Tavares (1980), "Optimal Generation Scheduling of Hydrothermal Power Systems," IEEE Transactions on Power Apparatus and Systems, PAS-99.

Steiner, P. (1957), "Peak Loads and Efficient Pricing," *Quarterly Journal of Economics*: 585–610.

Stott, B. (1974), "Review of Load-flow Calculation Methods," Proc. IEEE 62: 916–29.

Sullivan, J. (1990), "Private Power in Developing Countries: Early Experience and a Framework for Development," *Annual Review of Energy*, 15: 335–63.

Sullivan, R. L. (1977), *Power System Planning*, New York: McGraw-Hill.

Systems Europe (1986), "Energy Systems Analysis and Planning," Document 851.12-B, European Commission, Brussels.

TERI (1987), "The Energy Planners Software Package," Tata Energy Research Institute, Delhi, India.

"Thailand Energy Master Plan Project" (1982), Report by Robert R. Nathans and Associates and Systems Europe to the National Energy Administration and the Asian Development Bank.

Tims, W. (1975), "The Developing Countries," in E. Fried and C. Schultz (eds.), *Higher World Oil Prices and the World Economy*, Washington DC: Brookings Institute, p. 30.

Tokyo Energy Analysis Group (1985), "ENERPLAN User Manual," Report to the UNDP, Department of Technical Cooperation.

Tsinghua University (1984), "A Methodology for Energy Supply and Demand Evaluation," Report to the European Economic Community.

Turvey, R. (1968), *Optimal Pricing and Investment in Electricity Supply*, Cambridge, MA: MIT Press.

Turvey, R. and D. Anderson (1977), *Electricity Economics*, Baltimore, MD: Johns Hopkins University Press.

UNEP (1989), "The state of the World Environment, 1989," Nairobi, Kenya.

United Nations (1985), "Microcomputer Applications for Energy Planning in Developing Countries," Symposium Proceedings, Natural Resources and

Energy Division, Department of Technical Cooperation for Development, United Nations, New York.

US Agency for International Development (1988), "Power Shortages in Developing Countries," Washington, DC.

Vardi, J. and B. Avi-Itzhak (1981), *Electric Energy Generation: Economics, Reliability and Rates*, Cambridge, MA: MIT Press.

Wenders, J. T. (1976), "Peak Load Pricing in the Electric Utility Industry," *Bell Journal of Economics*, 7, Spring: 232–41.

Westley, G. (1981), "The Residential and Commercial Demand for Electricity in Paraguay," Inter-Amercian Development Bank, Papers on Project Analysis, 19, Washington, DC.

(1984), "Forecasting Electricity Demand: A General Approach and Case Study in the Dominican Republic," Inter-Amercian Development Bank, Papers on Project Analysis, 26, Washington, DC.

World Health Organization (1985), "Environmental Pollution Control in Relation to Development," Technical Report Series, 718, Geneva, Switzerland.

Wijesinghe, L. C. A. (1984), "A Sample Study of Biomass Fuel Consumption in Sri Lanka Households," *Biomass*, 5: 261–82.

Wijetilleke, L. and A. Ody (1984), "World Refinery Industry: Need for Restructuring," World Bank Technical Paper 32, Washington, DC.

Wilbanks, T. J. (1987), "Lessons from the National Energy Planning Experience in Developing Countries," *The Energy Journal*, 8: 169–82.

(1990) "Implementing Envrionmentally Sound Power Sector Strategies in Developing Countries," *Annual Review of Energy*, 15: 355–76.

Williams, P. B. (1990), "Rethinking Flood-Control Channel Design," *Civil Engineering*, 60 (1): 57–9.

Williams, R. H. (1990) "Expanding Roles for Gas Turbines in Power Generation," in T. Johansson, B. Bodlund, and R. Williams (eds.), *Electricity: Efficient End-use, New Generation Technologies, and Their Planning Implications*, Lund, Sweden: Lund University Press.

Williamson, O. E. (1966), "Peak Load Pricing and Optimal Capacity Under Indivisibility Constraints," *American Economic Review*, 56 (4): 810–27.

Willrich, M. *et al.* (1975), "Energy and World Politics," New York: Macmillan, Free Press, p. 116.

Wismer, D. A. (1971), *Optimization Methods for Large Scale Systems*, New York: McGraw-Hill.

Woodward-Clyde, Inc. (1981), "Decision Framework for Technology Choice: Case Study of One Utility's Coal-Nuclear Choice," Electric Power Research Institute, EA-2153, Palo Alto, CA.

World Bank (1981), *World Development Report 1981*, Oxford University Press.

(1982), "Malawi: Issues and Options in the Energy Sector," Report 3903-Mal, Washington, DC.

(1984), Ethiopia: Issues and Options in the Energy Sector," Report 4741-ET, Washington, DC.

(1988), *World Development Report 1988*, Oxford University Press.

(1989a), Environmental Assessment Sourcebook," Technical Paper, 139, Washington, DC.

(1989b), *World Development Report 1989*, Oxford University Press.

1989c), "Striking a Balance. The Environmental Challenge of Development," Washington, DC.

(1990), "Capital Expenditures for Electric Power in the Developing Countries in the 1990s," Industry and Energy Department Working Paper 21, Washington, DC.

World Commision on Environment and Development (1987), *Our Common Future*, Oxford University Press, London.

Index